A Modern Approach to
Graham and Dodd Investing

A Modern Approach to Graham and Dodd Investing

THOMAS P. AU, CFA

WILEY

John Wiley & Sons, Inc.

Published by John Wiley & Sons, Inc., Hoboken, New Jersey
Published simultaneously in Canada

For general information on our other products and services, or technical support, please
contact our Customer Care Department within the United States at 800-762-2974,
outside the United States at 317-572-3993 or fax 317-572-4002.

Wiley also publishes its books in a variety of electronic formats. Some content that
appears in print may not be available in electronic books.

For more information about Wiley products, visit our Web site at www.wiley.com.

Library of Congress Cataloging-in-Publication Data

Au, Thomas P., 1957–
  A modern approach to Graham and Dodd investing / Thomas P. Au.
    p. cm.
  ISBN 0-471-58415-0 (cloth)
    1. Investment analysis. 2. Portfolio management. 3. Graham, Benjamin, 1894- 4. Dodd,
  David L. (David Le Fevre), 1895- I. Title.

  HG4529.A9 2004
  332.6—dc22   2003065704

Printed in the United States of America

10 9 8 7 6 5 4 3 2 1

Disclaimer

The opinions expressed in this book do not necessarily reflect the investment policy
of the firm in which the author is employed. The author is solely responsible for its
contents.

Dedication

To Clara Weber Lorenz, a caregiver born in 1896, a contemporary of
Graham and Dodd

Ode to Investment

(Apologies to Ludwig van Beethoven and Henry Van Dyke)

Joyful, joyful, we all invest,
Not for pleasure but for greed.
Who wouldn't want to plant and harvest?
And take care of future need?
We will reap regret and sadness
If caution e'er is cast away.
But we will rejoice in gladness
Whene'er value rules the day.

—Tung Au (Author's Father)

Contents

PART VI
Some Contemporary Issues   271

Preface

As a child growing up in the 1960s, I always wondered what the cele-brated "Roaring" 1920s were like. This was said to be a wild and crazy time that most adults remembered fondly, like a favorite uncle, and yet the end of the decade had left a bad taste in everyone's mouth, as if that uncle had died a violent death before his time. How could such great times end so badly?

The "bad" 1930s immediately following were a distant time in the past to me, and yet well within the memory of many adults I knew (excluding my parents, who, as late 1940s immigrants, did not have the *American* experience of the 1930s). In contrast to the 1920s, the 1930s were a time of economic hardship, a step backward in the unfolding of the American dream. This was probably the least favorite decade for most people old enough to remember it. Could such times happen again despite the increas-ing sophistication of government economic policy? And were the wiser folks right when they whispered that the depressed 1930s were the natural result of the excesses of the 1920s, and not the fault of the government?

In the mid-1990s, I found some answers. An exciting new development called the Internet appeared to be playing the role that radio played in the 1920s—an apparent panacea for social and economic problems that was supposed to lead the world into a "New Era" or "New Paradigm." The giddy experience that resulted reminded me of what I had read of the ear-lier era. The stock market was already showing signs of overvaluation by the mid-1990s (see Chapter 18), but felt more likely to go up than down for some time to come. This, of course, would increase the probability that things would end badly, as they had in the 1920s. Was history repeating itself? And would this be a coincidence or not?

Browsing in a bookstore in Geneva, Switzerland (the world headquar-ters of my former employer) in 1995, I found a most convincing explana-tion of events in the most important book I would read in the whole decade of the 1990s, a paperback entitled *Generations* by William Strauss and Neil Howe. The book postulated a "Crisis of 2020" because recent elder gener-ations worldwide had been unwilling or unable to grasp the nettle of the festering global economic and political problems. This task would be left to America's Baby Boomers, born during and just after World War II, who were the modern incarnation of Franklin Delano Roosevelt's "Rendezvous with Destiny" generation (or what Strauss and Howe call the "Missionaries"). The recently dubbed Generation X were the "New Lost," and the child Millennial generation would soon become a facsimile of the civic-minded "World War II" generation, ideal for executing the Boomers' directives, less well suited for directing their own children in their old age. If this were the case, all these people would substantially repeat the respective life cycles of their analog generations, probably with similar results.

There were already a number of disturbing parallels to the earlier period. The successful Persian Gulf War (and the collapse of the Soviet Union) in 1991 functioned much like 1917 (when America entered World War I victoriously and emerged triumphant, almost unscathed). Both sets of triumphs left the United States as the world's sole political and economic superpower in their respective times. The world would be our "oyster" for perhaps a decade; after that, we would stop getting our own way, politically and economically (as was the case in 2003, when much of the world pointedly refused to support our invasion of Iraq). Meanwhile, dark clouds soon appeared in the late 1990s with the near collapse of Long-Term Capital Management, which in turn was due to crises in Russia, Korea, Indonesia, and other developing countries, just as Germany's collapse in the mid-1920s infected other parts of Europe. And yet the U.S. stock market and economy in both the 1990s and the 1920s went on their merry ways, perhaps buttressed, rather than hurt, by the near meltdowns in other parts of the world.

Strauss and Howe's historical secular crises (World War II, the Civil War, and the American Revolution) all had economic causes beginning over a decade earlier. World War II in the early 1940s was caused by the Great (and global) Depression of the 1930s; the Civil War of the early 1860s by the economic lagging of the South starting in the late 1840s; and the American Revolution of 1776 by British taxation beginning in the mid-1760s. These ominous developments had, in turn, followed secular triumphs in each era's respective preceding decade; the "Brave New World" of the 1920s; the annexation of Texas, California, and Oregon in stages between 1836 and 1848; and the successful French and Indian wars of the 1750s.

It appeared, then, that the secular crisis of "2020" (or slightly earlier) could easily have its roots in economic developments such as those identified in this book, and which will likely take place in the current decade. These stresses, in turn, follow logically from the 1920s-like 1990s. "Signs of the times" included such social phenomena as "instant" young adult multimillionaires and fantasy "reality" programs on national TV. More substantively, these times were marked by a blind and naïve public faith in the financial markets, an orgy of industrial and economic speculation, greedy CEOs, and a Wall Street that until very recently, at least, abandoned its fiduciary responsibilities in favor of its commercial interests.

Two investors, Benjamin Graham and David Dodd, yanked the investment world back to reality with their 1934 book *Securities Analysis*. (This book attempts to do the same for the modern era.) Perhaps their most important contribution was drawing a line between investment and speculation. But their antidote to the depressed 1930s market set a standard for their time and represents a high hurdle, even today. Their investment methodology works better at some times than others, best in stress periods like the 1930s and 1970s, least well in boom periods like the 1960s and 1990s, and quite well in intermediate periods like the 1950s and 1980s. If history teaches us that we are on the brink of the modern 1930s, it makes sense to revive the methodology that was most successful during the earlier time. Naturally, such a methodology should be dusted off and updated, but the end result should be a recognizable facsimile of the original.

A large number of people contributed at least indirectly to my professional development, and thus, to this effort, over an investment career spanning 20 years. It is impossible to thank or even identify them all. Here are the more important contributors, in order from the oldest to the youngest, or in descending order of generations.

The inspiration for this book comes from a childhood nanny, Clara Weber Lorenz, whose birth year, 1896, lies squarely between Ben Graham's in 1894, and David Dodd's in 1897, and who was the one member of the "Lost" generation that I got to know well. "Lorie" transmitted her vivid memories of the Great Depression to my family, and harbored no doubts that there would be another one, if not in her lifetime, then certainly in mine. She taught the spirit, if not the letter, of Graham and Dodd investing by playing what I call "Depression Monopoly" with me when I was seven years old. In this version of the game, we were not allowed to mortgage property and didn't get anything for landing on Free Parking (which is true to the official, but not unofficial, rules of the game). In such a "tight money" environment, the Graham and Dodd investments were the railroads and the utilities, which would yield a strong income stream in the here and now, without any further improvement or growth. And Lorie's insistence that "expensive" Boardwalk was a better buy than "cheap" Baltic Avenue had a sound basis: Boardwalk sells for eight times unimproved rent, Baltic for fifteen times.

First acknowledgments to a living person go to my World War II generation father, Tung Au, who helped me polish this book, making the prose far stronger, and the equations and tables more meaningful. He also pushed hard for dividing the chapters into sections, drew most of the figures, and composed the investment song. He was the first author of a previous book that I wrote with him, *Engineering Economic Analysis for Capital Investment Decisions,* but declined to be listed as the second author of this book. He and my mother, a pediatrician, also had the good sense to hire Lorie.

The Silent generation is best represented by the late Alan Ackerman of Fahnestock & Co. whose advice and encouragement I have always valued, though not always followed. Further along in the generational cycle is Nancy Havens-Hasty of Havens Advisory, whose birth year puts her on the cusp of the Silent and Boom generations. Nancy was the person who inspired me to pursue a career in securities analysis and portfolio management, and for this reason, this book would never have been written without her.

This book also owes a great deal to the many years I spent at *Value Line*, which shows in the large number of their reports cited here (the originals were not reproducible). A number of individuals, former employees of the company, and former bosses, also deserve particular mention. They include Baby Boomers such as Daniel J. Duane, who wrote the *Exxon* report cited in Chapter 7 and taught me much of what I know about the petroleum industry and natural resources in general; Dan's protégé, William E. Higgins, who wrote some key sentences in the *American Quasar Petroleum* report noted in Chapter 5, when I was a rookie analyst; and Marc Gerstein, who helped shape many of my views on cash flows and balance sheets. A lawyer, Marc once explained to me some of the legal issues discussed in the bankruptcy and workout section in Chapter 5. He also introduced me to my editor at Wiley, Pamela van Giessen, with whom he had worked.

In the area of bonds, where my experience is somewhat limited, I had a couple of mavens. These include Generation Xers Andrew Frongello of Cigna Corporation in Hartford, Connecticut, and David Marshall of Emerson Partners in Pittsburgh, Pennsylvania. Andrew walked me through some of the bond math, and David's forte is sovereign debt. Both are realistic "reactives" who have the clear vision of Lost generation's Lorie, as well as her wry sense of humor.

Thomas Au
Hartford, Connecticut, 2003

PART ONE

Basic Concepts

CHAPTER 1

Introduction

October 1929 marked a watershed of investing in the United States. Following a nearly decade-long bull market, the Dow reached a peak of 381.17. It then began a long and sharp decline, plunging to a sickening 41.22 in 1932, ruining many investors. Finally, the Dow recovered to the low 200s, which represented a "normal" level for the time. Serious investors wondered if these were random moves. Or could an intelligent investor determine "reasonable" levels for stock market prices and profit from this knowledge?

In 1934, a pair of investors, Benjamin Graham and David Dodd, began to make sense out of the wreckage. The problem during the late 1920s was that easy money, easy credit, and the resulting go-go era had turned the stock market from an investment vehicle into one of speculation. (This happened again in the mid-1960s and again in the late 1990s.) Stock prices had become divorced, in most cases, from the underlying value of the companies they represented. It took corrections of exceptional violence in the early 1930s, the early 1970s, and, by our reckoning, to come in the mid-2000s, to restore the link between stock prices and underlying values. In retrospect, one could, by careful analysis, find a reasonable basis for stock evaluations even in the Depression environment of the 1930s.

Graham and Dodd were among the first investors to make the transition from thinking like traders to thinking like owners. In the crucible of the Crash, they posed a set of questions that are still applicable today: What would a reasonable businessman, as opposed to a speculator, pay for a company and still consider that he was getting a bargain? What entry price would almost guarantee at least an eventual return of capital with good prospect for gains? Could a prudent investor reasonably allow for a margin of safety in his purchases?

If one believed the intrinsic value of a business was estimated to be worth $100, and the stock was selling at $95, it was no bargain. An estimate of the business value is just that—an estimate. The business might well be worth only $90. However, if the stock were selling at $50, it was clearly a bargain. A reasonable businessperson's valuation of a company might easily be off by as much as 5 to 10 percent. It would not likely be off by

50 percent. The difference between a price of $50 and an estimated value of $100 allows for a large margin of safety.

There are two types of risk in the stock market: price risk and quality risk. Price risk signifies the tendency to overpay for the stock of a perfectly good company. Quality risk involves buying the stock of a company that will never prosper, or worse, go into bankruptcy, possibly costing the shareholders their entire investment. Although the latter type of risk is more dramatic, because of its higher stakes, the former is more common, and hence more costly in the long run. Only a handful of companies actually default, and many of the ones that do experience financial difficulties make out all right in reorganization. Price risk routinely affects nearly all companies from time to time, particularly good companies, for which investors have overly high hopes. If you buy at the top and there is a subsequent decline, you could lose 30 to 50 percent on your investment in short order. That is why price risk is considered the greater danger, even though default risk is a serious matter. If debt holders get less than 100 cents on the dollar, shareholders may end up getting nothing (although in practice, shareholders rarely lose everything in a bankruptcy, because a few crumbs are usually thrown their way to ensure cooperation in a restructuring).

However, Graham and Dodd felt that even default candidates were likely to produce profits if they were purchased at a sufficiently low price and enough of them were owned to allow the law of large numbers to work in their favor. Indeed, these investors managed a bankruptcy/liquidation fund that did somewhat less well than the regular fund on a nominal basis, and much less well than conventional investments, after adjusting for risk.

Classic Graham and Dodd investing involves buying the stocks of average- to above-average-quality companies at a low price. If a stock is trading at the low end of its historical valuation band, the downside risk is lower than it would otherwise be, and the upside potential is at its maximum. This book will discuss some of the diagnostic tools used by Graham and Dodd to determine value, and then present updated versions used by modern practitioners.

GRAHAM AND DODD CRITERIA FOR SECURITIES SELECTION[1]

Graham and Dodd proposed stringent criteria for their investments, and because of the generally depressed valuations, found many securities that met these criteria in the 1930s.

The first of these requirements was for the stock to sell below its stated per-share net asset value or book value. Provided that book value was a minimum estimate for asset value (as verified by other tests listed below), an investor who purchased a stock below book value would be getting assets worth more than the investment.

It would be much better if the company could also meet certain liquidity tests. Graham and Dodd found a number of companies whose market value (stock price multiplied by the number of outstanding shares) was less than the company's *liquid* assets, such as cash, accounts receivable, and inventory, minus accounts payable and short-term debt, or what we would now call *working capital*. In an even better situation, working capital would be greater than the market value of stock plus long-term debt, or what we would now call *enterprise value*. An investor who bought the stock of such a company would effectively be paying less than nothing for the business as a going concern. Given the Depression nature of the time, this was not an unreasonable requirement.

Moreover, the company had to be profitable. The growth rate of profits, on which most modern analysts base their decisions, was much less important because, during the Depression, profits often fell. But some profitability ensured that assets, at least, would grow. So the company was expected to be an all-weather earner, able to generate profits even in tough times, not just a fair weather operator.

Nearly as important was the question of dividends. Provided that they were covered by earnings, the periodic payouts would guarantee a return, while the assets underpinning the principal would increase. If there were earnings, but the dividends exceeded them, then the distributions would be more in the form of a payback of invested capital, rather than that of a return. But at least the investor could be confident of getting back the original investment, plus a little more.

Graham and Dodd asked for a dividend yield (dividend divided by the stock price) of at least two thirds of the AAA bond yield. This requirement ensured that the stock had to be competitive with bonds as an income-producing instrument—a sensible criterion. Since bonds are inherently safer than stocks, one would have to have a reasonable assurance that the total return, dividends plus capital gains, eventually would be greater than bond returns. If there were dividend growth, a dividend yield that started at two thirds of the bond yield would eventually exceed the fixed income stream, leading to capital gains as well.

Alternatively, the so-called earnings yield had to be twice the AAA bond rate. The earnings yield (ratio of earnings per share of the stock price) is an outdated term, but it is the inverse of the much more commonly used price–earnings (P/E) ratio. This requirement meant that a qualifying stock's P/E could be no more than $1/2r$, where r is the AAA corporate bond rate, measured in decimals. If the AAA bond rate were 5 percent, the P/E ratio could be no more than 1 / (2 * 0.05) or 10. If the AAA bond rate were 10 percent, the P/E ratio could be no more than 1 / (2 * 0.10) or 5. This relationship had to be true to compensate for the risk that earnings might fall.

The economic conditions that make this form of investing viable have seldom existed since the 1930s. There are few, if any, stocks that satisfy all of Graham and Dodd's conditions simultaneously. But it is interesting that some stocks satisfy some of the conditions taken individually. After all, it is easier to hope for A or B or C than to hope for A and B and C. This book offers an updated form of Graham and Dodd, tailored to more recent economic conditions.

If, for instance, we can buy stock of sound companies around book value (or some alternative measure of asset value), we would overlook the likelihood that the company paid little or no dividends. We would, instead, look for evidence of rapid asset accumulation, expressed as a percentage of existing assets, as well as assurance that such accumulation would lead to good earnings and dividends or, alternatively, make the company a potentially attractive takeover candidate. This does not mean that a takeover must occur. Just the fact that a takeover is a possibility is often enough to push up the price of the stock, especially during the recurring periods of takeover mania.

If a growing company were paying a large dividend, however, we might overlook a paucity of assets on the theory that they had been paid out in the past in the form of dividends. Instead, we would look for evidence that, first, the dividend was secure and, second, there were good prospects for at least moderate growth. Here again, the test is how does the stock compare to bonds as an income-producing vehicle, not only in the present, but also over time. If the stock (at current prices) is likely to be a superior income-producing vehicle, say, in five years, based on a rising dividend, the stock is more likely than the bond to rise in price, thereby producing capital gains as well as higher income.

Suppose a company were selling at a high multiple—two, three, or more times the book value or asset value—and suppose it paid little or no dividends, so that it was also expensive on a dividend basis. Perhaps it is cheap based on earnings. This can happen if the rate of return on assets is high enough. We would, of course, test the quality of these supposedly high earnings, taking careful account of the company's strategy, track record, and how it stands in its industry. If there were good and sufficient reasons, we would make some allowance for earnings growth. We would, however, be especially wary of the competition that is likely to be attracted to a good business, and would want evidence that the company had a franchise that it had defended successfully over some years.

A high P/E ratio usually means that there are expectations of high growth built into a stock, which a Graham and Dodd investor would tend to distrust. However, we might occasionally make allowance for this fact if the stock were cheap on other measures such as sales or cash flow, and if rapid earnings growth were structurally determined by one or the other of these two factors.

We would be particularly interested if the calculated "economic earnings" were significantly above the accounting earnings reported in financial statements. After all, leveraged buyout (LBO) artists use "private market value" calculated on the basis of the cash flow as their proxy for business value.

Intellectually, we should give the greatest weight to facts that we are most sure about and less weight to data that are based on estimates or even educated guesses. The only thing that we know for sure about a company, at least on a day-to-day basis, is the stock price. We also know the dividend rate based on the most recent declaration, and hope that it will at least be maintained, if not increased, in the future. Provided that the accounting is sound, we also know the assets and liabilities on the most recently reported balance sheet (usually as of the last quarter), as well as historical earnings for the past quarter, the most recent year, and past years. Of course, this information becomes somewhat obsolete as the current quarter proceeds, at least until the next report is issued.

To the extent possible, we would try to avoid overly relying on forecasts of the future. Of course, the future must be forecasted, but more on an ongoing, monitoring basis, rather than something on which to base a stock valuation. Estimates of earnings are just that—estimates. They should be considered in the context of the past performance of earnings or of related variables such as sales and cash flow. Greater weight can be given to an earnings trend that has been stable and consistent in the past than to one on which earnings have fluctuated erratically. But investors ought to be particularly suspicious of a proposition that earnings will soon increase dramatically after a long-term trend of bad results. This is reminiscent of the motto of the Brooklyn Dodgers: "Wait till next year."

A certain cautious optimism is warranted, however. Over a five-year cycle, many companies can be expected to have perhaps two good years, two mediocre years, and one bad year, on the average. When things are going wrong for a short period of time (and stock prices are low as a result), there is a tendency for gloom-and-doomsters to extrapolate present conditions into the future. If there is a sound basis for believing that the present conditions are abnormal, one can reasonably believe that things will eventually revert to their long-term tendencies or trend lines. It is important to distinguish between the occasional pothole in an otherwise good road and the inherently bad road.

MODIFICATION OF GRAHAM AND DODD APPROACH TO MODERN PRACTICE

Having dispensed with the preliminaries, we can now concentrate on a discussion of the changes that have taken place in the financial world since the days of Graham and Dodd, and discuss the necessary modifications to apply their principles to value investing. Many recent examples are introduced later in the book to illustrate the modern approach and the similarities in the treatment of these cases and those in times past.

Nowadays, greater importance is attached to the income statement and less to the balance sheets than in Graham and Dodd's time, partly due to the changing nature of financial disclosure. Early financial reports would typically present balance sheets but only a brief income summary, not a full income statement. The third major document of today's annual report, the statement of changes in financial position, was not present. So Graham and Dodd had to base their early investment decisions on information available to them, which was mainly balance sheet information. Today's investors are much more fortunate. Now there are footnotes to most income statement items, together with management's discussion of operations. And the statement of changes in financial position will tell an investor what management is doing with the money they have earned, whether they are paying dividends, making acquisitions or capital expenditures, or doing other things. It also tells whether the spending program is financed internally or whether the company has to go into debt in order to expand.

The greater richness of the income statement, with detailed analyses of sales, cash flow, operating earnings, and other categories of earnings, allows for a greater battery of tests and screens. No one methodology works well all the time. Even Ben Graham admitted the shortcomings of his approach during the late stage of a bull market, such as those that existed in the late 1960s to early 1970s and the more recent one in the late 1990s. Under those circumstances, and perhaps against his better judgment, he loosened his valuation criteria to accommodate the exigencies of that time just before his death in 1976. We don't like the idea of changing the rules as we go along. Instead, we would rather have a large number of yardsticks that have proven their robustness in less demanding markets.

The other factor is the changing nature of the economy and society. When Graham and Dodd first wrote their book, their world was still one of brick and mortar. Now, we are moving into an information society. The new developments are based on intangible assets such as knowledge held by people and computers. The assets are far more movable than they used to be. They are, however, no less real, if less dependable. But intangible assets are less likely to appear on the books as financial items.

On the macro level, the economy is better managed than before. This is not to say that there will not be business cycles and recessions, but that they will likely be shorter and shallower than they were during the days of Graham and Dodd. Logically, it should follow that acceptable price/book and P/E ratios would also be higher.

Moreover, with the development of modern accounting, and most importantly, of accounting analysis, investors are more inclined to look past accounting definitions of earnings and asset value, and probe more deeply into the economic substance. Earnings that are hidden, let's say, for tax purposes, may well be as valuable to the company as more visible profits. The question, then, is whether, when, and how this extra value will be reflected in the marketplace.

In one respect, we are stricter than Graham and Dodd. We prefer a superb balance sheet, or at least a very good one. Except for inherently leveraged companies like banks and utilities, a debt ratio of more than 30 percent of total capital (debt plus equity) would be considered too high. In fact, a level of 20 percent would be more comfortable. If the investment case were based on asset value, then the ratios would be 30 percent and 20 percent, respectively, of asset values. A merely adequate balance sheet will protect investors against today's trouble, but not against unforeseen shocks that may occur in the future. We want the extra margin of safety that a very strong balance sheet will provide. A company that is all or nearly all equity financed will see fluctuations in its business fortunes, but offers a guarantee that it will retain at least part of its assets under even extraordinarily adverse conditions. However, it is a company that is overburdened with debt in which an investment may be lost.

It must be said that these rules and tests are a form of guidance. They are no substitute for good judgment. A master practitioner such as Warren Buffett realized his full potential only when he broke free of these rules and let his intuition supplement his logic. But these rules are designed for less talented investors as much to prevent harm as to produce winning investments. Or as Ben Graham put it, "Rule 1: Don't lose money. Rule 2: Never forget Rule 1."

REQUIREMENTS FOR VALUE INVESTING

Unlike Graham and Dodd, we do not advise conservative and aggressive investors to use different valuation parameters. Instead, the difference in our advice to each class of investors lies in the quality of the securities that can be admitted to the portfolio. For instance, we advise a conservative investor not to purchase the stock of a company that has a short earnings track record—one of less than 10 years—or a reported loss in the past five years. However, an aggressive investor can buy shares of a company that is currently losing money if the stock price has also been beaten down to an attractive level as a result, and he or she is convinced that the condition is temporary and most likely self-correcting.

In this regard, it is important to compare the company with others in the same industry. While different companies will have different sensitivities to a particular crisis, it is more comforting if the problem is industry-wide, rather than specific to one company. Then, it may be a question of choosing the survivors that will prosper after the industry consolidates. This is a task for which the Graham and Dodd methodology is geared. In this case, investors are advised to buy the highest-quality company in the industry, on the theory that it will be the last to fail and the first to gain market share from the failures of others. But a fallen issue may not be a good investment if many other companies in the industry are prospering, because then the fault lies with the company, not with the industry. The exception may occur when there is a new chairman or other change of control.

Likewise, a conservative investor is advised to stick to the securities that are not only currently paying dividends, but also have paid them for at least the past 10 years. The investor is getting at least some current return if the payout is covered by earnings, and a bird in hand is worth the proverbial two in the bush. The dividend also underpins the stock price in a similar way as a high coupon does for a bond. An aggressive investor can buy the stocks of companies that have only recently started paying a dividend, however, and may even consider the purchase of a security that has no yield if the stock meets other Graham and Dodd parameters. This is partly because some of the best securities are those of relatively new companies and partly because a fast-growing company may wish to retain cash for expansion, if the likely returns on investment are greater than the investors can hope for in most other securities. Certainly, it is better to see a company pay no dividend than to see it borrow to make a distribution to shareholders.

Conservative investors will pay more attention to asset values in trying to buy stocks "net" of working capital or, better yet, "net-net" of working capital and long-term debt. These issues derive their protection from asset values, which are known, rather than earnings prospects, which are less well known. However, aggressive investors need not worry so much about coverage of their investment by working capital or "quick" assets or even book value. Instead, they should focus on high returns on assets, which are usually generated by investing in higher-return fixed or tangible assets. Sometimes a company in this position may even be somewhat short of working capital.

Another set of requirements has to do with the nature of companies and securities. For instance, a company should be a certain size to be able to withstand economic vicissitudes and uncertainties. Here, one has the right to be quite demanding. In this day and age, hundreds of companies have sales, assets, and/or market capitalization of $1 billion or more. This one-time magic number carries far less prestige than it used to, much as $1 million for net worth of an individual is a far smaller number, relative to the overall economy, than it might have been some decades ago. Indeed, there is no shortage even of companies with profits of $1 billion or more. Given this fact, a qualifying investment for a conservative investor should have sales and/or assets of some significant fraction of $1 billion, say at least $500 million or more. An aggressive investor might shade these figures down to $100 to $200 million, but no lower than that.

Perhaps a more useful measure is net profits. For a conservative investor, a net income of $25 million in the most recent year, or an average of this figure in the most recent five years, gives a company at least some—though far from perfect—staying power against economic uncertainty. Again, an aggressive investor might shade this requirement down to $5 to $10 million. But a company with normal earning power below this level cannot be said to be an investment and must be regarded as a speculation.

A company also should have a sufficient corporate history in order for one to be able to form a judgment of its prospects. At the very least, the company should have been around during the last major recession (i.e., in 2001) and demonstrated its ability to manage tough times. A conservative investor should feel better with the stock of a company that has been in business for at least 20 to 25 years. An enterprise that has been in business that long has been through at least two or three recessions, several stock market cycles, and normally part of both halves of the 30- to 40-year-long cycle described in Chapter 20 of this book. Moreover, it takes a period of time for most companies to build up an asset base and establish a track record for inventory and other working capital components that will be satisfactory to a Graham and Dodd investor.

This minimum provenance is an important requirement for the conservative investor. A brilliant child of 12 or 15 may well have the mental capacity of an intelligent adult. In rare cases, he or she may be enrolled in college courses or participate in other activities far beyond the normal scope of his or her years. But this child will not legally be allowed to drink or drive or vote, even though a more pedestrian individual some years older will be permitted to do all of these things. These legal limits are imposed with good reasons because the child will not have enough of a life history to be relied on in such matters. Nor will this same child have the capacity to do certain things that are normally the province of adults until he or she goes through certain physical changes, typically during or just before the early teens. Likewise, a company with only a few years of history, however stellar, will not be "mature" enough for the conservative investor.

Beyond 50 years, the benefits of additional corporate age are small indeed. There are probably some advantages to a company that was around during or before the Great Depression of the 1930s, as opposed to having been started immediately after World War II. But a company established in the nineteenth century (in rare cases the eighteenth) offers no advantage over one founded in early twentieth century. In fact, too long a history may well be self-defeating. Things are changing at a faster rate than they ever have throughout human history, and a company confronting the twenty-first century with its roots in the nineteenth century may well find itself at a disadvantage. It is probably no accident that relatively recently banks such as Irving Bank and FleetBoston, which were founded over 200 years ago, about the time of the American Revolution, were taken over by others.

In addition to corporate age, the company's stock should have a trading history. Even allowing for the fact that stock market cycles are typically shorter than economic cycles, the trading history should not be less than two or three years. This would give investors some feel for how the stock will trade during periods of optimism and pessimism, and allow the establishment of upper and lower value bands.

We advise our investors not to participate in new issues, otherwise known as initial public offerings (IPOs). These issues are managed by large investment houses for the benefit of their favorite clients, usually institutions, but occasionally a wealthy individual customer such as a corporate chief executive officer (CEO). They are priced to sell or "move," which is to say that they are priced below the level where the favored customers can sell or "flip" them to less favored retail investors. Small investors may try to capture the initial momentum when a new issue hits the market, but by the time they place an order, the stock price may have already adjusted to a "normal" or even unsustainable level.

A final set of requirements has to do with liquidity or tradability. Preferably, a stock will be listed on a major exchange, either the New York or American Stock Exchange. Of course, some of the largest, most liquid names like Microsoft and Intel are traded at the national over-the-counter exchange, otherwise known as the National Association of Securities Dealers Automated Quotations (or NASDAQ for short), which has become a significant player in recent years. Other over-the-counter stocks (listed in financial pages simply as other OTC stocks) trade infrequently. The investor cannot be sure of getting the best prices on either the purchase or sale of such issues because the gap between the market maker's "bid" (or buy) price and his "asking" (or sell) price is large, typically a quarter of a point, sometimes more. Investors are also advised to stay clear of regional exchanges, especially those such as Spokane or Vancouver, which seem to have a disproportionate number of fly-by-night or "mousetrap" stocks sold by manipulative and unscrupulous promoters.

SUCCESS OF WARREN BUFFETT[2]

Perhaps the greatest living practitioner of the Graham and Dodd philosophy, although not exactly their methodology, is Warren Buffett. He was a former student of Ben Graham, but his investment method eventually evolved into a growth-at-a-reasonable-price style, rather than an asset-based approach.

Buffett's early achievements were in the Graham and Dodd style. He bought the controlling interest in a textile producer, Berkshire Hathaway, at a discount to book. Although textiles was a bad business, the working capital of the company was used to buy the stock of other companies, rather than reinvested in textiles. So Berkshire Hathaway became the vehicle for a very different type of entity—an investment concern.

In the early 1970s, Buffett bought stock of the *Washington Post*. The company, with double-digit margins, was selling at only two times sales. The P/E ratio was also low, in the mid to high single digits. Finally, the company had radio stations, newspapers, and other components, which had a total asset value of $400 million. Yet, the company was sold at a market value of only $80 to $100 million. This represented a discount of not 50 percent but 75 to 80 percent to takeover value. The market was low at the time and represented the most recent ideal Graham and Dodd environment.

Although the *Washington Post* paid only a small dividend, it did a related thing—it bought back stock. Given the gross undervaluation of assets, this was a smart thing to do. (If the money had been paid out as dividends, a shareholder would have to reinvest to get the same benefit.) Thus, although the newspaper business was inherently attractive, the *Washington Post* outperformed the *New York Times* and other newspaper stocks. At the same time, Buffett got a seat on the board and became a confidant of chairperson Katherine Graham. This enabled him to prevent the *Washington Post* from making the great mistake of its time—overpaying for high-priced media properties through the use of leverage. Instead, the company, despite its share buybacks, maintained a strong balance sheet.

Another Graham and Dodd–type investment of the time included GEICO, a turnaround situation. GEICO was technically insolvent until Buffett, working through Salomon Brothers, bailed it out by infusing $25 million of new capital at a bargain price. This was a rescue rather than a classic arbitrage situation, Graham and Dodd style. The idea was to hold on, rather than liquidate at a profit. (Berkshire Hathaway finally acquired all of GEICO in 1996.) Although the infusion of capital solved the problem that had depressed the stock price, the bargain remained.

In the mid-1980s, when GEICO stock moved from undervalued to basically fairly valued, there was a crossroads. At this point, Buffett decided that he would rather have a great company at a good price than a good company at a great price. He liquidated most of Berkshire's existing holdings except for the previously mentioned companies in order to help Capital Cities, headed by his good friend Tom Murphy, to finance the acquisition of ABC. Capital Cities was bought at a fair value, rather than at an undervaluation. So the investment case depended on Murphy's ability to generate growth by cutting ABC's costs. The combined company, Capital Cities/ABC, had a high level of leverage for several years because of the high purchase price, but Murphy took it down by selling assets, cutting costs, and using cash flow to repay debt.

Later in the decade, Buffett took a large position with Coca-Cola at a substantial premium to book. Because he was the most brilliant graduate of the Graham and Dodd school, he could afford to take these liberties, generating a total return of over 20 percent. More traditional Graham and Dodd practitioners earned somewhat lower percentages, in the high teens.

UNCERTAIN NATURE OF THE MARKET

A word of warning: While this book is about investment, all investments involve an element of speculation. The object is not to avoid speculation, but only to enter the market when the odds are favorable. The difference between a casino and the market is the odds. In the casino, the advantage lies with the house, and the game is rigged against the player. In the stock market, the odds are in favor of the investor, who will win on average, although not every time. In this regard, the stock market is more like farming or any other business than it is like a casino.

An example may illustrate the point. Suppose there were an even-money bet in which you and the croupier in a gambling house agreed on a number from one to six. Then you roll a fair die, winning if the number on the die is greater than the agreed-upon number, losing if it is less, and tying if it is the same. If the number were as low as three, you should take the bet. In this case, there are three chances out of six of winning, two of losing, and one of tying, so you are a three-to-two favorite on the bet. You would be ill advised to take the bet with a number of four or higher, because you would be an underdog.

Suppose, instead, that the croupier randomly called out numbers— mainly threes and fours, with occasional twos and fives, and rare ones and sixes—and the investor were allowed to choose which rounds to play. Rejecting the high-numbered rounds, you would willingly choose rounds in which the called-out number was three, and eagerly play rounds in which the called-out number was two, not to mention the ones. Even with favorable odds, you won't win all your bets. But a rational calculation of the chances indicates that these bets should be taken.

This is exactly the situation in the stock market. Ben Graham called upon the investor to imagine himself in business with a partner, Mr. Market, who would call out daily prices for a wide range of securities and allow the investor either to buy or sell (or do nothing). Being very temperamental, Mr. Market would call out vastly different prices on different days. Even allowing for the fact that the underlying values of the companies would move somewhat over time, the price–value relationships for a given company would be better on some days than others. It is up to the investor to pick the advantageous prices at which to "bet" on a purchase or sale.

Another analogy comes from poker. There is a saying in poker: "If you look around the table and can't identify the sucker, you are the sucker." Too many amateur investors get in at the top of the market, just when the "smart money" is selling. This process is called *distribution,* because the stock is being distributed by large investors to small investors, who are the buyers of last resort. So these small investors take the brunt of the losses that are likely to result. We prefer to be the grizzled veteran who perhaps drops a few hands by declining to call. But we will avoid being tricked into making large contributions to pots that we have little hope of winning.

Although Graham and Dodd investors are seldom the biggest winners, they tend to walk away with good gains at the end of the day because they have avoided large losses. The wins take care of themselves.

CHAPTER 2

Investment Evaluations and Strategies

People invest money today with the hope of earning more money tomorrow. They can do this by starting or investing in their own business. Alternatively, they can deposit money with a financial institution such as a bank or savings and loan. These savings may flow into public and private institutions through the creation of equity and/or debt securities for investment. *Equity* refers to the value of the stock of a corporation, and *debt* refers to the bonds or other loan instruments issued by an institution that will be redeemed at a later date. The investing public may choose to purchase these financial instruments—bonds issued by the government or bonds and stocks of corporations. A collection of stocks and bonds held by an investor is referred to as an *investment portfolio*.

Capital investment occurs when a corporation sells stocks or bonds to the public, usually through a brokerage house or other underwriters, and then commits the capital to corporate projects such as acquiring factories and equipment. Financial investment occurs when an individual buys the stocks or bonds of such a corporation through a brokerage house. Although such transactions are not investments in the strict economic sense, since no capital assets have been created, they assist the real investment process because they fulfill the expectations of the original investors, who advance capital to corporations in exchange for bonds or stocks, with the expectation of being able to resell the securities to others.

In this chapter, some basic concepts of investment will be examined and some mathematical measures for the calculation of investment returns will be introduced, before returning to the main issues of modification of Graham and Dodd's principle of value investing in the present financial environment. Although the focus of this book is on stocks, we will spend a considerable amount of time on bonds, because an understanding of the risk and return characteristics for bonds underpins an understanding of those for equities. As Ben Graham would say, "Investment is soundest when it is most businesslike." We would take off on the Graham comment by saying that "Equity investment is soundest when it is most bondlike."

CONVENTIONAL MEASURES FOR FINANCIAL INSTRUMENTS[1]

This section introduces a few simple concepts that underlie the measurement of investments. We need not worry about having to use the formulas associated with these measures, because the numbers derived from these formulas can be found in readily available compound interest tables or calculated directly by using commercially available software, such as Lotus 1-2-3 or its equivalent. Some formulas are included only to show the rationale that underlies the basic concepts. An appropriate financial instrument will be used as an example to illustrate the application of each of these concepts and measures.

One of the most common measures used by investors is the future value (FV) of an investment. Suppose that you invest, say, $1,000 at a (presumably) constant rate of return, r, per period (usually one year). How much money would you have at the end of 1, 2, 3, or more periods? If interest is paid only on the principal (because the investor withdraws interest payments), the gain at the end of each period is called *simple interest*. If interest is not withdrawn but reinvested at the end of each period, however, the original investment is compounded and accrued until the end of the specified period. The value of the original $1,000 investment at the end of the specified period is known as its future value. In the case of an investment receiving simple interest, the future value at the end of any period is the same as the original amount, but in the case of compound interest, the increased amount due to compounding at the end of a specified period is its future value.

Typically, an investment in a bond yields a steady stream of simple interest payments for some fixed periods (usually six months each) with a repayment of principal at the end of the specified duration. Thus, by purchasing a $1,000 bond with a specified interest rate r per period, the investment yields an interest of $1,000 * r$ per period. If r equals 2.5 percent every six months (5 percent a year), the semiannual interest payment would be $1,000 * (0.025)$. Normally, bonds do not allow one to reinvest in that same instrument, and other means are often used for the reinvestment of interest.

Money placed in a certificate of deposit (CD) will be compounded for the term of the CD. For a $1,000 initial investment, the value of the CD (before taxes) will be $1,000 * (1 + r)$ at the end of one year, $1,000 * (1 + r) * (1 + r)$ or $1,000 * (1 + r)^2$ at the end of two years, $1,000 * (1 + r)^3$ at the end of three years, and $1,000 * (1 + r)^n$ at the end of n years, where r is the annual percentage rate (APR). Note that interest is earned not only on the principal, but also on the interest. For an annual interest rate of 5 percent, the account balance (to the nearest dollar) is found to be $1,050, $1,102, and $1,153 after 1, 2, and 3 years, respectively.

The more commonly used concept in measuring investments is the present value (PV), which is the inverse of future value. In this case, the amount of the future receipt is known, and we solve for the present amount that is needed to generate this future amount. For example, the present value of a $1,000 Treasury bill a year before maturity is $1,000/(1 + r)$. If $r = 5$ percent, then PV = $1,000/1.05$, or about \$954.

If a series of payments is made at the end of each of period t (where C_t denotes the cash flow at period $t = 1, 2, ..., n$), the present value of these payments at a discount rate r (per period) is given by PV = $C_1/(1 + r) + C_2/(1 + r)^2 + ... + C_n/(1 + r)^n$. A special case in which all C_t (for $t = 1, 2, ..., n$) is equal to a constant amount A is referred to as a uniform series. An example is the regular payments on a mortgage taken out by a homeowner. Typically, the homeowner borrows a large sum and promises to repay in equal installments (usually monthly), over a period of 15 or 30 years. The mortgage repayment has to cover interest expense as well as the principal over the specified period of time. In each installment, a portion is paid for the principal and a portion for the interest. As time goes on, the interest portion of the mortgage payment is reduced, allowing for progressively larger portions of the installments to repay the principal.

However, if a series of payments is made at the beginning of period t (where C_t denotes the cash flow at period $t = 1, 2, ..., n$), the future value of these payments compounded at an interest rate r (per period) is given by FV = $C_1 * (1 + r) + C_2 * (1 + r)^2 + \cdots + C_n * (1 + r)^n$. A special case in which all C_t (for $t = 1, 2, ..., n$) are equal to a constant amount A is also a uniform series. An example of such a uniform series is the situation in which one tries to build up a sinking fund to replace capital in the future by depositing uniform payments over a number of periods until the time when the replacement is needed.

A uniform series that lasts forever is known as a *perpetuity*. There is, in fact, an instrument issued by the British government, which pays a fixed rate of interest forever. These obligations are referred to as *consol bonds* or *gilts*. The price (or PV) of such an instrument is based on A/r (the algebraic sum of the infinite series of payments), where A is the value of the coupon paid periodically, and r is the market interest rate per period. With the price adjusted to correct for the difference between the coupon and the market interest rate, the consol is priced to yield exactly the market interest rate at any given time.

Given the existence of inflation, a useful instrument might be an obligation in which the coupons are indexed to an assumed constant rate of inflation. We can determine the price of the instrument by taking into consideration all pertinent factors. Examples of various financial instruments that can be created for investors are endless. Only a few have been cited to illustrate the basic concepts without delving into the lengthy formulas for calculating the price of investing or borrowing by using such instruments.

EVALUATION OF PROPOSED INVESTMENT PROJECTS

The value of a firm depends not only on the amount of cash flow that it has, but also how that cash flow is allocated. The investment of capital in high-return projects will lead to rapid increases in a company's value and its stock price. If the investment alternatives available to a company are mediocre, management may be faced with tough choices. They may elect to return capital to the shareholders. Or they may choose to run in place, making investments that have a neutral effect, at best, on the company's fortunes. Unless they have strong incentives, often tied to the stock price to do otherwise, managers will usually choose this unattractive option.

Cash flow analysis is one of the newer methods that was not well developed in Graham and Dodd's time. But it has become popular in recent times as a valuation tool. Cash flow, not earnings, is what enables a business to run in the short term. Cash flow is also a gauge of the flexibility that a business has to redeploy assets in order to take advantage of new business opportunities.

A major difficulty of evaluating proposed investment projects from project cash flows lies in the quality of forecasting, which will be addressed in Chapter 6. Only the mechanics of making the evaluation, given reliable projected cash flows, will be considered here. Several conventional methods of evaluating proposed projects include the net present value (NPV) method, the internal rate of return (IRR) method, and the payback period (PBP) method.

Under the net present value method, the forecasted cash flows from a proposed investment are discounted using a specified discount rate, sometimes known as a *hurdle rate*. The investment is considered acceptable if the NPV of the cash flows is greater than, or at least equal to, zero; it is unacceptable if the NPV is less than zero. Raising the discount rate will reduce the NPV, while lowering the discount rate has the opposite effect. The main problem with this method is that managers have to specify the discount rate, which represents the cost of capital for a firm. The specification of a discount rate is properly the task of top management, one that should receive high priority. Managers are sometimes uncomfortable with their selected discount rate because in their eagerness to push an investment proposal, they have set an unrealistically low discount rate. Such self-defeating practices should be discouraged. As Warren Buffett points out, sometimes top management sets an appropriately high discount rate, but by communicating their eagerness to invest, they encourage middle management to come up with unrealistically high cash flow forecasts to meet the hurdle rate.

The internal rate of return method avoids this problem but creates others. In this method, the rate of return from a proposed investment will be calculated from the NPV of the given cash flows based on an unknown rate of return, which is to be solved. The method gives no consideration to the cost of capital external to the project (thus the name IRR). The first difficulty is a technical one if the interim cash flows change directions more than once (i.e., periods of net inflows followed periods of net outflows, or vice versa). Under those circumstances, the mathematical equation for solving the unknown IRR may result in more than one value. A related difficulty is that the IRR method makes the unrealistic assumption that the interim cash flows are reinvested at the same rate as the IRR, regardless of the number of changes in the cash flows.

The payback method is simply a crude way of measuring the time required to recoup one's investment. It suffers from a number of drawbacks. First, it gives no weight to the cash flows after the payback. Second, it gives equal weight to the cash flows before the expiration of the period, irrespective of the timing of such cash flows. Third, it does not estimate the rate of return for the project. These are the problems that the NPV and IRR methods attempt to address by using discounted cash flows. The saving grace of the PBP method is that it emphasizes the early recuperation of the investment to minimize the risk of exposure, and it becomes important under unstable economic and political conditions. Implicit is the assumption that the returns at the back end are gravy. As Will Rogers would point out, return of capital is more important than return on capital.

AN OVERVIEW OF FINANCIAL STATEMENTS

The financial statements are contained in the annual report of a corporation, which includes the balance sheet, the income statement, the statement of changes in financial position, and the auditor's report. The balance sheet summarizes the financial position of the corporation and lists the values of its assets and liabilities at the end of the reporting period (usually the end of the year). The income statement itemizes revenues and expenses for the reporting period (usually a year) and provides an overview of the operations for the period. The statement of changes in the financial position lists the sources and application of funds. The auditor's report is an independent appraisal of the financial statements of the corporation by a team of professional accountants.

The financial conditions of a firm that concern a prospective investor most are liquidity, solvency, and profitability. *Liquidity* is the ability of a firm to raise enough cash to pay its liabilities as they become due. *Solvency* refers to the long-term ability of a firm to meet its obligations, based on the structure of its debt in relationship to its assets. *Profitability* is the firm's capability to generate profits. Managers, lenders, and investors watch these conditions closely to make sure that the firm is able both to stay afloat and to provide a return on investment.

A share of stock represents a proportionate interest in a company. The exact proportion depends on the number of shares owned by the investor compared to the total number of the company's shares outstanding. For instance, the ownership of 100 shares represents a 10 percent interest in a private company with only 1,000 shares outstanding, but 100 shares represent only one ten-thousandth (1 percent of 1 percent) of a public company with a million shares outstanding.

By convention, a number of simple financial terms, such as *price, earnings, dividends,* and *book value* (or just *book*), refer to the per-share amounts of such quantities, rather than those that apply to the corporation as a whole. Terms such as *market capitalization* (or *market cap* for short), *net profit, dividends disbursed,* and *net worth* refer to their respective total values for the corporation, all of which can be found in the corporate financial statements. The per-share values of these items are obtained by dividing the respective total values by the total number of shares. As a check, market capitalization of a company (the value of the whole company) equals the quoted price (per share) multiplied by the number of shares. Net profits for the corporation are the earnings (per share) multiplied by the number of shares. Total dividends disbursed are the dividends (per share) multiplied by total number of shares. Corporate net worth is the book value (per share) multiplied by the total number of shares.

The value of the whole company changes in proportion to changes in the quoted price. While the individual investor is more interested in the stock price and the value of the shares she or he owns, a prospective acquirer of a company needs to know its total market cap in order to make a bid.

EVALUATION OF PUBLIC CORPORATIONS

We consider Graham and Dodd's evaluation procedure a three-legged stool of assets, earnings, and dividends, with earnings no more—and possibly somewhat less—important than either of the other two. That is partly because there is far greater uncertainty associated with earnings than with known quantities such as assets and dividends, but mainly because the end result of earnings is to determine the values of the other two. That is why it is distressing when the result of operation happens to be an outright loss, because then asset value is also impaired. If the company has any meaningful amount of debt, then the financial strength, expressed as a relationship between debt and equity, is also weakened. Finally, a disappointing earnings result reduces the support to the dividends.

To an outside investor, the best gauge of a firm's NPV is the stream of earnings. Future earnings, of course, are a guess, but the past stream of earnings can be found in financial statements. This stream of earnings can be broken down into two components: the portion of earnings that is distributed to stockholders in the form of dividends, and the part that is retained by the company and reinvested in projects.

Theoretically, the best way to value a firm is to estimate the NPV of the respective cash flows, but this is usually a difficult task for an individual investor who does not have inside knowledge of a firm's future plans, and who may not have a full understanding of the business environment in which the company operates. Instead, most investors base their calculations on known performance measures, such as assets and earnings reported recently, and their relationships to the current stock price.

The disposition of recent earnings is summarized in the statement of shareholders' equity. The statement starts with shareholders' equity at the beginning of the year, adds the current year's earnings, and then subtracts disbursements during the year such as dividend payments and stock buybacks to arrive at shareholders' equity at the end of the year. Although this statement of shareholders' equity is an abbreviation of several other financial statements, it is a very useful document. An example is the Statement of Consolidated Shareholders' Equity for Ashland Inc. in Figure 2.1.

One way of evaluating the return of a company is the return on assets (ROA). ROA is the net profit divided by the sum of all assets, current and fixed. Implicitly, it measures profitability against the sum of equity and all liabilities, both current and long term, on the right-hand side of the balance sheet. Its main weakness is that it does not distinguish among various components of capital.

A more widely used contemporary tool for evaluating the profitability of a company is the return on capital (ROC), which is the net profit divided by the capital. In this case, capital is the sum of long-term debt and equity invested in the company, but it excludes net current assets (and hence short-term debt). Instead, the denominator is the amount of permanent capital tied up in the company; the return number in the numerator is the sum of net profits, plus interest net of taxes. This ratio is a measure of underlying profitability.

Finally, the measure that is of greatest interest to equity investors is the return on equity (ROE). This ratio is just net profits divided by shareholders' equity. A large discrepancy between ROC and ROE is a signal that high returns and growth are being fueled by debt.

Some important concepts related to equity, earnings, and dividends deserve more attention than generally recognized, and are discussed briefly here. Let B denote the book value of the stockholders' equity, D the dividend paid, and E the net earnings. Then the ROE is represented

Ashland Inc. and Consolidated Subsidiaries
Statements of Consolidated Stockholders' Equity

(In millions)	Common stock	Paid-in capital	Retained earnings	Accumulated other comprehensive loss	Total
Balance at October 1, 1999	$72	$464	$1,710	$ (46)	$2,200
Total comprehensive income[1]			70	(26)	44
Dividends					
Cash, $1.10 per common share			(78)		(78)
Spin-off of Arch Coal shares			(123)		(123)
Issued common stock under					
Stock incentive plans		8			8
Acquisitions of other companies		3			3
Repurchase of common stock	(2)	(87)			(89)
Balance at September 30, 2000	70	388	1,579	(72)	1,965
Total comprehensive income[1]			417	(54)	363
Cash dividends, $1.10 per common share			(76)		(76)
Issued common stock under					
stock incentive plans	1	22			23
Repurchase of common stock	(2)	(47)			(49)
Balance at September 30, 2001	69	363	1,920	(126)	2,226
Total comprehensive income[1]			117	(68)	49
Cash dividends, $1.10 per common share			(76)		(76)
Issued common stock under					
stock incentive plans		16			16
Repurchase of common stock	(1)	(41)			(42)
Balance at September 30, 2002	$68	$338	$1,961	$(194)	$2,173

(1) Reconciliations of net income to total comprehensive income follow.

(In millions)	2002	2001	2000
Net income	$117	$417	$70
Minimum pension liability adjustment	(144)	(57)	2
Related tax benefit (expense)	56	22	(1)
Unrealized translation gains (losses)	19	(21)	(37)
Related tax benefit	1	2	10
Total comprehensive income	$ 49	$363	$44

At September 30, 2002, the accumulated other comprehensive loss of $194 million (after tax) was comprised of net unrealized translation losses of $63 million and a minimum pension liability of $131 million.

Source: Ashland Inc. 2002 Annual Report. Used by permission.

See Notes to Consolidated Financial Statements.

FIGURE 2.1. An Example of Statement of Shareholders' Equity.

by E/B. The percentage of earnings distributed as dividends is known as the dividend payout ratio, or D/E. If this percentage is multiplied by the ROE, the result is another percentage, which we call the dividend distribution rate (dividends divided by book value), that is, $(D/E) * (E/B) = D/B$. The percentage of earnings retained by the firm is $(E - D)/E$ or $1 - D/E$. The product of the retained earnings percentage and the ROE is $(1 - D/E) * (E/B) = (E - D)/B$, which is known as the *earnings reinvestment rate* (difference of earnings and dividends relative to net worth), or colloquially as the *earnings plowback rate*. Note that the earnings reinvestment rate is totally independent of the stock price, P. Note also that the dividend payout ratio and the retained earnings rate have to add up to 100 percent, that is, $D/E + (1 - D/E) = 1$ or 100 percent. The sum of the dividend distribution rate and the earnings reinvestment rate is just the ROE, that is, $D/B + (E - D)/B = E/B$.

For example, suppose that a company has a book value of $10. If it generates $1 of earnings and pays a dividend of 60 cents, then the associated ratios can be computed as follows:

ROE is $E/B = \$1/\$10 = 10$ percent.

Dividend payout ratio is $D/E = \$0.60/\$1.00 = 0.60 = 60$ percent.

Dividend distribution rate is $D/B = \$0.60/\$10 = 0.06 = 6$ percent.

Retained earnings rate is $1 - D/E = 1 - 0.60 = 0.40 = 40$ percent.

Earnings reinvestment rate is $(E - D)/B = E/B - D/B$
$\qquad\qquad\qquad\qquad = 10$ percent $- 6$ percent $= 4$ percent.

Note that the sum of the dividend payout ratio and the retained earnings rate is 60 percent $+ 40$ percent $= 100$ percent.

VALUE VERSUS GROWTH INVESTING

We now turn to the debate between value and growth investing. We will begin by making an important analogy between stocks and bonds. Early in the era of capital markets (the late nineteenth and early twentieth centuries), stocks were treated as substitutes for bonds. That is, stocks were owned primarily for dividend income, and secondarily for participation in the growth of the issuing companies, which would enable capital values to at least keep up with inflation, and hopefully exceed this level by a modest amount. Sophisticated investors such as Warren Buffett regard stocks as a special type of bond. Graham and Dodd would certainly agree.

A bond is more or less attractive depending on how its contractual interest rate (otherwise known as the *coupon*) compares with the market interest rate. For instance, a one-year bond may be issued with a coupon rate of 8 percent, thereby yielding $80 worth of interest, with a principal amount of $1,000 payable at the end of the year. If the market rate of interest suddenly drops to 7 percent, the bond's interest rate is very attractive relative to the current interest rate, and investors would be willing to pay more than $1,000 for it. Specifically, they would be willing to buy it at a price of $1,009 (= $1,080/1.07), where the numerator of the fraction is the principal and interest, and the denominator is 1 plus the market interest rate (expressed as decimals). The positive difference between the new market value of $1,009 and the original principal of $1,000 is known as a *premium*. Similarly, if the market interest rate suddenly rises to 9 percent, the old 8 percent coupon is not competitive with this new rate, and the bond would drop in value to $991 (= $1,080/1.09) before equilibrium is restored. The negative difference between the new market value of $991 and the original principal of $1,000 is known as a *discount*.

Similarly, a stock will typically sell at either a premium or discount to its book value, depending on how its company's ROE compares with the return required on the stock. This required rate of return depends on the prevailing bond rate, plus an additional risk factor to compensate for the fact that stocks are riskier than bonds. One useful measure of the cheapness or expensiveness of the stock is given by the ratio between the stock price P and the book value B, or the price–book ratio (P/B). This is in contrast to another, more common measure, the ratio of the price to earnings per share, or P/E.

To illustrate this point, consider a stock with book value $B = \$10$, and let us calculate P/B ratios, using stock prices $P = \$15$, 10, and 6.

For $P = \$15$, the P/B is $\$15/10 = 1.5$, yielding a premium to book value.

For $P = \$10$, the P/B is $\$10/\$10 = 1.0$, at parity with book value.

For $P = \$6$, the P/B is 0.6, yielding a discount to book value.

However, the dividend yield, which is the dividend divided by price of the stock, or D/P, depends on both the dividend D and the stock price P. Let us calculate the dividend yield of 60 cents at the stock prices of $15, $10, and $6.

For $P = \$15$, the dividend yield is $\$0.60/\$15 = 0.04 = 4$ percent.

For $P = \$10$, the dividend yield is $\$0.6/\$10 = 0.06 = 6$ percent.

For $P = \$6$, the dividend yield is $\$0.60/\$6 = 0.10 = 10$ percent.

If the stock price equals its book value (i.e., $P = B$), then the dividend yield is equal to the dividend distribution rate, or $D/P = D/B$. If the stock price is less than the book value (i.e., $P < B$), the dividend yield is higher than the dividend distribution rate (i.e., $D/P > D/B$). If the stock price is more than the book value (i.e., $P > B$), then the dividend yield is lower than the dividend distribution rate (i.e., $D/P < D/B$). These conditions are analogous to the fact that the current yield on a bond is less than or greater than the coupon, depending on whether it is selling at a premium or discount to par value (which is the bond analog of book value of the stock).

The earnings reinvestment rate has great theoretical importance, because it is the rate at which the company is expected to grow. If a company retained all of its earnings, book value in any given year would grow at the rate of the ROE. In fact, this is often not the case, because many companies pay out a portion of their earnings in the form of dividends.

The total (annual) return of a stock is the sum of capital gains and the dividend yield. Given the above theoretical relationship, the total return is $(E - D)/B + D/P$, where the first term is the earnings reinvestment rate, and the second term is the dividend yield. To the extent that stocks pay dividends, they are like bonds. What sets them apart from bonds is the reinvested capital, which is not disbursed in the form of dividends. The total (annual) return potential of a stock is the capital gains rate plus the dividend yield, which in theory, is the earnings reinvestment rate plus the dividend yield.

Why would a stock price exhibit a premium to book value? This is, in fact, the more common case, and is derived from the fact that companies typically have ROEs that are greater than the required rate of return for stocks. The successive revolutions in physical and social sciences in the twentieth century made it possible to have outsized returns on relatively small amounts of capital by substituting intellectual capital for physical assets. (Hence, the practice grew up in boom times of overlooking the protection to an investment offered by physical capital on the balance sheet.) Even so, intellectual capital needs to interact with physical assets to generate profits. This process can be measured by the ROE. For instance, Microsoft has an ROE of over 20 percent. This means that the computer programmers working at the corporate headquarters at Redmond, Washington, are more productive than most U.S. corporations. We can also use ROA as a measure, but stockholders are more interested in returns on *equity*.

It is true that value investing was not particularly successful for most of the 1990s. This was not because this form of investing had permanently gone out of style. Instead, one must realize that the most recent decade was an extraordinary period, the like of which appears perhaps once or twice in a normal lifetime. The first factor, which was generally overlooked, was the marked (and temporary) American political supremacy that followed the 1991 victory in the Persian Gulf War and the collapse of the Soviet Union. The nearest equivalent to this was the existence of the United States as the only fresh superpower after World War I (1918), when the other major powers had fought themselves to exhaustion and decline in influence. But this Persian Gulf War environment disappeared on September 11, 2001, when a terrorist attack on the bastion of capitalism reminded Americans (and the rest of the world) that American political power is not all-encompassing, nor is capitalism going to pervade the world in a steady fashion.

The second factor affecting the 1990s was the introduction of exciting new technologies. The new technologies are important, of course, but their contributions to profitability were generally overestimated. This was demonstrated in 2001 when companies like JDS Uniphase took billions of dollars of writedowns for earnings and book values accounted for in previous years that had, in fact, been largely illusory. Stripped of these paper gains, U.S. corporate profits were no higher in 2001 than they were in 1995; six years of profit progress had been wiped out. The problem was not that the technologies weren't real, but rather that the speed of their impact was overestimated. Investors had assigned much too high a PV to companies producing new technologies based on the belief that they would transform the world over two or three years, rather than two or three decades. Stock prices had nowhere to go but down when investors redid their calculations regarding the economics of the new technologies and came up short.

So what is the difference between a value investor and a growth investor? A growth investor wants the stocks of companies with the highest growth rates, at least 15 percent and hopefully more than 20 percent a year, and is willing to pay large premiums of price-to-book value (or large P/E ratios) in order to obtain such growth. Such a stock is characterized by a high or fast-growing ROE. This investor has a high degree of confidence in one's ability to identify such growth stocks and avoid the issues of those companies whose earnings will be disappointing. Assuming that this can be done (and it seldom can), then price is no object because the company's growth will eventually catch up to support the current stock price. In its extreme form, the philosophy can be described as "growth at any price."

A value investor, conversely, distrusts too much growth on the theory that all companies cannot be above average. Instead, the value investor looks for companies with characteristics of broadly average profitability, and then attempts to capitalize on them by purchasing some of their issues at a bargain price. A value investor may even accept the stock of a company with below-average economic characteristics if the price is right. That is, if the stock is cheap enough, and the dividend payout ratio is high enough, even the stock of a company with a low ROE can be attractive.

The debate between value and growth is largely a debate between views of the world. The growth investor believes, implicitly if not explicitly, that earnings will go up in a smooth pattern, and likewise, prices will fluctuate in a relatively narrow range around a perceived central value. Under such assumptions, the best thing to do is to get on the bandwagon and ride it to riches. In such a world, it is easy to do NPV calculations far into the future because estimates of the growth rate will not be far enough wrong to make a difference in the target stock price.

The value investor believes that earnings progress will take place in a disorderly, not smooth, fashion, and that this will be fully reflected in the stock price volatility. The value investor feels comfortable waiting for the right (low) price, based on a belief about price volatility, which is observable, rather than future earnings growth, which can only be guessed at. If anything, the doubting value investor who expects the worst will from time to time be positively surprised because of an unexpected upturn in the company's fortunes, or a "gift" in the form of a takeover bid from another company trying to obtain cheap assets with the expectation of improving their low returns.

Historically, the stock markets rise and fall in response to economic cycles. It is difficult to predict in advance exactly when the rise or fall will take place. A growth investor may ride on momentum of the tide for a short period of time but can seldom detect the perfect timing of the ebbs and flows to get out and lock in the gains. According to statistics, the stock market regresses to the mean in a long run, thus smoothing out the fluctuation or volatility of the short run. As Ben Graham would say, "In the short term, the market is a voting machine, but in the long term, it is a weighing machine."

As for the relative merits of growth and value stocks, a number of studies done at different times show that the capital appreciation on growth stocks outpaces that of value stocks by an average of one and a half percentage points a year, not as much as most people might think, but that value stocks yield an average of three percentage points more in dividends. So the value stocks provide a total return greater than that of growth stocks of one and a half percentage points a year. The contribution of dividends to total returns is unfortunately overlooked by too many investors.

Most investors invest in stocks as savings to buy a new home and to finance education for their children or for their own retirement. They should not gamble their money in a lottery-like atmosphere in order to chase hot tips. Like gamblers who do not know when to quit, they seldom win out in the end. That is why value investing is the sounder approach for those individuals who invest for the long run, particularly in periods other than the "exuberant" 1990s, 1960s, and 1920s.

Unfortunately, we are all too human not to be tempted by the urge to speculate on some "once-in-a-lifetime" opportunities. If you have adequate financial resources that will not be needed in the foreseeable future, you may be justified in spending a small portion of your wealth to invest in some risky but fast-growing stocks. According to John Bogle, an astute value investor and the founder and former CEO of Vanguard Funds, such speculative investment should be limited to no more than 5 percent of your wealth. Furthermore, you should recognize the risky nature of growth stocks and take some profits off the table by rebalancing your portfolio periodically to reflect the 5 percent limit. We will be well served by heeding such sound advice.

Fixed-Income Evaluation

Foundation of Fixed Income

Bonds are generally safer than stocks, based on the most common measurement of price fluctuations, because bonds carry a "money-back guarantee," as of the date they mature. This "guarantee," however, is only as good as the issuer. Still, investors during the 1930s who were spooked by the collapse of stocks took refuge in bonds. Indeed, the mantra of the late 1930s was "Bonds are the only sound investment."

At the risk of digressing from our main theme of investments in common stocks, we will begin our discussions with the evaluation of bonds. This is partly because bonds are important investment vehicles in their own right, and partly because the criteria for investments in common stocks are in many ways similar to those for bond investments. We believe that the average investor underestimates the degree to which bonds and stocks should and do behave similarly, a fact that has not been lost on Ben Graham and Warren Buffett. Moreover, an investor can get a "feel" for the dynamics of investments through purchasing "safer" fixed-income securities, especially those issued by governments such as the U.S. Treasury. Nonetheless, they carry important risks of their own. In fact, inexperienced investors will find them surprisingly risky because they are exposed to some, although not all, of the economic variables that affect stocks.

Interest rates fluctuate. This fact alone makes investments of money risky, even in the safest instruments such as U.S. Treasury bills, in which neither earnings variability nor risk of default is an issue. One must make a decision to purchase or not to purchase today with the near certainty that the rate of return will be different tomorrow. Naturally, if you were sure that the rate of return would be higher tomorrow, you would hold off investing until the next day, but then again, it might be lower. And if it were the same, you would have lost a day by waiting until tomorrow. (In this discussion, we omit consideration of management and transactions costs connected with frequent decisions.)

This chapter will deal with instruments carrying only the risks associated with the fluctuation of interest rates, but not credit risk—the chance that investors may not get their money back. The securities include the obligations of the U.S. government, plus those of other issuers, such as commercial banks, that carry some sort of explicit or implicit government guarantee. U.S. Treasury obligations are considered "risk free" because they are backed by the full faith and credit of the U.S. government. Barring the highly unlikely event of a political collapse, a return to investor of the face value of the investment is guaranteed. A more likely risk is that high inflation will erode the real value of investments, but that is a different matter that will be dealt with later in the chapter.

U.S. TREASURY INSTRUMENTS[1]

The "risk-free" U.S. Treasury obligations are the fixed income foundation against which the risks of all other investment vehicles are measured. Treasury instruments come in three varieties: bills, which mature in 1 year or less; notes, which have a maturity date in 2 to 5 years; and bonds, 5 to 10 years (formerly 30 years). Treasury bills come in $1,000 denominations, while notes and bonds are sold in denominations of $10,000 or more.

Treasury bills are sold at a discount to face value. That is, they will pay $1,000 at maturity so they are sold for a slightly lesser amount, say $900-plus. (This is important for tax purposes because the interest is not taxable until the maturity date or until the bills are resold.) These bills are quoted relative to the ending price of 100 (shorthand for 100 percent) and represent the percentage by which to multiply the final value of $1,000 to arrive at the purchase price. Thus, a Treasury bill quoted at 97 means that its purchase price is $970 or 97 percent of the $1,000 final value. Because they are short-term instruments, Treasury bills are considered almost the equivalent of cash.

For a $1,000 Treasury bill maturing in exactly one year that pays interest at an annual rate r, the quoted price Q (that is, the quoted percentage of $1,000 final value) can be calculated by dividing 100 percent by $(1 + r)$, or simply $Q = 100/(1 + r)$. Then, $r = 100/Q - 1$ (expressed in decimals). For example, given a desired r of 5 percent, the quoted price should be $Q = 100/1.05 = 95.24$. It represents 95.24 percent of the $1,000 final value, or $952.40. For a Treasury bill with $Q = 97$, $r = 100/97 - 1 = 0.0309$ or 3.09 percent.

Treasury notes and standard bonds are structured in such a way that they pay interest on a periodic basis and repay the principal on the maturity date. The annual interest rate is known as the coupon rate, because investors used to redeem these payments on and after their due dates by clipping coupons attached to the bonds and presenting them to the issuer for payment. (In the age of electronic transactions when most investors no longer hold the bonds physically, the term *coupon* is used figuratively to denote the transactions.) Treasury notes and bonds are quoted relative to their face values of 100 (shorthand for 100 percent) and represent the percentage by which to multiply the face value to arrive at the purchase price. So a Treasury note or bond quoted at 100 means that its purchase price is $10,000, or 100 percent of its face value of $10,000.

The interest payments are typically made on a semiannual basis, so each coupon actually represents only half of the annual interest. Because of this fact, if a bond bearing a coupon rate of r percent matures in n years, we often treat the instrument as maturing in $2n$ semiannual periods, with a semiannual interest rate of $r/2$ for the purposes of calculating the present value (PV) of the bond. Thus, an 8 percent 5-year bond would be treated as an instrument with a 4 percent yield for each of the 10 periods.

In this book, the *coupon rate* of a bond refers to its annual rate, while the *coupon* refers to the semiannual payment. However, for the purpose of calculations, the face value instead of the quoted price of the bond is used. Furthermore, a bond with a face value P will be characterized as a series of cash flows with payment c at the end of each period 1, 2, ..., $2n$, and a principal amount P payable at period $2n$. Given the interest rate $r/2$ per period, the PV of this bond may be obtained by using generally available interest tables or commercially available software in computers or even pocket calculators.

Since market interest rates change from time to time, the value of the bond varies with such changes. Consider an 8 percent five-year bond that yields 4 percent at each of the six-month periods for a total of 10 periods. If the market rate remains at 8 percent, you will get the market rate of return for the coupons plus the principal at the end. That is, for a $10,000 bond, the PV is simply $10,000. However, if the market interest rate goes down to 6 percent immediately after you purchase the bond and remains at 6 percent for the next five years, then the PV will go up; but if the market interest rate goes up to 10 percent, the PV will go down. The actual present values of the bond under these circumstances are shown in Table 3.1.

Coupon bonds may be sold before their maturity dates. Would you be able to recover the principal of a bond if it were sold before maturity? The answer is no if the market interest rate is higher than the coupon rate. A bond selling for 100 percent of its face value is known as *at par*. The difference between the face value and a lower selling price is called a *discount*; and the difference between a higher selling price and the face value is called a *premium*. When a bond is issued, it sells very close to par value because the coupon is set to approximate the market interest rate. As time passes, however, interest rates may change dramatically, producing a significant premium or discount in a particular bond issue. Coupons are a function of the years in which the bonds were issued. The 1970s were a time of high interest rates, so bonds of those "vintages" have high coupons. The early 1990s were a time of lower interest rates, leading to lower coupons for those "vintages." Thus, bonds issued in the 1970s will likely command premiums until they are retired.

TABLE 3.1 Present Value of a 5-Year 8% Bond

Part A. No change in market interest rate (4% semiannual)

Time Period	Cash Amount	Discount Factor	Present Value	Time Weighted PV
1	400	0.9615	384.60	384.60
2	400	0.9246	369.84	739.68
3	400	0.8890	355.60	1,066.80
4	400	0.8548	341.92	1,367.68
5	400	0.8219	328.76	1,643.80
6	400	0.7903	316.12	1,896.72
7	400	0.7599	303.96	2,127.72
8	400	0.7307	292.28	2,338.24
9	400	0.7026	281.04	2,529.36
10	10,400	0.6756	7,026.24	70,062.40
Total			10,000.36	84,357.00

Part B. Change of market interest rate to semiannual rate of 3% or 5%

Time Period	Cash Amount	3% Semi-Annual Market Interest Rate		5% Semi-Annual Market Interest Rate	
		Discount Factor	Present Value	Discount Factor	Present Value
1	400	0.9709	388.36	0.9524	380.96
2	400	0.9426	377.94	0.9070	362.80
3	400	0.9151	366.04	0.8638	345.52
4	400	0.8885	355.40	0.8227	329.08
5	400	0.8626	345.04	0.7835	313.40
6	400	0.8375	335.00	0.7462	298.48
7	400	0.8131	325.24	0.7107	284.28
8	400	0.7894	315.76	0.6768	270.72
9	400	0.7664	306.56	0.6446	257.84
10	10,400	0.7441	7,738.64	0.6139	6,384.56
Total			10,853.08		9,227.64

The return on a bond is measured by its yield, formally expressed in basis points, wherein one basis point is one hundredth of a percentage point. For example, a 2 percent yield is referred to as 200 basis points. The coupon is an accurate measure of the yield only when the bond is selling at par. If a bond is selling at a premium or discount, a more accurate measure is the current yield, which is the coupon divided by the price of the bond. If the bond is selling at a discount, the current yield is greater than the coupon rate because the denominator is less than 100. If the bond is selling at a premium, the current yield is less than the coupon because the denominator is more than 100.

The current yield calculation does not go quite far enough, because one also must factor in the effect of the premium or discount in a process called *amortization*. Given the maturity date and value, the coupon, and the current price of the bond, one can solve for the true interest rate, or yield to maturity. These calculations will not be performed here, but they can be done on computers or pocket calculators. If the bond is selling at a premium, the amortization factor is negative, making the yield to maturity lower than the current yield. If the bond is selling at a discount, the factor is positive, making this greater than the current yield. So do you want prices to be high or low as an investor? If you are a seller, you naturally want them to be high. As a buyer, you usually want them to be low.

Up to 2001, the U.S. Treasury sold coupon bonds maturing in 30 years with interest payments in six-month periods. However, some investment houses would "strip" the bonds of their interest payments and sell at a substantially lower price only the repayment of the principal at the end of 30 years. For an 8 percent 30-year coupon bond with a face value of $10,000, the buyer of the so-called strip bond will receive only $10,000 at the end of 30 years, without receiving any coupon payments at all. What price should an investor be willing to pay if the market interest is also 8 percent per year? This question can easily be answered by finding the PV of an amount of $10,000 payable at the end of 30 years. In our calculation, the result is found to be $994.

Strip bonds can also be sold before their maturity dates, and are similarly subject to price fluctuations as the standard coupon bonds when the market interest rates change over time. We can derive the PV of a strip bond at different market interest rates over different time periods. With such information, the investor can judge the merits and pitfalls of an offer to buy or sell.

In the final analysis, your goal as a bond investor is to maximize the total return. For any given coupon, the lower the bond price, the higher the yield. Put another way, if bond prices fluctuate because interest rates fluctuate, you want to be a buyer on days when the interest rate is higher rather than lower. Thus, capital gains on bonds are a mixed blessing. On the one hand, there is the increase in capital values, but the flip side of this is that money will be invested in lower rates of return. This condition is particularly hard on any new money that may come into the investor's possession.

A bond is an instrument that embodies a contract to pay a certain sum on a fixed date. A bond, unlike a stock, need never be sold in order to realize its ultimate value. Thus, you can work backward from the maturity date and the interest rate in order to buy the bond as cheaply as possible. The focus is to pose the question properly: "How low can I get it?" and not "Will it go up?" A value investor would apply the same principle to stocks.

MACAULAY DURATION

In 1938, Frederick Macaulay proposed a concept for measuring the weighted average time to recover the PVs of the amounts in the cash flows from a bond. Consider a coupon bond with a face value of P and a coupon payment c per period and the principal payment P at the end of n periods. Then the PV of the coupon for each period t is equal to c times the discount factor corresponding to t (for $t = 1, 2, ..., n$). The summation of these PVs equals the sum of all PV_t from $t = 1$ to $t = n$. The time-weighted PV is defined as $t * PV_t$ (for $t = 1, 2, ..., n$). Then the summation of time-weighted PVs is given by the sum of all $t * PV_t$ from $t = 1$ to $t = n$. Then, the weighted average time T is obtained by dividing the summation of time-weighted PVs by the summation of PVs, and that weighted average time is called Macaulay duration, named after the originator who proposed this measure. It can be expressed in a formula shown in Figure 3.1.

Consider an example of a five-year 8 percent coupon bond of $10,000 denomination, which consists of 10 six-month periods with 4 percent interest per period. The numerical values for various terms in the formula for computing the Macaulay duration are given in the columns for a 4 percent

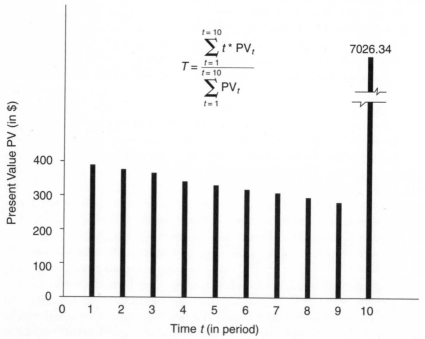

FIGURE 3.1 Macaulay Duration.

semiannual interest rate in Table 3.1. Thus, the Macaulay duration for this bond is found to be $t = 84,357/10,000 = 8.4357$ periods. Since this duration is based on 10 periods of six months each, the Macaulay duration in term of years is obtained by dividing this number by 2, resulting in $8.4357/2 = 4.21785$ years.

A similar calculation is carried out for both a five-year 6 percent coupon bond and a five-year 10 percent bond in Table 3.2. The Macaulay durations for these bonds are found to be 8.7861 periods and 8.1067 periods, respectively. The corresponding durations in terms of years are 4.39305 and 4.05335 years. It can be seen from these examples that, all other things being equal, the higher the interest rate, the shorter the duration, and the sooner the investor recovers the PVs of the amounts in the cash flows. In a sense, the Macaulay duration measures the riskiness of bonds, since the sooner the PVs of the amounts in the cash flows of bonds are recovered, the safer is the bond.

In the special case of a zero-coupon bond, the coupons all have zero values and the sum of present values of all intermediate periods is zero. Thus, the summation of the time-weighted PVs is identical to the summation of PVs times the period to maturity, which simply equals the PV of the repayment at maturity, and the Macaulay duration equals exactly the time to maturity. If there is even one coupon payment before the maturity date, the time-weighted PV of that coupon is less than the time-weighted PV of the principal; so the weighted "average" of the two pulls down the duration. If there are many coupons, the duration of the bond is much shorter than the time to maturity. It can be shown that, if there is a change in interest rate of x percent, a good approximation for the change in the value of the bond is the Macaulay duration times x percent. Since a bond with long duration is more sensitive to changes in interest rate than one with short duration, a 30-year zero-coupon bond with a Macaulay duration of 30 will rise or fall nearly 30 percent, given a 1 percent fall or rise in the interest rate.

After reviewing the risk and return characteristics of bonds, these characteristics can be generalized in five rules of thumb, as follows:

1. When prices go up, yields go down, and vice versa, because the maturity date and terminal value of the bond are known in advance.
2. Assuming times to maturity are equal, a bond with larger coupons has a shorter Macaulay duration than a bond with smaller coupons.
3. A bond's Macaulay duration is never longer than the remaining time to maturity, and is usually shorter except in the special case of a zero-coupon bond.
4. All other things being equal, a bond with a longer time to maturity has a longer Macaulay duration than a bond with a shorter time to maturity.
5. A long-duration bond is more sensitive to changes in interest rates than a shorter-duration bond.

TABLE 3.2 Present Values of 5-Year 6% and 10% Bonds

Part A. 6% Bond (3% interest per period)

Time Period	Cash Amount	Discount Factor	Present Value	Time Weighed PV
1	300	0.9709	291.27	291.27
2	300	0.9426	282.78	565.56
3	300	0.9151	274.53	823.59
4	300	0.8885	206.55	1,066.20
5	300	0.8626	258.78	1,293.90
6	300	0.8375	251.25	1,507.50
7	300	0.8131	243.93	1,707.51
8	300	0.7894	236.82	1,894.56
9	300	0.7664	229.92	2,069.28
10	10,300	0.7441	7,664.23	76,642.30
Total			10,000.06	87,861.67

Macaulay duration $T = 87,861/10,000 = 8.7861$ periods.

Part B. 10% Bond (5% interest per period)

Time Period	Cash Amount	Discount Factor	Present Value	Time Weighed PV
1	500	0.9524	976.20	976.20
2	500	0.9070	453.50	907.00
3	500	0.8638	431.90	1,295.70
4	500	0.8227	411.35	1,645.40
5	500	0.7835	391.75	1,958.75
6	500	0.7462	373.10	2,238.60
7	500	0.7107	355.35	2,487.45
8	500	0.6768	338.40	2,707.20
9	500	0.6446	322.30	2,900.70
10	10,500	0.6139	6,445.95	64,459.50
Total			9,999.80	81,076.50

Macaulay duration $T = 81,076/10,000 = 8.1076$ periods.

EFFECTS OF INFLATION[2]

U.S. Treasury bonds are protected by full faith and credit of the government against the erosion of their nominal values, but not necessarily against their real values. Even if one can avoid the effects of fluctuations of market interest rates by holding a bond to its maturity date, one cannot escape completely the market forces influencing its real value. In addition to the law of supply and demand, inflation is a major factor in affecting the outcome of investments, particularly in bonds of long duration.

Before considering the effects of inflation, we will consider the mechanism by which inflation creeps into the market interest rate. Let r be the "real" interest rate excluding inflation, and j be the interest rate including inflation (or deflation), usually referred to as the *nominal interest rate*. Let k be the average rate of price change (usually inflation but possibly deflation, for which k becomes negative). In calculating conventional measures of financial instruments, such as the present values of bonds, we use the discount factor $(1 + j)$ to account for inflation. This factor can be converted to the form of $(1 + r) * (1 + k)$, which contains separate elements to account for the real interest rate and rate of inflation. When we equate the two factors, that is, $(1 + j) = (1 + r) * (1 + k)$, we find $j = r + k + r * k$, and $r = (j - k) / (1 + k)$. If r and j (when expressed in decimals) are small compared to 1, as is usually the case, then we can drop the cross-product term $r * k$ in the equation for j, and eliminate k in the denominator of the equation for r without a serious rounding error. Then, the relations between r and j with respect to k can be approximated by $j = r + k$ and $r = j - k$. In other words, the nominal interest rate equals approximately the real interest rate plus the average rate of inflation.

With reference to bond investments, r in the above equations is called the *coupon interest rate,* which denotes the rate excluding inflation subsequent to the issuance of the bond, while j represents the real interest rate at a given time. Of course, the demand and supply for bonds also influence the nominal and real value of the interest rate. Thus, the market interest rate includes the effects of both inflation and the demand and supply of credit.

During the course of the 1970s, yields on Treasury bonds exploded from less than 5 percent to more than 15 percent, reflecting a corresponding increase in inflation. Such a process had never before occurred during peacetime in the history of the United States. The result was that bonds issued during the 1960s with sub–5 percent coupons offered negative real rates of return when inflation exceeded these levels in the 1970s, and bonds fell severely in value to restore to positive levels the real yield to maturity. Investors who had bought low-coupon Treasury bonds in the 1970s, 1960s, and even 1950s suffered unprecedented capital losses. Because rising interest rates were mainly a function of rising inflation, investors who held the bonds to maturity found that the principal values had been largely eroded by changes in price levels.

One instrument introduced in the late 1990s as a fighter against inflation was the Treasury inflation-protected securities (TIPS). Under the market conditions in early 2000s, these securities were priced to guarantee a real yield of over 3 percent. These instruments were largely ignored because inflation was, or at least was believed to be, below 2 percent at a time when the long bond was at times paying over 6 percent. Therefore, real rates were over 4 percent on the instruments, or more than the rate on TIPS. Many developing countries have local versions of inflation-protected bonds.

The inflation-protected bonds are issued at par, but the value of their principal is escalated according to the consumer price index (CPI). Thus, a bond issued at 100 might have a principal value of 110 several years later, based on the CPI. The interest is represented by coupons, which are fixed in value, and therefore the bond offers a declining current yield over time as a percentage of the escalated values of the principal. Quotations are taken as a percentage of the escalated, not the original, principal value. Thus, with a principal of 110, a quote of 99 really means a price of 0.99 * 110, or almost 109. If there is deflation, the principal value could go down, and a bond issued at par might find a principal value of only 99 if there is a 1 percent decrease in the CPI. This has not happened in the short time period since the TIPS were introduced, but Fed Chairman Alan Greenspan seemed to be worried about deflation as of early 2003.

The variation of the real interest rate is based on the nominal interest rate on one hand, and the inflation rate on the other. The risk of changing nominal rates could be avoided by locking in money for long periods of time. The risk of hedging against inflation by TIPS is far more difficult. Guessing inflation rates and, more importantly, changes in the inflation rate is a job that would fully tax the resources of a competent professional economist. To the extent that an investor has a lesser degree of skill, it might be safer just to place money in inflation-protected bonds in which there is no guesswork than in more traditional bonds quoted on a nominal basis.

Inflation protection is not perfect (except in a tax-deferred account such as an individual retirement account [IRA]) because the interest income is taxable, as is the accretion of the principal tied to the inflation rate (as would be the case in a zero-coupon bond). If there were outright deflation leading to a decline in the principal value, then the protection would be better because the decrease in principal would create a tax benefit. Inflation-indexed bonds could well be the instrument of choice for pension funds and other retirement vehicles that must guarantee the preservation of capital under all circumstances while earning as large a residual yield as possible.

MANAGING THE RISKS ASSOCIATED WITH TREASURY BONDS

Since investing in Treasury bonds involves both inflation risk and other risks implicitly or explicitly included in our discussions, how can we manage such risks? Problems implied by this question require serious consideration.

Changes in market interest rates have opposite effects on the principal, which is received far in the future, and on coupons, which are received currently. If the market rate goes up, the value of the principal goes down, but the coupons become more valuable because they can be reinvested at high interest rates. If the market rate goes down, the value of the long-dated principal goes up but the coupons become less valuable.

Many investors want to know how high or low the price of a bond should be before engaging in any transaction. If you are a seller, you naturally want them to be high so that you can reap the gain. As a buyer, you usually want them to be low for two reasons. One has to do with tax purposes. If a bond is bought at a discount, you get a capital gain on maturity or sale that is taxed at a lower rate than ordinary income from sources such as coupons. The second has to do with inflation. The principal value of a bond will probably be worth less on its maturity date than the same amount on its purchase, after taking inflation into account.

You might need to purchase a bond at, say, 90, in order to have the same "real" (inflation-adjusted) value when the bond matures at its face value. The downside of a discount bond is that your coupon and current yield are lower than those on a par or premium bond, because the difference appears in the form of a capital gain. But this exercise is just a reality check that shows that you ought to put aside part of the coupon (of a bond selling at par), just to make up for inflation. You really can't afford to spend the whole yield.

The advantage of a premium bond is that you get a fat current yield, but the disadvantage is that you get a capital loss if you hold it to maturity (and usually for shorter periods as well). Compounding this problem is the fact that there is no protection against inflation. So the high current yield actually encourages an investor to spend too much currently, and not to plow back money to compensate for the effects of inflation and loss of principal value. If investors hold such bonds to maturity while the interest rates go up, they suffer the so-called opportunity loss—the chances to invest the same money at higher interest rates.

An opposite situation involves reinvestment risk when market interest rates in the future will be lower than the coupon rates. For example, the interest rates were historically high in the early 1980s but fell during the course of the decade and into the 1990s. During this time, the coupons on bonds had to be reinvested at progressively lower rates of return. Fortunately, there was a solution to the problem: investing in strip bonds. Since the coupons have been removed from strip bonds, there are no coupons to invest, hence no reinvestment problem. Most brokerage houses issue Treasury strip bonds under such acronyms as LYON (linked yield option note) and TIGR (Treasury investment growth receipt). Meanwhile, interest would accrue at the rate implied by the discount until the time to maturity. Investors should note that the interest that has been accrued, but not paid, on such bonds is taxable on an annual basis (except in tax-deferred accounts such as IRAs).

In order to manage the risk of fluctuating market interest rates, an investor can diversify a bond portfolio in two ways. The obvious one is by buying the obligations of different issuers. But an equally important means of diversifying your holdings might be to buy a number of bonds of the same issuer (e.g., the U.S. Treasury) maturing at different times. This strategy is known as "laddering." You might buy bonds maturing in one, two, three, four, five, or more years in roughly equal amounts. This way, part of your bond portfolio will be maturing each year, and can be reinvested at different interest rates. You avoid placing all of your money at the top (or the bottom) of the market.

Another risk to bonds, including Treasuries, is taxes. U.S. obligations are free from state and local taxes, but federal taxes take their toll. To get around this, the U.S. Treasury also issues "zero-coupon bonds," for which the coupon payments will automatically be reinvested at a prespecified rate until their maturity dates. Thus, the investor will defer taxes on the coupon payments of a zero-coupon bond until its maturity. A special case known as EE bonds was introduced in the early 1980s to encourage ordinary people to save. Through commercial banks, U.S. Treasury offers EE bonds at a purchase price at 50 percent discount from par. The so-called first maturity is achieved when the accrued value of purchase price plus interest at variable rates reaches par at some unspecified time in the future. At this point, the investor can withdraw the par value without penalty or reinvest the amount at the quoted interest rate until the so-called final maturity, the specified term of the bond, say 20 years.

The EE bonds typically carry a variable interest rate that is lower than U.S. Treasury obligations of the same maturity, but they have several other attractive features that compensate for this fact:

1. An investor can sell back the bond at any time to the U.S. government based on the its accreted value derived from the stated, not the market, interest rate. Thus, there is no principal risk because the interest rate is known.
2. The investor can either pay taxes on the interest annually, as in the case with other stripped bonds, or else defer the tax until the bond matures or is sold.
3. If another Series E bond is issued at a higher rate, the holder of a bond with a lower rate can exchange it for the bond with higher rate, dollar for dollar, thereby capturing the higher interest rate.

Thus, Series E bonds combine a moderately high-yield, principal protection, as well as absolute safety of the credit and tax deferral features.

Because of all the considerations alluded to above (and a number that haven't even been mentioned), optimizing bond returns is a difficult job even for a sophisticated professional investor. The job involves trading, or at least positioning, a portfolio in ways that make it possible to lose money even in Treasury instruments with a money-back guarantee. To a professional investor, paper losses become real losses that are locked in as he or she tries to reposition for the next maneuver.

The amateur investor, however, should strive to obtain only acceptable, rather than optimal, results from bond investing. This means not continually trying to position the portfolio for maximum total return. Instead, a more appropriate goal is to manage on a "new money" basis, long the staple of institutions with steady cash flows such as insurance companies. That is, an amateur investor should try to maximize return on the "new money" as it comes in, while holding "old money" investments to maturity (and maintaining a high degree of safety for the portfolio as a whole all the time). Temporary paper losses due to fluctuations in interest rates should not be locked in, because these will be compensated for by higher yields (on the marked-down values). At the end of the day, the object is to get some return over time that will compensate for inflation and modestly increase spending power in real terms.

OTHER TYPES OF HIGHLY SECURED FIXED-INCOME INSTRUMENTS

Municipal bonds are conventionally treated as government bonds because they are issued by state and local governments or other governmental authorities. Like those of the U.S. government, municipal bonds are supported by the taxing authority of the municipality. But there are two differences. The first is that a city has a much smaller, and less stable, tax base than the country as a whole. People routinely move in and out of the jurisdiction to a far greater extent than they move in and out of the United States. The second is that a municipality, unlike the federal government, cannot bail itself out by printing money. The same is true for bonds issued by states.

There are two types of municipal bonds. The first is general obligation bonds (or GOs), which are supported by the taxing authority of the municipality. The second is revenue bonds, which are tied to the revenues of a specific project (sometimes referred to as an authority or some other name), and are really a form of project finance. In most cases, GOs are safer because of the larger revenue (read "tax") base. But a large investor might prefer a revenue bond that was tied to a specific project.

Municipal bonds are far less safe today than when Warren Buffett wrote to his investors in 1970, "I cannot imagine the City of New York not paying its bills."[3] First, a number of municipalities including New York City went to the brink of default shortly after Mr. Buffett made his assessment. Second, the federal government passed a law in 1979 allowing municipalities to default (rather than raise taxes to pay their obligations). Third, there were the interrupted payments or temporary default of a number of authorities, such as the Washington Power Supply Service (sometimes referred to as WPSS before its default, and "Whoops" afterward). Incidentally, Warren Buffett made a pile of money buying those bonds at a discount. Finally, there have been cases of municipal bankruptcy and default, such Orange County, California, which lost millions on derivative contracts by a rogue treasurer, Robert Citron.

More conservative investors often favor municipal bonds. As per the Constitution of the United States, they are exempt from federal taxes. Bonds of many jurisdictions are "triple tax free," which means that they are exempt from state and local taxes also if the buyer lives in those jurisdictions. Their real advantage is the tax shelter that they provide. The measure of a bond's return is "taxable equivalent income," the amount of income before taxes it would take to match the untaxed sheltered income. For instance, if the investor were in a 33 percent tax bracket, counting federal, state, and local taxes, and earned 6 percent on a municipal bond, the taxable equivalent income would be 9 percent. This 9 percent yield, taxed at 33 percent, would work out to 6 percent after tax, and the 3 percent difference represents a tax subsidy. However, such obligations are sensitive to changes in tax rate, which in turn changes the tax subsidy. Moreover, municipal bonds have credit and interest rate risk.

There are a number of government-related agencies that have a call on the U.S. Treasury, the most famous of which is the Government National Mortgage Agency (Ginnie Mae for short). There are also a number of agencies that are chartered by the government but are owned by private stockholders that also issue paper. These include Federal National Mortgage (Fannie Mae), and Federal Home Loan Mortgage (Freddie Mac). Formerly, this category also included Student Loan Marketing Association (Sallie Mae), but this agency has been fully privatized. These institutions are known as government-sponsored entities (or GSEs). Unlike Ginnie Mae, their bonds do not have a legal guarantee against default, but it is hard to imagine the U.S. government defaulting on such paper because of the economic and political ramifications for the programs. As such, they yield about 100 basis points or so more than Treasuries, meaning that their bonds are considered quite safe, although not as safe as U.S. Treasuries. One important risk is a political one—that the program (e.g., subsidized housing) may be discontinued. In that case, existing bondholders would be paid off during the winding down of the program, but no new investors could be admitted.

It must also be noted that although they derive protection from their sponsorship by the U.S. government, these agencies function as business enterprises. As such, their objectives are to maximize profits rather than minimize risk. In fact, some of them compete with private-sector companies, capitalizing on their government affiliation in order to gain a competitive advantage. In at least one case, a GSE took on leverage ratios in this new century comparable to those assumed by Long-Term Capital Management, a prestigious international hedge fund, in 1998. The rationale was that government-backed assets were financed by government paper, but a similar match in "government" paper (albeit in those of foreign sovereign entities in many cases) brought about the demise of the hedge fund. As was the case with municipalities such as New York in the 1970s, there probably won't be "ultimate" failure for government entities, but there could be a period of anxiety for bondholders.

Bank deposits will be discussed in this section because we can now treat them as if they were government-guaranteed securities. This has not always been the case. Until the Great Depression, depositors could lose all their deposits in a failed bank. As a result, the biggest fear up to the early 1930s was a "run on the bank"—people losing confidence in a particular bank and taking all their money out, leaving the bank unable to conduct routine operations. Under these circumstances, there wouldn't be enough money to take care of the last group of depositors. The knock-on result was the fact that businesses suddenly lost access to credit just when they needed it the most, and went bankrupt in far larger numbers than was justified even by the grim economic conditions of the time.

The Federal Deposit Insurance Corporation (FDIC) was created to prevent this from happening again. Currently, every depositor in a participating bank is insured up to $100,000 by the federal government. This $100,000 applies to each *depositor*, not to each account. Thus, a married couple with a joint account would be insured up to $200,000, but a person with $75,000 in each of checking and savings accounts would be insured up to only $100,000, even though the accounts totaled $150,000. (The banks pay the insurance as a cost of doing business.) This is a provision that protects "small" savers. Large investors will do well to spread their deposits in a number of different banks, keeping the account sizes near or below the $100,000 insured amount. But for our purposes, bank deposits can be considered "safe."

Banks offer several deposit plans to meet various financial needs. The first is checking, or demand deposits. These accounts generally do not pay interest because money can be withdrawn from them on demand (typically through a check). A variation of a checking account is a Negotiable Order of Withdrawal (NOW) account, which is an account bearing interest (on a daily basis) that also confers check-writing privileges. The drawbacks to these accounts are that interest rates on them are comparatively low, and they require minimum balances of money that could otherwise be put into other, higher-yielding accounts. For instance, a depositor may have a choice of putting $10,000 into a NOW account yielding 2 percent annually, that is, $200 in all, or of having a checking account with an average of $2,500 yielding 0 percent and the remaining $7,500 in a savings account yielding 4 percent for a total of $300. For most investors (except those with large paychecks of more than $2,500 and large monthly expenditures from the checking account), the second alternative is preferable.

A second type of account is a savings account, otherwise known as a time deposit. These are 90-day accounts, insofar as the rate of interest is set every 90 days. In theory, the bank may also require the depositor to give notice of up to 90 days before withdrawing the money, although in practice, this is almost never done. Because of the theoretical 90-day maturity, interest rates on savings accounts are higher than those on NOW accounts, and they certainly beat the 0 percent rates on ordinary checking accounts. As a practical matter, the disadvantage of the time deposit is lesser convenience; a depositor has to visit an automated teller machine (ATM) or human teller at the bank in order to withdraw money, instead of merely writing a check.

For long periods of time, typically six months or more, and larger amounts of money, typically $1,000 or more, banks will offer certificates of deposit (CDs). These instruments "lock in" money for a stated period of time, say five years, and also lock in a stated interest rate for the whole time. Therefore, rates are usually higher than on time deposits. The drawback is a penalty for early withdrawal. Typically, the bank turns around and makes investments, in Treasury bonds or loans, of roughly the same maturity. The penalty to the early withdrawer is to compensate the bank for costs incurred in early liquidation of investments, or for causing a "mismatch" in maturities. Unlike bonds or most other fixed-income instruments, a CD is not negotiable.

CHAPTER 4

Fixed-Income Issues of Corporations

Corporate bonds are obligations of corporations. Unlike U.S. Treasury securities, they have the credit risk of nonpayment because the companies have to earn, rather than merely print, the money to pay interest and principal. This risk ranges from very slight to significant. The bonds of an Exxon Mobil or a Johnson & Johnson are far safer than most. IBM was once in this category too but dropped a couple of levels when it lost its leadership in the computer industry.

The evaluation of corporate bonds (as well as stocks) begins with an analysis of financial statements of the issuing corporation. Bonds that are backed by the full faith and credit of corporations, rather than the United States or some other major sovereign government, must be analyzed in much the same way as the equity of those same corporations. The key difference is that bonds have repayment priority over any form of equity. But they are typically junior to bank debt, especially that which already existed at the time of the bond issuance. Hence, bonds often are not the most senior securities in a corporation's capital structure.

INFORMATION FROM FINANCIAL STATEMENTS[1]

Useful information may be extracted from financial statements of corporations. We will focus on the items that are pertinent to bondholders and defer further explanation of some others until later.

The document that measures the financial position of a firm is the balance sheet, because it balances the company's assets and claims against assets. According to convention, the balance sheet has a standard form that lists the assets on the left-hand page and liabilities and stockholders' equity on the right-hand page. Other formats are sometimes used, but they are less common. Usually, a balance sheet presents the information for the most recent year just ended, and the previous year's data is given in the annual report for the purpose of comparison.

Assets and liabilities are listed in descending order of liquidity on the balance sheet. At the top of the assets column on its left-hand side are current assets such as cash or other items that can be quickly converted into cash, such as marketable securities, accounts receivable, and inventory. Noncurrent assets include fixed assets such as plant, property, and equipment and so-called intangible assets such as patents, trademarks, and goodwill.

The top portion on the right-hand side of the balance sheet is structured much the same way. Liabilities are debts incurred to acquire assets. At the top of the list are current liabilities, such as accounts payable, short-term debt, and wages or taxes payable, that must be paid within a few days or weeks, and in any event, no more than one year. In the middle of the column are long-term debt and other long-term liabilities that can be paid over one or more years. These debts include bank loans and bonds. Stockholders' equity is represented by what's left over, the difference between assets and liabilities, which belongs to investors. This is a "plug" number that makes the balance sheet balance. If liabilities are greater than assets, stockholders' equity can be negative, which is usually a sign that the company is in trouble.

Another document of interest to a bondholder is the income statement, which shows how much the company has been earning. The typical income statement will begin with sales or revenues, followed by several categories of expenses, the explanation of which will be deferred until Chapter 6. The statement continues to reach a line called earnings before interest and taxes (EBIT), which is of greatest interest to bond investors. The most important fact about this line is that interest is deductible from income for tax purposes, so if interest expense equals or exceeds EBIT, no tax is paid. After the subtraction of interest expense from EBIT, taxes are assessed, and what is left is net profit.

MEASURES OF BOND SAFETY

The financial aspects of a firm that concern a prospective debt investor the most are liquidity, solvency, and profitability. Investors in equities, or stocks, have similar concerns, but the order is often reversed—profitability, solvency, and liquidity.

Liquidity can be determined by the relationship of current assets to current liabilities. One measure of liquidity is the difference between the two, which is called *working capital*. However, this measure is often misleading. For example, a firm with $200,000 in current assets and $100,000 in current liabilities and another firm with $1.1 million in current assets and $1 million in current liabilities have the same amount of working capital (i.e., $100,000), but it is intuitively obvious that, percentage-wise, the first firm is more liquid.

A better measure of liquidity than working capital is the current ratio, which is defined as the ratio of current assets to current liabilities. In the preceding example, the current ratio for the first firm is 2 while the current ratio for the second firm is 1.1. Generally, the current ratio should be above 2. If it is much below this figure, the company may have some trouble generating enough cash to meet its short-term obligations, because some of its inventories and accounts receivable included under current assets may not be convertible into cash quickly. A more rigorous test is the "quick" ratio, resulting from cash, marketable securities, and accounts receivable compared to current liabilities.

Working capital (current assets minus current liabilities) will be a positive number as long as current assets are greater than current liabilities. If this number is negative, it is often a sign that the company is having liquidity problems. A condensed balance sheet would show working capital (or what Graham and Dodd would call *net working capital*) at the top, fixed assets on the left-hand side, and the debt and equity on the right-hand side. Graham and Dodd would also compute another quantity, current assets minus all liabilities, which they called *net-net working capital* (or "net-net" for short). They preferred that this number be positive when making either a debt or an equity investment.

The three main measures of bond safety are: (1) debt to total capital, (2) times interest earned, and (3) the pretax return on total capital. Taken together, they give a fairly comprehensive picture of the safety of any bond issues, particularly if they are supplemented by industry- and company-specific information.

Solvency can be measured in two different ways. The first way, debt to total capital, is just a measure of strength of the balance sheet based on the relationship of debt and shareholders' equity. *Total capital* is conventionally defined as the sum of shareholders' equity plus long-term debt. Working capital is excluded from total capital. The second way, the interest coverage ratio, is the ratio of EBIT to interest payments. It is also called *times interest earned*, and is a gauge of the company's ability to meet its interest payments.

In Graham and Dodd's day, the ratio of debt to shareholders' equity, or debt–equity ratio, was the measure of debt financing, or leverage. The more modern measure of leverage is debt as a percentage of total capital (debt plus equity). These are really two different ways of saying the same thing. For instance, Graham and Dodd would say that a company's debt-to-equity ratio should be no more than 1 to 1. The modern expression of this concept is there should be no more than a 50–50 relationship between debt and equity, or debt should amount to no more than 50 percent of total capital. In fact, we would consider 50 percent an outer limit of acceptability for debt (except for inherently leveraged operations such as banks and utilities). The lower the debt-to-total-capital ratio, the safer the bond.

Times interest earned, or interest coverage, is the ratio of EBIT to interest payments. Because interest expense is deductible from income for tax purposes, the higher the ratio, the greater the safety of interest payments. In this calculation, one does not count equity income (which is earned through partial control over other companies) or other noncash income items. Interest coverage must be considered not only in the context of things as they stand currently, but also in terms of reasonably foreseeable economic scenarios, down as well as up. On balance, an interest coverage ratio of three times may be considered barely adequate, four to five times as moderate, and one should not feel totally comfortable with coverage of less than six to seven times. We would regard situations in which interest is covered only two times as being inadequate even on an ongoing basis, with no margin for error if things go wrong. Many companies are in such straits; some are so-called "fallen angels" through circumstances beyond their control, but others, upon initial founding or a major expansion, through conscious decision. As Warren Buffett would point out, the second situation is far more dangerous than the first because of the willful nature of the management rather than economic vicissitude. Such a condition is sometimes known as *moral hazard*.

The worst situation is one in which interest is not being covered at all, because the company is losing money on an operating basis. An apparently sound Graham and Dodd investment, Baldwin United was selling at five times reported earnings in late 1982. But there was an important footnote in the Capital Structure section (interest not covered) of the Value Line report at the time, indicating an operating loss. The reported earnings came from the sale of insurance products that the company assumed would provide tax benefits that were later disallowed. Against the guidance of his company's ranking system, a young analyst at Value Line named Jeff Vinik, who later went on to do greater things, came up with a brilliant tongue-in-cheek recommendation against the stock in the written report whose statistics are shown in Figure 4.1. The company went bankrupt when its illusory "earnings" could not be used to service debt.

The pretax return on total capital (PROTC) relates income statement and balance sheet amounts. This is the ratio of EBIT to total capital and is a measure of the return that the company is earning on its capital, or its profitability. It is stated before taxes, because interest is deductible for tax purposes. (Equity investors are more interested in measures of after-tax profitability since they get what is left over after the creditors and the government have been paid.) This ratio is less important than the other two measures of bond safety (i.e., debt to total capital and times interest earned) because of the seniority of debt. If debt is less than 30 percent of total capital and the interest coverage ratio is favorable, it will then be the equity

1980	1981	1982E	1983E	Year
47.63	124.94	**169.90**	154.75	Sales per share
2.97	4.40	**8.50**	8.55	"Cash Flow" per share
2.36	3.48	**5.45**	7.00	Earnings per share
0.68	0.80	**0.84**	0.85	Dividends per share
12.61	15.32	**21.35**	28.90	Book Value per share
19.73	19.95	**20.50**	21.00	Shares (mill.)
12.90	18.40	20.3		Share price (Year low)
255	367	**416**		Market Cap (mill.)
7.9	6.5	**5.9**		P/E Ratio
1.0	1.2	**1.0**		P/B Ratio
3.60%	3.55	2.80%		Dividend yield
939.6	2492.1	**3500**	3250	Sales (mill.)
7.7	10.3	**13.5**	15	Depreciation (mill.)
53.7	79.3	**120**	165	Net Profit (mill.)
NMF	NMF	**NMF**	NMF	Income Tax Rate
2591	4957	**9900**	18500	Total Assets (mill.)
140.5	303.1	**550**	600	Long Term Debt (mill.)
275	325.7	**550**	775	Shareholders' equity (mill.)
14.7%	15.8%	**16.5%**	15.0%	Return on Capital
19.5%	24.4%	**22.0%**	21.5%	Return on Equity
13.8%	19.0%	**18.3%**	17.8%	Reinvestment rate
5.7%	5.4%	**3.7%**	3.7%	Dividend Distribution Rate
71%	78%	**83%**	83%	Retained Earnings Rate
29%	22%	**17%**	17%	Dividend Payout Ratio

Bold figures were Value Line estimates, or derived from them.

Capital Structure as of 9/30/82
Total Debt: 1631.4 mill.
LT Debt: 530.2 mill.

(Interest Not Covered)   *(57% of Capital)*

Preferred Stock   (2% of Capital)
Common Stock   (41% of Capital)

Source: Value Line Publishing Inc.; author's calculations.
The italics in the capital structure section are the author's.

FIGURE 4.1   Summary Statistics for Baldwin United 1980–1983.

holders who will be "short-changed" by the company's low profitability. Even so, low overall profitability can be an "early warning" signal for debt holders that their investment is not as safe as it might be otherwise. A low PROTC is an indication of very limited borrowing capacity.

RATING OF BONDS

Bonds are graded by rating agencies such as Standard and Poor's (S&P), Moody's, or Fitch. A handful of bonds of the highest quality, those that carry practically no risk of nonpayment, receive an AAA rating from S&P or the equivalent Aaa rating from Moody's. Only very few companies currently fall into this category, including Exxon Mobil, Johnson & Johnson, Pfizer, and Warren Buffett's Berkshire Hathaway, as well as several others that probably do not deserve this sterling rating. They are immune to any except the worst cyclical shock, such as another Great Depression or worse. Bonds that carry only a slight credit risk receive the next highest rating, AA. Obligations in these top two levels are sometimes referred to as *gilt-edged securities,* and are considered suitable even for very conservative investors, such as the proverbial "widows and orphans." To reflect this fact, their yields are barely more than the Treasuries, typically a fraction of a percentage point in the case of AAAs, and just over a percentage point in the case of AAs.

Bonds of medium quality are called *investment grade.* They are slightly or somewhat speculative, but are suitable for most investors. These include A-rated bonds, which are fairly well protected, and hence are predominantly investment vehicles with moderately speculative elements. The next lower level, BBB, refers to investments that have significant, but not predominant, elements of speculation, and moderate levels of protection.

Bonds rated below investment grade are considered to be predominantly speculative vehicles, and are often referred to as *junk bonds.* Because many institutions are prohibited by mandate from investing in bonds rated lower than BBB, such bonds are less liquid than higher-rated issues. The highest of these levels, BB, represents a speculation with some redeeming investment features, and instruments rated in this category are sometimes described by the oxymoron *quality junk.* Bonds rated single B are considered very speculative, because of their lack of protection from economic uncertainty, but without imminent risk of default. Bonds rated lower than this, such as CCC, CC, and C, are believed to carry varying degrees of default risk.

Junk bonds are known more formally as high-yield bonds. BB-rated bonds typically pay a least three to five percentage points (300 to 500 basis points in finance lingo) more than Treasury bonds of comparable maturity, and lower-rated bonds sometimes 10 or more percentage points more than the Treasuries. Their main risk is credit risk, rather than interest rate risk.

They may actually offer some protection against rising interest rates if these changes are the result of an improvement in business conditions that upgrades the quality of junk bonds. In this regard, junk bonds are more like equity than bonds. The yields are typically in high single- to low double-digit percentages, and if an investor purchases them at a significant discount to par, the prospective returns are equity-type returns in the low to mid-teens. If a company's financial position improves, however, the bond will go up in value just because of the company's greater "ability to pay." That's because the yield to maturity will fall to reflect the bond's lower risk, and the bond will sell at a premium or lower discount.

Ratio analysis is usually the key to arriving at bond ratings, although the rating agencies will sometimes consider other factors such as the nature of the industry or the quality of management. The ratios used by rating agencies include: debt to total capital, times interest earned (interest cover ratio), and pretax return on total capital. (In the case of Enron, they may have given too much weight to the reported numbers and the nature of the industry, and not enough to poor quality of management, which used all kinds of tricks to report distorted numbers.) Typical ratios required by rating agencies for the three main measures of safety in each rating category are shown in Table 4.1.

If anything, the safety of bonds must be of even more paramount importance than is the case for stocks, because bonds pay a fixed rate of interest and no more. While an equity investor who purchases several speculative stocks may be bailed out by a large gain on one of them that makes up for his losses on the others, a bond investor who has even one default is apt to suffer tremendously because returns on the other investments will just pay for themselves and not recoup losses on the wayward one. Hence, a policy of "zero tolerance," or something close to it, must be the rule regarding credit losses on bonds bought around par.

Graham and Dodd advised conservative investors not to buy bonds of companies with an interest coverage ratio of less than three times, but to

TABLE 4.1 Bond Rating Model

Metric/Rating	AAA	AA	A	BBB	BB	B	CCC or Lower
Interest Earned ($\times$)	>15$\times$	5–15$\times$	4–5$\times$	2–3$\times$	1–2$\times$	0–1$\times$	Negative
Debt/Total Capital	<15%	15%–25%	25%–35%	35%–45%	45%–55%	55%–65%	>65%
Pretax Return	>30%	15%–30%	12%–15%	10%–12%	8%–10%	0%–8%	<0%

Source: Modified version of a table presented in an article by Jane Tripp Howe, "Corporate Credit Analysis," cited in F. Fabrozzi, ed., *The Fixed Income Handbook* (Chicago: Irwin Press, 1995): 388.

buy bonds with credits of BBB or better. We would strengthen this prohibition for the average investor to single A or better, which implies an interest coverage ratio of four to five times, and a debt-to-total-capital ratio of no more than 25 to 35 percent.

On the whole, we would not look to assets as securities for debt, if the company is losing money. Such losses are usually an indication that the assets are not worth their stated value. An exception might be liquid working capital assets such as marketable securities and accounts receivable. A lender would have to be much more cautious on inventories, with industry-specific knowledge of the ultimate liquidity of the items in question, rather than the mere ability to read a balance sheet. It is the key to real understanding.

In taking up a debt issue, you must ask why the company wants to issue bonded junior debt, rather than borrow senior money from a bank. The prospectus, a document that accompanies the issue, should give a reason. The one we would most like to see is that the company plans to boost working capital, perhaps by retiring short-term (and senior) debt and extending maturity of the overall debt burden at a fixed rate. In such an event, the very issue of the debt would make it senior to most, while improving on the status quo regarding liquidity. Again, we would be more wary of a debt issue for a major expansion or acquisition, unless we were comfortable with the specific proposed use of the funds.

It must be pointed out that the interests of a bondholder and a stockholder are by no means identical, and in some cases, even adversarial. A stockholder is more often than not primarily concerned about the size of a potential gain; a bondholder, whose returns are limited to interest, plus a gain resulting from a discount to principal at purchase, is much more concerned about the *likelihood* of these gains, plus the safe return of principal. They would logically have different feelings about most forms of earnings growth, for instance. The interests of bondholders and stockholders are identical if the growth occurs in the most favorable way (i.e., because of improved pricing for the company's main product). This is normally reflected in healthier cash flows that are unequivocally good for both types of investors. Too often, however, growth is achieved through capital spending or corporate acquisition programs that benefit the stockholder at the expense of the bondholder. With rare exceptions, the debt-to-capital ratio will rise and the interest coverage and pretax return ratios will fall after such activities. The stockholder, who reaps both upside and downside (and more of the former), will often take heart in such a result; not so for the bondholder, who is often called to foot the bill (through a new debt issue by the company) and will be exposed to all risks of such expansion without participating in the rewards.

Bondholders in the 1990s and the early part of the 2000s often lost sight of this fact and evaluated an issuer's creditworthiness on earnings growth. This practice seemed to work only because bonds were issued mainly to finance growth plans with great expectations, but their safety depended on the success or failure of these initiatives. In fact, bondholders should not permit themselves to be placed in such a position. Newly issued bonds should be bought only when they carry adequate safety *at the time of issue,* based on earnings power *then* available, and giving *zero* weight to prospective increases. Unlike equities, their quality should never be voluntarily subjected to the vagaries of an uncertain future. If interest and equity coverage are not adequate in the present, there is no guarantee that they will be in the future. As a practical matter, most managements are equity friendly, especially in the "equity culture" of the 1990s; a few are bond friendly, but practically none is substantially even-handed to holders of both equities and bonds. A fixed-income investor should take note of this fact when choosing issuers of such instruments.

PURCHASE OF DISCOUNTED BONDS[2]

Graham and Dodd normally took the conservative position that bonds (and stocks) should be bought for income and asset support rather than capital gains. In this case, they would reverse their normal conservative rule by saying that none but the highest-quality bonds should be bought unless there is the prospect of a considerable capital gain as well as income. In fact, the vast majority of bonds do repay principal, sometimes with the greatest difficulty, but the intervening travails often cause the prices to be heavily discounted from par when the bond is poorly secured. Anticipating this fact, Graham and Dodd would warn investors to wait until after the discount has taken place, by perhaps 30 points, to 70. At such a level, an issue becomes very interesting even on current yield. (For example, a 7 percent coupon gives a current yield of 10 percent based on a price of 70.) But the prospect of a large capital gain serves as an additional "sweetener." That's because while a price of 70 represents moderate default risk (and a workout typically takes place at a price between 40 and 60), the 30-point potential upside may well be adequate compensation in the case of a somewhat shaky security. This 30 percent discount is not adequate in the case of a very shaky issue, that is, the junkiest of junk bonds such as WorldCom. It does, however, apply to some of the higher-quality junk bonds and many that are considered to be BBB by the rating agencies.

One issue that should be considered more often than actually practiced is whether one should buy corporate bonds at a premium, or whether investment should be limited to discount bonds, provided that one can get a comparable yield to maturity. Our preference is decidedly in favor of discounted bonds and against the premium bonds. One reason is that the amortization of the discount provides at least some protection against inflation and it represents a form of forced savings. The trade-off, of course, is a lower coupon and current yield. Another reason to prefer discount bonds is the structure of the original bond itself. Although the bond might have a large discount because it was issued during a period of much lower interest rates, a more likely reason is that the credit of the issuer had deteriorated in the meantime and the bond had fallen to reflect this fact. Such issues are referred to as *fallen angels*. But a bond selling at a premium because of its high yield is likely to be that way because it was a low-credit "junk" security at issuance that has become, perhaps temporarily, respectable. Given an approximate equality of yields to maturity (for that is how return is measured), we would generally prefer the discounted fallen angel over the newly respectable higher yielder. A fallen angel, by definition, is an issue that had once been investment grade, and as Warren Buffett would point out, probably has a management that would like to regain that status. However, an issue that was junky coming out of the box probably represents a company with a corrupt management (unless top management has been changed in the meantime), a fact that may probably be overlooked during the course of a good year.

Investors who buy bonds that have fallen significantly in price, and are therefore really buying an instrument with equity-like characteristics, are often reminded of this fact by the discounted price. It is less likely to be so for the purchaser of a high-yield security selling near par, who may instead underestimate the risk in pursuit of a high payout that may, in fact, prove illusory.

A second issue is the amount of bank debt that is senior to the bond. A good bond covenant will strictly limit the amount of bank or other debt that is senior to it. A bad situation is one in which a bondholder is pushed down in priority by piling on the more senior (usually bank) debt so that the bonds, in effect, become almost equity, with little of the upside associated with stock.

A third issue of concern is the amount of equity at both (historical) book value and (current) market value. Just as an equity holder wants to see a relatively small amount of debt when looking up the right-hand side of the balance sheet, a debt holder wants to see a large amount of junior paper when looking down. In a sense, the two purposes are complementary. The owner of debt wants to see a large amount of junior securities to support his prior claims, while the owner of equity wants to see the amount of debt limited in order to be able to "live to fight another day," no matter what the economic vicissitudes, rather than to see the future chances of a capital gain extinguished through the untimely demise of the corporation.

A fairly important protection is the size of the corporation. A corporation should have sales several times the size of its total debt. In a particularly egregious case in 1984, American Quasar Petroleum had long-term debt of over $100 million and annual sales of only $40 million or so, as indicated in

1982	1983	1984E	1985E	Year
2.76	2.00	**1.70**	**0.90**	Sales per share
1.12	0.58	**0.20**	**0.15**	"Cash flow" per share
0.08	-0.57	**-0.60**	**-0.20**	Earnings per share
0.00	0.00	**0.00**	**0.00**	Dividends per share
3.01	1.37	**0.75**	**0.75**	Book value per share
19.19	19.25	**19.50**	**40.00**	Shares (mill.)
5.00	5.90	1.90	1.10	Share price (Year Low)
96.0	113.6	37.1	44.0	Market Cap (mill.)
NMF	NMF	**NMF**	**NMF**	P/E Ratio
1.7	4.3	**2.5**	**1.5**	P/B Ratio
0%	0%	**0%**	**0%**	Dividend Yield (mill.)
53.0	38.5	**34.0**	**36.0**	Sales (mill.)
20.0	16.2	**15.0**	**14.0**	Depreciation (mill.)
1.5	-7.0	**-11.5**	**-8.0**	Net Profit (mill.)
-19.8	0.2	**-5.0**	**0.0**	Working Capital (mill.)
121.0	122.9	**105.0**	**95.0**	Long Term Debt (mill.)
57.7	25.3	**15.0**	**7.0**	Shareholders' equity (mill.)
6.80%	NMF	**NMF**	**NMF**	Return on Capital
2.7%	NMF	**NMF**	**NMF**	Return on Equity
2.7%	NMF	**NMF**	**NMF**	Reinvestment rate
0%	0%	**0%**	**0%**	Dividend Distribution Rate
100%	NMF	**NMF**	**NMF**	Earnings Retention Rate
0%	0%	**0%**	**0%**	Dividend Payout Ratio

Capital Structure as of 9/30/84
Total Debt: 126.6 mill.
LT Debt: 115.0 mill.

(Interest Not Covered)   (90% of Capital)

Common Stock   (10% of Capital)

Source: Value Line Publishing Inc.; author's calculations.
Boldfaced numbers were Value Line estimates or derived from them.
The italics are the author's.

FIGURE 4.2   Summary Statistics for American Quasar Petroleum 1982–1984.

the Value Line array in Figure 4.2. There was no way that the company could retire the debt based on the past and reasonably foreseeable earnings. (The company had vast unexplored leased acreage that did not produce anything before the leases expired, but it had served as security for debt.)

Ironically, junk bonds are not the most dangerous bonds for individual investors, and even for many professionals. Rather, it is the medium-grade issues, those in the lower single-A category, all of BBB rating, and the higher reaches of BB rating, that are likely to prove most treacherous. An issue with an unquestioned high degree of safety—AA or better—will probably live up to its billing as a conservative investment. A low-rated bond is known and understood to be "junk." The problem with many medium-grade issues is that by being located in the middle of a spectrum, they are most likely to go either higher or lower. In general, it is difficult for a bond to be somewhat, but not overly, speculative. Only the most astute professional investor will be able to judge which way the bond is going. Other investors are likely to be deceived as to the merits of such an issue. This is particularly true nowadays when events (such as the collapse of Enron) often transpire faster than the rating agencies seem to respond.

Still, it must be noted that the disadvantage of high-yield bonds to an ordinary investor is the potential for capital loss, which balances out the potential for gain, and in this regard is more nearly like an equity than a high-grade bond. As in the case of stocks, diversification is the rule here, both as to issuer and as to the industry or economic sector; a portfolio of, say, high-yielding telecommunications bonds can hardly be said to provide adequate safety any more than a portfolio of telecommunications stocks will protect an equity investor. The average individual investor is perhaps less equipped to invest in high-yielding bonds than in similarly junky stocks, if for no other reason than the chances of "getting lucky" are less for a fixed-income vehicle. Hence, the only prudent method is to buy a high-yield bond fund.

An obnoxious variation of the already speculative junk bond is payment-in-kind bonds. These are bonds on which interest will be continually accrued, rather than paid periodically. Under such circumstances, the company has essentially admitted that it will not be able to pay interest for the foreseeable future. In effect, the investor is being told, "Trust us, you'll get your money, principal and interest, someday, when economic conditions improve, or our cost-cutting plan takes hold, or we put our competitors out of business." Or as the Red Queen said to Alice in Wonderland, "Jam yesterday or jam tomorrow, but never jam today." (To which Alice sensibly replied, "It must some time come to jam today.")

OTHER FIXED-INCOME INSTRUMENTS

Most other fixed-income instruments represent a hybrid, explicit or implicit, between bonds and stocks. In theory, they are intermediate in both risk and return between one and the other, but in reality, you have to be careful not to get the worst of both worlds.

Convertible bonds are bonds that can be converted into shares of the company's common stock at a fixed exchange rate. For instance, if a $1,000 bond is convertible into 25 shares of stock, the conversion price is $40 per share of stock. The conversion price is set above the stock price prevalent at the time the convertible bond is issued (e.g., the stock price might have been $35 or so when the convertible was sold). In fact, the bond will typically sell at a premium to the value of the underlying stock (which is the price of the stock times the number of shares the bond is converted into). In this example, the $1,000 bond is worth substantially more than the value of the underlying stock costing $35 * 25 = $875, and if the stock rises to $40, the bond will sell for more than $1,000.

The reason for this relationship is that the convertible bond pays an interest rate that is higher than the stock's dividend yield. For instance, the interest rate on the convertible bond might be 4 percent while the dividend yield on the underlying stock is 2 percent, giving the bond a two-percentage-point yield advantage. The so-called breakeven time is the number of years that the yield advantage must persist before it amortizes the premium that the buyer has paid on the bond, assuming that the dividend remains constant. The true breakeven time is usually longer than the theoretical one, if the common stock dividend rises, thereby eroding the yield advantage and lengthening the time it has to persist in order to bring about a breakeven result. As long as the yield premium persists, the convertible bond will command a price premium that will rise and fall at a slower rate than the common stock, making it less risky. If this relationship breaks down because the company is unable to pay interest (or dividends), the bond is said to be "busted." At very high prices for the stock (and bond), the yield advantage of the bond over stock practically disappears, and the bond becomes almost as risky as the underlying stock.

Preferred stock is equity that ranks below debt but above common stock in the capital structure of a company. It has a dividend that is set higher than that of the common stock, giving it a yield advantage. As such, they are fixed income instruments that, in most cases, are more like bonds than like common stock. Corporations, but not individuals, can deduct a large chunk (currently 85 percent) of the preferred dividends from taxable income. Therefore, preferred stock is usually priced in such a way that it is more suitable for corporations than individuals.

This disadvantage does not apply to the preferred stock of some foreign companies, where economic rights are equal, and the rights on preferred stock are in fact superior to those on common stock when dividend preference is taken into account, and where the sole offset is the superior voting rights of the common. American preferred stock, however, pays a dividend that is fixed, and generally does not rise even when dividend increments accrue to the common. In the rare event that the preferred participates in any dividend increases, it is called *participating preferred*. And if the preferred is convertible into common, then it is a special case of a convertible bond. Barring these cases, a preferred stock is an intermediate instrument that pays a dividend somewhat higher than the interest on a bond, but has a lower claim to assets in liquidation. It is widely and mistakenly considered senior stock when, in fact, it is normally a junior bond.

Following the advice of Ben Graham, we cannot generally recommend most American preferred stocks for individual investors. Such stocks can be brought only if the current yield is attractive and/or there are good prospects of a capital gain through resale to the ultimate end holder, a corporation. This circumstance will occur only when the investing public believes that the company is in trouble, and then the investor has to be able to look farther enough ahead than others to realize that this is not the case, or at least not to the degree generally believed. This is a daunting task for a professional, never mind an amateur investor. Although there is a rule of "never say never," the purchase of a preferred stock must fall into the "almost never" category for the individual investor.

The problem arises in a distressed situation because the payment of dividends on preferred stock represents a moral, rather than legal, obligation. Interest on bonds and other debt such as bank loans will be paid first, and this is a legal obligation set by contract. However, management may often elect to pass dividends on stock. In some cases, this will affect only the common stock, while the preferred will be spared, at least for a time. But in general, preferred stock tends to have the worst of both worlds, with little more upside and far less safety than debt, and barely more safety and much less upside than common stock.

There are several ways that a preferred stock can be made more attractive. One kind of preferred stock that is worth considering is cumulative preferred stock. In this variety, omitted dividends must be made up in the following years before any dividends can be paid on the common stock. Sometimes an investor may buy a fallen preferred stock at a discount to par with several years of cumulative dividends to boot. Then the trick is to guess how soon the company will be restored to profitability and pay its arrearages. The cases in which there are meaningful cumulated preferred dividends are so rare as to be almost textbook cases. Otherwise, if a preferred stock is almost like common stock because of a participating dividend or convertible feature described above, that might make it attractive.

Just as bonds can be converted into stocklike instruments, stocks can also be converted into bondlike instruments. The link between these two instruments is a third instrument called an *option*. Options come in two varieties: calls and puts. A call option is an instrument containing the right, but not the obligation, to buy a stock at a particular price known as the strike price (usually higher than the current one), by a certain maturity date.

A put option is an instrument containing the right, but not the obligation, to sell a stock at a particular price (usually at a strike price lower than the prevailing one), by a certain date. Such rights cost money because they provide a form of insurance against uncertainty to the buyer.

For every buyer of an instrument, there must be a seller. In the case of a call option, such a seller might be the owner of a stock that he or she would not be willing to sell at the current market price, but would be willing to sell at a somewhat higher price that he or she might wish for. In the meantime, there are buyers who want to speculate on a higher price for that stock within a specified maturing date, usually several months. Selling the rights to potential price appreciation enables a conservative investor to trade two birds in the bush for the proverbial bird in the hand. For instance, if stock X is selling for $25 a share, a seller of a call option pledging to sell the stock at $30 will receive a premium of a small percentage of the current price, say 8 percent or $2, from the buyer. This is a good plan for the seller if the stock is fully priced at $25. However, there may be a buyer who speculates that the stock price will soon exceed $32 (within the maturity date). If the targeted "strike" price ($30 in this case) is not hit, the call writer (seller) is left with the stock, but at least has garnered an additional income of $2. But if $25 is a bargain price and $30 is a fair price, the seller will pocket $32 for the transaction when the option is exercised at the strike price.

One can also sell a call option without owning the underlying stock, but that is akin to selling short (selling stock one does not own)—a dangerous practice. If the stock goes up past the strike price, the seller of the option must either buy the stock in order to fulfill the obligation to deliver or else must repurchase the call option itself, which will have skyrocketed in tandem with the underlying security. In either case, one will suffer a loss similar to a short seller who must repurchase a stock at a higher price than the one at which it was sold. This is known as a *naked call*.

The seller of a put option pledges to buy a stock if it goes to a strike price below the current price. The writer (seller) of a put option will receive a premium of a small percentage of the current price if the stock never hits the targeted strike price, or will buy the stock if it hits the strike price before the maturing date (often at the most inconvenient time for the seller of the put option). A buyer of a put option, however, is purchasing portfolio insurance, which would have been a good idea before a big collapse of the market, say in early October 1987. An example of a seller of a put option was Warren Buffett, acting as chairman of Berkshire Hathaway. In 1993, Berkshire Hathaway was the single largest owner of Coca-Cola's stock, and Buffett sat on its board. When Coca-Cola's stock was trading in the low $40s, as quoted at the time, Berkshire sold a put option contracting to buy the stock at $35. Buffett had determined that the stock was worth that much, but not the $40-plus at which it was trading. The stock never dipped to $35, but Berkshire collected a premium of $1.50 on every put it sold, yielding an extra income on a slightly overpriced stock on top of the underlying dividend. Berkshire thus profited from the exuberance of other investors, who kept the price of Coke above what the company was willing to pay. But in committing to pay a price of $35 a share (actually $33.50 after subtracting $1.50 premium that was earned), Buffett was making a strong statement about the value of the Coke stock, one that would have been tested if the price had plummeted to, say, $30 a share.

Most corporate bonds have a so-called "call" provision; that is, after a certain date, they can be redeemed at the company's option, usually at a slight premium to par. This premium is typically not enough to compensate for the lower interest rate the investor will get upon reinvesting the funds. If interest rates go up, however, the investor is stuck with a below-market rate and a capital loss. Ordinarily, there is no way for the investor to "put" the bond back to the company at face value and get back the original investment. This is a case of "heads you win, tails I lose." A few bonds do have this put option, but they are mostly lower-rated issues, especially of foreign borrowers.

A few corporate bonds do have "poison put" provisions. This gives the holder the right to sell the bond back to the company at a specified price, usually at par, if certain conditions are met. A typical condition is a hostile corporate takeover, which is often financed by borrowing that depresses the value of the combined company's bonds. The put provision allows bondholders to sell the bonds back to the acquirer at par as an obligation of the acquisition, thereby protecting them from the vicissitudes of the merger—an "event risk" (and making the takeover more difficult because the acquirer has to purchase the bonds).

If a preferred stock offers an individual investor the worst of most possible worlds, convertible debt often offers the best. This is an issue of subordinated debt, which is convertible into the underlying stock of the company based on a strike price somewhat higher than the prevailing one, say 20 to 30 percent. In compensation for this feature, which is really a call option on the stock, the interest rate is set two or three percentage points lower than the prevailing rate on a noncallable bond, although the convertible debt usually enjoys a yield advantage over the stock.

CHAPTER 5

Distressed Fixed Income

This chapter will discuss truly distressed, as opposed to merely high-yielding, fixed-income securities. These issues mostly fall under the category of bankruptcy candidates, and subsequent workouts, or of those that only threaten to go into workout. Ben Graham, in his time, and more modern investors like Martin Whitman of Third Avenue Value specialized in these situations. This type of investment is not to the taste of many investors. Even so, it is an exercise in taking apart financial statements and analyzing business value.

A more compelling reason for exposing an average investor to this topic is that she or he may hold bond mutual funds. That is to say that the average mutual fund investor may be indirectly holding such fixed-income issues, willy-nilly. If corporate securities with a high chance of default are listed in a major index, it is a certainty that most funds will be invested in these issues for index management purposes. Funds have been notoriously pusillanimous in not wishing to "mistrack" their indexes, even to avoid a strong prospect of capital loss. Managers have a greater fear of bad relative performance than bad absolute performance, an attitude that many private investors will not share.

Workout situations fall into three categories. The first is when a company is forced into bankruptcy or the brink thereof, through a one-time shock event. The second is when the company is basically healthy but has taken on too much debt. The third is when a company is not overly indebted but has a weak business position. It is possible to have a hybrid of the last two when a company has both a bad business position and a heavy debt load, and such is the kind of situation that value investors want to avoid.

Bankruptcy also falls into several corresponding categories. The first is a technical bankruptcy, such as that of Texaco in 1987 after its $10.5 billion court judgment to Pennzoil. The second type is chapter 11, or debtor-in-possession bankruptcy. Third type is chapter 7, or liquidation. Different types of debt and other claims have different priorities in a bankruptcy proceeding, and sometimes the struggle over priority can get contentious. For instance, management pay is usually an "administrative claim" that gets the highest priority, but occasionally, excessive CEO pay or legal fees can be disallowed by a bankruptcy judge or reduced to a lower priority. Workout-type investments are usually made by bankruptcy specialists, who often have a legal background and are capable of litigating their claims in court, or at least of predicting the likely outcome of a court fight.

BANKRUPTCY AND WORKOUT PROCEEDINGS

A bankruptcy can be filed in any one of eleven regional court circuits. (Each of these circuits has several legal districts under its jurisdiction, making up a national total of 93 legal districts. The circuit got its name from the nine-teenth century practice of having judges make the circuit of each district in the region.) Each circuit has its own way of treating bankruptcy cases, and judges have wide discretion within the precedents of the particular circuit. For instance, during the late 1980s bankruptcy of Texaco, the company was able to get bankruptcy relief in the Second Circuit (White Plains, New York) where it was headquartered, after having lost the original judgment in Harris County (Houston), Texas, which was Pennzoil's hometown.

A company declaring bankruptcy must file a statement of assets and lia-bilities. Later on, it must file a plan of reorganization that includes, among other things, five-year forecasts of earnings and cash flows. These filings are useful for information purposes, because they contain key facts and assumptions that would otherwise be considered proprietary corporate information and not shared with the public.

As a practical matter, claims in a bankruptcy are not usually settled in strict order of priority, which means that shareholders often get something, even at the expense of bondholders, including senior bondholders. That is because of the ability of even junior claim holders to delay the liquidation process through litigation claims that workout rather than liquidation is in everybody's best interest. Also, interest does not accrue on debt during a bankruptcy proceeding. So debt holders in a high-interest-rate environment may well prefer to accept 85 to 90 cents on the dollar relatively quickly, rather than 100 cents on the dollar some months or years later, that actu-ally have a lower net present value. In a low-interest-rate environment, the debt holders will have less reason to be in a hurry, and therefore bankruptcy proceedings may be more contentious. If the parties cannot agree among themselves, the judge can "cram down" a settlement as a last resort. That is, he or she can force a satisfaction of claims at fair value, beginning with the highest priority until the money runs out, leaving the junior debt holders with nothing.

The advantage of liquidation is that it is relatively fast. Assets will be sold or otherwise disposed of, and the proceeds will be gathered and distributed to investors, mainly debt holders. This is particularly true where the business position is so bad that there is no point in trying to continue. If there is only a moderate amount of debt, a substantial portion of it will likely be paid, and, occasionally, the disbursements will be 100 cents on the dollar or something close to it. In any event, people will quickly find out where they stand, get paid accordingly, and be able to move on.

More often, a reasonably strong business will have taken on more debt than can be paid, at least at a time of distress. If the company can continue, with or without temporary relief, then obligations will eventually be paid in full. This is not assured in advance, of course, and while the purchase of such obligations at any discount from par is likely to produce some return, one must buy the bond at a large enough discount to make it worth the wait and worry.

In a true workout situation, the proceeds will be substantially less than 100 cents on the dollar, even after a prolonged struggle. In such instances, an immediate liquidation will result in a fire sale. Of course, equity holders stand to lose everything, but even debt holders stand to take a major "haircut" from par. One solution may be for debt holders to convert their obligations into equity and take their chances in the equity market. In such instances, a buyer of bonds around par will likely suffer an actual loss. An investor in such cases will have to estimate the final workout value (rules of thumb usually lead to "worst case" values of between 40 and 60 cents on the dollar) and then buy at large enough discount from this value to compensate for the time and trouble of waiting for the final resolution. It is not only the final amount that is in question in such cases, but also the timing, which makes it especially hard to do net present value (NPV) calculations. The only plausible, if imperfect, solution is to employ a high hurdle rate.

Some of Warren Buffett's greatest successes have been in the area of distressed securities, but this was more true in the 1980s and early 1990s than in late 1990s.[1] One example was the purchase of Washington Power Service (Whoops) bonds, then yielding over 16 percent to maturity. The problem basically resolved into what is often called a binary or zero-one decision. Will the authority ultimately repay its bond or won't it? The company had to take large write-offs for two failed nuclear power plants, Numbers 4 and 5, on which it could not collect rates, and had to default on bonds associated with these plants. When this happened, the bonds of plant Numbers 1, 2, and 3 fell to distressed levels even though they were still paying interest, on the fear that they, too, would default. As it was for a number of other nuclear utilities in the late 1980s, such as Long Island Lighting (or Lilco), the question then was whether the regulators would let them cover enough from their other investments to make up for the losses on the failed ones. In most instances during that time, the answer was yes. Buffett had gotten it right on this one and reaped a handsome return.

Warren Buffett also took a position in bonds of Texaco, which had declared bankruptcy to prevent its assets from being attached, after a jury had awarded Pennzoil $10.5 billion in actual and punitive damages for Texaco's "tortious" interference with the other's attempted takeover of Getty Oil. The bonds were cheap, assuming that a "reasonable settlement" could be reached. The case was finally settled for $3 billion, which roughly represented the economic value of the transaction. Having bought the bonds at a discount, Berkshire Hathaway was able to sell them at a premium.

Another Berkshire Hathaway coup was an investment in RJR Nabisco bonds at the turn of 1990. This was a problem of overindebtedness of a healthy operation. The company's basic problem was that it had taken on too much leverage in the 1989 leveraged buyout, so aptly recounted in *Barbarians at the Gate*.[2] So even a modest downturn in sales and profits during the 1990 recession caused a plunge in the value of the bonds. At Buffett's purchase price of around $60, the yield to maturity was about 15 percent. But the company was busily selling assets to raise cash, and planned an equity issue that would enable it to retire the debt. This it did several months after Buffett's purchase, and gave Berkshire a gain of 75 percent (counting interest) during that time span.

One of Warren Buffett's biggest mistakes (by his own admission) was the purchase of USAir's 9 percent convertible preferred stock, which had been issued especially to him. This was the "true" workout situation, in which competition from other airlines, some of them operating in bankruptcy, placed USAir in an unenviable position. As he ruefully admitted, he had been lulled into a false sense of security by the structure of the issue, to the point where he had overlooked the underlying economics of the business. This was something that Ben Graham had specifically warned against—that the conversion feature served as an illusory compensation for an inadequately protected issue. In a fixed-income investment (and preferred stock at par is just that), one is hostage to the ability of the underlying business to produce income. And this was precisely what USAir failed to do at the time.

PREMISES FOR INVESTING IN DISTRESSED BONDS

There are several premises regarding an investment in distressed bonds. The first premise is that the investment must pay equity-like returns, typically 10 percent or more. Risks are typically slightly lower than for equities. The return profile is somewhat different, however. On one hand, you have a high but not potentially unlimited return because the boundaries set by the issuer's par value. On the other hand, the seniority of bonds over equity makes it more likely that you will receive something if the company goes bankrupt.

The second premise is that the debt should be senior enough in the capital structure to offer a reasonable expectation of being repaid. Our rule for equity investment is that debt should be no more than about 30 to 40 percent of total capital, the sum of debt plus equity. That is to say, no more than 30 to 40 percent of the total capital should be senior to the equity in the form of debt or preferred stock. For a quasi-equity debt instrument, the amount of senior debt should be no more than 40 to 50 percent of total capital. Like equity, such debt is junior to senior debt, but unlike equity, it is actually above, rather than equal to (*pari passu*) equity. The cushion offered by the existence of junior capital makes it possible to bend the rules a bit regarding the amount of senior capital.

Liquidation value can be estimated from the balance sheet. Only cash and high-quality marketable securities can be counted at 100 cents on the dollar. Accounts receivables are usually worth 80 to 90 percent of face value, after allowing for bad debts and factoring costs. Inventories can be worth 50 cents on the dollar or less. Ironically, commodity inventories such as steel and other raw materials and intermediate goods, which are worth the market price and carried at the lower end of cost or market price can be worth close to full value, if market value approximates this figure. It is the high "value-added" inventories that have sustained processing costs such as clothes that are worth a small fraction of the cost if there are no good alternate uses for items that are out of style or otherwise obsolete. Values for plant, property and equipment vary widely. In rare cases, it is worth 100 cents on the dollar or even more. Obsolete machinery may be worth very little, perhaps only as much as scrap value.

ANALYSIS OF FINANCIAL STATEMENTS OF DISTRESSED COMPANIES[3]

For distressed companies in a workout situation, a far more important financial statement than the income statement is the statement of changes in financial position, often referred to as the *flow-of-funds statement*. This is because a distressed company generally has no income. In a few cases, the idea is that income is temporarily depressed and will improve when the economy turns around. In such situations, forecasts of the future are helpful. In general, the company is not profitable, and senior debt holders are likely to be paid off at the expense of junior debt holders and equity holders. Then the two issues are the availability of future funds, in the form of cash flow, and whether the debt is senior enough to be paid. Cash flow can also be determined by comparing the balance sheet of the current year with that of the previous year.

The flow-of-funds statement is divided into three parts. The first part of the statement contains the cash flow from operations. This consists of net income, plus depreciation, plus deferred taxes, adjusted for components of net income or other items that do not produce cash. For example, income from equity holdings in other companies is subtracted from cash flow from operations because it is a noncash income item. In essence, one "backs into" cash flow from net income, reversing the process of taking out noncash charges from cash flow to arrive at net income. The net income figure represents the most recent addition to net worth, and the depreciation number is the most recent addition to accumulative depreciation on the balance sheet.

The second part of the statement is an itemization of changes in the components of working capital other than cash at the top of the balance sheet. Increases (decreases) in current assets such as accounts receivable and inventory represent a use (source) of cash, while increases (decreases) in liabilities such as accounts payable or short-term loans represent a source (use) of working capital items. The final number represents the cash that is "squeezed out" of (or used up in) working capital items. In earlier (historical) versions of the sources and uses of funds statements, these items were broken out, but the more modern practice is to list the net amounts as a single line under the sources of funds.

The third part of the statement regards "uses" of funds in investing and financing activities, which is subdivided into two sections. The first section refers to funds from or used in financing activities. It analyzes the long-term liabilities on the right-hand side of the balance sheet. Increases in debt or other long-term liabilities are a source of funds, while debt repayments are a use of funds. Dividend payments are a use of funds because they represent a reduction of net worth. The second section describes funds used in or from investing activities. It reconciles the changes in long-term assets such as plant, property and equipment, or other investments. Investment in capital assets is a use of funds while sales of assets are a source of funds.

The sum of the cash flow items represents the change in cash from one year to the next. Thus, the net income number is actually a managed number based on cash flows, depreciation, and taxes. A choice of depreciation method does not affect cash flow, but it does affect earnings. The discussion of various depreciation methods will be deferred until Chapter 6.

It is important to note that changes in the balance sheet items from one year to the next are net amounts, while the amounts listed in the flow of funds statement are gross amounts. For instance, if a company refinanced a $100 million debt obligation with $150 million, it would show up as a net increase of $50 million on the balance sheet, but the two gross amounts would both be listed in the flow-of-funds statement.

When the changes in long-term assets, long-term liabilities, equity accounts (income minus dividend), and noncash working capital items have all been netted out, the result is the increase or decrease in cash for the year. The strength of the financial position of a firm cannot be judged by the increase or decrease of cash alone. A decrease in cash may reflect the use of available resources to fund a major capital investment for expansion. Improved management of inventories, accounts receivable, and accounts payable may lead to an increase in cash. Consequently, an evaluation of the changes in financial position of the firm must include a detailed analysis of the inflows and outflows of funds, and an itemization of changes of the components of working capital on a year-to-year basis. It is imperative that the statement of changes in financial position be viewed within the larger context of the firm's overall operations. However, a steady decrease in cash year after year may be an indication that a firm is in financial trouble, and a steady increase in cash over time, whether or not the firm as a whole is growing, is usually a good sign.

Sometimes the financing has gotten so "fancy" in forms such as derivative contracts that it may appear under other labels. The most egregious example of this practice is Enron, but many other companies have similar financing arrangements whose function, if not primary purpose, is to mislead investors. One bad feature of fancy forms such as derivative contracts is that they were really external financing sources but were listed as sources from operations. This misreporting did not impact the company's total liquidity, but did present a misleading picture of its internal liquidity, that which would have existed if it had lost access to outside financing.

Note that a company's internal financing should be relied on most exclusively for the repayment of debt. It is unwise to assume adequate liquidity just because a company theoretically has sources of external financing, either through refinancing or through asset sales. If the company does that, financial soundness is hostage not only on the company's ability to continue its operations, but also on the state of the financial markets. Indeed, this is how most distressed companies get into trouble in the first place. By and large, the typical distressed situation is bred in times of easy money, and comes to a head in times of tight money. Disaster strikes when the refinancing window closes down, as it inevitably does from time to time. That happens usually when asset buyers also disappear (because they can't get financing).

Another big danger is short-term debt, particularly commercial paper. This is because it is easy enough to roll over in good times, but there is no guarantee that external capital will be available in bad times. News Corp tried to finance a modernization of its presses and at the same time start up Sky Broadcasting (which later merged with another company). The company got caught in the liquidity crunch around the time of the Gulf War in

TABLE 5.1　Bond Rating Model, Extended

Metric/Rating	AAA	AA	A	BBB	BB	B	CCC or Lower
FFO/Net Income	>125%	75%	45%	25%	15%	10%	<5%

Source: Modified version of a table presented in an article by Jane Tripp Howe, "Corporate Credit Analysis," cited in F. Fabrozzi, ed., *The Fixed Income Handbook* (Chicago: Irwin Press, 1995): 388.

1990–1991, an unexpected but bona fide external shock, and was almost forced into bankruptcy. Finally, a consortium of banks, led by Citicorp, itself in none too good financial shape, bailed the company out.

A look at the flow-of-funds statements showed that a number of companies were taken in by the false technology-related boom in 1999, and ramped up capital spending and acquisitions that year and later. These include the obvious workout candidates such as Enron, Global Crossing, and WorldCom. Companies that were potentially solvent were bankrupted through the greed and overreaching of their chief executives, who let go of the corporate purse strings and loaded up unnecessarily on debt. In fact, cash flow as described by funds from operations (FFO) is so important in the analysis of distressed company debt that it should be added as a criterion for bond rating as shown in Table 5.1.

A workout situation must be distinguished from others that are hopelessly gone. Enron turned out to be such a case, while WorldCom and Qwest threatened to fall into the latter category. Another case was Adelphia, a media company, which was riddled with self-dealing by the founding family. The investment case was made on asset transfer value. In all these situations, the quality of management is a major factor in the demise of the companies. An article in a business magazine at the end of 2001 cited the three CEOs who were the worst managers of their personal affairs. They were Kenneth Lay of Enron, Bernie Ebbers of WorldCom, and Stephen Hilbert of Conseco. Each of these executives had managed his personal affairs in an aggressive and risky manner that would reflect in the way they ran their companies.

Enron was perhaps the most publicized of the scandals. It was in fact a money-losing company for some years. However, false accounting had made it appear profitable, not only to the outside world, but probably also to most people within the company. To fund its true losses, the company had to take on large amounts of debt, much of which was not treated as such. So the company overextended itself without fully realizing it. Such action is similar to a high-wire artist who thinks there is a net below when in fact there isn't. As Warren Buffett put it, a company executive that lies to others in public will eventually lie to himself in private. If the results of operations had been accounted for honestly, the stock would have fallen, but probably not to zero, and there would have been a chance for management to take appropriate corrective action. But there were so many things going on, so poorly accounted for and reported, that top officers such as Kenneth Lay, the long time CEO, and Jeffrey Skilling, his short-lived successor, could probably say "legally accurately" that they did not have the whole picture. They probably knew of some individual transactions and should have been able to make educated guesses as to their likely impact, but that is a different story.

In all fairness, Kenneth Lay did not sell all of his Enron stock on its way down. His urging of his employees to hold on to their stocks because of his faith in it therefore had some substance. Lay did sell a significant portion of his holdings in order to invest in other new economy companies, most of which tumbled as badly as Enron. Although he and his wife were not broke, contrary to his wife's public claims, it was true that they lost most, perhaps 90 percent, of their fortune from its peak value, and were in fact "fighting for liquidity." Kenneth Lay had managed his own affairs as badly as he had managed his company, but did not feel the workers' pain because he was starting from such a high economic base.

Enron was so deep in the hole and so overextended that it probably could not have been saved even with new management, whose job is to ensure an orderly liquidation of assets. Another factor was a large number of potentially illegal corporate acts that made it a party to litigation and brought down its auditor, Arthur Andersen.

Bernie Ebbers leveraged himself to the maximum to buy WorldCom stock for his own account. When the stock went down, he was saved from a margin call by a personal loan made by the company, a potential conflict of interest. He had made a number of other investments outside of WorldCom with mixed results. At the end of the day, he had stocks and other assets probably worth tens of millions of dollars and debts in hundreds of millions. WorldCom was being run by a leader who was all but personally bankrupt. This was reflected in the attempted but aborted purchase of Sprint and the completed acquisition of Skytel. Stockholders found out about his misdeeds after the fact, but their plight would have served as a warning to bondholders. The personal situation of the CEO (on whose performance the value of stock depended) was known by bondholders. Unfortunately, few of them availed themselves of the warning to save most of their losses.

Let's look at the financial statements of WorldCom, starting with the flow of funds statement as shown in Table 5.2. An analysis of this document shows that beginning in 1999, WorldCom spent much more on capital spending and acquisitions than it took in from operations. This is the first sign of a troubled company. These expenditures, of course, had to be funded with massive amounts of long-term debt. Turning to the balance sheet at the end

TABLE 5.2   Cash Flow Summary, WorldCom (U.S.$ millions)

	12/1998	12/1999	12/2000	12/2001
Net Income	−2725	4013	2598	1524
Deprec & amort	2289	4354	3280	4121
Other non-cash adj	5148	3629	1790	1203
Chg in non-cash wc	−530	−991	−2338	−243
Cashflow-operating acct	4182	11005	5330	6605
Disp of fixed Asset	148	1940	0	0
Capital expenditures	−5486	−8716	−10984	−7619
Sale LT invest	0	0	0	0
Purchase LT invest	0	0	0	0
Other investing accts	−4160	−2779	−2628	−1199
Cashflow-investing acct	−9498	−9555	−13612	−8818
Dividends paid	−42	−72	−65	−83
Inc (dec) St borrow	0	0	0	0
Increase: LT borrow	6390	0	6377	3526
Decrease: LT borrow	0	−2894	0	0
Inc capital stock	472	886	585	124
Dec capital stock	0	0	−190	−200
Other financing accts	48	−221	1489	−249
Cashflow-financing acct	6868	−2301	8196	3118
Net changes in cash	1552	−851	−86	905

of 2001, shown in Table 5.3, it appears that the company was not badly capitalized, with some $57 billion of equity supporting $24 billion of long-term debt. However, of that equity, some $45 billion was goodwill from the cash-eating acquisition binge of previous years. If one subtracted this amount (which was later written off) from the net worth, there was only $12 billion of tangible net worth supporting twice as much debt. Meanwhile, the stock had gotten hammered as the telecommunications–media–technology bubble began to unravel. Then the issue was whether the acquisitions were wise or foolish. The stock price collapse clearly spoke the answer. But knowledge of Ebbers's personal situation should have tipped the balance. Anyone who had managed his own affairs this poorly probably made serious misjudgments on behalf of the company as well.

An analysis of the income statement of WorldCom in Table 5.4 has been left for the last. With the benefit of hindsight, we know that the income figures for the period from 1999 to 2001 were fraudulent. But even if they hadn't been, so what? Accounting standards are sufficiently malleable so that even what is legally reportable as income can be highly debatable.

TABLE 5.3 Balance Sheet—WorldCom (U.S.$ millions)

	12/2000	12/2001		12/2000	12/2001
Cash & near cash	720	1409	Accounts payable	3584	2751
Marketable sec	0	0	St borrowings	7200	172
Acct & notes rec	4980	3734	Other St liab	3429	2992
Inventories	0	0	**Current liabilities**	**14213**	**5915**
Other cur assets	2392	3036			
Current assets	**8092**	**8179**	LT borrowings	11696	24533
			Other LT Liab	3648	3742
LT inv't & LT rec	0	976	Noncur liabilities	15344	28275
			Total liabilities	**29557**	**34190**
Depr fixed assets	34422	39386			
Non-depr fixed ass	6727	5576	Preferred equity	798	1993
Accum depreciation	5972	8170	Minority interest	2592	101
Net fixed assets	**35177**	**36792**	Share capital	0	0
			Retained earnings	52946	55617
Other assets	42624	45954	**Shareholder equity**	**56336**	**57711**
			Total liab & equity	**85893**	**91901**
Total assets	**85893**	**91901**			

TABLE 5.4   Income Statement, WorldCom

	12/1998	12/1999	12/2000	12/2001
Net Sales	18169	35908	22755	21348
Cost of goods sold	8534	14739	8745	8120
Sell, gen & adm exp	6852	13289	8969	10179
Operating inc (loss)	2783	7880	5041	3049
Interest expense	692	966	458	1029
Net non-op L (G)	3681	−250	−385	−412
Income tax expense	877	2965	1990	943
Income before XO items	−2467	4199	2978	1489
XO L (G) pretax	265	0	118	0
Tax effect on XO items	−100	0	−43	0
Minority Interest	93	186	305	−35
Net Income	−2725	4013	2598	1524

Source: Copyright © 2003, Bloomberg, L.P., all rights reserved. Reprinted with permission.

Investors in bonds as well as in stocks were so mesmerized by the "concept" in this case that they basically believed what they wanted to hear (and the company crossed the line of propriety in order to tell them that story). In a situation in which a company is in trouble, cash flow, not book income, will decide the difference between survival and death. Profit is an opinion; cash flow is a fact.

Bernie Ebbers was dismissed when the bonds went down to the low 40s, or bankruptcy levels, and the stock approached zero. Only this move finally gives the company a fighting chance of survival. When new management was installed, the company finally drew down its last $2.5 billion line of credit. It also exchanged parent company stock for the "tracking" stock of MCI, thereby eliminating a burdensome dividend requirement on the latter. The ability of WorldCom (since renamed MCI) to survive going forward would depend on its ability to manage itself for cash.

Conseco was another go-go story. It had been founded by Stephen Hilbert in the early 1980s, and had expanded very aggressively. As often happens in such cases, it made one aggressive move too many, specifically the acquisition of Green Tree Acceptance in 1996, with a huge pile of mobile home loans, a relatively risky security, at a fancy price. This was the last straw for a corporate structure that was probably already overextended. Hilbert had found his personal leveraged account under water when his stock tumbled. Gary Wendt of GE Capital was brought in to fix the situation but made little headway during his tenure as CEO.

SOVEREIGN DEFAULT

One potential source of default on foreign bonds is sovereign default. Contrary to the dictum of one former chairman of a major U.S. bank that "countries don't go bust," they do. Although average investors are not likely investing in such bonds for their own account, they may be investing in mutual funds that hold bonds issued by foreign governments. Another reason for knowing about sovereign default is that defaults in foreign markets have ricochet effects on the U.S. markets as well. For instance, the U.S. bear market of 1982 was brought about by Mexico's going to the brink of default before being bailed out. A similar occurrence took place in Mexico in 1995, but with no apparent ill effects on what was then a very bullish U.S. market.

Countries are rated by the rating agencies in much the same way as companies are. The agencies look at slightly different things such as the ratio of gross domestic product (GDP), the trade balance, or foreign exchange reserves to national debt, but otherwise they follow much the same process. Sovereign ratings come in two varieties: local currency debts and debts denominated in U.S. dollars (or other developed market currency such as the euro or yen.) The sovereign rating acts as a ceiling on the ratings for local corporate debt in U.S. dollars. That means, with rare exceptions, the corporate debt cannot be rated higher than the sovereign debt in which it is domiciled. The exceptions occur for commodity-based companies that earn money in U.S. dollars rather than local currency *and have significant operations outside the country where it can keep the dollars* without having to repatriate them.

An example is Argentina, in Latin America. This is a country that was the envy of the developing world at the end of the nineteenth century to early twentieth century. However, the country was not only forced to default on its debt early in the twenty-first century but also to prevent its otherwise solvent corporate borrowers from paying debts denominated in U.S. dollars or other foreign currencies. This was the result of a long period of slow economic growth; the mid-single-digit annual growth in foreign debt exceeded the growth of the local economy. A massive balance of payment deficit also hurt. The final linchpin of the collapse was, ironically, a structure designed to lead to sound money by pegging the peso, the local currency, to the U.S. dollar. When the dollar proved to be one of the strongest major currencies during the 1990s, the Argentina currency became "too strong" to allow its local producers to compete in world markets. Productivity growth in Argentina had been slow for three quarters of a century, removing one potential underpinning of the currency.

A more important troubled sovereign credit is Japan. Following a decade of prolonged recession and unsuccessful government pump-priming in the 1990s, this country has the largest national debt as a percentage of GDP—between 130 percent and 140 percent, which are basically levels of Third World debts, among developed countries. The redeeming feature is its large stock of foreign exchange reserves, which, if offset against local debt, would bring the net debt down to a more normal 40 to 50 percent. The country's sovereign credit rating has been slipping from AAA to AA, then toward A, and may fall to BBB at some point.

Given the level of foreign debt in the United States and its switch in the domestic posture from budget surplus to deficit in early 2000s, there is a real question as to why the United States retains its AAA rating. The answer (apart from the fact that all major rating agencies are based stateside) appears to reside in the fact that the U.S. dollar is the world's de facto fiat currency. In essence, the U.S. government can print money to pay its foreign debt and have this paper accepted without question. Even so, this has not been without cost. There has been a yield premium, typically averaging 2 percent or so a year between interest rates on American sovereign debt and those of other developed countries. This more or less compensates for the fact that the American dollar fell by about one half against most European currencies between 1950 and 2000, and by about two thirds against the Japanese yen during the same period.

Paradoxically, sovereigns have historically been least likely to default on bonds, somewhat more likely to default on bank loans, and most likely not to pay intergovernmental obligations. After World War I, only Finland among America's allies repaid its debts to this country incurred during that war. All other major countries failed to pay, citing as their excuse that Germany defaulted on its reparation payments, which they had counted on to pay the United States. When the Great Depression hit in 1930s, both the reparations of Germany and the outstanding loans to the United States were forgiven.

In the 1980s, there was a wave of defaulted Third World loans from foreign banks in developing countries, mostly in Latin America. These loans were worked out through Brady bonds, an instrument named after the U.S. Treasury Secretary Nicholas Brady, who is credited with inventing it. The idea behind the Brady bonds is that the defaulting country would purchase enough zero-coupon U.S. Treasuries to repay the principal at maturity, and cover from one to three future interest payments with security. The Brady bonds would set interest rates of 4 to 6 percent of the face value, which were significantly lower than the high-single-digit levels of interest rates for the defaulted loans. The foreign banks would accept the Brady bonds as repayment of the defaulted loans, knowing that the principal would be secured by the backing of the U.S. Treasury. Thus, the foreign bankers were bailed out and could report that there were no accounting losses, because principal repayments were guaranteed—a more important point than the fact that they had suffered large economic losses. In the meantime, the debts had been restructured and would support the payment of part of the future interest of Brady bonds.

Investors in Brady bonds would be speculating only with interest, not with principal. These bonds were sold at a large discount from par, typically at 60 to 70 cents on the dollar because of their low interest rates, especially in relation to the risk. Their total yields are a blend of implied Treasury yields, based on the present value of the Treasury zero-coupon bond that secures part of the Brady bond, and the "local yield," based on the unsecured portion of the reconstructed bond, quoted as "stripped yield." For instance, if the Brady bond is quoted at 70 and the present value of the Treasury security is 40, the unsecured portion of the bond is 30. That is, for a 6 percent bond of $1,000 face value, the market price is $700 (70 percent of $1,000), of which $400 is secured by the U.S. Treasuries and $300 is the portion backed by the reconstructed local bonds. The interest attributable to the Treasuries may amount to perhaps $20 of the $60 coupon. With the local payment for the difference (e.g., $60 − $20 = $40) and a local bond value of $300, the real local interest rate would be $40/$300 or over 13 percent. These so-called stripped yields are typically higher than the yields on U.S. dollar bonds issued directly by the same local governments. Brady bonds, by definition, have a history of default, and the local bonds typically do not. This is a rare exception that the (defaulted) bank loans carry higher rates than local bonds.

PART

three

Equity Evaluation

CHAPTER 6

Cash Flows and Capital Expenditures

In applying Graham and Dodd methodology to stock valuation, a basic premise is that cash flows are ultimately what give value to a stock. This chapter will begin with a discussion of operating cash flows derived from volume, price, and cost relationships, and then derive a measure of available cash flow from the income statement. An examination of the interaction between cash flows and capital expenditures will be used to measure "economic earnings" that are related to—but by no means identical with—accounting earnings. Finally, the chapter will conclude with a discussion of the role of cash flows in two key areas of corporate decision making, mergers and acquisition, and the choice of debt versus equity funding of the balance sheet.

VOLUME, PRICE, AND COST RELATIONSHIP[1]

Pretax profit is a function of volume, price, and cost, as shown in Figure 6.1. The revenue from sales, R, equals unit price, P, times volume, V, or $R = P * V$. The profit (or earnings), E, then is given by $E = P * V - C$, where C represents various costs.

Costs come in two varieties, fixed costs, F, and the variable cost $M * V$, where M is the marginal cost of producing an additional unit. In this linear model, the marginal cost is measured by the slope of the cost line in Figure 6.1, and is a constant number. Fixed costs, otherwise known as sunk costs, do not vary with the level of output. This includes things like plant and equipment (especially the depreciation thereon). The costs to build and install these items are fixed and have already been incurred in the past. Variable costs are those that arise when the number of units produced increases. These include direct costs such as units of raw material and labor that go into making units of finished products. Most capital costs, including interest expense, are basically fixed, although some have both fixed and variable components. For instance, a telephone has a flat charge for installation and

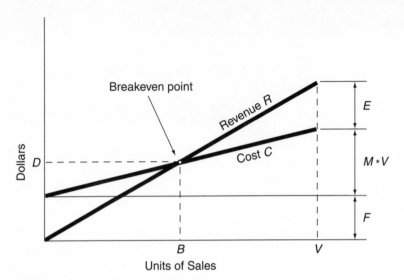

FIGURE 6.1   Volume, Price, and Cost Relationship.

an hourly usage charge. Selling, general and administrative expenses or "overhead" are also hybrid costs that contain both fixed and variable components. They may be fixed or variable costs, depending on the corporate culture and how the corporation manages them.

As shown in Figure 6.1, the breakeven point occurs when the earnings line E crosses the cost line C (i.e., the operation goes from loss to profit). The critical volume of sales (expressed in units of goods sold) is the breakeven volume B which can be found by setting $V = B$ (i.e., $P * B = F + M * B$), resulting in $B = F/(P - M)$. The corresponding dollar value D at breakeven point is given by $D = R * B$. The difference between the revenue from sales and variable costs is known as contribution. When fixed costs have been fully "absorbed" by contribution, additional sales lead to profits. At a given volume V, the profit $E = P * V - (F + M * V) = (P - M) * V - F$, in which $(P - M)$ is the contribution per unit and $(P - M) * V$ is the total contribution. (The ratio of the revenues per sales to the variable costs is P/M, which is called the contribution margin. The larger the contribution margin and the smaller the fixed cost, the lower the volume needed to break even.) Beyond that point, the contribution becomes profits through a process known as spreading out of fixed costs, because the fixed cost per unit is less than the contribution per unit.

Although the linear model of volume, price, and relationship is imperfect, it is sufficiently robust to illustrate qualitatively, and within limits, even to estimate pretax profit quantitatively.

ANALYSIS OF CASH FLOWS

The top line on the income statement is the revenue from sales (or sales for short), and the next two expense lines include direct cost (also called *cost of goods sold*) and an overhead item known as *selling, general and administrative expenses* (or SG&A for short). By managing the items represented by these three lines, the company can maximize the earnings before depreciation, interest, and taxes (EBDIT for short). This number is often referred to as "cash earnings," and is one measure of corporate cash flow.

From these three lines, gross margin and earnings before depreciation, interest, and taxes (EBDIT) are computed as follows:

Gross margin = Revenues − Direct cost (labor and materials)

EBDIT = Revenues − Direct cost − SG&A (Overhead)

These are operating charges, all cash.

The next items to be computed are earnings before interest and taxes (EBIT) and pretax income:

EBIT = Revenues − Direct cost − SG&A − Depreciation

Pretax income = Revenues − Direct cost − SG&A
− Depreciation − Interest

Note that depreciation is not a cash charge but a book entry. Interest expense is a cash charge (except for capitalized interest, which goes to the books as a capital asset). Since capitalized interest is infrequently used, it will not be included in the analysis.

The next two lines in the income statement are for taxes. They are: cash taxes (payable shortly) and deferred taxes (payable after more than one year). We will not discuss the management between cash and deferred taxes, because this specialized function requires the services of a tax specialist from an outside accounting firm, or one hired from such a firm. Occasionally, a member of the Treasury Department or an academic may be employed to perform this task. For the time being, other income, which can be either cash or noncash, and equity income/minority interest from subsidiary operations, which are noncash items, will be disregarded. Then,

Net income = Revenues − Direct cost − SG&A − Depreciation
− Interest − Taxes

By taking out only cash expenses from the EBDIT, the available cash flow is given by:

$$\text{Available cash flow} = \text{Revenues} - \text{Direct cost} - \text{SG\&A} \\ - \text{Interest} - \text{Cash taxes}$$

Alternatively, the available cash flow can be obtained by noting the noncash charges (deferred taxes and depreciation) in the income statement as follows:

$$\text{Available cash flow} = \text{Net income} + \text{Deferred taxes} + \text{Depreciation}$$

The income statement can be recast by beginning with the EBDIT line, and then taking out only cash expenses. EBDIT minus interest expense is before-tax cash flow. Interest expense reduces both earnings and cash flow, so it is taken out. Then, before-tax cash flow minus cash taxes is after-tax cash flow. Deferred taxes and depreciation have been left in, leaving the same cash flow quantity as before. Thus, the net income number is actually a managed number based on cash flow, taxes, and depreciation.

One problem with reported earnings is that it does not take into account interperiod difference of cash flows. For instance, if a transaction will give rise to a tax liability in the future, this tax liability is charged against earnings today.

An expanded cash flow number incorporating information from the statement of changes in financial position would be:

$$\text{Expanded available cash flow} = \text{Net income} + \text{Depreciation} \\ + \text{Deferred taxes} +/- \text{Changes of working capital}$$

EFFECTS OF DEPRECIATION ON CASH FLOW ANALYSIS[2]

Let's now consider the effects of the choice of depreciation methods on pretax earnings since the larger the depreciation expense, the smaller the pretax earnings (all other things being equal). Although inventory can be adjusted to reduce pretax earnings through different inventory valuation methods, the inventory, unlike depreciation, does not affect the allocation between cash taxes and deferred taxes.

Several methods to calculate depreciation, including the straight-line method and other so-called accelerated methods, can be found in any standard accounting text. However, while the more aggressive (accelerated) depreciation methods reduce accounting earnings, they actually produce higher after-tax cash flows! That's because higher depreciation charges result in fewer taxes being taken out of the pretax cash flows. The allocation of cash flow between depreciation, taxes, and after-tax earnings is somewhat arbitrary, although it is governed by generally accepted accounting principles (GAAP) and the Tax Code.

To see how this works, consider the case of $1 million of assets with a 10-year life, and $250,000 of pretax cash flow.

Under the straight-line method, the depreciation equals the value of assets divided by the life of the assets in years, or in this case, the depreciation is $1,000,000/10 = $100,000 in each year of the 10-year life.

Under the double declining balance method, depreciation is progressively declining in succeeding years as a fraction of the book value of the previous year where the fraction equals to 2 divided by the life of the assets. Thus, in the first year, the book value of the previous year is the full value of the assets and, therefore, the depreciation is calculated as 2/10 of the assets or $200,000. In the second year, the depreciation coefficient of 2/10 is applied against the reduced asset base of ($1,000,000 − $200,000) for a total of (2/10) * 800,000, or a total of $160,000. The depreciation is similarly reduced in each subsequent year.

Under the sum-of-the-years method, depreciation is calculated as a fraction of the value of assets, where the fraction equals the years of remaining life divided by the sum of the numbers of all years. In this case, the sum of all numbers from 1 to 10 is 55, and for the first year, the remaining life is 10 years. Thus, the depreciation for the first year is 10/55 of the $1 million asset, or $181,000, and that for the second year is 9/55 of $1 million, or about $164,000.

Note that under the accelerated depreciation methods, depreciation is highest in the first year and lower in subsequent years. For instance, under double declining balance, the second-year depreciation of $160,000 is less than $200,000 in the first year. Likewise, under the sum-of-the-years method, the second-year depreciation of $164,000 is less than $181,000 in the first year.

Referring to Table 6.1, we can compare income and cash flows under each of the depreciation methods for the first year of the life of the assets. Depreciation is subtracted from pretax cash flow to arrive at taxable income, which is taxed, say, at 34 percent. Net income is what remains after taxes are taken out. After-tax cash flow can be found by subtracting the taxes from taxable income, or by adding net income after tax to depreciation.

Note that while the straight-line method of depreciation maximizes net income, the other two "accelerated" methods produce higher after-tax cash flow. That's because the latter methods save on taxes. Or looking at it "bottom up," the lower net income under the accelerated methods is more than offset by the higher (tax-sheltered) depreciation charges. It is often stated in the accounting textbooks to the effect that "depreciation is a source of

TABLE 6.1   Effects of Depreciation Method on After-Tax Cash Flow

Account/Method	Straight Line	Double Digit	Sum of Years
Pretax cash flow	$250,000	$250,000	$250,000
Depreciation	$100,000	$200,000	$181,000
Taxable income	$150,000	$ 50,000	$ 69,000
Taxes @ 34%	$ 51,000	$ 17,000	$ 23,500
Net income	$ 99,000	$ 33,000	$ 45,500
After-tax cash flow	$199,000	$233,000	$226,500

funds." Such a statement is misleading, and a more accurate statement is that depreciation *represents* funds, specifically funds that are not counted as earnings.

A variation of these methods is another measure, called *cash recovery rate*, which was proposed by Professor Yuji Ijiri of Carnegie Mellon University. The cash recovery rate (CRR) is defined as follows:[3]

Cash recovery rate
    = Expanded cash flow/(Assets + Accumulated depreciation)

Note that, by definition, the expanded cash flow in the numerator includes depreciation. The denominator includes accumulated depreciation, indicating the amount of money that has historically been spent on plant (the number on which depreciation is calculated), not just the current, written down, value of the plant. The CRR tends to be a more stable measure of company performance than return on equity (ROE), partly because of the higher bases for both the numerator and denominator of the ratio, and partly because of the removal of the arbitrariness of the calculation when cash flow, instead of earnings, is used in CRR.

Under an adjusted CRR, changes in working capital in the cash flow are excluded in computing the ratio. Note that changes in working capital are equal to the difference between investment activities (such as the purchases and sales of equipment and other assets) and financing activities (the borrowing, repayment of debt, and stock buyback programs). In any given year, one can raise cash by working down inventory, speeding up receivable collection (or factoring it out), or extending payables. But this can't happen every year. Changes in working capital should be included if rising sales habitually required increase in inventory.

The difference between cash flow and capital expenditures is called "free cash flow." This is the cash available to pay dividends or do a *capital shrink* through a retirement of debt or equity. Warren Buffet's *owner earnings* is a variation of this term because it takes out only replacement capital expenditures, leaving the option of capital spending for expansion.

USES OF CASH FLOWS AND CAPITAL EXPENDITURES

Available cash flow can be used to enhance the value of the company in one of four ways:

1. To increase regular dividends or to pay a one-time special dividend
2. To raise the level of ordinary disbursements, such as debt repayments and stock buybacks
3. To make acquisitions, which have short-term and long-term effects on the company
4. To finance growth through capital spending

A rise in the dividend provides an immediate payoff. Investors value the increase because it raises the income stream available for consumption, or else provides an opportunity to redeploy some capital without selling stock. So valued are these disbursements that stock of a company often rises when management signals its willingness to raise its dividend payout, at least at a faster rate than historically.

The other disbursements work in a more indirect way. Repayment of debt makes the company more valuable by strengthening the balance sheet and reducing the debt component of enterprise value. Assuming that enterprise value remains constant or increases, the equity component must increase. A stock buyback typically reduces the total amount of equity outstanding but increases the earnings and cash flow per share to the remaining shareholders and takes out the more impatient shareholders. A share buyback signals management's belief that the stock is undervalued and puts the company's money where its mouth is. If this program is soundly conceived, it is one of the best ways to increase shareholder value.

Acquisitions or leveraged buyouts occur when the discounted value of cash flows of a company is far above the market value of its stock. This may occur, for instance, when interest rates fall, allowing a given cash flow stream to service a higher level of debt. The stock price may not have risen nearly enough to compensate for this fact. This is an unusual case in which it makes economic sense to substitute debt for equity. Managements of companies with excess cash flows want to make acquisitions. Sometimes, an acquisition makes good sense, for instance, if the acquirer has excess plant capacity and does not need to replace the plant of the acquired company, so that it can treat all cash flows as free cash flows. In a few cases, a stock buyback paves the way for a takeover. An unusual example of this was General Foods, which was taken over by Philip Morris in the mid-1980s.

A company can also expand its growth through capital spending. This is accomplished by capital expenditures on plant beyond replacement needs. Capital expenditures (capex for short) may be for replacement financed by cash flow available from depreciation, or may be for expansion financed in other ways above the amount of depreciation.

Total capital expenditure of a company is the sum of the amounts for replacement and for expansion. That is, from uses of funds,

Total capex = Replacement capex + Expansion capex

This equation pinpoints how much capex is going to actual expansion rather than replacement. Alternatively, from sources and uses of funds,

Total capex = Depreciation + Additional capex (above depreciation)

If the total capex is less than replacement capex, the company is shrinking. Thus, a growing company will provide additional capex beyond the funds available from depreciation. If the replacement capex is higher than depreciation, there will be no expansion capex unless the additional capex is large enough to compensate for the difference between replacement capex and depreciation. The problem of a large replacement capex confronts all transportation companies, including autos, airlines, railroads, and shipping.

Table 6.2 shows the comparison in the computation of accounting earnings and economic earnings. If depreciation equals replacement capex, accounting earnings and economic earnings are equal. If replacement capex is less than depreciation, economic earnings are seen to be greater than accounting earnings. Conversely, if replacement is greater than depreciation, then economic earnings are less than accounting earnings. It is misleading to look at accounting earnings without reflecting on economic earnings of a company.

The divergence of accounting earnings versus economic earnings is, in fact, the rationale behind investments in cable and other media that have high fixed costs and low variable costs. The fixed costs are incurred up

TABLE 6.2   Accounting Earnings vs. Economic Earnings

Arithmetic Signs	Accounting Earnings	Economic Earnings
	Pretax cash flow	Pretax cash flow
−	Depreciation	Replacement capex
−	Tax	Tax
=	Accounting earnings	Economic earnings
−	Additional capex	Expansion capex
+/−	Changes in work. cap.	Changes in working capital
=	Available cash	Available cash
	(for dividends)	(for dividends)

front. The depressed accounting income results from the arbitrary matching of today's cash flows with depreciation on last year's capital expenditures. If one uses the depreciation from today's capital expenditures, the economic income picture becomes very different.

If a company has no sustained cash flow over a period of time, it has no value. There is no cash to pay dividends, buy plant and equipment, or do anything to create shareholder value. Even the short-term viability of the company is in doubt. If the company has positive cash flow, but economic earnings are zero or less, it has a value less than book value and is a wasting asset. There is enough cash to pay interim dividends, but the net present value (NPV) of the dividend stream is less than book value. Only if a company has positive economic earnings, as opposed to accounting earnings, can it be said to be creating shareholder value.

That is why Warren Buffet and many modern investment practitioners would not favor investment in capital-intensive businesses like auto companies. And in the case of a slow-growth industry like automobiles, most capital spending is replacement or maintenance capital spending. Value Line's reviews on the auto companies will illustrate this point. A typical example is recent Value Line reports on General Motors (not reproducible here). In good years, their cash flows modestly exceed capital spending. In bad years, capital spending is maintained, even while earnings and cash flow plummet. The net of it is that over the course of a whole business cycle, the auto companies spend more cash than they take in. The result is that they have to use ever-increasing amounts of debt to keep the companies running in place. The same is true with most other transportation companies such as airlines, railroads, and shipping.

Capital allocation, as Warren Buffett would point out, is one of the two most important jobs of top management. It ranks in importance with managing day-to-day operations (or hiring others to do so). His test was: Does each dollar of capital expenditure generate at least one dollar of market value (hopefully much more)?

THE ROLE OF CASH FLOWS IN MERGERS AND ACQUISITIONS

Occasionally, the incentives to retain earnings are so strong that managers will make investments that actually destroy value. This often occurs when there are windfall cash flows that are high relative to the investment base. An example of this phenomenon was the oil companies in the late 1970s and early 1980s. This gave rise to people like T. Boone Pickens, who realized that the prices of oil stocks were significantly less than the value of their cash flows. In order to force companies to change their ways and distribute cash, he went on the takeover path.

This period was characterized by several phenomena. First of all, oil price hikes had led to strong cash growth. Second, they had led to commensurate increases in capital costs, notably land leases and "day rates" for drilling rigs. These expenditures were usually capitalized into the cost of drilling wells (and then depreciated), which means that it took some years for them to be realized in expense.

A renewal of this debate was seen more than a decade later during the attempt by Kirk Kerkorian to take over Chrysler in 1996. Kerkorian favored a higher dividend, while management argued that a stronger balance sheet was necessary to tide over the company during the downturn. In substance, as opposed to form, the two sides of the argument were not that far apart. At least they agreed on the basic premise—that capital spending ought to be capped. In form, at least, the debate was about whether shareholder interests were better served by keeping the cash on hand to shore up the balance sheet or disbursing the cash. There were merits to both arguments, but this depended largely on one's holding period. Long-term investors would want to see more cash on the balance sheet, while short-term investors would want a higher total return now, with less safety down the line (for future investors).

Cash flow analysis is a favorite tool of leveraged buyout (LBO) operators. In preparing a bid for and taking over a company, the most liberal depreciation rules are applied. Then, deferred taxes are used to the maximum extent possible. The plug number is supportable interest expense. The idea is to borrow enough money so that EBDIT minus the sum of depreciation and interest expense will make earnings before taxes approximately zero. Under this formula, the more that can be borrowed, the richer the payout to shareholders.

Why does this formula work? The reason is that "stepped-up" depreciation overstates the true physical depreciation of assets. Capital spending is less than the artificially high depreciation expense, which is just a book entry. But this book entry creates a tax shelter for cash flow. Similarly, the (NPV) of deferred taxes is less than their nominal value. So book earnings may be approximately equal to zero. But the resulting tax benefits are piled on top of positive (and carefully hidden) economic earnings.

This principle was abused in some LBOs. Having successfully manipulated depreciation expense, LBO operators tried to justify higher prices for acquisitions by deferring interest charges through payment-in-kind (PIK) debt. This action was said to "conserve cash." However, unlike capital spending, debt had to be amortized. (LBO operators cut capital spending so close to the bone that businesses suffered.) This was the case with companies like Macy's and Federated, which succumbed to the competition. RJR Nabisco barely escaped a similar fate, only because KKR, its buyer, accepted subpar returns.

Why is goodwill paid? Because the company is earning a superior rate of return on assets, perhaps mostly due to superior management. Let us consider a numerical example to illustrate the point. Suppose the market ROE is 12 percent. Company X, which has assets of 100 (in whatever base unit) earns 24, for an ROE of 24 percent. An acquirer would logically pay up to 200 in order to get the earnings of 24, because then he would earn the market ROE of 12 percent on this investment. Of the payment of 200, an amount of 100 is covered by the purchased assets. The remaining 100 goes into goodwill. The impact on the acquirer's balance sheet of the transaction might indicate:

Credit (reduce) cash	200
Debit Plant, property & equipment	100
Debit Goodwill	100

Let's say, arbitrarily, that the annual goodwill charge worked out to 4 (a 25-year amortization). So the actual income accrual would be $24 - 4 = 20$. Since this amortization charge is an arbitrary one, it would be ignored by cash flow–oriented analysts. If the goodwill asset were a Coke franchise, for instance, there would probably be an appreciating asset.

The above example was done using after-tax numbers. More likely, pre-tax numbers would be used in the analysis done by the acquiring corporation. That's because amortization is not deductible for tax purposes. A cash flow–minded acquirer might not mind the hit to earnings by amortization but would care about the lost tax deduction. So the purchase price in this example would be a bit less than 200.

EQUITY VERSUS DEBT SECURITIES OF A FIRM

The question of whether an investor should buy the equity or the debt securities of a firm ought to be considered in light of the trade-off between one's needs for returns and safety. Debt instruments pay a fixed rate of interest that is generally, but by no means always, lower than the returns that can be earned on the stock, and they have the first claim to a corporation's assets and cash flows. Owners of stock take most of the risks in investing but they get only what is left after the claims of the debt holders have been satisfied. This can be a lot, in the case of a company like Microsoft, which has had high returns over its corporate life and no debt; or very little, in the case of a heavily indebted steel company that struggles to make interest and principal payments on its debt obligations, never mind about doing anything for the shareholders.

The question of the optimal mix of debt and equity is also important for a corporation. In fact, the two questions are opposite sides of the same coin. Debt is cheaper than equity for the corporation, so companies often prefer to issue as much debt as is consistent with the needs and financial viability of the corporation. However, corporations risk bankruptcy by taking on too much debt, so they need to have some equity as a safety cushion. This result occurs because when a company sells debt, it takes on risk by guaranteeing interest and principal payments to the lender, whereas when it sells equity, it is the stockholders who take on the risks inherent in a variable rate of return, while the company has no further obligations except to make good-faith efforts to earn money.

Even so, a number of academics have tried to argue that the mix of debt and equity doesn't matter. Based on the assumption of perfect capital markets, Modigliani and Miller, two Nobel Prize winners, derived two basic propositions with respect to the valuation of the securities with different capital structures, and their theory is often referred to as the MM model. In spite of their assumptions, which cause some discrepancies between theory and real-world observations, it is important to understand the conditions under which the MM model is valid so that we know what to expect under different conditions of market imperfections.

Proposition I of the MM model states that the market value of a firm is independent of its capital structure, and is given by the expected return from its assets at a rate appropriate to its risk class. This proposition allows the complete separation of the capital investment decision from the use of financial leverage. In the MM model, firms are divided into "equivalent return classes" with similar operating characteristics, meaning that firms having similar risks without using leverage (debt) belong to the same risk class. As long as the rate of return used to compute the present value of the assets of a firm is equal to that of other firms belonging to the same risk class, we can ignore the financing decisions because no single combination of debt and equity is better than any other combination. If the MM model's proposition I holds, the simplest financing plan is to use all equity financing. Hence, the market value of the firm can be determined by the NPV of the stream of cash flows from operations using the firm's assets, discounted at a relatively high rate of return appropriate to equities.

Although borrowing by a firm increases the rate of return on shareholders' investment, by substituting cheaper debt for equity, it also increases the firm's risk. The MM model postulates that the increase in expected return by holding shares of a levered (indebted) firm is offset exactly by the increase in its financial risk. In perfect capital markets, an investor can borrow as freely and at the same rate as a firm. Therefore, an investor who wishes to assume a higher risk level through financial leverage to get a higher expected return can obtain a personal loan and buy more shares of an unlevered firm to achieve the same result, to offset the fact that the returns to an unlevered firm are less than that of a levered firm in the same risk class. Thus, it makes no difference whether the investor assumes the financial risk indirectly by holding the shares of a levered firm, or directly by borrowing money to buy more shares of an unlevered firm. Conversely, an individual can reduce the risk of a risky security by creating a portfolio consisting of that security plus cash.

Proposition II of the MM model states that the expected rate of return, r_e, on equity of a levered firm, is corresponding to the risk class with all equity financing, plus a financial risk premium equal to the debt-to-equity ratio times the spread between r_a and r_d, where r_a is the expected return on the unlevered asset itself and r_d is the expected rate of return on debt. That is,

$$r_e = r_a + (D/E)(r_a - r_d)$$

where D and E are market values of debt and equity, respectively. The above equation is based on the assumptions of no taxation and perfect capital markets. This proposition indicates that the expected rate of return on the stock of a levered firm increases in proportion to the debt-to-equity ratio. (In the real world, tax refunds on interest expense give corporations a significant incentive to use debt rather than equity financing.) Solving for r_a from the preceding equation, the expected return on a firm's assets with all-equity financing is given by

$$r_a = r_e * E/(D + E) + r_d * D/(D + E)$$

If an investor's portfolio included all of a firm's stock and debt, he or she would be entitled to all of the firm's operating income generated by its assets. Then, the expected return on the portfolio is equal to the weighted average of the expected rate of return on its stock r_e, and the expected rate of return on its debt r_d, with the proportions of equity and debt, respectively, as weights, as expressed by the preceding equation. Consequently, r_a is sometimes referred to as the *weighted average cost of capital*. This is the "hurdle" that a firm must beat in order to provide a worthwhile return to investors.

In fact, capital structure does matter. The main assumption behind the academics' theory was that in a case of financial distress, the original shareholders would be wiped out, and the debt holders would be more than willing to convert their loans to equity. But debt holders looking for safety are usually unwilling to accept risky equity in satisfaction of their claims, nor should they be forced to. That's because in the real world, they normally cannot "reinsure" the risk that they are taking, so their investment may end up with a different risk (and return) profile than they bargained for. Also, a corporate restructuring is not "frictionless" as the academics hypothesize.

In a bankruptcy situation, employees get laid off to reduce the corporation's costs, and various classes of creditors, and even equity holders squabble about how to divide the claims. In the end, everybody is a loser except the lawyers and "workout" artists. Thus, it is reasonable for a firm to maintain a debt level that is low enough to avoid bankruptcy in all but the most exceptionally bad circumstances.

The ivory tower MM theory met its most severe test in real life in 1998 by the near failure of Long-Term Capital Management, which was headed by John Meriwether, former Vice-Chairman of Salomon Brothers, and included Myron Scholes, a Nobel Prize winner, as a senior partner. The firm had borrowed some 30 times its capital to take large bets to place trades with very thin profit margins. The profit potential of the trades was so small as to make them not worth doing, unless their returns were magnified by large amounts of borrowed money. When real-world events caused actual returns to fall slightly below the cost of the borrowed money (as well as expected returns), the effect of the large borrowings was like investors buying on margin and getting it wrong. There are limits, nowadays, to how much individuals can buy stocks on margin, but there were practically no rules against Long-Term Capital's doing what it did.

The risks of Long-Term Capital's strategy were best depicted in the novel *Bonfire of the Vanities,* in which the hero, Sherman McCoy, and his fictitious firm Pierce and Pierce bet $6 billion in the hope of earning one sixteenth of a percentage point, or less than $4 million, and actually earned one eighth of a point, or just under $8 million.[4] In real life, of course, a firm could easily earn one sixteenth of a percentage point less than expected, which would cause the $6 billion trade to only break even; and a shortfall of one eighth of a point would have caused a loss of several million dollars, all in one afternoon. In fact, this portion of the novel was a parody of Salomon traders, including several alumni who staffed up Long-Term Capital.

It took nothing less than the intervention of the U.S. Federal Reserve Board, plus some deep-pocketed investors such as Warren Buffett standing by, to rescue Long-Term Capital. Thus, a failed private investment (speculation is actually a much better description) almost turned into a public liability funded by American taxpayers, including those who do not invest in the stock market. Hence, it is not inappropriate for public policy to discourage the excessive use of debt by private firms, even though this decision is usually made at the corporate level.

A modified and more reasonable version of the MM capital theory is that capital structure does not matter as long as debt is no more than 30 percent of total capital, with equity making up the remainder. As long as debt remains below the 30 percent level, the chances of financial failure are indeed generally small enough to be neglected, and in the unlikely event that it happens, debt holders will likely recover all, and equity holders at least a portion of their investment. This 30 percent standard is the amount that we are willing to allow as being suitable for a conservative investor to commit his funds in an industrial firm, and is, in fact, stricter than the original Graham and Dodd rule of thumb, which required that debt be no more than equity, or a 50–50 debt-to-equity ratio in the capital structure.

This idea of using debt securities as investments in lieu of equity is not nearly as preposterous it may seem to those investors whose experience is limited to the so-called equity culture of the late 1990s. When public investing first made its debut over a century ago, an investment in stocks was very similar in nature to investments in lower-grade bonds for a higher yield and prospects of a modest capital gain, at some sacrifice of safety, compared to ordinary bonds. The capital gains on the bonds were largely limited to the discount from par value, but the potential for gains on stocks was customarily limited by the payment of the majority of earnings as dividends, with the reinvestment of the smaller part of disposable funds, as well as practical limits on the returns on invested capital. The successive revolutions in physical and social sciences in the twentieth century changed that from time to time by making it possible to have outsized returns on relatively small amounts of capital, especially intellectual capital. Hence, the practice grew up in boom times of overlooking the protection to an investment offered by physical assets on the balance sheet. (For instance, Jeffrey Skilling, former CEO of Enron preached the virtues of an "asset light" company.) In harder times, investors will probably rediscover the value of hard assets.

CHAPTER 7

Analysis of Asset Value

Assets give value to a firm. They are the purpose of capital expenditures and give rise to cash flows. In general, assets should not be overlooked in the evaluation of a business, as they too often are nowadays. These assets, together with a dividend stream, form the foundation of investment value. Moreover, both quantities offer a more reliable, if less forward-looking, guide to valuation than the much used and abused earnings stream. In the final analysis, the more that stock purchase decisions are based on what is known, and less on what is merely guessed at, the more such decisions amount to investment rather than speculation.

THE MARGINAL EFFICIENCY OF CAPITAL[1]

A public corporation normally seeks to invest its money at the highest possible rate of return. Economist John Maynard Keynes expressed this in a concept called the *marginal efficiency of capital* (MEC), which is an application of the better-known law of diminishing returns. The first batch of available money is invested at a very high rate of return, the second batch at a somewhat lower rate of return, and so on. The last amount of money may earn only a CD rate in a bank account. (An MEC curve is shown in Figure 7.1.) Sometimes, overly eager or aggressive managers may actually make investments at a negative rate of return, thereby diminishing the value of the corporation.

Investors generally want to identify the corporations that will give them the best returns for their money. This is not an easy task because such investors are not privy to a corporation's projects or cash flows. (Prior to the Securities and Exchange Commission's [SEC's] regulation FD or Fair Disclosure, very large investors such as mutual funds or sell-side analysts were sometimes given private information about corporate projections.) Therefore, they have to review publicly available financial statements and make educated guesses about the future profitability and liquidity of the firm of their choice, based on the past, plus what is known about the present.

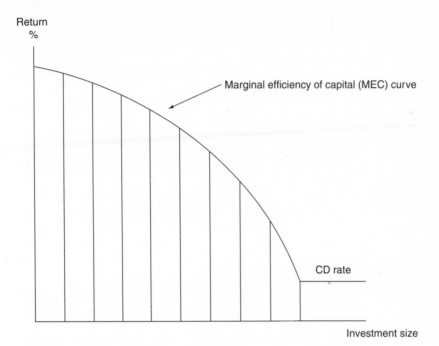

Return
%

Marginal efficiency of capital (MEC) curve

CD rate

Investment size

FIGURE 7.1   Marginal Efficiency of Capital.

Since stocks of fast-growing companies are characterized by high return on equity (ROE), would a value investor find a high ROE desirable? All other things being equal, the answer is yes. A high ROE can support a high dividend distribution rate and a high retained earnings rate, with its implication for a high growth rate. But all other things are seldom equal. High ROE stocks typically command large premiums to book value. The first disadvantage is that the dividend yields are much lower than the dividend distribution rates. Also, a company might not be able to grow as fast as the reinvestment rate might theoretically allow. Why is this the case? It refers to the marginal efficiency of capital. The first 1 percent of capital investment could produce a growth rate of greater than 1 percent; the last 1 percent of reinvestment will probably produce a growth rate of less than 1 percent.

An examination of the Value Line array on Coca-Cola (dated February 8, 2002) as shown in Figure 7.2 will illustrate this point. The company's ROE is over 30 percent. But the price-to-book (P/B) ratio is over 10. The company retains 60 percent of its earnings, leading to an earnings reinvestment rate (what Value Line calls retained to common equity) of nearly 20 percent. And it distributes about 40 percent of its earnings in the form of dividends, leading to a dividend distribution rate of over 10 percent, which

Year	1997	1998	1999	2000	2001	2002
Sales per Share	7.64	7.63	8.01	8.23	7.06	7.92
"Cash Flow" per Share	1.92	1.69	1.63	1.79	1.92	1.99
Earnings per Share	1.64	1.42	1.30	1.48	1.60	1.66
Dividends per Share	0.56	0.60	0.64	0.88	0.72	0.80
Book Value per Share	2.96	3.41	3.85	3.75	4.57	4.78
Shares (mill.)	2470.6	2465.5	2471.6	2484.8	2486.2	2471.0
Share Price (year low)	50.0	53.6	47.3	42.9	42.4	42.9
Market Cap (mill.)	123530	132151	116907	106598	105415	106006
P/E Ratio	30.5	37.7	36.4	29.0	26.5	25.8
P/B Ratio	16.9	15.7	12.3	11.4	9.3	9.0
Dividend Yield	1.1%	1.1%	1.4%	2.1%	1.7%	1.9%
Sales (mill.)	18868	18813	19805	20458	17545	19564
Depreciation (mill.)	626	645	792	773	803	806
Net Profit (mill.)	4129	3533	3233	3669	3979	4134
Working Capital (mill.)	-1410	-2260	-3376	-2701	-1258	11
Long-Term Debt (mill.)	801	687	854	835	1220	2700
Shareholders' Equity (mill.)	7311	8403	9513	9316	11365	11800
Return on Capital	51.2%	39.1%	31.5%	36.4%	31.9%	29.1%
Return on Equity	56.5%	42.0%	34.0%	39.4%	35.0%	35.0%
Reinvestment Rate	37.3%	24.4%	17.3%	21.3%	19.3%	18.2%
Dividend Distribution Rate	19.2%	17.6%	16.7%	18.1%	15.8%	16.8%
Dividend Payout Ratio	66%	58%	51%	54%	55%	52%
Dividend Payout Ratio	34%	42%	49%	46%	45%	48%

Source: Value Line Publishing Inc.; author's calculations.

FIGURE 7.2 Summary Statistics for Coca-Cola 1997–2002.

can be found by subtracting the earnings reinvestment rate from ROE. But the historical and forecasted growth rates, which can be found on the left-hand side of the page, under "annual rates," are less than the reinvestment rate, or theoretical growth rate. Note also that the dividend yield is not much more than 1 percent, a fraction of the dividend distribution rate, because the P/B ratio is so high. So investors do not get the full benefits of Coca-Cola's high ROE.

All in all, growth stocks are much more susceptible to earnings disappointments than value stocks. That's because of where such companies operate on the marginal efficiency of capital curve. The main assumption is that growth will be maintained by investments at the high end of the curve, and that the law of diminishing returns will not apply. If such a company is forced to move down the MEC curve to the next level of profitability, the result will be an earnings disappointment that punishes the stock. However, it is the stock of a company with below-average ROE, and hence below-average expectations, that is likely to surprise on the upside. Almost inevitably, an opportunity comes along with average or even above-average ROE that even a "sleepy" company is not likely to miss. The result will be the production of a high ROE (relative to the company's history), as well as analyst expectations, that pushes up the price of the stock.

THE BASIC GRAHAM AND DODD APPROACH TO ASSET VALUE

Let's begin with the basic Graham and Dodd approach, which is based on asset value. Asset value is most easily measured by book value, which is just net worth, or shareholder's equity per share, when there is no preferred stock. (If there is preferred stock, it is subtracted from net worth to get net worth for common stock.) This figure is just the sum of all capital that has been invested and retained in the company over its history. It is a conservative estimate of assets because it gives no effect to franchises, "going concern" value, intellectual property, or other intangible assets (except for goodwill established through the purchase of other companies in arm's-length transactions.) Graham and Dodd recommended the purchase of stocks based on the relationship of price to equity without considering the returns to the underlying assets. Although this approach has some flaws, they hit upon an approach that is reasonably useful, given "normal" returns to assets. After discussing their methodology, we will try to measure the returns on assets and equity, and try to relate these returns to investment values.

Assets can be financed either by equity or debt. A corporation's debt should be considered in much the same light as mortgage on a house. If you were to purchase a house for $100,000, all cash, and the value of the house were to decline to $70,000 (a not uncommon occurrence in recent memory in many parts of the country), the reduction in owner's equity would be some 30 percent. You would suffer a painful loss but by no means would come close to losing your entire equity under such circumstances. Indeed, there would probably be enough of an asset remaining for you to take out a home equity loan in order to stay afloat. However, if the financing were 20 percent down, 80 percent debt, an arrangement generally considered prudent, a 30 percent decline in value of the house would more than wipe out the owner's equity. In the event that you wished to move and wanted to dispose of the house, you could not get anything for it in a sale. (Indeed, under the terms of many mortgages, you, the mortgagor, would have to make up the difference between the sales price and the mortgage.)

Because the true value of a company, its so-called enterprise value, is the sum of its equity and debt at market value, not merely the market capitalization of its equity, a company that is heavily indebted is really operating with a large mortgage, so to speak. This is all well and good when a company's fortunes are all the way up and up, because the returns to the small equity piece are magnified by the large amount of leverage employed. However, when conditions are bad and the value of the equity collapses, an enterprise value that is composed of too much debt and too little equity is likely to be catastrophic to an investor. Warren Buffet has likened the operation of a highly leveraged company to driving a car with a knife attached to the steering wheel. Such a sword of Damocles would make for a very alert driver in one instance and a very aware management in the other, but a single pothole in the road could occasion serious, and potentially fatal, consequences in either case.

Leverage is a tricky matter because some forms of leverage are more onerous than others. The most dangerous form of leverage is bank debt. It is theoretically due on demand, although borrowers have forgotten this because this provision has seldom been enforced. In the event of a general collapse of financial markets, however, borrowers will be sternly reminded of loan covenants. This, in fact, is already beginning to happen in Japan. Almost as dangerous is commercial paper, which is mainly sold by corporations to other companies. The expectation is that it will be renewed, but this is not always the case, as a number of issuers found out during the last credit crunch around 1990. Less onerous is deferred taxes, and the reason is simple. If a company does not earn a profit, it not only avoids paying most taxes, but it can in many cases even recover cash taxes that were previously paid, or cancel deferred taxes that were booked and not paid. If none of these options is available, a money-losing company can carry forward net operating losses (NOLs) for a number of years that can be used to offset future profits. In extreme circumstances, a company can sell these NOLs to other concerns or the NOLs can benefit a potential acquirer.

In fact, if a common stock is depressed because the company has too much debt, and its bonds, which are senior to the stock, have a sufficiently attractive yield, it is possible that the bonds should be brought in lieu of the stock. In a default situation, the equity holders get wiped out (or have their percentage of ownership of the stock severely reduced in order to give priority to the debt holders, who become equity holders). Before this occurs, the debt will be priced to yield equity-like returns of 10 percent or more. The equity of such a company has taken on the characteristics of very risky securities such as options and warrants, that effectively represent a "call" on the recovery of the company, not its value as things currently stand. This level of risk is too great except for all but the most astute of professional investors. In such a situation, the way to get equity-like returns is through the debt, not the equity, and you have to consider the seniority of the bonds relative to all the other debt claims above it. The whole purpose of investing in debt is to get a security that is senior to all forms of equity, and ideally is equal to (*pari passu*) all forms of debt.

When buying the stock of a company for which working capital represents a large portion of the market value of the stock, you should look very carefully at the individual items. It is best if working capital consists mainly of receivables, cash, and marketable securities. These are liquid assets on which a distribution to shareholders can be made. You must be careful of a high level of inventories, particularly if they are rising. On the liabilities side, we would prefer to see a low level of accounts payable and short-term debt.

Among inventories, raw material inventories are the best. A high ratio of work in progress or finished goods inventory to the total could be a sign of trouble. Raw materials can usually be sold for something close to their purchase price. Finished goods inventory, on the other hand, consists not only of raw materials but also labor and overhead. If they can't be sold to an end user, they will have to be sold as scrap at a loss. In such a situation, they might not fetch as good a price as "unspoiled" raw material, even though their costs are much higher. Inventories are particularly dangerous if the company has to issue new long-term debt—or worse, short-term debt—to "carry" them. With the development of just-in-time inventory management, large inventories may be a sign of poor management.

In addition to buying stock below book value, Graham and Dodd advised investors to try to get the stock below net working capital, that is, below the value of the current assets minus current liabilities. In this way, you would be paying only for the liquid assets and getting the business for free. In a special case of high degree of safety, net working capital would exceed the market value of stock plus long-term debt. Since the enterprise value of the firm is just the market cap of the equity and debt, minus liquid assets, the enterprise value in this case would be zero. To get stock of such high safety is referred to as buying net-net.

In 1965, Warren Buffett bought a controlling interest in Berkshire Hathaway for less than its book value of $17 a share and just over its net working capital, thinking that he would thereby get its textile business for practically nothing. This was, in fact, a mistaken premise, because the textile business turned out to be worth zero or less, due to foreign competition. But he had successfully "leveraged up" because his investment partnership's 70 percent holding of Berkshire translated into control of 100 percent of the assets, once he was elected chairman. By liquidating most working capital items and severely limiting reinvestment in textiles, Buffett actually had gained a larger pool of assets to recycle into other, more productive investments.[2]

Book value will ideally represent tangible assets. Often, a company may have a large book value based on the premium paid over book in the purchase of other concerns. While we would not discount such intangible assets altogether, they must in many cases be considered to have been purchased on a wing or a prayer. This may contrast with the opposite case, that of acquiring a valuable franchise such as Coca-Cola. In such a case, intangible assets may have equal or greater economic value than fungible tangible assets of a similar dollar amount. As a compromise, we will allow the inclusion of intangible assets in the calculation of book value, and let a high or low ROE, as discussed in the next section, be the judge of their value.

Believing as they did that stocks should be bought like bonds, Graham and Dodd wanted the protection of a good balance sheet and a stock price that was at a discount from book value, much as they might want to buy a good corporate bond at a discount from par. They assumed that most firms would pay out large proportions of their earnings as dividends (as was the custom of their time), and that the earnings would generally be adequate to pay reasonable dividends. In the next section, we will measure vigorously a company's "ability to pay," and its implications for stock returns. Chapter 8 will explain how to select stocks whose value lies primarily in their dividend payments.

THE SPECIAL CASE OF OFF-BALANCE-SHEET ASSETS AND LIABILITIES

Sometimes book value will considerably understate asset value. In this case, buying a stock based on fully stated asset value would still meet the Graham and Dodd tests.

In the case of oil companies, book value is typically a minimum value for the asset value that is disclosed in the annual report. The SEC requires the companies to estimate the so-called net present value of reserves. This is based first on "proved and probable" reserves as of the prevailing prices at the end of the year. The estimate of physical assets, in turn, is based on engineering standards. Future production is forecasted and multiplied by the prevailing price, while associated production costs are subtracted. The resulting earning stream is discounted at 10 percent. These are pretax numbers, on the theory that a potential acquirer would finance the purchase with debt, and write off the resulting interest expense. The NPV of the reserves is over and above the value of the fixed assets required to produce them, because depreciation of these assets is factored into the cash flow.

A Value Line report on Exxon in January 1983 illustrated this point. It calculated that the reserve-adjusted book value was $52, versus the net worth of $35. So there was $17 per share in reserves. With a stock price in the high $20s, the stock was selling for roughly half of asset value.

What is the significance of the additional asset value? In 1982, the company earned $3.10 per share and paid $3.00 of dividend per share. So it looked like earnings barely covered the dividend, and there were fears of a cut. The ROE, based on $3.10 of earnings and $35 of book value, was $3.10/$35 or just under 9 percent. If one took the view that true asset value was $52 rather than $35 a share, the investor would have gotten a bonus by the way of assets, but the reconstructed ROE would have been diluted to $3.10/$52, or a bare 6 percent. But wait. In order for asset value to be greater than book value to the tune of $17 a share, there must have been a rise in asset value that did not flow through the income statement. Suppose, arbitrarily, we took the view that the asset value premium doubled every 10 years, or compounded at a rate of 7 percent per year. Then, taking 7 percent of $17, there would have been roughly $1.20 a share of "earnings" that took place off the book through an increase of asset value. If this were the case, Exxon's true earnings for 1982 would be somewhere over $4 a share, not the reported $3.10. This higher figure covered the 1982 dividend far better than $3.10 a share. A rough ROE calculation would be about $4.30/$52, or just over 8 percent, not so far from just under 9 percent on the traditional measure. As one would expect, a much higher asset base would earn a slightly lower return. Thus, the asset accumulation significantly improves true asset-based earnings without a meaningful dilution of returns on the higher asset value. All in all, an investor who can identify such situations is getting more for the money.

In another instance, Philips Electronics traded close to book value for most of the late 1990s. It controlled not only its own operations, but also interests in Polygram Records, ASM Lithography, and Taiwan Semiconductor, all of which were publicly traded. One must first evaluate Philips's interests in these three companies at market value, and then compare them with the carrying costs of the investment. The difference should be added to book value to arrive at an asset value. This idea was borne out by the fact that when Philips sold its interest in Polygram in late 1998, the gain on the sale temporarily increased the book value above the (admittedly depressed) price in the fall of 1998. The market value of the retained interest in the other companies only added to the pot.

Another example is Sears, which announced the spin-off of Allstate Insurance in order to emphasize its retailing operation again. This was to be effected through the distribution of 81 Allstate shares for every 100 Sears shares. An analysis undertaken in early 1995 showed Sears to be fairly priced and Allstate overpriced as of the time of announcement. (It turned out not to be the case in hindsight.) But if you bought 100 shares of Sears, and then sold short the 81 shares of Allstate that were to be received in the distribution, you could get Sears for 8 times the earnings of the retailing operations. This is a Graham and Dodd–type investment. And the analysis has been simplified by canceling out the Allstate exposure, the less well understood of the two.

To further illustrate, in mid-1995, Seagram sold for a price of $29 with a book value of about $14. It also owned DuPont stock worth about $15 a share pretax ($10 a share after tax). Seagram resolved to dispose of its DuPont holdings, which later lifted the book value to $24 after tax. This made for a potentially interesting investment story. Seagram used the proceeds of its DuPont sale to buy Universal Studios from Matsushita of Japan. The latter was a "motivated seller" because of problems both at Universal and at its core operations in Japan. So Seagram's purchase price was $7 billion, about $1 billion less than similar assets might have commanded elsewhere. Under these circumstances, a purchase of Seagram's stock was considered and rejected by the author. Although the Universal Studios purchase was tactically brilliant and might have made sense given the prevailing enthusiasm for media properties, paying a high absolute price for entertainment properties did not seem prudent, since they could also fall in value. A conservative investor would have much preferred to see Seagram invest in its core liquor business, or better yet, repurchase stock. In fact, it took several years for the market to reward Seagram, and only after several restructuring moves that ultimately included the final sale of the company to Vivendi Media of France. With the benefit of hindsight, the DuPont stock that was divested doubled in the next two and a half years; its retention would have lifted Seagram's asset value to the mid- to high $30s per share. Seagram did not do as well with its venture into entertainment, and its stock languished in the low $30s for some time.

Liabilities can also lie off the balance sheet. This is particular true for capital-intensive companies. For instance, there may be heavy use of leased assets that actually amount to a form of borrowing. So-called capital leases are considered debt and are included as such on the balance sheet. But shorter-term operating leases are not treated this way. Yet, if the company is dependent on such leases, the payments may be every bit as onerous as interest and principal payments.

Another important liability is unfunded retiree health care benefits. Pension assets have been settled, but this liability is a relatively new area. In theory, the liability should be accounted for as it is incurred. But the normal practice has been on a "pay as you go" basis. The gap between accrued liabilities and actual payments is bridged by actuarial assumptions. If these turn out to be overly optimistic, the company is not on a sound footing even from an accounting standpoint. An example of this trend is the U.S. auto companies. Until the early 1990s, they typically sold at significant discounts to book value. But then they were forced to take a hit for retirement benefits in 1991. The difference represented a large part of book value; so stock prices that had previously represented discounts became premiums. This one-time adjustment increased ROE, but this was partly offset by the fact that earnings, both past and prospective, had to be adjusted downward as well.

THE SPECIAL CASE OF AN UNUSUALLY HIGH RETURN ON EQUITY

The reader might ask, "What about the company that is selling at a multiple of book value because its ROEs are high, say in excess of 20 percent?" By definition, this would be one of the faster growers and a most promising investment if the high ROEs, and hence growth, can be maintained. In many cases, the shareholders' equity has been reduced by the payment of a generous dividend, and Chapter 8 will explain how to adjust the book value upward to account for the payout. But this is not a consideration for an Intel or a Microsoft, the former of which pays only a nominal dividend, and the latter of which paid no dividend at all until 2003.

Graham and Dodd would have distrusted paying a multiple of book value for high growth or for its proxy, a high ROE. We would, too, but not to the degree as the original value investors. Since we allow ourselves to pay a premium over book value when the ROE is high enough, we set forth our own modification for evaluating a security with a high ROE (and no dividend). Based on considerable theoretical deliberation and practical testing over several years, the author suggests the following formulas for companies with ROE less than and greater than 15 percent, respectively:

Investment value (price) = Book value, for ROE < 15%

Modified investment value = (book value) * $(ROE/15\%)^2$,
for ROE > 15%

Note that a high hurdle rate (15 percent) is required before allowing a premium to book value. Such a requirement screens for a very good company. Once a superior return is earned, however, the factor is squared. That is because a high ROE will help in two ways: through high growth and through the high-price earning multiple that will likely result from it. For example, if ROE is 21.2 percent, then (21.2 percent/15 percent) squared equals 2. In other words, it requires an ROE of 21.2 percent before we would feel comfortable paying as much as twice book value for an issue. An ROE of about 26 percent is required for us to pay three times book value, and an ROE of 30 percent for four times book value.

There is no guarantee that such a high ROE can be maintained or that it will lead to high earnings growth. The first observation is that because of the marginal efficiency of capital, high ROEs do not lead to comparably high rates of growth. In fact, high rates of ROE cannot be maintained unless a company pays out a significant portion of earnings in the form of dividends. A case in point is Coca-Cola Company, which maintains its astronomical ROEs by paying out two thirds of its earnings as dividends. But this has the effect of reducing the retained earnings rate, and hence the growth rate, to a more "normal" level.

The second observation is that high ROEs provide a margin of safety that an above-average growth rate will be maintained. Unless it is generated by an undue amount of leverage, a high ROE is a natural sign that the underlying economics of the business are attractive. Within limits, therefore, management can adjust growth rate through its dividend payout policy or through a moderate use of debt.

High-tech stocks are among the most promising investment area for Graham and Dodd analysis. The originators of this type of analysis actually distrusted technology stocks because such stocks were in a field that they (and their greatest acolyte, Warren Buffett) could not relate to. The fortunes of tech companies, and hence their equities, are notoriously volatile. But it is just this volatility that often brings the valuations within reach. In a forced-choice situation, we would rather hazard the vicissitude of a rapidly changing business and technological environment under normal conditions than we would with a more pedestrian issue under the extreme stresses of, say, a Great Depression. We don't mind taking risky bets if the odds are in our favor. Many tech stocks (but not Microsoft, which basically broke the mold) satisfy our modified requirements; a few even qualify on more traditional Graham and Dodd grounds.

IBM (in the 1990s) was a case in point. Long a traditional growth stock, it had become a value stock in the closing decade of the twentieth century. Few people believed that it could go below book value, but of course it did. The company turned itself around. Although it basically lost its leadership in many product lines to younger, hungrier companies, it worked its way back into the mainstream and earned a normal return for the industry. This enabled the stock to return to a "normal" multiple above book.

Wall Street has long been unable to make up its mind as to whether information technology stocks are commodity or growth issues. These include producers of computers and parts such as silicon "chips" that make up the guts of computers, or software that makes the machine run. In addition, advanced telecommunications technology falls under the tech label. They are actually a hybrid of the two, called *commodity growth* or *cyclical growth* stocks. Their long-term prospects, nowadays at least, are better than today's "deep cyclicals," such as autos and chemicals (which were high-tech stocks in their own day). When priced at comparable valuations to autos and chemicals, as they often are, high techs are more attractive. But this was seldom the case around the turn of this century.

Because of their inherent operating volatility, tech companies often have less debt than average, which is an attractive feature under our version of Graham and Dodd. Beware of exceptions to this rule, because these companies run the risk of getting the worst of both worlds—high operating risk and high financial risk. It is probably a sign that the company is not well run.

The tech stocks have high ROEs. This supported an underlying industry long-term growth rate of 15 to 16 percent. Yet until the mid 1990s, their price–earnings (P/E) ratios were much lower, perhaps even in the single digits, reflecting expectations of a much lower growth rate. They generally pay few or no dividends. So the stocks don't get dividend support. But the cash is retained on the balance sheet, sometimes in excessive quantities. Some of the most cash-rich companies around are high-tech companies, including Microsoft. Capital spending is often surprisingly low. The whole idea of such companies is substituting technology for monetary capital.

It is noteworthy that tech stocks generally attract equity investment because of the prospect for high returns. Such new capital is important in securing the investment of existing shareholders. In fact, the capital infusions lead to increases in book value above what earnings would produce. From the discussion of the statement of stockholders' equity in Chapter 2, the relationship measuring the effect of earnings on book value can be expressed as follows:

Ending book value = Beginning book value + Earnings − Dividends

or

Earnings = Ending book value − Beginning book value + Dividends

This relationship holds true if the number of shares doesn't change, and there are no accounting adjustments. We use this relationship to measure the impact of a new stock issue at a price higher than book value. If the new shares are issued above book value, ending book value is boosted by this premium, thereby creating a "dividend" and additional "earnings" for original shareholders. Companies that routinely issue stock at a premium show changes in book value per share greater than earnings per share.

A case in point is the information on Tech Data in the Value Line report of July 21, 2000, as reproduced in Figure 7.3. At the end of fiscal 1997, the company had a book value of $14.56. The following year, fiscal 1998, the company earned $2.29. Theoretically, its ending book value should have been $14.56 + $2.29 − $0.00 = $16.85. But, in fact, ending book value was $18.93, more than $2 higher. This was the result of the issue of almost three million new shares at a premium to book. Similar stories could have been told in previous years. Note also that the growth rate of book value over the past 10- and 5-year periods shown in the "Annual Rates" table in Figure 7.3 was several percentage points higher than the growth in earnings.

This relationship is shown in prospectuses for initial or secondary public offerings to new shareholders. The following amounts are quantified: beginning book value, purchase price, and dilution to new shareholders by the excess of purchase price to old stockholders. That's how "insiders" of start-up companies get rich, and if a company repeatedly issues new shares, early outside investors can also benefit. So in this way, a high ROE eventually results in balance sheet strength as well. The stated book value can be increased by new share issues, and in fact has often been significantly upgraded by off-the-book asset gains such as goodwill.

Price volatility can also benefit companies that buy or sell shares of stock from time to time. An alert company with a low price-to-book (P/B) ratio can generate steady growth of per-share book value, and to a lesser extent, of earnings, merely by buying stock at a discount from book, just as a company favored by a high P/B ratio can increase book value by selling shares at a premium. Book value is a more stable measure of a company's well-being than earnings, which merely form the major part of changes in book value. For this reason, master investors like Warren Buffett often judge a company by its ability to increase book value.

When stock investments are based on book value or asset value, they become much like bond investments. A stock that is secured by assets, particularly liquid assets, virtually promises a return on principal. If the stock is further paying a substantial dividend, it assumes the character of a convertible bond. It is like a bond that promises income and a return of capital in a stormy weather scenario and offers the capital gains of a stock in fair weather.

Year	1993	1994	1995	1996	1997	1998	1999
Beginning Book Value per Share	3.70	5.84	6.90	7.56	10.13	14.56	18.93
Ending Book Value per Share	5.84	6.90	7.56	10.13	14.56	18.93	19.41
Change in Book Value per Share	2.14	1.06	0.66	2.57	4.43	4.37	0.48
Earnings per Share	0.83	0.91	0.56	1.35	1.92	2.29	2.34
Shares (mill.)	36.55	37.81	37.81	43.29	48.27	51.10	52.23
Stock Price (year low)	10.60	14.00	8.30	12.50	19.80	33.80	14.50
Price/Book Ratio	1.8	2.0	1.1	1.2	1.4	1.8	0.7

Source: Value Line Publishing Inc.; author's calculations.

FIGURE 7.3 Earnings versus Changes in Book Value for Tech Data 1993–1999.

THE GENERAL CASE OF UNSUSTAINABLE
EARNINGS FOR CYCLICAL STOCKS

Cyclical stocks get their character from two economic forces. First, the demand for oil, steel, and automobiles is unsteady. Second, production is characterized by high fixed costs and low variable costs. It is costly to introduce a new plant, but once it occurs, the best strategy is to sell high volumes at low variable costs and high contributions (the difference between sales and variable costs) in order to "absorb" fixed costs. For this reason, returns on equity at the peak of a cycle are very high. By definition, though, commodity producers have few defenses against the entry of new products from competition, which is attracted to these high returns. This contributes to a "feast or famine" environment of varying degrees. Therefore, a commodity company must be evaluated against its average, rather than peak or trough earnings. The problem with cyclically high earnings is that implied earnings growth expectations, as expressed in the ROE, are too high at their peaks.

The best tool for evaluating cyclical stocks might not be earnings but ROE. A cyclical company in a good year will earn a very high ROE, typically 30 percent or more, and in a bad year something close to zero, maybe even a loss. Therefore, the natural analytical tendency to "straight line" the most recent earnings forward must be strongly resisted in the case of a cyclical. (Such a practice may do only minimal damage to the analysis of a stable company in the food or utility industry.) If one is using history as a guide, it must be a long history, encompassing at least 5 years, and more like 10 or 15. Only by examining a company's record and taking average performance over both good and bad years can such a company's prospects be fairly estimated. In any event, one should not expect more than an ROE much above 10 percent over the course of a whole business cycle, and if one wanted to be conservative, even an estimate of a high-single-digit percentage ROE might not do such a company injustice. Given the fact that most companies will retain earnings (and this alone should cause earnings to grow over time), we would use an average ROE, applied to the most recent book value, rather than average earnings, as the best indicator of the company's normalized earnings power.

The compensation to a low rate of return is that cyclical companies do not need to reinvest as much as they actually do. Demand for a commodity grows slowly but steadily over time, and absent new supplies, prices should keep pace. The problem is that a strong industry-wide reinvestment program causes supply to grow at a faster rate than demand, pushing prices down. This affects everyone, of course, not just those companies that overinvest, but the pain is more likely to be felt by companies with a relatively high proportion of fixed assets (earning a low return), matched by debt at a fixed rate, than by companies in a more liquid position. Indeed, it is better for companies in a cyclical industry to have a strong dividend payment (or stock repurchase) program because they can participate fully in the vagaries of the industry with a minimum of investment. Over the course of a whole business cycle, a cyclical company would most probably maximize shareholder returns through a lesser, rather than greater, amount of investment and returning its generally ample cash flows to stockholders.

It should be a first principle that a company engaged in this kind of business should be conservatively financed. This rule alone will virtually ensure that other companies that follow it would not contribute to a significant overcapacity. That's because expansion would, by definition, be limited by what could be supported out of internally generated funds, which in turn would be limited by demand, and the earnings that would result there from.

The use of asset value analysis can allow investors to make otherwise "dangerous" investments in technology and cyclical stocks relatively safe. Such commitments may in the end be better secured, if more volatile, than the issues of popular consumer plays, not to mention Internet stocks that sell for a high multiple of asset value based on unsustainably high returns (or worse yet, expectation thereof).

An ROE is a check of reasonableness for earnings growth, which is a measure that the average modern investor focuses on the most. Everyone knows that earnings can grow quickly off a low base. Likewise, an ROE can shoot up dramatically from the low single digits, creating the impression of rapid earnings growth. In a recovery situation, a company can "grow" earnings per share just by doubling its ROE. Suppose a company has a book value of $50 a share, and first-year earnings are $2 a share. Then the ROE would be 2/50, or a paltry 4 percent. Assume that the dividend is also $2 a share so that all of year 1 earnings are paid out, leaving book value of $50 a share. In year 2, earnings double to $4 a share. This is better but still a mediocre 8 percent ROE. The doubling was possible because it took place off a depressed base. (If part of the year 1 earnings were retained, increasing the year 2 book value above $50, the math would differ slightly but the principle would remain the same.)

Assuming that all of year 2 earnings were paid out in the form of dividends, what would have to happen to double earnings again? The ROE would have to double, this time to a healthy 16 percent. The first doubling of ROE from 4 percent to 8 percent is the easiest, and the second may be doable, but ROE isn't going to continue to doubling to 32 percent, 64 percent, and so on. After one or two doublings from a low-single-digit base, ROE is likely to settle down in the low to mid-teens, or even in the high single digits. Just as trees do not grow to the sky, there are limits to ROEs. A value investor is always conscious of this fact, which growth investors overlooked around the turn of this century.

CHAPTER 8

Some Observations on the Value of Dividends

In the final analysis, the purpose of investing is to obtain a dividend stream from the stock. First, you get the income itself. Second, you can obtain a capital gain that accompanies either a rising dividend or an upward revaluation of the existing disbursement. Dividends are an important component of the total return, which historically has averaged almost 11 percent a year for stock. Of this amount, just about 4 percent reflects inflation over the years; 2 percent is due to real growth in stock values, and almost 5 percent, or just under half, is the result of dividend payments. This chapter will first present some of the more conventional wisdom regarding dividends. Then it will conclude by presenting our own model for investment value, which incorporates both the value of the dividend stream and book value, while showing how earnings contribute to the process.

Well-priced dividend-paying stocks of good quality are generally more attractive than bonds. Fixed income is just that—a level payment stream. However, dividends can grow over time if profits grow. That's why the dividend yield requirement of Graham and Dodd is only two thirds of the AAA bond yield. (The dividend yield is just the dividend divided by the stock price.) If the dividend grows at all, at some point the dividend yield on original cost will exceed the bond yield.

There are other reasons why dividends make a stock attractive. First, one can be somewhat surer that earnings are real if a dividend makes up a large proportion of them. Second, American companies in the twentieth century have displayed a notable lack of willingness to cut the dividend stream (even sometimes when, in fact, it should be cut). Instead, they have tried to keep faith with stockholders by maintaining and even increasing the dividend when possible. A dividend cut or omission almost always indicates that something is seriously wrong with the company.

This point was made most persuasively by Geraldine Weiss in her book, *Dividends Don't Lie*.[1] First, dividends are paid in cash. Unlike earnings, they are not subject to arbitrary accounting principles and other standards.

112

Second, they represent the best-guess estimate of distributable earnings as determined by the company's financial officers and ratified by the board of directors. Naturally, a dividend is only as good as the board of directors who declared it.

Dividend-paying stocks are among the most liquid and tradable of all. First, they provide income, and hence, a means for the investor to redeploy funds without selling the stock. Second, they can be resold to a larger group of investors, those who want income, more easily than other issues of comparable size and quality that don't offer as generous a yield.

A dividend yield will rise (through a drop in the stock price) when the growth rate falters. Under these circumstances, investors demand greater compensation in the form of a higher yield (and lower price–earnings [P/E] ratio) for lost growth. If growth, in fact, stabilizes at the lower level, the increasing cheapness of the stock and the resulting higher yield will often be sufficient compensation. And if growth returns to previous levels, the required dividend yield will fall, causing a rebound in the price of the stock.

The question of how much of earnings to pay out in dividends is a most important one for a company. Here, unlike the case of interest coverage, which we would want to be high, the amount of dividend coverage has a wide range of acceptable answers. About the only unacceptable answer is that dividend policy has been established by default, without a consideration for the company's particular circumstances.

MEASURES OF DIVIDEND COVERAGE

The measure of dividend coverage in the United States is known as the *payout ratio* and equals the amount of dividends paid divided by the net profit. If there is no preferred stock (with its preferred dividend), this just reduces to the ratio of dividends per (common) share divided by earnings per share. This is the reverse of the British practice, which puts earnings in the numerator and dividends in the denominator to arrive at a dividend coverage ratio. Thus, a 50 percent payout ratio under American usage corresponds to a dividend coverage ratio of two times under the British style.

Obviously, a lower payout ratio or, conversely, a higher coverage ratio means that the dividend is more secure. This could be a good policy for a highly cyclical company whose earnings vary widely from one year to the next. Another type of company that pays out little or, in many cases, no dividend is a very fast grower that can earn high returns on reinvested capital. In such a case, retention of all earnings and payment of no dividend is decidedly preferable to borrowing money to pay dividends.

Dividend payout ratios are typically in the 40 to 50 percent range. A payout of 60 percent is a sign of incipient maturity, and it means that the company is paying out more of its earnings in dividends than it is reinvesting in the company. It is very mature companies like electric utilities that pay out 80 percent or so of their earnings as preferred and common dividends. This means that most of the total return is coming from dividends rather than growth. But the theoretical payout level is less important than the more important question of what dividend level is appropriate for the company.

The Graham and Dodd preference is for higher dividends: first, because dividends provide an up-front, tangible return; second, because the income stream gives a high-yield stock something of a bondlike character; and third, because cash disbursed by companies cannot be reinvested foolishly. It returns the prerogative of the reinvestment of the funds to the shareholder, who has the option of buying more of the company's stock. Most businesses can't support a high level of reinvestment. Then the question is: Will management act in the best interest of shareholders by returning capital to them?

Dividend yields ought to be compared to the interest rates. In Japan, for example, interest rates for much of the 1990s were about 1 percent. So yields of 1 percent, or slightly more, compared favorably with prevailing interest rates, and a Japanese investor could have bought Japanese stock on Graham and Dodd grounds, because 1.0 percent was more than two thirds of the AAA bond yield. At the bottom of the interest rate cycle, the "carry trade" for those brave souls who didn't worry about stock market fluctuations was to borrow money at 0.5 percent, buy a stock yielding 0.9 percent, and pocket the difference. The difference was enough to service both the interest and principal on debt, so eventually the investor would have gotten the stock for "free." (A similar situation existed in the United States after World War II.) Other investors placed such funds in the U.S. Treasury at 6 percent and got both an interest rate differential and a gain on the subsequent rebound of the U.S. dollar against the Japanese yen.

Dividend growth can be supported in two ways. Dividends can rise in line with earnings growth. However, dividends can rise faster than earnings if management pays out increasing proportions of earnings. It is best not to count too much on a rising payout ratio unless it is very low to begin with. If, for example, the dividend payout ratio is 25 percent, and the management is inclined to raise it, one can reasonably expect it to rise to 40 percent within a reasonable period of time. One can't make the same assumption that the payout ratio will double from 40 percent to 80 percent soon, if ever.

In one sense, dividend growth for a company with a below-average payout is more assured than earnings growth. You can count on either moderate earnings growth and a rising payout or a strong earnings growth and a constant payout for good dividend growth. Either outcome can assure dividend growth over the medium term. But, of course, the strong earnings growth and constant payout will lead to larger capital gains.

You must also be aware that dividends can be cut. This could be the result of the economic cycle, and is a particularly severe problem for cyclical companies. More often, it is a result of a company's overleveraging. While you should not be particularly concerned about a high payout ratio or a low dividend coverage ratio, you should be concerned about a low coverage of interest on debt. If a company is experiencing difficulty in meeting interest payments, which are a contractual obligation, the first thing that is likely to be sacrificed is the dividend payments to shareholders, which represent only a moral obligation to investors who are junior, at any rate, to debt holders.

An example of this occurred with nuclear utilities in 1980s. They, like many operators in other industries, borrowed heavily to finance major plant construction. But nuclear power is a controversial item, at least in the United States. So there is a large chance of a nuclear power plant's being "disallowed" by regulators. When this happens, the plant can't be put to use, nor can the cost of the plant be factored into rates charged on other power sources. So the assets had to be written off. The liabilities, however, were just as real as before, and their burden on a reduced asset base necessitated dividend cuts.

Because they were dividend-paying entities operating in stable businesses, the typical dividend cut for a utility was typically no more than one half, or more generally only about one third. This is because the pressure comes from only part of the business, say one of several power plants. (Beware of utilities or other companies that seem to make one bad investment decision after another.) Cyclical companies, however, may eliminate the dividend entirely if their income statement goes from profit to loss, because their whole business is affected by the vagaries of the business cycle on their particular commodity.

At any rate, you want a stable, not an erratic, dividend payer. When a company has a habit of declaring, then cutting, then eliminating dividend payments, it can't be considered a dividend payer at all but must be analyzed as a special situation. Such analysis is outside the scope of this book, and such investments are not suitable for Graham and Dodd–type investors.

DIFFERENT DIVIDEND SITUATIONS

There are three dividend situations. The first is one featuring a very low growth rate. These can be considered almost as bond investments and typically pay the highest yield of all. Electric, gas, and water utilities generally fall into this category.

Power utilities have for so long had the reputation of being high-yielding issues that they've gained a reputation of suitability for "widows and orphans" that is not always wholly deserved. Up to, and for some time after World War II, producers of electric and gas power in the United States had been classic growth stocks. The market for power was expanding all through the first half of the twentieth century, during which many American families did not have access to electric power or central heating. Indeed, bringing electricity to rural areas was one of the aims of the New Deal of the 1930s. After the war, when most households did at least have access to such facilities, the demographics of the Baby Boom era ensured that the number of users would continue to grow, at least until these children grew up and started forming households in the late 1960s and early 1970s. Moreover, the demographic boom was accompanied by a surge in the number and sophistication of appliances, which in turn fueled demand for more power. All in all, the dispensers of electricity and gas were moderately fast growers well into 1960s when the favorable demographics and the economic transformation of society came to an abrupt slowdown. The mid-1960s acceleration of the rate of inflation was the final straw. Until this time period, utilities did offer a combination of moderate to relatively high growth that more than offset inflation, combined with large dividend yields and a high degree of safety. In short, they were "perfect" investments for the average investor for a long time.

As sellers of a basic commodity product whose rates were set by regulators, utilities were unable to fully compensate for the effects of the price inflation that afflicted the world after the mid-1960s. Indeed, insofar as inflation was caused by skyrocketing in the price of oil and other fuels that took place through most of the 1970s, utilities were caught in a cost–price squeeze. Coupled with the effects of slow demand growth, they were barely able to increase earnings in nominal terms, and profits actually decreased after adjusting for inflation. Utility stocks' one saving grace was their large dividends, the result of limited opportunities for capital investment. Between the mid-1960s and the mid-1990s, the earnings growth of utilities was held by regulators below the rate of inflation during periods of both rapidly and moderately rising prices. Productivity gains, meanwhile, partly but not entirely, compensated for this fact. Thus, the dividends were not wholly spendable, because a portion of them would have to be reinvested in order to preserve capital in real terms.

Oddly enough, utilities regained some of their relative attractiveness in the late 1990s, when inflation decelerated greatly. Although nominal earnings growth was still limited to 2 to 3 percent in most cases, the rate of general inflation had fallen to comparable levels. So earnings growth and resulting stock price appreciation could maintain the value of an investment after inflation. The entire dividend could now be safely spent; or, if reinvested, the whole rather than just a part represented an addition to capital. Under such circumstances, the prevalent dividend rate of 4 to 5 percent was more attractive than the higher nominal dividend yield of 6 to 7 percent was a decade ago.

The second group of companies has slowly growing earnings but offers dividends that are growing faster than earnings, at least for a time. Companies in this category include many of the standard heavy industrials including autos, chemicals, oil, and steel. These commodities are subject to the vagaries of wide swings in the balance between demand and supply, and hence price, but at least they are not directly regulated, as is the case with electric utilities. One of two things will happen. Most often, a cyclical surge enables earnings growth to catch up to past dividend gains. If this doesn't happen, the company will fall into the first category of stocks.

This is a situation in which the 30-odd-year-long cycle theory expounded in Chapter 20 may come into play. The commodity companies were flush with cash in the 1970s when commodity prices were rising. This caused them to make unwise acquisitions. Exxon's purchase of Reliance Electric was an over $1 billion mistake, in money of the time. To avoid such temptations, the better-managed companies used their hefty cash flows to raise their dividend payments. (Exxon and others also bought back shares, which is a disbursement of cash and may be considered almost a dividend payment.) These disbursements increased at a rapid clip through the 1980s, which were an indifferent decade for commodities, and at a slower but still substantial pace in the 1990s, which were actually terrible for commodities. Commodity prices will probably boom in 2000s, thereby enabling the companies to regain ground that they lost in the past two decades. If this is the case, dividends will likely grow more slowly than earnings over the next 10 years. Commodity companies used to pay out less than half of earnings, versus two thirds or more today, and if earnings explode, this ratio may go back to below 50 percent. If not, the rate of dividend growth will slow to that of earnings growth, as companies reach the limits of their capacity to pay.

A dividend of this kind of commodity company provides a form of inflation protection because a commodity company usually can raise prices, and hence earnings and dividends, at least as fast as inflation. In such a situation, the stock has characteristics corresponding somewhat to cash instruments as well as bonds. Specifically, in times of rising inflation and interest rates, a dividend that grows at least as fast as inflation will give the stock cashlike characteristics, while in times of falling inflation and interest rates (which hurts earnings growth), the dividend will give the stock bondlike virtues, as long as the payout is maintained. A modestly growing dividend will lead to capital preservation, and in some cases, capital growth. In such cases, an investor will be able to spend most or all of the dividend and still expect that capital is being preserved in real terms.

Other companies with shorter cycles include banks, as well as food and formerly telephone utilities. These cycles may last only a few years. Steady increases in dividend payments, usually in high-single-digit percentage terms, merely help to smooth out the year-to-year volatility in earnings.

The third class of companies includes those with fast-growing dividends, supported by fast-growing earnings. In this case, the dividend growth is a likely driver of a high stock price. Only under very adverse circumstances will dividends rise without driving up the stock price.

Growth should start from a significant base. In an extreme case, Wal-Mart in the early 1980s yielded 1 percent. But earnings and dividend growth were both so dramatic that 10 years later, the dividend had risen 15-fold, yielding 15 percent on the original cost. At its peak, the stock's P/E ratio had risen so high that the yield was a paltry 0.5 percent. And the growth rate had slowed down, meanwhile. Hence, it would have been 20 or 30 years, not 10, before the early 1990s dividend would have led to a meaningful future yield.

Companies such as Wal-Mart will almost never be Graham and Dodd–type investments. Even so, Graham and Dodd–type guidelines may still be useful to the very venturesome investor who wishes to undertake such investments. Such an investor should be in a position to hope that some years hence, no more than three or five, it will qualify on Graham and Dodd grounds relative to the original purchase price. If such a purchase is in fact indicated by subsequent events, the superior growth characteristics will operate to allow a more rapid accumulation of wealth than would otherwise be the case. But it is a lot to hope for, to make an expensive investment that is justified by subsequent events. More likely, the proverbial bird in the hand is worth two in the bush.

Occasionally, it is possible to purchase the stock of fast-growing companies with good dividends that fall within reasonable value parameters. A case in point is that of the large pharmaceutical companies after the election of President Bill Clinton in 1992. Their stocks fell sharply because of the so-called "Hillary effect," a reference to the widespread belief that the very vocal and visible First Lady (now Senator) would try to impose sweeping health care regulations in the name of "reform." In this context, we are referring to the effect on long-established concerns such as Bristol-Myers Squibb or Merck, not Amgen or any of the emerging growth vehicles.

DIVIDEND SAFETY

As in the case of other Graham and Dodd characteristics, the safety or sustainability of the dividend is as important as its size or any other consideration. Based on the past payment record, is the dividend likely to be maintained at the current level, and possibly increased if things get better for the company? The second and related concern is the strength of the balance sheet. Can it support the dividend and needed capital expenditures if there is a moderate earnings disappointment? Third, does EBIT (earnings before interest and taxes) comfortably cover the interest payments to bondholders who are senior to the equity holders? If the company has to struggle to meet interest payments, the first thing that is likely to give is the dividend payments. Fourth, do earnings adequately cover the dividend at this point in time? This question is more forward-looking than the previous ones. A one- or two-year downturn might be weathered successfully, but a prolonged slump in earnings is likely to cause the directors to pare the dividend in order to preserve the balance sheet.

The drug companies met all these tests in spades in 1992–1993. They yielded as much as 5 percent, well above the market average of less than 3 percent, and above most stocks other than utilities. At the same time, most of the companies had embarked on a cost-cutting regimen that salvaged their bottom line in a period of slow growth. In essence, stocks of good quality should be bought when the price is right, as signaled by the unusually high dividend yield (just as an unusually low yield might be a signal that prices are too high). This period should have been a signal of a historic opportunity in the pharmaceuticals.

First, dividend increases had gone back about 40 years, and the dividends had actually been paid much longer than that, in most cases, for the better part of a century. Second, nearly all of the major drug companies had exceptional balance sheets. This was reflected in a Value Line Safety Rating of 1 (Highest) or 2 (Above Average). Financial Strength Ratings were A or higher. Interest coverage was hefty, in some cases over 100 times. Dividend coverage was less exceptional, but more than adequate. As a group, no more conservative investments could have been found, even among utility issues.

The big question mark was growth. Even without the "Hillary effect," growth had been slowing at least to the average for industrial companies. Here, the large yield advantage, along with the strong financial characteristics alluded to earlier, weighed heavily in the drug companies' favor. In any event, they were yielding only a percentage point or so less than electric utilities, but had prospects for earnings and dividend growth distinctly better than that of the 3 to 4 percent that was then typical of the power generators. At an absolute minimum, there should have been a large crossover from utility to drug issues among income-oriented accounts.

Because of historically large payouts, the drug companies had a smaller proportion of assets to share price than typical industrial companies. But their high returns on equity (ROEs) were more than adequate compensation. Many of the drug stocks would have met our test for modified investment value set forth at the end of this chapter. (This test, unfortunately, was not available at the time, so it was not then apparent how cheap they were.) Given a chance to do it again, the author probably would have bypassed Merck, which was still too expensive, but invested more in American Home Products (now called Wyeth) and Bristol-Myers Squibb.

PRACTITIONERS OF DIVIDEND VALUATION

We now present two other methods of using dividends in valuation. These include dividend valuation band, first popularized by Geraldine Weiss, and the "Dogs of the Dow," popularized by Michael O'Higgins.

The dividend band was put forward by Geraldine Weiss in *Dividends Don't Lie*.[2] These bands hold for individual stocks, and are derived relative to the stock's own price history. (The higher the yield, the greater value in the stock.) Thus, a 3 percent yield may signal undervaluation for a fast-growing stock, and overvaluation for a slow grower. The trick is to buy near the bottom of the band and sell near the top. This same technique is often used for earnings, and specifically, P/E ratio. (For example, buy stock X at a P/E ratio of 10 and sell at a P/E ratio of 20.) But Weiss believes, and Graham and Dodd would concur, that dividends are a more reliable indicator of value than earnings.

The Weiss strategy is essentially a blue-chip strategy. To qualify for purchase, a stock should have been paying dividend for two or three decades or longer. At the very least, the stock should have been paying dividends for the several years it takes to establish value bands on the high and low sides.

The Weiss book was written in 1987, so the examples are somewhat dated, but an example will illustrate the method. Over the 10 years to 1996, the stock of Philip Morris (now called Altria) has traded with a dividend yield as high as over 5 percent, based on the dividend divided by the low price, and a yield of less than 3 percent, based on the dividend divided by the high price, as indicated in Figure 8.1. Noting the high prices for the respective years, there were "sell" signals in 1990, 1991, and 1992, based on the high prices of 51.8, 81.8, and 86.6, and their respective yields of 3.0 percent, 2.3 percent, and 2.7 percent. However, there were "buy" opportunities in 1993, 1994, and 1995, based on the low prices of 45.0, 47.3, and 55.9, and their respective yields of 5.8 percent, 6.4 percent, and 6.5 percent.

Another popular dividend strategy is the "Dogs of the Dow," which has several leading proponents. That is, buy the 10 Dow stocks with the highest yields at the beginning of each year. First, by definition, a Dow 30 concern is a well-established company, one that's probably considered "too big too fail." Second, the Dow 30 stocks are all issued by basically mature companies. Thus, the long-term growth prospects of one are not significantly

Year	1987	1988	1989	1990	1991	1992	1993	1994	1995	1996
High Price	10.4	8.5	15.3	17.3	27.3	28.9	25.9	21.5	31.5	39.7
Low Price	6.1	6.7	8.3	12	16.1	23.4	15	15.8	18.6	28.5
Earnings per Share	0.65	0.74	1.01	1.28	1.51	1.82	2.17	2.56	2.17	2.56
Dividend per Share	0.26	0.34	0.42	0.52	0.64	0.78	1.22	1.47	1.22	1.47
Div Payout Ratio	40%	46%	42%	41%	42%	43%	56%	57%	56%	57%
Yield at Low Price	4.26%	5.07%	5.06%	4.33%	3.98%	3.33%	8.13%	9.30%	6.56%	5.16%
Yield at High Price	2.50%	4.00%	2.75%	3.01%	2.34%	2.70%	4.71%	6.84%	3.87%	3.70%

Source: Value Line Publishing Inc.; author's calculations.

FIGURE 8.1 Price and Dividend Relationships for Philip Morris 1987–1996.

different from the others. What distinguishes one from the other, therefore, is an above-average yield. A high yield might be a signal that the stock price is fundamentally cheap, and, if so, management and the board of directors might be eager to do something about getting the stock price up. (Dow 30 companies have their pick of people on both counts.)

A strategist, Michael O'Higgins specialized in buying Dow stocks. He has used a variation of the "buy the highest yielders" strategy.[3] He would make a list of the 10 cheapest stocks on dividends (highest yielders), then the 10 cheapest on a P/E basis, and 10 cheapest on other measures such as price/book, and buy the five to seven stocks that overlap on the different lists. This variation tends to screen out stocks that are cheapest only on dividends (because they are paying out a high proportion of earnings), but less cheap on earnings themselves.

Alternatively, another trick is to buy the stocks that are the second and third cheapest on the various measures, on the theory that there may be one cheap Dow stock that deserves a low price (e.g., Johns Manville, with its asbestos liabilities), but not more than one in such a distinguished group.

Even the Dow stocks have had their share of beaten down "turnaround" plays, which are marked by a high dividend. These included Union Carbide in the mid-1980s after the Bhopal nuclear disaster in India, Texaco a few years later after its bankruptcy declaration following a $10.5 billion "tortious interference" award to Pennzoil, and Eastman Kodak when its bloated cost structure in the early 1990s led to an earnings decline.

The Dogs of the Dow strategy did not provide good relative returns during the late 1990s. This was probably not the result of any newly found popularity that reduced returns. Instead, the Dow itself significantly trailed the Standard & Poor's (S&P) 500 during an exceptional period when the latter turned more than 20 percent for four years in a row. In this kind of environment, the yield advantage of Dogs stocks becomes relatively insignificant. And the returns on the S&P were skewed toward high-technology issues, precisely the companies that don't pay much, if anything, by way of dividends.

It is probable that a dividend stream lends value to the stock independently of assets and earnings. In fact, dividends are so important that some of our earlier evaluation rules can be expanded to incorporate the effects of annual disbursement of dividends. Thus:

■ Expanding the PEG ratio, which is the P/E ratio divided by the growth rate, some investors and others derived the PEGY ratio, which is the P/E ratio divided by the sum of the growth rate G and dividend yield Y. That is,

$$PEGY = (P/E)/(G + Y)$$

We consider this a reasonable growth formula for earnings valuation, because the addition of the dividend term in the denominator reduces the value of the fraction, hence making the stock cheaper at any given price. We justify this by rationalizing that it is only retained earnings, not those paid out in the form of dividends, that support growth. In the case of no dividend, the PEGY ratio simply reduces to the PEG ratio.

■ For asset value, a stock is considered to be of investment value if it could be obtained for book value plus 10 times the annual dividend or less. Thus,

$$\text{Investment value (price)} = \text{Book value} + 10 * \text{Dividends}$$

■ If the company in question is a high ROE generator (with ROE greater than 15 percent), we can modify our formula proposed in Chapter 7 to include an extra dividend term as follows:

$$\text{Modified investment value} = (\text{Book value}) * (\text{ROE}/15\%)^2 \\ + 10 * \text{Dividends}$$

Generally, we prefer to use the investment value formula. By allowing a factor of 10 times the dividend to be figured in the purchase price, we are just saying that a 10 percent return is satisfactory. This is certainly true for a bond investment (except in the high-interest-rate environment of the late 1970s). It is arguably less true for stocks. But a large dividend payment makes the stock safer. Given that the long-term return on stocks is 11 percent, a return of 10 percent for the "safer" bondlike component of the stock investment is adequate. And this assumes that the dividend will remain level and not grow meaningfully. By allowing a maximum of book value for the remainder of the purchase price, we are saying that we will endeavor to pay no more than the face value of retained earnings for this portion of the stock, without regard to goodwill, franchise value, and other intangible assets. In fact, the concept of investment value is central to the rest of this book. We make the following observations:

■ An investor who purchased a stock at investment value and held it for some years is almost certain to realize a satisfactory return on investment, provided that earnings and leverage ratios are also satisfactory.
■ A purchase cannot be considered a bargain unless it is undertaken at roughly one half of investment value.
■ An acquirer is often willing to pay roughly twice investment value for control of a company.

The first issue regards the likelihood of a satisfactory return on invest-ment value. Much of the problem has been solved by an insistence on a sat-isfactory leverage ratio (debt less than 30 percent of capital in most cases), and satisfactory earnings, expressed as a return on equity of at least 10 to 12 percent. A holding period of several years would smooth out the fluctu-ations of price and allow enough time for the investment to "work out." And the entry price ensures that one will not have overpaid to get this return.

Second, why is an acquisition at one-half investment value usually a bargain? Because it multiplies any prospective return by two. For instance, if the appreciation on the underlying investment is 10 percent a year, $100 will rise to $259 in 10 years. An investor who paid $100 or half price for $200 of investment value will end up with $518 of investment value. This represents a gain of 18 percent per annum instead of 10 percent. Likewise, if the underlying appreciation were 12 percent a year, the actual return based on a half-price purchase will be 20 percent. This is illustrated by the fact that the Dow bottomed in 1932, and again in 1974, at one half of investment value. (This phenomenon will be discussed in more detail in Chapter 18.)

Third, why would an acquirer be willing to pay twice investment value for a company? It's probably because the acquirer can increase the invest-ment value in several ways. The most obvious is by cutting costs. Another is to generate production and/or marketing synergies with the acquirer's exist-ing business. Finally, the acquirer can finance part of the acquisition with debt, obtained at a lower interest rate than the likely return on the business, even after taking into account the premium purchase price. Such a purchase is like purchasing a house wherein the cost of servicing the mortgage is less than the rent, or the rent savings.

When Warren Buffett purchased General Foods in 1981, he bought it for just over half of investment value. Book value at the end of the year was $30.86 and the dividend was $2.20, giving total investment value of nearly $53. The price range in that year was between 27 and 32, not far from the theoretical bargain price of $26.50. By 1985, the investment value had risen to just under $60. Philip Morris paid $120, or twice investment value, for General Foods.

In the late nineteenth century, Andrew Carnegie turned a "small" fortune for his day, of about $1.5 million, into a very large fortune of his time. He bought an interest in a steel company at a bargain price, watched it double to investment value, compounded it at roughly 15 per-cent per year for a period of roughly 30 years, and sold his holdings to J.P. Morgan at about twice the going market price, the premium that Morgan was willing to pay for control in order to fold Carnegie's steel company into what became U.S. Steel. Note, however, that the enlarged company had a market cap of about $1 billion dollars in 1900, and a market cap of $1 to $2 billion dollars in the year 2000, after running in place for 100 years!

A 15 percent compounded return represents a trifle more than a doubling every 5 years. Over a period of 30 years, this is 2 to the sixth power, or 64 times. Carnegie got two more doublings on his investment—one for the bargain purchase and one for the transfer of control. Multiplying 64 by 2 twice more gives 2 to the eighth power, or a 256-fold increase in capital. Carnegie's sale proceeds of $412 million was an increase of more than 256 times (which would be $384 million), because we have used round numbers in doing the math, but at least they illustrate the point.

We would not be quite so dogmatic as Graham and Dodd regarding dividends. But our model is robust enough to give credit to earnings that are retained by a company, provided that such retained earnings do not dilute the ROE. In the rare instances that a superior return on equity is actually achieved, our model encourages the retention of earnings by squaring that portion of the ROE that exceeds 15 percent. Most important is that the management should fairly assess the company's internal reinvestment prospects versus those available in the marketplace and make the value-maximizing choice, relinquishing the option to shareholders in doubtful cases. It is noteworthy, though, that the shareholders of Berkshire Hathaway, among others, elected not to receive a dividend because it is unlikely that most of them could reinvest the funds more effectively than could Mr. Buffett.

The 15 percent hurdle for modified investment value is based on the experience of Carnegie, Buffett, and other successful investors. The modified formula also explains why Coca-Cola was a good investment for Berkshire Hathaway in the late 1980s. The purchase price seemed high relative to book value based on our multiplier of 10 times the dividend, assuming a level of dividend stream. But the ROE was high, assuring that the dividend would grow. So a multiplier of 4 times book value of $1.07 based on an ROE of 30 percent or an asset value of $4.28 seemed reasonable. Adding up these two factors gives an investment value of $5.78, which exceeds the 1988 high.

One of the most profitable investments Warren Buffett has made for Berkshire Hathaway is See's Candy. In 1972, he paid $25 million for an operation with only $7 million of book value. Twenty years later, See's had a book value of only $25 million. But with only $18 million of additional retained earnings, See's disbursed $410 million pretax income over the 20-year period. So it turned out to be a highly profitable investment after all. What was its attraction? In a word, its "dividend"-paying capacity.[4]

You may ask: What about earnings? The answer is that the model indirectly incorporates earnings. That's because a company can pay them out as dividends or reinvest them. This was demonstrated in Chapter 2 by the analysis of the statement of shareholders' equity. The model values each component of earnings separately and calculates an investment value that is the sum of the two components. What has been downplayed is not earnings but earnings growth as expressed on a year-to-year basis. Dividends, and to a lesser extent, book value, are good indicators of sustained earnings. It is on this figure, and not short-term performance, that a Graham and Dodd investor wants to focus.

CHAPTER 9

Some Warnings about the Use of Earnings in Valuation

Since the heyday of Graham and Dodd, the income statement has been given greater prominence than the balance sheet in securities analysis. Most investors nowadays make their decisions based on their valuation of *estimates* of future earnings, rather than the value of assets or even dividends, which are *known*. While the focus on earnings has merit, in large part because earnings give rise to both assets and dividends in the final analysis, the lesser certainty that one can attach to the earnings stream causes this book to give relatively less weight to earnings and greater weight to the other two variables than do most authors or financial analysts.

The emphasis on earnings per share means that an investor should be much less concerned about corporate profits per se. Indeed, one of the best uses that a company can make of its earnings and related cash flows is to buy back its own stock when its price–earnings (P/E) ratio is low. This reduces interest income, and hence earnings, but it reduces number of shares by a larger percentage. Because the denominator is sinking faster than the numerator in the fraction, earnings per share will rise. Conversely, a company will benefit existing shareholders by selling stock when its P/E ratio is high, especially if it can put money to good use. If a company reduces earnings per share by issuing new shares, the transaction is said to be dilutive to earnings. If earnings per share are raised by an acquisition, the transaction is said to be accretive. In a typical acquisition, the deal is dilutive for the first year or two, and then accretive in the following years, as cost-cutting measures take effect. An example of this point is Cadbury Schweppes (shown in a Value Line array in November 1998 [Figure 9.1]), wherein corporate profits grew but share issues canceled out all the benefits, so earnings growth per share (and the stock price) went nowhere.

Investments based on current and prospective earnings are founded on the dual propositions that most companies will earn money in any given year, and that these earnings will grow over time. Then the question becomes: How large a weight should be attached to earnings growth per se,

1990	1991	1992	1993	1994	1995	1996	Year
17.35	17.21	13.96	13.29	15.17	14.94	13.98	Sales per ADR
1.54	1.58	1.18	1.30	0.84	1.47	1.49	"Cash Flow" per ADR
0.73	0.89	0.59	0.70	0.59	0.71	0.71	Earnings per ADR
0.44	0.55	0.59	0.49	0.59	0.64	0.66	Dividends per ADR
6.68	6.93	6.64	7.09	7.92	4.95	8.28	Book Value per ADR
350.00	351.19	364.80	414.90	416.95	495.50	507.14	ADRs (mill.)
13.4	16.1	19.2	15.6	16.3	17.6	17.9	ADR price (year high)
4690	5654	7004	6472	6796	8721	9078	Market Cap (mill.)
18.4	18.1	32.5	22.3	27.6	24.8	25.2	P/E Ratio
2.0	2.3	2.9	2.2	2.1	3.6	2.2	P/B Ratio
3.3%	3.4%	3.1%	3.1%	3.6%	3.6%	3.7%	Dividend Yield
6072.0	6044.0	5092.3	5512.7	6326.5	7402.8	7087.9	Sales (mill.)
281.4	245.3	230.3	272.0	312.6	392.2	403.2	Depreciation (mill.)
265.2	325.9	216.2	278.5	359.5	350.3	360.0	Net Profit (mill.)
305.0	543.1	107.4	-93.1	88.6	-837.0	-799.4	Working Capital (mill.)
787.0	1013.5	697.6	571.9	633.5	1339.2	1346.9	Long-Term Debt (mill.)
2633.0	2723.5	2651.0	3169.3	3585.6	2626.0	4199.7	Shareholders' Equity (mill.)
9.2%	10.2%	8.1%	8.7%	9.3%	10.9%	8.0%	Return on Capital
10.1%	12.0%	8.2%	8.8%	10.0%	13.3%	8.6%	Return on Equity
3.9%	6.0%	2.9%	3.1%	4.0%	3.5%	0.0%	Reinvestment Rate
6.2%	6.0%	5.3%	5.7%	6.0%	9.8%	8.6%	Dividend Distribution Rate
39%	50%	35%	35%	40%	26%	0%	Earnings Retention Rate
61%	50%	65%	65%	60%	74%	100%	Dividend Payout Ratio

Source: Value Line Publishing Inc.; author's calculations.

FIGURE 9.1 Summary Statistics for Cadbury Schweppes 1990–1996.

and differing rates of earnings growth among companies as opposed to historical or current earnings?

It is of prime importance that investors consider current earnings reports in the context of the company's overall profit record. Thus, a single year's result should not be given undue weight. History shows that the market will eventually pay more for total profits posted more or less evenly over a period of 10 years than for the same earnings bunched up in one or two years. Within this context, the result of any one year may differ significantly from the norm. So one should not be overly enthusiastic about a single good year, or overly discouraged about a single bad year, unless it persisted long enough to be the harbinger of a trend.

Graham and Dodd warned investors not to expect too much of earnings growth, and instead to look to asset values and dividends as a basis for making investments. Their first rule, that earnings yield (the inverse of the P/E ratio) should be twice the AAA bond yield, basically assumed that earnings would not grow at all (which investors feared during the Great Depression). As time went on and it became clear that "a (postwar) rising tide lifts all ships," the very stringent earlier rule was relaxed. Lower earnings yields (or their inverse, higher P/E ratios) based on "normal" earnings growth could be accepted. Even this posture contrasts with that of most earnings-oriented investors, who seek out companies with above-normal earnings growth, even at high P/E ratios, on the theory that the above-average growth will support the premium valuation if it lasts long enough.

Earnings are stated under generally accepted accounting principles (GAAP). These principles deal with the accounting treatment of largely discretionary items such as revenue recognition, depreciation and amortization, research and development expenses, and leasing and financing charges, among others. This is not a perfect measure of earnings but at least has the merit of being a "least common denominator" used by all companies. (Perhaps a more reliable measure of earnings than the GAAP number is the number reported to the Internal Revenue Service as taxable income, which companies have every incentive to minimize, and which is seldom disclosed by companies.) Managers in the 1990s who wanted to pump up the stock price and raise the value of stock options and bonuses found GAAP measures too stringent and put all sorts of pressure on accounting authorities to water down standards. They also constructed inflated "pro forma earnings" by excluding expenses (or occasionally by including revenues) in ways not allowed by GAAP, and presenting these inflated number to the analysts. They also presented operating income numbers (before the deduction of interest) and EBDIT numbers (income before the deduction of depreciation, interest, and taxes) to show lower price–income ratios, by pretending that depreciation and interest expense did not adversely affect a company's prospects.

After the turn of this century, it appears that management at a number of companies such as Enron have been manipulating reported earnings. Almost as bad, many other companies have been reporting "legally accurate" earnings that are misleading because they "do not volunteer information." For instance, the negative impact of executive stock options has been omitted from most earnings reports, while bull-market paper gains on pension plan assets were included. A complete discussion of the ways that earnings can be presented to investors would take up a book in itself. For now, it will be assumed that investor and public concerns will force companies to "clean up" earnings reports as time goes by. The rest of the chapter will try to address other, long-term issues faced by investors in properly interpreting actual and estimated profits.

MEASURES OF EARNINGS MOMENTUM

There are a number of tools purported to measure earnings growth, but do so over such short periods of time that the results of such calculations cannot sensibly be called earnings growth, but rather short-term earnings momentum. The use of earnings momentum as a substitute measure for growth is a common tool of analysts. This was first popularized by Value Line, which ironically started as a value house, but has since become part of the mainstream.[1] We begin with earnings momentum, not because it has the blessings of Graham and Dodd, but precisely as a warning as to what they would not do.

The measure of the cheapness or dearness of a stock, measured in terms of earnings, is the price–earnings ratio. This is just the price per share, divided by the earnings per share. The P/E ratio can be computed in several ways, depending on which E one uses. (The P, for price, is a known quantity.) In one case, the earnings used are trailing 12-month reported earnings, which at least has the advantage of being a known quantity. More commonly, the earnings used in the P/E calculation are the *estimated* earnings for the current calendar year (or sometimes the following calendar year if the estimate is being undertaken in the fall of the current year). Value Line uses a hybrid measure, earnings for the past six months, which are usually known, plus earnings for the upcoming six months, which is an estimate.

One way of computing earnings growth is to compute year-over-year earnings changes on a quarterly basis. This is generally preferred to linked quarter comparisons because of the problem of seasonality. One wants to compare the fall of this year to the fall of last year, rather than the summer of this year. Improperly used, however, this method falls right back into a seasonality trap. A simple analysis of the quarterly earnings of Zale

Sales

Year	Oct. Quar	Jan Quar	Apr Quar	July Quar	Fiscal Year
1999	254.2	568.0	289.7	326.0	1428.9
2000	322.6	735.9	361.3	373.8	1793.6
2001	371.8	861.4	418.0	435.5	2086.7
2002	409.9	897.1	449.1	435.6	2191.7

Earnings Per Share

Year	Oct. Quar	Jan Quar	Apr Quar	July Quar	Fiscal Year
1999	0.06	1.75	0.17	0.23	2.21
2000	0.15	2.33	0.30	0.32	3.10
2001	0.16	2.52	0.14	0.09	2.89
2002	-0.10	2.64	0.22	0.15	2.92

Source: Value Line Publishing Inc.
Totals may not add due to rounding.

FIGURE 9.2   Zale Corp. Seasonality of Sales and Earnings.

Corporation (as indicated in a Value Line array dated November 15, 2002) will show why. Referring to the lower left corner of the array (Figure 9.2), a low percentage gain is indicated in the seasonally strong January quarter comparison, precisely because it has the highest base. However, there is a large percentage gain (or loss) in the seasonally weak April quarter because of the low base. For example, from 1999 to 2000, the rate of earnings growth was $(2.33 - 1.75)/1.75 = 33\%$ in the January quarter, while it was $(0.30 - 0.17)/0.17 = 76\%$ in the April quarter. If one were to take these two comparisons at face value, one might be tempted to think that the rate of earnings growth was speeding up during the April quarter. But in fact, it's all because of the bunching of earnings in the strong season.

For other reasons set forth later in this chapter, even a proper application of earnings momentum method has a limited usefulness at best. But if one were to use such an approach correctly, one should take the sum of the most recent four quarters of earnings, divided by that of the previous four quarters of earnings. (Again, using the example of 1999 and 2000 earnings numbers of Zale Corporation, we obtain a sum of 2.21 for the earnings in four quarters in 1999 and a sum of 3.11 for those in 2000. The resulting rate of earnings growth becomes 41 percent.) Then, at least a comparison in any given quarter would have only one fourth of its previous weight. This rolling comparison process is similar to the moving average approach that is generally well accepted in economic work.

Even this revised methodology has pitfalls. The closure of a large sale on the last day of quarter A rather than the first day of quarter B could have a significant impact on both quarters' earnings. Certain holidays, such as Easter, could fall into either the calendar first or second quarter. (Many retailers have a fiscal year beginning after January 31 so that the April quarter will end on April 30, just to avoid such problems. Zale's fiscal year carries the same idea.) If the year-over-year method is used, it must be with an awareness of the pitfalls that arise from timing differences rather than performance issues.

RECURRING AND NONRECURRING EARNINGS

It should go without saying that earnings used in P/E calculations should be recurring in nature. One-time write-offs or gain should be excluded. Their impact should be duly noted as it relates to asset value, or book value, but not in the earnings stream. The last thing an investor would want to do is to capitalize such proceeds by multiplying it by a P/E ratio in her calculations. Things like gains or losses on the sale of assets would fall into this category (unless, of course, a company makes a habit of trading assets). Value Line is very conscientious about excluding nonrecurring items from its earnings presentation, noting the differences between its computed earnings and company-reported earnings in footnotes to its reports. Rather than treating such items as earnings, they should be considered adjustments to book value. The associated effects on investment income (either actual, in the case of gains, or forgone, in the case of losses) would be recurring.

Graham and Dodd, as well as Warren Buffett, warned about the tendency of companies to "kitchen sink" their losses in a bad year by taking write-offs (for corporate restructurings) to either atone for past errors or to "clean up" the balance sheet for the future. This will cause results to be understated in a year that managers and investors had written off anyway. If the restructuring is based on past problems, then it means that previous years' earnings in the aggregate were overstated to the degree that current earnings are understated. If the charge is a reserve for future expenses, such as severance, then future earnings are unduly relieved of expenses that were brought forward into the current year. Even so, charging past losses to the current year might be the least of several evils. This might be a sign of attitudinal changes at the company and a desire for a fresh start.

It also goes without saying that recurring earnings should have a normal tax rate. If a company is using tax loss carry-forwards to shield current income from taxes, tax is booked at the normal rate, and the amounts shielded are treated as extraordinary income. But suppose a low tax rate is the result of credits. How then should earnings be treated? If it is the result of a current credit such as an investment tax credit (in years that are allowed), or others such as job training credits that are results of normal operations, then one might consider such tax-advantaged earnings to be recurring. But if a number of credits were taken in one year that are unlikely to be repeated, then the artificially inflated earnings cannot be considered to be fully recurring. Tax credits, of course, represent an additional income to shareholders' equity, but should not be capitalized as part of the income stream.

THE PROBLEM WITH ERRONEOUS EARNINGS AND GROWTH ESTIMATES

As alluded to in Chapter 6, earnings growth can come from one of three sources: price increases, volume increases, and falling costs. A fourth issue, product mix, is really a blend of all three. The idea is to replace a low-margined product with a high-margined product.

Graham and Dodd would issue the same warning about earnings estimates, and then say that if the investor were suitably conservative, overvaluation would become less of a threat. In fact, aggressive earnings estimates are likely to cause disappointments when the actual results come in.

Although—or perhaps because—most measures of growth are short term rather than long term, Graham and Dodd would advise investors to base their estimate of earnings growth on the long-term record. This is a good starting point but not quite adequate for our purposes, since the future is often materially different from the past. To this, we would add an analysis of underlying structural factors:

- What is the industry's growth rate in the company's current markets?
- What are the chances of the target company's rising above this growth rate by expanding into related product markets?
- What are the chances of the company's rising above this growth rate by expanding into new geographical markets?
- Is the company in question growing faster or slower than the industry as a whole? How does it stack up against its competitors?
- If the company is growing "faster," at what point does the company get to be a proxy for the industry?
- Are earnings growing faster than sales? If so, how long can this continue and why?

Earnings estimates are most often treated by analysts and investors as single-point estimates. In a handful of cases, with very stable businesses, perhaps in consumer goods, this treatment may be adequate. This situation occurs when prices and volumes and costs are all completely forecastable within very narrow limits. More often, when earnings exactly hit target, it is a situation in which earnings are managed. Certain expenses are deferred until the end of the quarter, or in some cases after, then booked or withheld retroactively, in order to manage earnings. In earlier years, as Graham and Dodd warned, companies had been in the habit of setting up reserves, suppressing earnings in good years and tapping reserves in bad years in order to smooth earnings and not disappoint investors, but ultimately misleading them. The accountants have long since put a stop to the most egregious abuses of this sort, so they are generally limited to the amounts that are not "material" (i.e., by definition of less than 3 percent). Unfortunately, analysts and investors, by obsessing on earnings and rewarding or punishing a company for quarterly variances of as little as a penny a share, have made formerly immaterial amounts material.

In general, however, earnings possibilities ought to be treated as a range, rather than as a point. Certainly, a company that delivered only one half, say, of an earnings number blessed with corporate "guidance" ought to have a very good explanation. An estimate, by definition, should be based on the most likely scenario, but one that should nevertheless have every expectation that actual results will differ slightly, though perhaps not materially, from the estimate. The very elaborateness of earnings "models" that are now commonplace may lend a false sense of precision, and hence, of comfort, to what must be a very imprecise process.

An earnings estimate should also be accompanied by an explanation of the likely sources of error. This is standard procedure in scientific experiments, whereas actual results will differ at least slightly from theoretical ones. This is even true in a field such as chemistry or physics wherein scientific laws are verified by empirical evidence. This must be even more true in economic endeavors, wherein events behave more like a so-called random walk, rather than according to predetermined formulas like $E = MC^2$.

The most common distribution of events such as earnings is the so-called "normal" distribution or bell-shaped curve. This is the one that analysts assume to be the case. Normality is an easy, comfortable assumption to make, from a mathematical and economic standpoint. As a result, this type of analysis fails to properly consider situations that are abnormal, but this is a mistake. If there is a type of situation in which the chances of things behaving normally are 90 percent, it takes only six such situations to produce a 50–50 chance of *at least one* of these six abnormal things occurring.

Graham and Dodd warned investors not to expect too much earnings growth in general. A reasonable expectation for most companies might be nominal gross domestic product (GDP) growth, that is, real (reported) GDP growth plus inflation. For a company that is well positioned in a fast-growing, cutting-edge industry, particularly with a large international presence, a rate of growth sustainable over the medium term might be one and a half to two times world GDP growth, which may well exceed U.S. growth.

The danger is that while almost any given company could grow earnings at rates of 15 percent, 20 percent, or higher, it is unlikely that all of them would. Less than a quarter of companies can grow at rates of 15 percent or more. Only a handful can grow at rates above 20 percent. Yet plenty of companies have P/E ratios of 20 or higher. Put another way, the range of percentage gains is much narrower than the range of P/E ratios. If the earnings component of the P/E ratio is so susceptible to estimate error, then any analysis based on such an unreliable input must be undertaken with a certain degree of caution, if not outright skepticism.

David Dreman has done numerous studies to the effect that low-P/E stocks taken as a group outperform high-P/E stocks. Specifically, if one divided a universe of stocks into fifths, or quintiles, ranked by P/E ratios, the two lowest quintiles would outperform the two highest quintiles.[2]

Why might this be? One answer lies in a statistical phenomenon known as the *regression to the mean*. At any given time, there are some low-P/E stocks that are priced appropriately, given earnings prospects. But there are other stocks whose performance will shortly be average, or even above average, and are therefore pegged too low when priced below the median. When the market realizes this fact, it will close the value gap between the below-average P/E and the market rating. Naturally, there will be a handful of low-priced issues that for some reason will go lower, but these will not be numerous in comparison with issues in the other two categories. Conversely, while there are some high-P/E stocks that properly reflect their good prospects, these will only carry their own weight. Meanwhile, there will be a number of companies in which earnings are disappointing. In that case, not only does the price fall as the result of the earnings shortfall, but the P/E ratio is likely to contract as well.

How would Graham and Dodd undertake an earnings growth analysis? They would consider a period of years, using a methodology of averaging past earnings. An earnings surprise should not be held against a company if it merely disappoints unreasonable expectations. A more important situation occurs when a company has a history of disappointing earnings, particularly one that does not cover the existing dividend. Then the interaction of earnings and dividends (adding the former and subtracting the latter) impairs asset value, and most likely financial strength.

THE PROBLEM OF EARNINGS SURPRISES

The problem of earnings surprises is the corollary of errors in earnings estimates. Any deviation of true earnings from earnings estimates constitutes a surprise, either in the positive direction if the earnings estimate was too low, or a negative direction if the earnings estimate was too high relative to actual. In theory, any result reasonably close to the estimate, say within 5 percent, or a nickel a share, should not be considered a surprise, although many times it will be treated as one. In practice, earnings surprises tend mostly to be in one direction—negative—because earnings estimates were too high to begin with. The result is that there are vastly many more buy recommendations from analysts than there are sells, or even the sum of sells and holds if one takes the position that a "hold" recommendation is really a euphemism for "sell."

Anyone who has had any experience with a real business will know that there are plenty of unforeseen events and contingencies that will prevent results from being exactly in line with the plan. The difference has to be considered one of materiality. But if a stock sells off because earnings per share were off by a penny (in many cases a rounding error), it suggests that analysts and investors have been cutting their estimates very fine. When an earnings number affects both terms of the P/E over G in calculating the PEG ratio, the effects of even small differences in the earnings term can be quite dramatic with regard to the whole ratio.

Sometimes a stock sells off anyway, even when earnings meet targets. This is the result of an unfortunate practice where the targets published by analysts were merely the official targets. The unofficial and true hurdle is a higher number bandied about by analysts and large investors, either with or without the blessing of the company, called the "whisper" number. Being unpublished (except later in a retrospective analysis in the financial press), this number is generally not available to individual investors, even though they are impacted by it. Graham and Dodd, were they alive today, would not rely on such numbers and may actively discourage their use.

Another problem sprang from the use of earnings and the market sensitivity to this information. Companies used to give out critical earnings information or sometimes hints known as "guidance" to select brokerage house analysts and institutional investors in meetings or conference calls that were not generally open to the public. It was a situation that former Securities and Exchange Commission (SEC) Chairman Arthur Levitt termed *unacceptable*. It is a form of market manipulation much like that of the 1920s when leading investment houses gave stock "tips" to favored investment trusts that enabled them to buy when the public was selling, or vice versa. Since the promulgation of SEC regulation FD (Fair Disclosure) in 2001, corporate announcements are much more open to the public, putting individuals on a more equal footing with large investors.

THE VALUATION OF SUSTAINABLE EARNINGS GROWTH

The buzzword for the search for value in growth stock investing is growth at a reasonable price, often abbreviated as GARP.

The first variation of this rule is: Don't buy stock with a P/E ratio higher than that of the market, or at most, higher than a modest premium to the market multiple, say 25 percent. Thus, if the market P/E ratio is 20, the highest permissible P/E ratio would be 20 in the first case, and (1.25) * (20) or 25 in the second case. In this event, you want companies with earnings growth above the average and with a P/E ratio of not more than 25 percent above the average. This is a step in the right direction. The intent is to limit the risk to market risk, which is the possibility that the market as a whole might be too high. It then seeks to find growth stocks that are "cheap," if not in absolute terms, then relative to their superior prospects, on the theory that they will either appreciate more or fall less than average. Compared to "the market," such an investor will do "all right" in most instances. It's just that the investor will have overlooked the possibility that capital could be deployed more safely, and ultimately more profitably in other types of investments such as bonds or real estate.

Another common and misleading practice is a rule that the P/E ratio should not be higher than the growth rate (in percentage terms). This rule then reduces to the formula that the so-called PEG ratio (i.e., P/E divided by the growth rate, g) should be less than 1. This is liable to lead to *reductio ad absurdum*. When the earnings number affects both terms of P/E over growth rate g, the effects of even small differences in the earnings term can be quite dramatic with regard to the whole ratio. Does it mean that a company with a 1 percent growth rate should be capitalized as one times earnings? In practice, this means that the rule will apply, in the base case, to the old formula that a 10 percent grower can support a P/E multiple of 10 times earnings, and a somewhat faster grower can support correspondingly higher P/E multiple.

The issue that is often overlooked is how long growth must be sustained in order for this rule to hold. Too many investors make their purchases based on the assumption that is only for the current year. And they use an earnings estimate of that year for both the numerator and the denominator of the PEG ratio. If E_e is this year's estimated earnings and E_a is last year's actual earnings, then the growth rate $G = (E_e - E_a)/E_a$. Thus, the PEG ratio can be replaced by the modified ratio as follows:

$$\text{Modified PEG} = (P/E_e)/((E_e - E_a)/E_a) = (P/E_e) * E_a/(E_e - E_a)$$

Hence, the rule for buying stock requires that this ratio must be less than one.

In order to reach a decision for buying a stock, it is of the utmost importance to consider the growth rates for the subsequent years. It is no less
important to consider whether the immediately succeeding earnings will be
almost as robust as the ones examined or whether they will drop precipitously. This is precisely the question overlooked by the now old-fashioned
and rightly discredited "payback period" method of investment analysis.
Yet investors will blithely use a similarly flawed methodology just because
it appears to be more "modern."

Once we have established a sensible measure of sustainable earnings
growth, then the question is: How do we value it. In their later years,
Graham and Dodd would say that one must be most conservative in esti-
mating earnings growth rate, but having done so, one could be more
aggressive in assigning a price–earnings multiple. The Graham growth
formula was

$$P = E * (8.5 + 2 * g)$$

where P is the stock price, E the earnings, and g the expected growth. Or,
put another way, the P/E ratio would be $(8.5 + 2 * g)$. Thus, a company
with no growth would be a bond equivalent selling for 8.5 times earnings
or an earnings yield of about 12 percent; a company with 10 percent
growth might sell for $(8.5 + 20)$ or 28.5 times earnings. This would be
placed at the upper limit of sustainable growth.

A more sophisticated model was set forth by Warren Buffett. In fact,
he has demonstrated that the P/E ratio may reasonably be well above the
growth rate in some cases. This is true primarily when the growth rate can
be estimated with a high degree of accuracy and certainty for a company
such as Coca-Cola. And this comes from the company's oligopolistic pricing power and a product that can be sold worldwide. Buffett admits that
finding such situations is harder than it might seem, even for him.
Although he labels companies such as Coca-Cola and Gillette the
"Inevitables," he doubts that he can find a "Nifty Fifty" or even "Twin-
kling Twenty" of them. Buffett's formula for the correct price for such
companies is

$$P = E/(r - g)$$

where P is the stock price, E the "owner's earnings," r the risk-free interest
rate, and g the long-term growth rate. By definition, a mature company
should have a growth rate less than the risk-free rate, and the term $(r - g)$
is always positive for such a company.

Of course, Buffett's formula is nothing more than a variation of the
so-called Gordon model commonly taught in most business schools. The

Gordon model places the dividend D instead of the earnings E in the numerator so that the equation is

$$P = D/(r - g)$$

There are some slight but important differences between the original Gordon model and the Buffett version. First, when Buffett considers a growth rate, he is thinking of an "autonomous" growth rate, the one that would take place without the addition of any new capital, assuming only reinvestment of cash flow attributable to depreciation. Then in such case, all of the earnings can be paid out in the form of a dividend, thus making all reported earnings distributable earnings or "owners earnings." That is why E in Buffett's model can be treated as D in the Gordon model.

The Buffett version of the formula points out an omission of the original Gordon model. In practice, any amount of earnings growth can be generated by the retention or infusion of new cash. For example, if an investor has a bank account, there are two ways that it can grow. One is for the account to earn the market interest rate. The other is for the depositor to add new money. But the more relevant variable is the market interest rate, the return on one's original capital. If you doubled your original deposit, it would appear to result in a "return" of 100 percent in the account. But the true growth rate would be the low-single-digit return on a constant amount of capital.

If the autonomous growth rate were 0 percent and the risk-free interest rate were 10 percent in Buffett's formula, the stock's P/E ratio should be only 10, that is, $P = E/(0.10 - 0) = 10E$. Then the company cannot grow without the retention of earnings. If the company distributed all of its earnings as dividends, the dividend yield would be 10 percent, based on a P/E ratio of 10. Alternatively, the company could retain all of its earnings and pay no dividend. Then the value of the company, and the associated stock investment, would grow by 10 percent a year. In either event, or any intermediate case, the investor would realize a return of 10 percent per annum.

However, a company with an autonomous growth of 6 percent a year and a risk-free interest rate of 10 percent should sell for perhaps 25 earnings, according to Buffett's formula, that is, $P = E/(0.10 - 0.06) = 25E$. For a company that could grow at 6 percent a year without additional capital, it could pay out all of its earnings as dividends. Based on a P/E ratio of 10, the yield would be 10 percent, and there would in addition be a capital gain of 6 percent. The total return would be 16 percent, or well above the 10 percent target. The P/E ratio could be higher than 10 (and the yield correspondingly lower) to bring about a satisfactory total return. How much higher could the P/E ratio be? Well, at a P/E ratio of 25, the distribution of all earnings would lead to a yield of 4 percent, which, combined with the 6 percent autonomous growth, leads to a total return again of

10 percent. Buffett showed that a stock with a P/E of 25 need not have a growth rate of 25 percent, but mid-single digits would suffice, as long as it was both autonomous and sustainable.

Companies occasionally can grow with no net capital reinvestment. This is not because capital investment is identically zero, but rather, because the company can expand by reinvesting only the portion of cash flow that is attributable to depreciation, without appropriating additional monies that are the product of earnings. This could be the result of "hidden capital" investment (e.g., through technological innovation). Indeed, technology is the main driver of investment. That is why some of the greatest profits have been generally been made in the "high-tech" stocks of any given era, information technology in our time, chemicals or iron and steel in another age.

In practice, the autonomous growth factor is hard to forecast reliably, as Warren Buffett ruefully admitted in his 1991 annual report. In a case in which the autonomous growth rate was presumed to be 6 percent, the issue would certainly sell at a premium to the base-case P/E multiple of 10, but normally at less than 25 times earnings. This is, of course, to make allowance for the hazards of a guess.

Occasionally, popular enthusiasm will carry multiples to a ridiculously high valuation. This occurs when predictions become very sanguine, and people feel sure of these forecasts. This, in fact, happened to stocks in the late 1990s. Chapter 20 will point out when these kinds of moods are likely to occur, at least in American society, during periods of crowning achievements such as the journey to the moon in the 1960s and the technology boom of the 1990s.

But the main argument against companies selling at 25 times earnings is the risk factor or potential for disappointment. In order to compensate for risk, companies ought to sell at a discount to their theoretical P/E ratio, with a large discount for larger risk. Indeed, Buffett's genius probably consists not of finding companies with high potential growth rates (as any number of other investors can do this), but of identifying concerns with reliable growth. For starters, these companies are identified at the bottom right corner of the typical Value Line report which includes indexes of a company's financial strength (ranging from a low of 5 to a high of 100) on earnings predictability, price stability, and price growth persistence. We would add a fourth measure: earnings growth persistence.

Earnings growth persistence is added to the list because, in order to merit a high P/E ratio, steadiness is as important as growth. That's why a prime food or beverage company such as General Mills or Coca-Cola will command a higher multiple than most tech stocks even if the latter has better near-term growth prospects. Warren Buffett can buy the fast growers in the former category because he can evaluate them with a high probability of success. (His mistakes have been with bargain merchandise.) As the

Buffett formula showed, the premium that an investor can pay for sustainable growth is surprisingly high. Even Graham and Dodd would concede that sustainable growth should command a high multiple, but warn that rates of growth that are much beyond the mid-single digits are probably unsustainable. We would amend this by saying that autonomous rates of growth beyond the mid-single digits is unsustainable.

Too few investors question the premises for growth without examining its sources. For instance, many investors are willing to pay a fancy P/E multiple for debt-fueled gains. This occurs when a company loads up on debt and then earns a return slightly above the servicing costs. In such a case, the more debt the better. The problem then occurs when the relationship between debt service and earnings change, either because the debt is floating rate or because earnings take a tumble. In such a case, the whole superstructure will totter, jeopardizing the investment at least of the equity holder. This was the case in the early 1980s with any number of oil companies, perhaps the most prominent being Dome Petroleum, and more recently, in the 1990s, with retailers such as Caldors. Debt leverages earnings growth (or collapse) in much the same way that a mortgage leverages the return on a house. The historical appreciation on U.S. houses has been 7 percent, but this can represent 35 percent ROE on a 20 percent down payment, provided that the income from the house is enough to service the mortgage. To use the modern-day vernacular, we would consider debt, at least in large quantities, a form of economic steroids, a short-term boost to performance that jeopardizes the normal function of the body down the road.

SPECIAL CASE: HIGH-GROWTH FRANCHISE STOCK

Often, the high growth is a result of a franchise. A company has a unique product or service that can't quite be replicated, and thus gives the company considerable latitude to determining its product pricing, quantities sold, and resulting profit margins, with minimum regard to conditions in the economy as a whole. Investors will pay a premium for such franchise stocks, as well as issues of companies that merely appear to have franchises. Questions to distinguish the former from the latter include:

- Have there been large outlays that have appeared as expenses on past income statements that could be reasonably capitalized if permitted?
- Has the franchise been around for a while?
- Is it based on a unique, hard-to-copy concept, or is it something that anyone can do?
- Are there independent transactions that establish an arm's-length market value for the franchise?

The quintessential franchise stock is Coca-Cola. In 1989, the company estimated that it would cost $100 billion to recreate its franchise. The company had been around over 100 years—one of the few, actually, in American industry. Its product is not unique, but the special formula is a secret that can't be copied exactly. More important than the formula itself is the mystique that has grown up around it. And independent transactions for bottlers and for competing franchises have largely established a market value for Coke franchise.

McDonalds was a surprisingly strong franchise until recently. Its founder, Ray Kroc, took the assembly line method that was used to produce cars and applied it to fast food. He did so in a postwar era when families began to eat out more to free the mother from the drudgery of household tasks. Conceptually, a McDonalds store is easy to understand. Operationally, it is hard to apply because the average Western world worker does not want to do the boring and repetitive tasks of the assembly line. The food itself is unexceptional. But a certain mystique was planted in the minds of the customer about a standard but satisfying product, and this mystique had been drilled into the workforce. Both customer taste and employee service were managed superbly.

Stocks such as these are regarded as "one decision" stocks to be bought and put away. This is not a bad posture for most 30-odd-year-long cycle. But P/E ratios can get out of hand, even for a genuine franchise stock. It is when the merits of franchise stocks are most widely recognized, as reflected in P/E ratios of 30, 40, or more—as was in the case in the late 1970s and at the turn of the twentieth and twenty-first centuries—that there is a time of maximum danger in those stocks, and for the market as a whole. As worthy as these stocks are, they would be even better investments if one could avoid a once-in-30-year loss by selling them and purchasing lower-quality but cheaper investments, especially ones with significantly higher yields, or putting money into cash.

CHAPTER 10

Sales Analysis

This chapter will be concerned with the top of the income statement. The so-called top line is sales. And the two lines underneath are cost of goods sold (COGS), and selling, general and administrative expenses (SG&A). By subtracting the two expenses lines from sales, we get earnings before debt, interest, and taxes (EBDIT), as discussed in Chapter 6. The purpose of generating revenue is to maximize the EBDIT, but this is accomplished by managing the top line on sales as well as the two expense lines on the income statement.

CONTROL OF SALES AND COSTS

The ethos of the 1990s emphasized the maximization of profits through the control of costs more than the increase of sales. These cost controls were the main reason for the record high levels of prosperity. The result was profit gains that came from harvesting of sales built up in earlier years, and therefore cannot be repeated.

This differed from the ethos of, say, the 1960s, when many costs were considered fixed, and advertising and marketing programs were used to control the rate of sales gains. The costs incurred in these programs led to building of "brands" based on recognition and awareness of products. Companies that had large selling and/or many brand-name products possessed franchises. This strategy works best when purchasers have large amount of discretionary income, as they did after World War II.

The problem with cost cutting is that it leads to rates of earnings "growth" that are unsustainable in the longer term. In the long run, earnings growth can only come from sales growth. This is a lesson that executives learned too well in the 1960s and 1970s, when they let go of cost controls in the pursuit of sales. But in the short to medium term, earnings growth can come from margin expansion. Still, one has to be especially careful when earnings are growing faster than sales, not to extrapolate the excess earnings growth too far into the future. After all, one way to put it is that gross profit margins can rise only to 100 percent, after which earnings will not grow faster than sales. Earnings growth is then really the result of a rebound in margins, which are temporarily depressed. But when margins rebound to normal levels, there is no reason to expect that earnings will grow faster than sales.

A learning curve effect occurs when per-unit costs go down as more units are produced. This is because workers learn to work faster and more skillfully with greater practice. Learning curve effects are most pronounced in cutting-edge industries such as information technology in the late twentieth century and, prior to that, railroads, steel, and machine tools in the nineteenth century. Put another way, the linear relationship in the cost model is an imperfect representation of reality.

The strategies for managing sales are high growth and high margins (the rarest), high growth and low margins, low growth and high margins (the most common), and low growth and low margins. High growth and high margins tend to attract competitors. However, heavy spending on advertising and selling expense involves a trade-off between increasing sales and depressing EBDIT margins. There is also a competitive factor involving the low margins as well as the resulting "goodwill," both of which create a barrier to entry by potential competitors. Rapid sales growth can also increase margins by allowing the spreading out of fixed costs.

In constructing a pro forma income statement, analysts start with a forecast of sales growth. Then they continue with margin assumptions, leading to a cost of goods sold number. SG&A expenses are next. The easiest items to forecast are those that are most under the company's control (i.e., depreciation accruals and interest expense), which are the result of capital expenditure policies.

One thing to note is that while depreciation is sometimes broken out separately in the income statement, more often it is included in the inventory, and thereby in the cost of goods sold. In this case, the depreciation number can be found in the flow of funds or statement of changes in financial position and subtracted from the reported cost of goods sold to get the true cost of goods sold. A large number of fixed costs may be included under depreciation.

Interestingly, margins may be harder to forecast than sales. A multiproduct company will have items of varying profitability. Knowing the state of the economy, it may not be too hard to arrive at a sales figure because variations in sales between one product and another will often cancel out. What is less likely to cancel out is the exchange of one product for another. For instance, cash-strapped consumers will continue to buy clothes, food, and other essential items, but they may substitute cheaper brands for more expensive ones. The cheaper brands, by definition, are the ones that have a higher ratio of cost to price.

The quality of sales is important in forecasting future earnings growth. The following four questions give some clues:

1. Is the sales growth due mainly to price or volume increase?
2. What are the margins?
3. Are there a large number of repeat sales, or are customers mainly first timers?
4. Is there underutilized capacity for products with low variable costs so that most of the contribution margin goes straight to the bottom line?

Price increases are better in the shorter term because they lead to faster and bigger margin gains, at least temporarily. Unit volume gains are a better foundation on which to build long-term growth. A well-situated company has the ability to grow both price and volume. Of the two, investors like Warren Buffett prefer to see sales gains come from price increases, because it is a sign that the company has little competition and can pretty much charge "what the traffic will bear." Buffett's descriptive metaphor for such a situation is a "toll bridge."

A related question is: How large a factor is the company in its industry? The advantage of being a large player is the ability to control the industry. For instance, one can be a price leader—the one that everyone else follows. But, a small company is at the mercy of larger concerns that may be able to underprice it by achieving economies of scale and passing them on to customers. However, there is an advantage in not being too large. Dell Computer was able to grow at its phenomenal rate because it was a small part of its industry. It gained market share from other computer vendors, including and especially IBM, not so much by taking away their existing sales as by getting a disproportionate share of new sales in a fast-growing industry.

For a company of a certain size, one must look at the ratio of total sales to gross domestic product (GDP). An example is Wal-Mart, the great growth story in retailing of the 1980s and the 1990s. In its earlier years, Wal-Mart's sales were concentrated only in a small part of the country, and its sales represented a minuscule proportion of the U.S. GDP. By the end of the period, Wal-Mart's sales were nationwide and, in fact, were beginning to go international; its sales were beginning to represent a meaningful part of the U.S. GDP. By the early 1990s, Wal-Mart was dominant in its industry, representing one quarter of the sales of the retailing industry as defined by Value Line. Table 10.1 compares Wal-Mart's sales versus U.S. GDP in the period 1985 to 2001.

TABLE 10.1   Wal-Mart Sales vs. U.S. GDP

Year	Wal-Mart Sales ($million)	U.S. GDP ($billion)	Wal-Mart Sales as % of GDP
1985	8452	4039	0.21%
1986	11909	4269	0.28%
1987	15959	4546	0.35%
1988	20649	4906	0.42%
1989	25811	5251	0.49%
1990	32602	5546	0.59%
1991	43887	5725	0.77%
1992	55484	6026	0.92%
1993	67345	6343	1.06%
1994	82494	6947	1.19%
1995	93627	7265	1.29%
1996	104859	7636	1.37%
1997	117958	8080	1.46%
1998	137634	8782	1.57%
1999	165013	9274	1.78%
2000	191329	9825	1.95%
2001	217799	10082	2.16%

Source: Value Line; author's calculations.

RATIOS FROM SALES FIGURES

The sales figure is a particularly important number. Its relationships with other accounting variables can be expressed as ratios. Traditionally, the following three ratios are regarded as the most important measures:

1. Sales-to-assets ratio (sales/assets), known as the *asset turnover ratio,* which measures how efficiently assets are being utilized. Turnover ratios can also be calculated for individual components of assets, most commonly accounts receivable and inventories.
2. Net income-to-sales ratio (net income/sales), known as *net margin,* which measures the profitability of sales.
3. Assets-to-equity ratio (assets/equity), known as the *leverage ratio,* which adjusts for the balance impact of leverage employed.

In the past decade or two, the trend is to replace "assets" in the first and third of the above ratios with "capital," which is defined as assets minus working capital. Thus, sales-to-capital ratio (sales/capital) is the capital turnover ratio. And the leverage ratio becomes capital-to-equity ratio (capital/equity).

All other things being equal, the higher the turnover ratios the better, because they represent high utilization of assets (or capital). A particularly worrisome feature is a low or falling sales-to-inventory ratio (sales/inventory). In that case, it may indicate that inventories are piling up and become obsolete, necessitating writedowns along the way. Similarly, higher net margins are better than lower margins. But high profit margins sometimes come at the expense of low sales growth, which in turn may be reflected by low sales/assets or sales/capital. An ideal situation would occur if both the turnover and leverage ratios were high and net margins were also high. But such situations are seldom seen.

Putting these ratios together, we can derive the all-important return on equity (ROE) relationship. That is,

$$ROE = Turnover * Net\ margins * Leverage$$

Substituting the appropriate terms into the above equation (following the traditional practice of using assets),

$$ROE = (Sales/Assets) * (Net\ income/Sales) * (Assets/Equity)$$
$$= Net\ income/Equity$$

If "assets" is substituted by "capital" in the preceding equation, the result will be the same.

Can companies distort the sales figures? Unfortunately, there are a number of ways to do this. For instance, sales are supposed to be recorded when goods are shipped. But some companies depart from this rule. For instance, they will book orders as sales. In some cases, they may make assumptions about follow-on sales and book some of these volumes when an initial sale is made. It stands to reason that reported earnings based on these figures will also be inflated. In a number of accounting scandals in recent years, most notably at Enron, the so-called mark-to-market method of accounting allowed the companies to derive fictitious asset values by making overly optimistic estimates of future sales to be generated by those assets. Warren Buffett called these practices "mark to myth."[1] What's worse, Enron and other companies inflated their top lines by booking profitless "sales" to each other, in order to impress gullible growth-oriented analysts and investors, by giving the impression of business activities when there were none.

Another problem occurs with what is called *channel stuffing*. Many manufacturers sell to distributors of their products rather than directly to customers. For one or several quarters, the producers can maintain a high degree of "sales" by pushing product into distributors' hands, even when level end-product demand is soft. This process becomes progressively harder as distributors' inventories build. Eventually, the process stops because the distributors can't accept any more inventory. Then one of two things happens. In some cases, sales skid to a screeching halt, bringing earnings down with then for several accounting periods. In other instances, inventories have to be written off, in one accounting period, making a big dent in earnings and book value. These problems were particularly acute in the fictitious turnaround of Sunbeam Corporation by "Chainsaw Al" Dunlop. *Clue:* Why would sales of barbecue grills be strong in the winter months? *Answer:* Because of channel stuffing.

A less common situation occurs when a company wants to understate sales (and earnings) in a given quarter, so that it will have easier comparisons in subsequent years and maintain a smooth growth trajectory. This kind of situation occurs most often in the beginning of a product cycle. What happens when a new, pioneering product is accepted instantly is that the initial "rush" might cause a disproportionate number of sales to occur in the beginning, thereby making future improvements hard to achieve. In such circumstances, companies may establish a "reserve" for possible returns. Fewer items are booked than actually sold, on the theory that some of them may be returned. For certain types of new products, this is a real risk. In other cases, the company was just using this concept in order to be overly conservative in recording sales and earnings. Again, this is just to manage the earnings report to Wall Street, where beating earnings "estimates" (actually expectations supplied by management) by a penny or two is the best way to "manage" (push up) the stock price.

For new technologies, market penetration potential is sometimes considered more important than current sales. One measure of such penetration potential is the number of population units. The theory is that a certain percentage of people in a "typical" population will accept the product if it is marketed to them properly. Items that lend themselves to this method of analysis are usually upgrades of basic services already in wide use such as wireless phones or cable TV. Even assuming such a method of analysis to be valid (and we often have doubts on this point), this has to be undertaken with a certain amount of care. For instance, a population with a disproportionate number of old or young people will likely represent a significantly better or worse market than one in which there is more balanced age distribution.

A region in which wealth is unequally distributed will probably have a lower eventual penetration rate (unless it is a low-budget item) than a region in which wealth distribution is more typical of national average. This is particularly a problem in developing countries for advanced products such as cellular phones or cable TV, where only a small percentage of the population has U.S.-type income levels needed to purchase such items.

The concept of penetration can also boomerang. For instance, the primary buyers of electronic chips have been computer companies. Now, however, there are new entrants such as cellular phones, automobiles, and others. These are sectors with economics that are very different from the computer industry. During the penetration period of a new market, sales growth can take place above the historical rate for the core market. But after the penetration process is well under way, an add-on market can actually dilute growth if it is fundamentally less robust than the original core market. (Occasionally, the new market is actually more robust than the core market, as in the case of over-the-counter drug manufacturers that found their way into prescription drugs around the second World War, but that is rare.) For instance, if they are of equal size, the average of a 16 percent growth rate in the core market and 8 percent growth in the new market is 12 percent. Growth will be higher than that as the new market is entered, but after the initial penetration of the new market, further penetration will take place at a lower rate than the original 16 percent, albeit off a higher base.

VALUATION OF SALES AND OTHER TOP-LINE MEASURES

In the long run, profits and dividends, not sales, are what drive up stock prices. But to the extent that these variables derive from sales, sales can be an important valuation metric, along with others.

Ken Fisher, the author of *Super Stocks,* uses an analytical tool called the price-to-sales ratio.[2] Based on the fact that the average company has margins of 5 percent, his rule of thumb is to buy companies of good quality (with margins of 5 percent to 10 percent) at a price-to-sales ratio of around 0.75 (i.e., with a price–earnings [P/E] ratio of 15 or less), and sell them when the price-to-sales ratio is 1.5. For a mature or mediocre company with margins of 2 to 5 percent, the rule is to buy at 0.4 times sales and sell at 0.8 times sales. For companies with excellent margins of between 10 and 20 percent, the rule can be stretched to buy at 1.5 times sales and sell at 3.0 times sales. These ratios are mainly based on an "average" net profit margin of 5 percent. Under these circumstances, a price-to-sales ratio of 0.5 translates into 10 times earnings. If the price-to-sales ratio were 1, this would translate into 20 times earnings.

One way to find value stocks is to look for very low price-to-sales ratios, say 0.2, 0.1, or even less. In a turnaround situation, profitability is in question anyway, so the trick is to buy stocks cheaply enough so that if the turnaround succeeds, you will be adequately rewarded. Suppose a stock has typically commanded 1 times sales in a bull market. Then if the price-to-sales ratio were 0.2, a reversion to 1 times sales would mean a fivefold increase in the ratio. Assuming that sales were growing as the valuation corrected itself, the gain would be more than five times. In playing a turnaround situation and buying at low price-to-sales ratios, it is often helpful to make assumptions about "normalized" profit margins, just as you would make bets that ROEs would return to normal in the case of low price-to-book (P/B) ratios.

Ideally, sales growth will be in the 15 to 20 percent range. If there is margin expansion, earnings growth could be 20 percent or more. If there is also an expansion of the price-to-earnings or price-to-sales ratio, price appreciation will exceed earnings growth. Price-to-sales ratios work best for start-ups or turnaround situations. In these kinds of situations, you look at where margins will be, not where they are currently. In the case of a new company, it is a matter of spreading out fixed costs. In the case of a turnaround, it is a case of cutting bloated costs. Thus, a price–sales analysis grounded on hypothetical margins and earnings could indicate a bargain even as actual margins are so thin and earnings are so small, that the price-to-earnings ratio is very high, or even a nonmeaningful figure.

If a company has more than one line of business, one or more of those businesses is likely to be more important than the others. Very often, a highly diversified company has low-margined sales that boost the top line but do little or nothing for the bottom line. These are known as *junk sales.* (Some managers may strive for unprofitable sales just to get a higher ranking on the *Fortune* 500 list of companies. Enron, for one year the "seventh largest" corporation in America, was a case in point.) A straight price-to-sales ratio analysis for the whole company in such situations is meaningless, and may even be harmful. A more useful exercise is to do a price–sales valuation for the individual businesses, then add up the valuations and compare the sum with the company's market value. This is basically a sum of the parts analysis, using sales rather than asset values.

A related topic to line-of-business or segment analysis is geographical analysis. A company can operate in its home market, other developed markets, and emerging markets. By definition, the home market is the most mature, other developed markets are less penetrated, and emerging markets offer the best possibilities for growth.

Unilever was a case in point. Despite the fact that it sometimes satisfies Graham and Dodd–type evaluations, the composite company is so mature (with single-digit sales and earnings growth) that it is only occasionally an attractive investment. Its home European markets are the most mature; the Americas, only slightly less so. But individual subsidiaries in developing countries often manage 20 percent or better sales and earnings growth. Then the stocks of individual subsidiaries based in emerging markets may be more attractive, at least to growth-oriented investors, than an investment in the parent company. However, one advantage of its exposure to the rest of the world is that their growth rates will be incorporated into fortunes of the parent, whose stock may be selling more in line with Graham and Dodd multiples.

At some point, a corporation may decide that a sensible thing to do is to divest its noncore businesses. After all, its marginal business is someone else's core business. As a result, the business is likely to be worth less to the prospective seller than to a strategic buyer. Somewhere in between is a price that represents a good deal for both parties. Unilever demonstrated this point, selling its chemical and cosmetics businesses during the 1990s and concentrating only on foods.

In another instance, Denmark's Novo-Nordisk is the leading insulin provider in Europe, and America's Eli Lilly is the leader in the United States. When each company has reached the saturation point in its home market, the natural thing is to try to raid the other party's market. Novo-Nordisk has been the more determined player in the other's home market. It supports its sales of insulin with insulin pens, which are easy-to-use injectors with premeasured doses. In addition, the pens account for sales in their own right. It's like the Gillette formula: Sell the razor and get a market for the blades. For this and a number of other reasons, Novo-Nordisk gained worldwide market share by penetrating Lilly's home market more than Lilly could penetrate Novo-Nordisk's home market.

Another way to analyze sales is to consider sales and market capitalization per unit volume. This is often done for commodities like metals, cement, and even soft drinks. A global comparison works best for products that can be marketed internationally because they have a relatively high value-to-weight ratio. It doesn't work quite as well for more local products such as cement. This analysis leads to two interesting questions:

1. Why can a company charge better/worse prices than peers in different regions?
2. Why is a company's operating performance better/worse than that of its peers per unit of sales?

Answers to such questions will offer useful guides to the management.

TYPES OF SELLING SITUATIONS

The best sales plan is based on what is called a "unique selling proposition." It refers to something that a company does better than anyone else, at least in relation to the target customer base, for a quoted price. This is a natural source of monopoly-type power, and one that is not likely to be regulated.

Whether it is a monopoly or a commodity producer, a company's operating position is of paramount importance. Management must raise and answer the following six questions:

1. What is the industry growth rate in the company's current markets?
2. What are the chances of raising this growth rate by expanding into related product markets?
3. What are the chances of rising above this growth rate by expanding into related geographical markets?
4. Is the company in question growing faster or slower than the industry rate? How does it stack up to competition?
5. If the answer to question 4 is faster, at what point does the company get to such a size as to be a proxy for the industry?
6. Are earnings growing faster than sales, and if so, how long can this last?

Sales can be described in terms of the current sales base versus new add-on sales. In retailing, the current sales base is referred to as "same-store sales." New-store sales are important component of growth. But the health of the company, or at least of the industry, is best measured by same-store sales growth. However, a sales-oriented organization will strive mightily for new product development. At 3M, for instance, there is a corporate goal of at least 25 percent of sales coming from products developed within the past five years. That is why the company created an "intrapreneurial" culture that invented, among other things, Post-It note pads.

Companies typically opt for either a value-added premium-price strategy or a high-volume commodity strategy. This can be seen in the retailing industry. Companies like Wal-Mart and, before it, Sears made a virtue of preaching everyday low prices and then delivering a wide variety of goods in spite of that fact. This was made possible by a high-volume strategy aimed at a mass market. Premium producers like Williams-Sonoma earn higher margins, however, but at the price of lower sales growth. For a multiproduct company, a strong sales effort is typically supported by a strong research and development (R&D) effort. Although Wal-Mart is characterized by good merchandising, it is also strong in technology, with point-of-sales scanning contributing to both good inventory control and good marketing.

A company that is a monopoly is in a better position to control sales. By definition, it can charge what the market is willing to bear without having to worry about competition, at least locally. As a result, it has the capacity to maximize profits. Although a true monopoly will either be broken up or regulated by the government, there are a number of companies selling products for which there are no real substitutes. These companies operate in a quasi-monopolistic position, subject only to competition from different competing products. Warren Buffett likes these types of situations, with Coca-Cola being a case in point.

A oligopoly exists when there are only a few competitors in an industry. An important condition is that barriers to entry are high (i.e., it is hard for new firms to enter the market). One measure of oligopoly is the so-called concentration ratio—the amount of market share occupied by the top three or four firms. If it is 50 percent or more, the industry is an oligopoly.

The communications industry became less of an oligopoly and more of a commodity situation during the course of the 1990s, because new technologies introduced by new companies were being brought to bear. (The classic instance of this was when Time Warner, an old-line media company, merged with America Online [AOL], an Internet service provider, in order to stay ahead of the new media companies, but did not succeed.) In spite of many problems in the transition, they may still increase total industry profits by lifting volumes, while reducing the share of each individual provider. Another unfortunate example was the telecommunications industry, in which local, long distance, and wireless providers became virtually interchangeable. Overinvestment in all these segments almost ruined the whole sector.

In times of booming pricing for commodities, there is a temptation to bring new capacity on stream. The problem is that such investments take several years to complete and that capacity additions that are undertaken at the top of the boom will come on-stream at the bottom of the cycle. These moves aggravate the tendencies of an inherently cyclic industry. These dynamics hold for most raw materials, including oil, forest products, and most building materials. Such companies thrive during a period of secular shortage, especially if it is worldwide, such as what happened in the 1970s and may be about to happen in the 2000s. In such periods, prices rise rapidly. The greatest beneficiary is the highest cost producer that has survived the previous shakeout. That's because the effects of a price increase go straight to the bottom line. Then the company that had the lowest margins before the price increase will enjoy the largest percentage gains.

The best situation is one in which commodity producers evolve into an oligopoly. This has occurred over the past 50 years in the pharmaceutical industry. At first, there were a large number of drug manufacturers producing relatively simple compounds, such as aspirin and analgesics. Then the drug companies started specializing in more complicated applications, such as heart disease, ulcer, or anticancer medications. Finally, a number of more developed drug companies merged into multiline companies (e.g., Bristol-Myers Squibb, Glaxo SmithKline) at a time when health maintenance organizations (HMOs) and other health care providers started to look for "one-stop shopping." These behemoths gained critical mass to maintain R&D efforts for increasingly expensive and complex drugs.

As John Kenneth Galbraith pointed out in *The New Industrial State,* demand is now managed.[3] This phenomenon showed up after World War II as the American economy went from one of a few suppliers and many customers to many suppliers chasing a relatively smaller number of customers. (The problem of producing goods had been solved by the mass-production techniques developed in the 1920s and earlier, the full implementation of which had been delayed by the Great Depression.)

Marketers have a number of tools with which they can manage demand. One of these is advertising and promotion. Although this endeavor is recorded on the income statement as an expense, it is often a form of investment. Such expenditures are usually worthwhile because they tend to make the market larger than it would be otherwise. And while it might lengthen the time to achieving the profit breakeven point, the advertising makes profits and profit growth somewhat more stable than might otherwise be the case. Hence, they add market value to a company's stock. More traditional ways of managing demand are to create a better product and/or sell at a lower price.

SALES GROWTH AS A LIMITING FACTOR IN EARNINGS GROWTH

In assessing the prospective sales growth of a relatively new product or process, one must hew to a realistic estimate of sales potential, based on the demand for even remotely similar products. It's only rarely that a new product will generate a lot of new demand, as opposed to displacing demand from existing products. Let's take the assumption that Amazon.com can eventually displace a non-Internet competitor such as Barnes and Noble. Then the market value of Amazon.com should eventually rise to Barnes and Noble's peak market cap, maybe somewhat (two or three times) more, through greater efficiency, a number of years in the future. But that is not what the market was saying around the turn of this century. Instead, it was expecting that the Internet companies would not only displace their competitors, but also would generate sufficient additional sales over and above what the established companies would have generated in the same field, when companies like Amazon.com were valued at a multiple of 10 times or more of Barnes and Noble's valuation.

One must also be careful about using the price-to-sales ratio with an inherently low-margined high-volume business, such as a grocery store. So a low price-to-sales ratio gives an understated view of the P/E ratio. One method is to "adjust" the sales by dividing them by 5, so that the 1 percent profit margins translate into "normal" 5 percent "margins" on adjusted "sales." This method has the advantage of yielding a top-line number that is comparable to those in other industries for easy comparison. In 2000, William Miller of Legg Mason Value Trust found grocery stores Albertson and Kroger bargains; the price-to-adjusted-sales numbers seem to bear this out. Thus, the price–sales methodology can be adjusted to work even for unusual industries.

Technology and health care companies have high profit margins, typically 15 percent, 20 percent, or even more. They also have high returns on equity, 20 percent or more as a rule. So price-to-sales ratios are higher than the norms for such companies. Even so, they have to be taken with a grain of salt. If 1 times sales is a high price for a stock based on 5 percent margins, then 10 times sales is an expensive valuation for a hypothetical company that can earn a 50 percent net profit margin. No major company has achieved this, although some tech companies such as Microsoft have achieved margins of between 30 and 40 percent. In fact, price-to-sales ratios were the ultimate test of how overvalued the tech stocks were at the end of 1999. Note that margins in most cases were actually above average, because the products were so unique and, in most cases, the companies had relatively few direct competitors. So the companies deserved to have high price-to-sales ratios, but not ratios of 30 or more. If the net margin were 100 percent, meaning that all of the sales became earnings (no taxes for anybody?), the stocks would still be overpriced. In fact, the prospects were for margins, and hence earnings, to go down.

A simple mathematical example will illustrate the point. The number 4 can be expressed as the sum of 2 and 2, or as a product of 2 and 2. Superficially, the two treatments appear to make no difference. However, if 2 and 4 represent the first two terms of a sequence, the next term will be vastly different depending on whether 4 is the sum or the product of 2 and 2. A sequence of arithmetic progression of 2, 2 + 2, 2 + 2 + 2, etc., yields 2, 4, 6, 8, 10, a linear function. A sequence of geometric progression of 2, 2 * 2, 2 * 2 * 2, etc., yields 2, 4, 8, 16, 32, an exponential function. It is probable that many investors, in evaluating the "new economy" around the turn of this century, were looking at 4, which equaled 2 + 2, and thinking that it was a function of 2 * 2. They were therefore fooled into paying up for exponential growth. Our valuation methodologies would only assume that the "new economy" is basically linear, as was the old economy.

Special Vehicles for Investment

CHAPTER 11

A Graham and Dodd Approach to Mutual Funds

Most investors want to own a number of stocks. A holder of a single issue may do extremely well or poorly because of factors involving the one company, regardless of how well the market is doing overall. However, if you own a basket of equities, the basket will act somewhat more like the market as a whole. One stock will zig while the other will zag. Although some investors would rather try to beat the market by owning only a handful of shares, most prefer to reduce risk to the extent that it is reducible, while still participating in the market.

Two stocks are safer than one, and ten are safer than two. In addition, you may want to be diversified between asset classes, including both U.S. and foreign stocks, government and corporate bonds, and cash. A broader definition of equity-like instruments might include real estate and/or gold.

The problem is that most investors don't have the inclination or know-how to buy a well-diversified portfolio of stocks. They may buy stocks one at a time, concentrating in one industry or making one sector bet. One way around this is through the purchase of a mutual fund, a professionally managed operation that buys and holds stocks.

Mutual funds come in two basic varieties. They are closed-end funds, and the much more common open-end funds, which are "true" mutual funds.

A closed-end fund has a fixed number of shares. Such a fund was established by an initial public offering of these shares at a given price. The proceeds of this offering were then invested in stocks, bonds, or other financial instruments. Depending on the success of the investments, the value of the fund, and hence of the shares, can go either up or down, and the dividends and interest of the funds will be paid out in the form of income. Moreover, depending on how management is perceived, the fund shares may sell at either a premium or discount to the per-share value of the assets under management. This premium or discount is established when investors buy and sell shares from and to other investors in the same fund. In this regard, a closed-end fund operates much like a stock, except that the "company" is an investment portfolio.

After its initial establishment, an open-end fund will take new money directly from investors on a daily basis, by issuing shares, including fractional shares, corresponding to the money invested on a particular day. It will also redeem the shares of any investors who want to withdraw money on the same day on a pro-rata basis. Thus, an investor in such a fund will buy shares from and sell shares to the fund itself (actually the fund management company), rather than other investors. Like a closed end fund, the value of the fund shares will go up and down with the value of the underlying investments, but unlike a closed end fund, the shares will theoretically never sell for either a premium or discount, because purchases and sales of the fund are supposed to be made at the pro-rata net asset value at end of each day. Buy and sell orders must be placed no later than 4 P.M. on each business day, and the settlement will take place during the evening hours, after the fund's holdings have been priced and the share values have been computed.

Some flagrant exceptions to the above rule became a national scandal after they were exposed in 2003 by states' attorneys general, especially New York's Eliot Spitzer (who had earlier prosecuted Wall Street firms for conflicts of interest in allowing research to be unduly influenced by investment banking considerations, using a half-forgotten 1920s-era state law known as the Martin Act). The two most egregious offenses were known as "late trading" and "market timing."

Late trading was a process in which favored (usually large) investors were allowed to place buy and sell orders after the 4:00 P.M. deadline, thereby capitalizing on information (e.g., earnings reports) that was released after 4:00 P.M. This could occur because the settlement period extends for several hours after the 4:00 P.M. close. For instance, one particular hedge fund manager would "propose" trades to the mutual fund administrator, thereby generating the appropriate paperwork, before 4:00 P.M. The hedge fund manager then left in trades that he liked and pulled trades (and related paperwork) that he disliked an hour or two after the deadline, based on what had transpired in the meantime. What was worse, there was usually a *quid pro quo* regarding other business relationships in cases like this.

Market timing refers to frequent in-and-out trades by a given party, which are disruptive to the management of a fund, by forcing the fund to manage around, and cope with an unusually large number of purchases and redemptions. It is a particular problem for international funds, in which investors try to anticipate tomorrow's developments in foreign markets (which are closed), based on what is happening in U.S. markets today. Although market timing is not illegal in and of itself, it is illegal for a fund to punish ordinary investors (by locking them in or out of the fund or by imposing extra charges) for frequent trades, and then allowing favored investors to make similar trades without such penalties. In some particularly egregious examples such as the Putnam Funds and the Strong Funds, the funds' managers themselves were allowed to make frequent trades in their own funds for their personal accounts when the same privileges were denied to others.

U.S. MUTUAL FUNDS

Mutual funds had an inauspicious beginning. They were started shortly before the Great Crash of 1929, just when popular interest, hence the market averages, were near their peak. Created ostensibly to serve the interests of the investment public, they were caught up in, and contributed to, the feeding frenzy. Worse yet, they would buy stocks on margin, even while the investors bought the mutual funds on margin. So the investor was leveraged two ways with twice the risk. When the bear hit, mutual funds collapsed even faster than the underlying stocks, bringing investors down with them.

The Securities and Exchange Commission (SEC) changed that during the Great Depression. Funds now have to file for a charter that spells out investment objectives and the methods they will use to achieve those objectives. If they register as a "diversified fund," they may invest no more than 5 percent of their funds in any one stock and 25 percent in any one industry. If they want to use margin or derivatives, or any other aggressive techniques, they must spell that out in the charter. Shareholders are at least forewarned.

One important fund document is the prospectus. The prospectus will give a great deal of important information on expenses, turnaround time for redemption, historical performance, and other matters. You should not be unduly swayed by the fee structure. It is better to own a well-performing fund that charges high fees than a poorly performing fund that charges lower fees. What counts is the net return after fees. Unless two funds are nearly alike in performance, the size of the fee won't make a difference in this calculation.

Another important document for the mutual fund is the statement of assets, which will give a good flavor of the fund's investment style and a historical perspective of recent results. While past performance is no guarantee of future success, the statement of assets is instrumental in helping an investor find out whether the style, at least, is suitable. One word of warning involves a practice known as window dressing; portfolio managers sometimes buy good-performing stocks or sell poor performers near the end of the quarter or year in order to show the most advantageous holdings, even though they were unrepresentative of the portfolio for most of the time period in question. A more complete disclosure would reveal asset purchases and sales for the period in question.

INTERNATIONAL FUNDS

How should the average investor go about choosing a fund? One common way is to read the newspapers or financial magazines, which depict the best- and worst-performing funds over various periods of time. This is better than nothing. Studies have shown that managers of best-performing funds tend to have an above-average level of skill and will continue to outperform other similarly situated funds, though not necessarily remain at the top. The down- side is that funds with the most eye-catching returns have capitalized on a particular "hot" sector or theme that may be about to turn "cold" by the time the average investor learns of it. On the whole, the style/theme decision is the more important one, and one that investors must make on their own.

Another way is to respond to advertisements. Again, this is better than nothing. SEC regulations do ensure that "truth in advertising" does work somewhat better than in many other industries. The companies that spend the most money on advertising generally are the larger, more established firms. This doesn't guarantee outperformance, of course, but does give some promise of stability of management and style.

A number of services evaluate mutual funds. Perhaps the most widely followed mutual fund evaluator is *Morningstar*. Value Line which publishes a voluminous stock guide, followed with a "me-too" product that is about as good, and may be more useful for someone who is already accustomed to the format in the stock survey. Business magazines such as *Fortune* and *Forbes* also publish commentaries on funds from time to time, although they do so from a general business perspective rather than a strictly mutual fund view.

In recent years, international investing has gained in popularity. This is, first, because of the wider variety of instruments that are available to Americans and, second, because of the growing recognition of the advan- tages of investing abroad. A whole battery of mutual funds has arisen to take advantage of this trend.

There are also mutual funds, both open and closed end, on single coun- tries. Some people prefer to choose countries much as they might choose sectors. Perhaps they have business or cultural ties to a particular country. This gives a very concentrated exposure that could benefit, or be harmed by, economic and political reform. Apart from these considerations, country funds lend themselves all too well to flavor-of-the-year strategies. Investors pile into the fund of a country that is "hot." This makes them more volatile than most. However, well-managed country funds can earn average returns of roughly 20 percent for a number of years. This is more than can be said for all but the best-managed U.S. funds.

In 1989, country funds went to huge premiums, as much as 50 to 100 percent of underlying assets. This represented speculation, especially from

Japanese investors. In a number cases, it was possible to come up with proxies for the individual countries just by buying a handful of the largest stocks. Sometimes there will be several funds in the same country or region, some of which sell at premiums and others at discounts. For instance, the one with the discount may be the newer of the two, while the one with the premium is the older. Or one may be traded in the United States, and the other in London. All other things being equal, it is better to buy the one with the discount, especially for the smaller countries, where most investors own the same handful of stocks. One should pay the premium only if the manager is particularly well regarded.

CORPORATE MUTUAL FUNDS

From time to time, there will be operating companies that will also own large portfolios of stocks, or significant minority interests in companies, which are of equal or greater importance than operating assets. This is far more common in Europe and Asia, where banks and even industrial companies will often have large holdings in industrial companies, than in the United States. Nevertheless, several companies have become famous, and justly so, for their investment prowess, which complements and adds materially to results from operations.

The top executives of such firms often see their primary function as capital allocators rather than operators. The advantage is that they are focused on the bottom line and will refuse to operate at a loss. The disadvantage is that they have to go outside the company for operators.

Warren Buffett's Berkshire Hathaway may be more or less a closed-end fund in all but name. It consists of a mix of insurance companies, industrial businesses, and large stock holdings in large companies, with equities often making up the single largest part of firm's value. Its stock holdings include blue chips such as American Express, Coca-Cola, Gillette, the *Washington Post*, and Wells Fargo, which were originally bought at a discount to fair value. The company made even more money from restructuring situations, namely insurance company GEICO, rescued from bankruptcy in 1976 and finally taken private 20 years later, and Capital Cities, which bought ABC in 1986 and allowed itself to be acquired by Disney 10 years later. More speculative holdings have included Freddie Mac and General Dynamics. Most of the privately owned industrial holdings are in mature businesses that post single-digit percentage sales and profit gains, but throw off significant cash, allowing Berkshire to invest in other businesses or in stocks.

At least one brokerage analyst disputed this assertion, and attributed the bulk of Berkshire Hathaway's value to its operating businesses, coming up with a value of over $90,000 a share. Taking the book value (which is represented by investments) at just under $40,000, this would leave over $50,000 as the value of the underlying business and support the assertion that the majority of the value of the company is from operations, not the portfolio. But this asset value has not been supported by the stock price.

So we came up with our own estimate as of the turn of the century. (Because of the weak stock market, these values didn't change much between 1999 and 2001.) The first assumption was that Berkshire Hathaway's asset value is more or less the value of its investment portfolio. This is a greater amount than book value, because part of the portfolio is supported by insurance reserves and other liabilities. A good guess is that these liabilities can be serviced by the insurance business, effectively allowing Berkshire to own its investment portfolio free and clear. But make no mistake about it. If there were a catastrophe in the insurance business, the stock would suffer. The value of the investment portfolio was, in round figures, $50,000 a share.

What value should be assigned to the operating business of Berkshire? Our formula is 10 times pretax operating earnings (not look-through earnings of consolidated subsidiaries, which are already included in the asset value) of almost $1,000 a share. Call it $10,000 a share for good measure. Then our conservatively estimated investment value for Berkshire Hathaway was $60,000 a share. (This figure probably rose to nearly $70,000 a share in 2002, due to the company's successes in insurance operations and corporate buyouts.) Early in 1999, the stock was selling for $70,000 a share. As the portfolio could be estimated with considerable accuracy, there was $20,000 a share to be distributed between the implied value of the insurance company and a "Buffett premium," for his historically superior management skill. Analysts had made the argument that the operating businesses alone were worth $50,000 a share, based on comparables. It's true that the operating assets were somewhat larger than the investment assets. But we (perhaps artificially) assigned all the liabilities to the operating business as well, which would greatly reduce their net worth. Put another way, the value of the assets may well have been worth $90,000 a share, but the company wasn't worth that much after subtracting the liabilities.

Another corporate quasi–mutual fund is Leucadia National. Like Berkshire Hathaway, it had insurance and industrial operations. Unlike Buffett, its top managers do not buy passive investment positions. The company's modus operandi is to buy undervalued assets, turn around the underlying companies, and in many, though not all cases, sell stock back to the public. In a number of instances, Leucadia bought controlling, but not full, interests in the companies it turned around. Successful turnarounds included Phlcorp, the successor to Baldwin United. It had occasional foreign investments, for instance, in the Bolivian Power Company, and in a joint venture in Russia with Pepsi-Cola's bottling operation. Its portfolio management style is more active than Berkshire Hathaway's. When it ran out of investment opportunities, it distributed $12 a share in cash in 2000, a move that business magazines rightly likened to Buffett's dissolving his partnership in 1970. This represented 40 percent of its asset value, the maximum amount allowable without creating unpleasant tax consequences.

Another such "fund" is Loews Corporation. It owns the CNA Insurance Company, Lorrillard Tobacco, Loews Theaters, and miscellaneous other businesses such as Diamond Offshore (drilling). In addition, it has a short-selling operation. This might be an interesting investment for the trying times that may be ahead. Tobacco, petroleum production, and cinema were among the fastest-growing industries in the stressed-out 1930s, and short selling may be the order of the day in the upcoming environment. The insurance company is the glue that holds the whole thing together, performing much the same functions as Berkshire Hathaway's insurance businesses. Most of these businesses suffered through the 1990s, which were not good times for them. The downside is that the stock is only modestly, not hugely, depressed as a result, even considering its single-digit price–earnings ratio (P/E) ratio.

These corporate funds, by definition, are "focus" funds, concentrating on a handful of companies that fit a highly defined profile selected by management. As such, they do not offer enough diversification for the average investor if bought in isolation, although they could form a significant part of a portfolio. Their attraction is the high degree of professionalism, by managers who have general business as well as portfolio management experience.

DISTRIBUTIONS

A mutual fund must distribute all of the dividend income earned by its stocks during the course of the year. A fund must also distribute capital gains realized during that time, and may distribute unrealized gains (by borrowing the money). All of these distributions are taxable, unless the fund is held by a tax-advantaged entity such as an individual retirement account (IRA). This is true even if the investor purchased a fund too recently to have a gain on the fund shares. But the value of the fund drops after a distribution. That's why funds trade at a discount if they have large amounts of unrealized gains. Of course, if a fund has realized losses, distributions will be tax sheltered. That said, the best time to buy a fund is right after a distribution, to have a lower cost base and to avoid these tax problems.

One of the issues regarding a mutual fund is tax efficiency. If taxes result from turnover, then the lower turnover incurs fewer taxes and hence is more "tax efficient." This was an important consideration during the 1990s, when corporate earnings grew steadily and stock prices expanded even faster because of rising P/E ratios. Then the best strategy was to let stocks compound as many times as possible before selling and paying taxes on the capital gains.

The 2000s decade probably will be much different, assuming a stressful economic environment. Earnings will not grow steadily, and even if they do, P/E ratios are so high that they are likely to fluctuate wildly, leading to high volatility in stock prices. On balance, P/E ratios are likely to fall in the coming decade, balancing out most, if not all, of the earnings growth. If one can earn 50 percent on a particular investment during a period of sub–5 percent annual price gains, why shouldn't one sell it and take a profit? Put another way, many stocks will see a whole decade's worth of price appreciation bunched into one or two years.

Even as conventionally measured, however, higher taxes are seldom directly proportional to higher turnover. That's because tax efficiency is not based on the absolute turnover, but rather the retained portion of the portfolio. Most portfolio managers work with "core" and "trading" portions of the portfolio. That is, one may retain 75 percent of the holdings (by market value) in any given year, and then trade 25 percent of the fund two or three times during the course of the year. In this admittedly extreme example, there is almost no difference between 25 percent turnover and 50 percent or 75 percent. Most of the tax liability is incurred on the gains realized from the previous years on the first 25 percent of turnover. Similarly, if everything that was held on January 1 was sold, then it doesn't matter whether turnover was 100 percent, 200 percent, or 300 percent, because nearly all gains on the portfolio (except unrealized gains on stocks held at the end of the year) would be taxed anyway.

WHEN TO SELL A FUND

Even though you want to be a "long-term" investor, there are good reasons for selling a fund, particularly when it changes in character. Examples include the following:

- *The manager may be changed.* Well-performing managers often go on to new positions. Some of them retire in any given year, and a few have been known to die on the job. In any event, there may be a change of philosophy and discontinuity of performance as a result. This is a particular concern if the replacement is being brought in from the outside (unless, of course, you know of and like the new manager). It may be less of a concern if the replacement comes from inside the organization, particularly if he or she has been helping to manage the fund all along.
- *The philosophy may have changed.* This is unlikely to happen with the same manager, but it is not out of the question. This could be the case

with a manager who has been conservative and is suddenly starting to get aggressive, or vice versa.

■ *The investor's needs may have changed.* This is more likely than the above. Perhaps you have been investing in equity funds for a number of years and are now about to retire. Thus, capital preservation is of prime importance. You may want to switch to a bond fund or even a cash fund. If the investor has suddenly come into a large sum of money, however, he or she may want to take more chances and switch to a more aggressive fund.

■ *The instrument may no longer meet the return objectives.* For instance, cash yielded high-single-digit (in some cases low-double-digit) returns for most of the 1980s. In the 1990s, yields dropped to the low single digits. (If you had known this was going to happen, you would have bought bonds and reaped a large capital gain.) Even so, it would not have been too late to switch into a bond fund or a stock fund.

■ *A fund may underperform similar vehicles over an extended period of time.* Almost no fund performs well all of the time. A few perform well most of the time. But most investment themes are occasionally out of favor. For instance, value funds may languish at a time when growth funds are prospering. If your manager is sticking to what he or she knows best, underperformance will probably occur occasionally. (Even Warren Buffett underperformed the Standard & Poor's [S&P] 500 four or five times in the past 30 years.) The trade-off is that you will get management compatible with your personal goals.

The thing to avoid is a case in which a fund is underperforming other funds of similar philosophy and objective (e.g., other value funds). Then the fault may lie with the fund manager, rather than the investment style. An investor who changed funds could get a higher return with a similar, or even lesser, amount of risk.

If there are new fund instruments that offer a higher return, they may be attractive. After you've invested happily in U.S. funds for a number of years, they suddenly begin to lag foreign funds. Most countries will be "hot" every now and then. The test is: Have the country and its stocks done well over time? Alternatively, you may decide to put a certain proportion of money into a Europe or Pacific fund just to diversify away from the U.S. market.

Many investors aren't in a position to manage their own investments but want participation in the stock market because of equities' superior long-term returns. Even Warren Buffett conceded the merits of an index fund for such people. "Paradoxically, when dumb money acknowledges its limitations, it ceases to be dumb."[1]

The question then arises: What kind of benchmark should you use? An S&P index fund would give broad representation to U.S. stocks, using its most standard gauge. But this is only one asset class: large-cap U.S. equities. There are other benchmarks for other categories of funds, such as various small-cap indexes and the EAFE (Europe, Australia, Far East) index for international funds.

One variation of this strategy is to use mutual funds to reach those sectors that the investor cannot access because of either lack of knowledge or lack of suitable instruments. For instance, an investor may be quite comfortable purchasing U.S. equities but use mutual funds to get representation in foreign countries when this seems desirable. Within the international group, U.S.-listed issues of Asian countries are far less numerous than those of European or Latin American countries. Despite our experience in money management, we would use Asian country funds to buy into that part of the world.

EVALUATION OF MUTUAL FUNDS

In order to get superior investment performance using mutual funds, you have to evaluate the investment styles, as well as the basic skill level of the manager. As Mr. Buffett would say, "If you don't know jewelry, know the jeweler."[2] Graham and Dodd funds are managed based on a radically different, and hopefully clearly stated, proposition from those that underlie the investments of most other managers. No matter what the skill level, in the final analysis, the likely success or failure will correlate closely to the degree that the fund manager's view of the world economy matches the reality. One word of warning: An "extreme" position such as ours is likely to be either wildly right or wildly wrong, compared to those of others.

There are really two bases for choosing mutual funds. One is to try to get a mix of assets that will replicate the "market," however defined. A whole consultant industry is being built around this phenomenon. They are trying to identify different "styles" and force managers to choose and stick to one, in large part so that they can blend mutual funds in order to come up with a reasonable proxy for the market. Of course, they want superior performance overall and try to achieve that by selecting outperforming managers within each category. Thus, each manager is measured against others with similar objectives, as much as or more than the market as a whole.

One variation of trying to track the results of the overall market is to try to mimic the results of a particular reference group. We believe that this due to a phenomenon that we label "the retirement imperative." Many people are concerned that their investments will give them a similar lifestyle and retirement as their friends or some other reference group. Thus, if a person's family and friends are all buying technology or Internet stocks, it is a rare individual who will not be similarly invested, because he or she otherwise may end up with a new group of friends. A similar rule applies to a group of people who all have most of their assets invested in their company's stock. If such investments prosper, terrific! If not, "misery loves company."

The analogy generally used to illustrate this investor herd mentality phenomenon is the story of lemmings. These are small, furry creatures often found near the Arctic Circle in Europe. They reproduce dramatically, and every few years their numbers outrun their food supply. When this happens, these generally individualistic creatures get together in packs in search of fresh food. Leaving their natural habitat, they head for the ocean, allowing nothing to stop them. Larger animals that get in the way are trampled by the herd. Upon reaching their destination, they all jump into the sea and, of course, drown. One way of looking at this is that the lemmings all die. A more enlightening view is that every lemming who dives into the ocean gets to retire in the same style as every other lemming who does the same.

The more appropriate manner is to choose a style that is compatible with your temperament as well as your investment objectives. The greatest style divide is probably not between small cap and large cap, but between value and growth. These two metrics form the basis of "style" for mutual funds. A group of fund evaluators, mainly pension plan consultants, classify funds as value or growth (or blend) and small, medium, or large cap. Small-cap stocks tend to have better growth prospects, while large caps have more liquidity and sustainability.

The difference between the GARP funds and the so-called growth funds is that GARP stands for *growth at a reasonable price,* while an aggressive growth investor would pursue growth at almost any price, making aggressive assumptions about the potential for growth to justify the high, and sometimes astronomical, prices paid. For the time being, at least, the GARP school of thought must be considered as being closer to "growth" or at least "blend" style than to a true Graham and Dodd style.

A word must be said about the so-called value funds. The kind of value that Graham and Dodd preached, and that is advocated in this book, is called *deep value.* This is in depressed, often cyclical issues in which earnings growth prospects are limited. In such a case, stocks are valued much as bonds might be, on their ability to sustain dividends and maintain their "principal," their asset value, through a wide variety of economic scenarios including downturns. The more typical value fund measures value by earnings, specifically the P/E ratio, rather than assets or dividends. In only comparing the P/E ratio to its growth rate, such a fund minimizes or ignores factors considered important here.

Probably only a handful of major value funds follow a true Graham and Dodd–type style. The following three characteristics will distinguish such a fund from others that call themselves value funds:

1. Graham and Dodd investors are unwilling to pay for growth, so with rare exceptions, their stocks will have growth prospects no better than average (high-single digits). Instead, they look to the dividend and asset values for compensation. High dividends, when combined with average growth prospects, provide high total returns and may also signal undervaluation. A Graham and Dodd–type fund will have a high dividend yield because such a fund relies on income as much as growth for its total return.
2. A Graham and Dodd–type fund will often have high turnover, because a large percentage of its holdings will be undervalued asset plays that are taken over, or that are sold when they go to a premium to book value, typically one to two years after purchase. In some cases, the fund may actively seek out such "risk arbitrage" situations; in others, the takeover process will follow as a natural consequence of bargain purchases.
3. P/E ratios in a Graham and Dodd fund aren't necessarily low because the stocks they would favor are often those that are out of favor because of poor earnings prospects. The price will be low relative to other measures such as book value and sales, to provide room on the upside if there is a turnaround.

Ralph Wanger, manager of the Acorn Fund (which uses the GARP style), compared the imperatives of investment managers to those of zebras. "If you are a zebra and you live in a herd, the key decision you have to make is where to stand in relation to the rest of the herd. The aggressive zebras, on the outside of the herd, eat much better. On the other hand, or other hoof, there comes a time when lions approach. The outside zebras end up as lion lunch . . . An institution such as a bank trust department cannot be an Outside Zebra."[3]

Herein lies a paradox. Ordinarily, a conservative investment strategy would characterize such investors as inside zebras. But in one important sense, they were on the outside because they had only modest exposure to the technology sector that represented the "inside" in the late 1990s. Warren Buffett summed it up best. "Be fearful when others are greedy and be greedy when others are fearful." The late 1990s stock market ethos can be summed up primarily by greed, with the occasional hiccup in the fall of 1997 and 1998. Hence, Mr. Buffett was running scared during that time. If, a crash comes, however one should step up to the plate, using the methodologies outlined in this book, because there will be numerous, as opposed to scarce, candidates for this style of investing. In the 1930s, the then

State of the World ⟍ Strategy	Continued Boom	Crash
Aggressive Growth	**Great Wealth**	Poverty
Conservative Value	Modest Wealth	**Relative Wealth**

FIGURE 11.1   Consequences of Various Strategies.

conventional wisdom was that "bonds are the only safe investment." The time to say that was before, not after, the crash, which is what this book has tried to do. Such a posture, outlined in Chapter 17, with heavy concentrations in cash and dividend-producing issues like real estate investment trusts (REITs), was bondlike in 1999, in anticipation of just such a crash. After the crash, the author plans to use a relatively aggressive strategy that may run counter to the newly established wisdom.

The technology boom had two effects: It raised overall market returns, but paradoxically, it lowered the prices of nontech stocks, which fell because they had to meet higher prospective return hurdles posed by the tech stocks. The following represents an illustration of how a conservative value investor would select mutual funds. (Aggressive growth investors, of course, would take the opposite view at every turn.) This dilemma can be summed up in a two-by-two decision matrix as shown in Figure 11.1. There are two states of the world, continued boom and crash, and two possible investment strategies: aggressive and conservative. There are four possible outcomes, depending on the interaction between strategy and state of the world. The "correct" decisions relative to the state of the world are indicated in boldface.

If you followed the aggressive growth strategy, you could become "seriously" rich, a millionaire or better, over a period of a few years, with starting capital in perhaps the tens of thousands of dollars, provided that the boom continued. But you could lose most of your investment in the event of a crash and end up poor if this investment strategy had involved most of your capital.

If you followed a conservative strategy such as that outlined in this book, you could still aspire to modest wealth, over several years, turning a starting capital of tens of thousands into hundreds of thousands, or starting capital of hundreds of thousands into the low millions. This strategy would, of course, work somewhat better in a boom, but would provide very substantial protection in the event of a crash. On a relative basis, this strategy would actually work better in a crash, because it would enable you to compare more favorably to people who had been impoverished using the aggressive growth strategy.

The lightfaced outcomes demonstrate the results of wrong guesses. But note an important difference between the two. The conservative value strategy still gives "modest wealth" for an incorrect choice, a good consolation prize. The aggressive growth strategy, however, leads to poverty—a heavy penalty for a misguess.

For many people, the conservative strategy would be preferable if the "crash" scenario had as much as a 30 percent chance, even with the probabilities favoring the continued boom. But for reasons outlined in the last section of the book, we believed that the chances of a crash were considerably more than 30 percent—at least 50–50, and perhaps even a probability by the early 2000s. Under these circumstances, only the most daring or desperate investors should opt for the aggressive growth strategy.

The distinction between large and small caps is largely, but not wholly, artificial. At the turn of the twenty-first century, small caps represented value and large caps represented growth. But in the mid-1970s, the opposite was true. Both small and large caps were hammered in 1973–1974, but the earnings and stock prices of small caps bounced back faster from the oil shock of 1973. On the whole, the value side of the investment paradigm, which now calls for investing in small-cap value stocks, probably ahead of their period of relative outperformance, is more attractive.

This book sets forth a theory as to when and why small and large caps outperform. It is based on the generations model in Chapter 20. The theory is that large caps perform better when "strong" generations, such as the World War II and Baby Boom generations, consolidate the economy as midlife managers. The weaker intervening generations, the Silent generation and Generation X, distrust size, at least for its own sake, and disperse the economy when they are in their forties and fifties. Thus, large caps were favored in the 1960s and 1990s; small caps were favored in the 1970s and probably will be favored in the decade of the 2000s, particularly the second half.

ARGUMENTS AGAINST USING MUTUAL FUNDS

This chapter has made the standard arguments in favor of owning mutual funds. So what are the disadvantages of using mutual funds, when the alternatives are to hire an investment advisor, or to manage a portfolio on one's own?

First, the selection of mutual funds is almost an art within itself. An investor who lacks the capability to buy individual stocks may also feel a lack of capability in choosing a mutual fund. In such a case, you may be best off by hiring an advisor or a consultant.

Second, one won't get the personalized service with a mutual fund that one will with an advisor. Ideally, the advisor should know all about the investor's needs and personal circumstances and tailor the portfolio accordingly. In the old days, an investment advisor was second only to the family doctor in what he knew about the investor's personal affairs. And this is not surprising because, in fact, the advisor is the family's "financial doctor."

Third, mutual funds will often engage in investments such as emerging markets securities or junk paper that are wildly unsuitable for a particular investor. But an advisor can be prevented from doing these things. Also, an advisor is not normally under pressure to keep up with the latest trend nor should he or she be put under such pressure. To do so would be to sacrifice one of the major advantages of having an independent advisor.

Fourth, some mutual funds are now more popular than stocks, and they can be even harder to buy and sell. In fact, some fund families severely restrict purchases and sales, because they force cash inflows and outflows that may be inconvenient for the fund manager. If many investors wanted to buy or sell at the same time, there may also be delays and tie-ups on the phone. The same can be true of a broker, but then there is likely to be a problem with the whole market (as was the case on Black Monday), rather than with a particular fund. In any event, mutual funds cannot be "day traded" the way stocks can, because investments are made as of the closing value at the end of a day.

All but the busiest investors should manage at least a portion of their own portfolio, in order to get a taste of the business of investment, thereby learning what a mutual fund manager or an advisor can or cannot do. Some investors will find that they will do better on their own than in a mutual fund. In a few cases, they might consider going into the investment business for themselves.

CHAPTER 12

A Graham and Dodd Approach
to International Investing

This chapter is about investing in international stocks using the Graham and Dodd approach. There are some obvious differences between valuation methods in different countries. But the Graham and Dodd method can be used abroad, with modifications, as well as at home.

Immediately after World War II, the United States had roughly one half of the world's gross national product (GNP). Now, the total is under one third and declining, as much of the rest of the world grows at a faster rate. The United States, with fewer than 300 million people, has less than 5 percent of the world's population. Not all of the other five billion-plus people in the world practice capitalism or engage in economic activities that are reflected in the stock markets. The 300-odd million people in western Europe and the 100 million people in Japan form the exception, not the rule. Stock markets in western Europe and Japan together have a little over one third of the world's market capitalization, with the United States representing most of the remainder. But there are emerging parts of the world, such as the Pacific Rim and Latin America, that are likely to repeat the process of industrialization followed by capitalization that occurred in developed markets. This provides investment opportunities. All other things being equal, higher country growth rates will lead to faster growth rates of individual companies and stocks representing a cross-section of these markets.

ADVANTAGES OF INTERNATIONAL INVESTING

What are the benefits of international investing? First, there are the benefits of diversification. Simply put, you can benefit from the wider selection of stocks offered abroad, including an expanded number of potential Graham and Dodd selections. Many foreign companies have lower price–earnings (P/E) or price–book (P/B) or price–cash flow (P/C) ratios than comparable U.S. firms. Even if valuations are comparable, there will sometimes be higher-quality foreign firms with a higher growth rate than the U.S. firms in the same industry.

174

Second, there is a wider range of industries in which Graham and Dodd–type investments are most often found. Industries that produce basic materials such as cement and steel are mature and cyclical in the United States. This is much less the case in many countries abroad. Very few investors made money in American cement stocks in the past decade, and only a few brave investors would have tried the steel companies. By contrast, you could have earned average annual returns of over 20 percent in Latin American stocks such as Cemex (Cementos Mexico), or even Puerto Rico Cement, which, although technically American, was something of an emerging markets play until its acquisition by Cemex in 2002.

A third possible reason to invest abroad is to capture the gains that occur when a country moves into a higher level of development more nearly like that of neighboring countries. This phenomenon is known as *convergence*. It is the articulated rationale for investing in emerging markets. But the most important beneficiaries of the convergence phenomenon in the late 1990s were the moderately developed countries in Europe, such as Spain, Portugal, and Ireland. This was even true of Italy to a certain extent.

A final reason for investing abroad is to hedge against a weak home currency, which, for an American investor, would mean the U.S. dollar. The greenback was weak for most of the period between the early 1970s and the early 1990s (apart from a period of strength in the mid-1980s on the back of the Reagan economic boom), because of the deficit financing of the Vietnam War, and has become weak again in the early 2000s. If earnings are growing, say, 10 percent in euros for a European company, and the euro is rising 5 percent against the dollar, then the company's earnings are growing 15 percent in dollar terms.

DISADVANTAGES OF INTERNATIONAL INVESTING

There are some disadvantages to investing abroad. For instance, it is harder to get information about foreign companies than it is for U.S. firms. But this is where the Graham and Dodd methodology confers an advantage. With its emphasis on assets and the balance sheet, it was designed for a more primitive disclosure culture. And investors in the home country are laboring under many of the same handicaps that Americans face. This creates inefficiencies in the market that will reward analysis. Another way to put it is that mature markets have been more efficiently priced. There are armies of analysts, both domestic and foreign, covering major U.S. stocks, so "everything" that one should know about the more visible companies, at least, is known. This is generally not the case in most foreign countries, so it is often easier to find suitable value investments abroad than in the United States.

There is usually a difference between U.S. generally accepted accounting principles (GAAP) and foreign GAAP. For foreign companies with U.S. listings, the differences in the computation of earnings and book value are listed in the back of the financial statements. Thus, the American investor gets to see earnings and assets with his own eyes. Foreign companies have to report every half year, but most of them are now reporting on a quarterly basis. American Depositary Receipt (ADR) issuers generally have to meet Securities and Exchange Commission (SEC) standards regarding segment and geographical reporting and footnote disclosures.

The differences often aren't material, but sometimes they are. Most of the time, the differences deal with depreciation and goodwill amortization or deferred taxes. Some countries allow more contingency reserving than the United States, which tends to lower reported earnings but makes them more stable. Note, however, that the local people will be focusing more on their home country accounting, and in cases in which the local investor is dominant, these may be the more relevant numbers.

Another problem arises with foreign exchange when the U.S. dollar is strong, as it was around the turn of the century, as well as in the late 1980s. In 2000 and 2001, when the greenback was particularly strong, the stock markets of a number of countries fell in line with the U.S. averages in local currency terms, but fell several percentage points more than the Standard & Poor's (S&P) 500 after translating these moves into dollars. The issue of currency fluctuations is so important that it will be dealt with in a separate section.

One word of warning: As markets become globalized, international stocks have been trading more in line with U.S. stocks in terms of valuation. This is true if, as is more and more the case, the same pools of money are being shifted out of U.S. stocks and into international stocks, or vice versa. Major brokerage houses are beginning to organize their research and trading globally by industry, rather than by country. Stocks of companies producing commodities such as oil, which is denominated in dollars, have long been moving more or less in tandem around the world. But as this trend continues, stocks in other industries will move more nearly alike.

THE PROBLEM OF CURRENCY FLUCTUATIONS

One reason that U.S. investors distrust international stocks is currency fluctuations. This is less worrisome than is generally perceived. For one thing, most major U.S. stocks have significant foreign operations, so investors in those stocks are already implicitly taking on foreign currency risk. Likewise, their foreign counterparts often have significant U.S. operations. A U.S. drug company might have 60 to 70 percent of its sales stateside and

TABLE 12.1 Effects of Currency Fluctuations on Net Income

	Local Currency		U.S. Dollars	
Account	Year 1	Year 2	Year 1	Year 2
Sales	100	200	100/5 = 20	200/10 = 20
Cost of Sales	50	50	50/5 = 10	50/10 = 5
Depreciation	10	10	10/5 = 2	10/10 = 1
Interest	10	10	10/5 = 2	10/10 = 1
Pretax Income	30	130	30/5 = 6	130/10 = 13
Tax (50%)	15	65	15/5 = 3	65/10 = 6.5
Net Income	15	65	15/5 = 3	65/10 = 6.5

30 to 40 percent foreign exposure, while a British firm, Glaxo SmithKline, will have 30 to 40 percent U.S. sales with the balance overseas. Thus, the difference in U.S. or foreign exposure would be only about 30 percent between the U.S. and foreign company, not 90 to 100 percent.

Indeed, U.S. multinationals also incur currency risk when they invest abroad. Coca-Cola, for instance, does almost two thirds of its business outside the United States. These sales will be exposed to the fluctuations of local currencies against the U.S. dollar. The good feature about Coke's case is that sales are so broadly diversified that no one currency or group of currencies will have an isolated impact on the bottom line. The foreign exposure would be hurtful only if nearly all currencies were falling against the U.S. dollar.

A weak currency may actually have benefits on the operating side. This is particularly true if a company with a weak home currency sells a product such as oil or metals, which is denominated in U.S. dollars. Consider the example shown in Table 12.1, assuming that in year one, there are 5 currency units to the U.S. dollar, and in year 2, there are 10 currency units to the U.S. dollar. Note that the company actually does better in U.S. dollar terms when its home currency is weak than when it is strong. That is because its revenues are fixed in U.S. dollars (doubling in local currency) whereas its costs are in home currency.

Note that sales remained constant in dollar terms (doubling in local currency terms), but that dollar costs declined in year 2 because of the weakness of the local currency.

THE USE OF AMERICAN DEPOSITARY RECEIPTS IN INTERNATIONAL INVESTING

American investors can buy foreign stocks mainly in the form of ADRs. A not-insignificant proportion of foreign stocks are available in the U.S. market in this form. They usually include the largest, most visible, companies.

Many of them are mature concerns that make good Graham and Dodd–type investments. Occasionally, a retail broker may be able to fill an order for a stock on the more common exchanges like London or Tokyo. It is another thing to buy stock on the Santiago, Chile exchange. So the discussion will focus mainly on ADRs.

In many cases, countries will not allow the shares of their companies to leave their country. So these shares will be held through a foreign depositary in the home country, which may be the local branch of an American bank. The bank will then issue ADRs equivalent to its actual holdings. The three largest banks in the business are the Bank of New York, Citigroup, and J.P. Morgan Chase.

ADRs come in several varieties. First of all, there are unsponsored ADRs. These are created by banks for trading by large institutional investors without the sponsorship of the company. Unsponsored ADRs are beginning to go out of fashion because they are so cumbersome to deal with, even for institutions.

A second group of ADRs are known as sponsored ADRs. In such cases, the company will bear the record-keeping, transfer, and other costs. The lowest-level ADRs, level 1, aren't listed on the U.S. stock exchanges. Instead, they are traded over the counter in the "pink sheets." Level 2 ADRs, which are accompanied by greater disclosure, are eligible for listing stateside, and level 3 ADRs are eligible for both listing and new public offerings in the United States because the disclosure requirements are even more stringent, and essentially equivalent to those in force for American companies. ADRs are most commonly created when a foreign company (or a selling shareholder such as the government of the country) wants to do an offering while gaining access to the U.S. market. Most of the ADRs are listed on the New York Stock Exchange, and others on the American Exchange or NASDAQ system. Their prices are quoted in U.S. dollars, but they reflect quotes in their home country, in local currency, adjusted by the exchange rate between the home currency and the U.S. dollar. Often, the U.S. dollar value of an ADR will differ slightly, say 1 to 2 percent, from the dollar equivalent value in its home market, but these differences are temporary. On the rare occasions that the difference is significantly more, it will be arbitraged away.

Other variations on ADRs are available only to large institutions because of their insufficient disclosure and/or liquidity. There are the ones that come under SEC Rule 144A regarding private placements. These are traded over the electronic portal system. Global Depositary Receipts (GDRs) allow a company to issue shares simultaneously in several parts of the world. They may qualify under Rule 144 in the United States, and Rule S1 in Europe. European Depositary Receipts must meet European disclosure requirements.

ADRs offer many of the conveniences of the regular American stocks. Brokerage fees and settlement rules are similar to those regarding ordinary U.S. stocks, not the underlying foreign shares, which are already in the custody of a bank. Likewise, transfer arrangements and dividend payments (in U.S. dollars at the prevailing exchange rate) are taken care of by the bank. But the value of the dividend fluctuates with the exchange rate between the date of declaration in the foreign currency and the date of payment, unless they are simultaneously declared in U.S. dollars. (British Petroleum [BP], for one, accommodates its U.S. investors in this way.)

ADRs also offer a means of bringing the issues' price ranges into levels that are comfortable for the average U.S. investor. Share prices are different in most foreign countries than in the United States. Stateside, they are measured in the tens of dollars. In Asia, they are often measured in local equivalents of single dollars. In Europe, where liquidity is low, and only a small proportion of the population trades, they are measured in the equivalent of hundreds of dollars. Thus, an ADR may represent 10 shares of an Asian issue. Likewise, it may take 5 or 10 ADRs to equal one share of many European stocks.

EUROPEAN COMPANIES

Europe is slowly but surely opening up to American investors. A few companies listed ADRs existed before 1990, a large number were listed in the 1990s, and more will be listed in the 2000s. This will hold true as more companies raise capital (and make acquisitions) across borders. Although European companies have traditionally been insular, the European Monetary Union is forcing companies to think on a regional, and in some cases, global, basis.

The United Kingdom has the largest number of listed American Depositary Receipts of any country. That's largely because the language is the same, and the accounting is in most respects similar to ours. The business ethos is a cross between the traditional European and the American philosophies.

Most of Britain's energy companies are listed on the U.S. stock exchanges. These include BP, Shell (the sister company of Royal Dutch), and BG (formerly British Gas). In the telecom industry, the BT Group (formerly British Telecom) is the cheapest, relative to assets. Vodafone is neither the cheapest nor the best run. Cable and Wireless lends itself well to the sum of the parts analysis because it has two subsidiaries, CWP (formerly Mercury) and the former Hong Kong Telecom.

Food and drug companies include Diageo and Cadbury Schweppes, as well as Astra Zeneca and Glaxo SmithKline. Their stocks and ADRs generally sold outside of Graham and Dodd parameters for most of the

1990s. Imperial Chemicals better lives up to its name following the 1993 "demerger" (divestiture) of Zeneca Pharmaceuticals, and is also a better value play, but its weak balance sheet tends to put us off.

Utilities include Power Gen and National Power. These often fit our parameters but are mediocre investments nevertheless because of the severity of British regulators. The best Graham and Dodd investments are often the water utilities, but being local in nature, they have little incentive to list on the U.S. exchanges. Britain also has a number of bank ADRs, including HSBC and Barclays. But Lloyds Bank, arguably the best bank investment, is not listed in ADR form, nor is Prudential PLC, the insurance company.

The best Graham and Dodd investments available to U.S. investors are often found in heavy manufacturing. These include conglomerates such as Hanson and Tomkins. The Corus Group (formerly British Steel), is perhaps the quintessential Graham and Dodd investment in Britain from time to time. One might also consider Anglo American, or RTZ, the global mining companies.

In services, the Rank Organization has a major "hidden" asset in its joint venture with Xerox. WPP, the advertising agency, met Graham and Dodd parameters during its turnaround days in the early 1990s, although it moved out of this environment in the late 1990s.

A number of France's most prominent companies are listed in ADR form. These include Total, the oil and gas company. This company and Elf Acquitaine, the former state-owned company, listed ADRs in the early 1990s, but Total acquired Elf after first merging with PetroFina. Serge Tchuruk, the former chairman of Total, went to Alcatel (formerly Alcatel Alsthom), where he spearheaded a turnaround that lifted its price out of Graham and Dodd territory. This was a major rescue, because the previous chairman had plunged the company into legal difficulties with the French government. In technology, ST Microelectronics stands out.

Aventis (formerly Rhone Poulenc), the chemical company, sold around its book value for much of the mid-1990s. And book value understated asset value because of the company's majority holding of Rhone Poulenc Rorer, the American pharmaceutical company formed by the merger of Rorer with Rhone Poulenc's U.S. operations. In fact, in early 1996, the company sold for just the value of its interest in the U.S. drug subsidiary, meaning that an investor got a major chemical company for free. This was highlighted by the 1997 buyout of the minority interest of this subsidiary. Subsequently, the company divested many chemical businesses in order to focus on health care, following its merger with Germany's Hoechst. This is an example of monetizing and reinvesting assets to create shareholder value.

French financials are not generally represented among ADRs. The major exception is AXA, an insurance company formed by the merger of Axa and UAP in 1996. In the food and beverage area, Group Danone and

Louis Vuitton Moet Hennessey are expensive, reflecting the nature of this industry, especially the branded goods portion, worldwide. The lack of value also extended to France Telecom and Equant up to the turn of this century, but these became cheaper, if troubled, companies by 2002.

The Netherlands now has most of its major stocks listed in the United States. This market has been one of the best-performing markets in the past 20 years, because most of the stocks had Graham and Dodd–type valuations before they were listed and/or became popular with American investors. Royal Dutch Petroleum (and its British sister Shell) was arguably the cheapest major oil stock until the mid-1980s. Akzo, the predecessor to Akzo-Nobel, was a classic Graham and Dodd play in the early 1990s. Aegon, the insurance company skyrocketed out of Graham and Dodd territory during the mid-1990s. Ditto for the banks, ING and ABN-Amro. Unilever, the major food company, benefited from a major restructuring about that time. Philips Electronics has often remained a Graham and Dodd–type play, especially after adjusting for the value of its interests in other semiconductor companies. This was seldom the case for KPN, the phone company, or NT Post, the postal operation. Heineken, the brewer, is the largest Dutch company that does not have an ADR, but it is usually not a Graham and Dodd–type investment.

The Iberian countries had a number of Graham and Dodd–type investments until the European "convergence" phenomenon of 1996, which affected both bond and stock prices. In Spain, these included electric utility Endesa and Telefonica. Telefonica has interests in telephone companies in Argentina, Brazil, Chile, Peru, and Venezuela. There are also a number of banks, including Banco Bilbao-Vizcaya (BBV) and Santander, which later merged with Banco Central de Honduras (BCH) to form BSCH. Banking used to be a troubled sector in Spain in the early 1990s, because of high interest rates and market share wars, but both sets of pressures abated in the middle of the decade. Both BBV and BSCH have investments in the Americas. These issues became better Graham and Dodd investments after their prices were depressed in the early 2000s by their Latin American operations.

Repsol, the energy company, sometimes comes close to Graham and Dodd parameters, after adjusting its balance sheet for the value of its reserves and investments in Gas Natural and in Latin America. Predominantly a downstream-oriented company in Europe, it expanded its exploration and production operations through an acquisition of Argentina's Yacimientos Petroliferos del Fisco (YPF), which had earlier acquired America's Maxus Energy. The Argentine exposure caused Repsol shares to take a beating early in 2002.

Portugal's contributions included Portugal Telecom and Banco Comercial. They were pulled out of Graham and Dodd territory in the late 1990s by the convergence phenomenon previously discussed.

In Central Europe, Germany has a few companies listed in ADR form. Perhaps the most famous is Daimler Chrysler, which has an American as well as German component. It is arguably the classic Graham and Dodd investment. Other listed companies that meet this book's criteria from time to time are Eon (formerly Veba), the electric utility, and BASF, the chemical company. SGL Carbon was listed at Graham and Dodd valuations as a German share in 1995, but not when it listed as an American ADR two years later. Other listed German ADRs, which include SAP, the software company, and Fresenius, the medical products company, are often interesting to growth, but not value, investors.

Italy long featured a Graham and Dodd choice in Fiat, the auto company. The range and quality of choices expanded dramatically in 1995 with the ADR listing of ENI, the energy company, and Telecom Italy, the telephone company. Listings of INA, the insurance company, and San Paolo, the bank, followed. Other choices include Natuzzi Industries, Benetton, Fila Holdings, Gucci, and Luxotica in consumer goods.

In the Scandinavian countries, Sweden's Ericsson, the telecom company, was a Graham and Dodd investment as far back as 1987, but not since the early 1990s. Longer-lasting Graham and Dodd plays include heavy manufacturing companies such as Electrolux (white goods), Volvo (automobiles), and occasionally, Asea Brown Boveri (ABB), the engineering company. In Finland, Nokia, the telecom equipment company offers better growth, but Stora Enso, the forestry concern, is more of a classic value play. Norway features two energy companies, Norsk Hydro and Saga Petroleum, that are often good Graham and Dodd choices. The two listed Danish companies, Novo-Nordisk and TeleDenmark have not been within Graham and Dodd parameters as of the mid-1990s, although they were earlier.

ASIAN COMPANIES

Oddly enough, Japan is a fairly good Graham and Dodd market. This is because interest rates have been very low, 1 to 2 percent, for some years. So rules comparing earnings and dividend yields relative to such low rates have substantial applicability, even though P/E ratios were very high until the early 2000s. Many Japanese companies are also cheap based on book value and cash flows. So it's possible that Japanese companies have been "hiding" earnings, despite the wretched economy that has prevailed since 1990. And it was a cardinal principle of "Japan Inc." to seek market share, even at the expense of near-term profits. Asset levels for Japanese companies were artificially high because of what were, in effect, government-encouraged (and -subsidized) bank loans. This social contract helped fuel a large expansion of assets, especially real estate, and paper wealth through the 1980s. But the bubble burst in 1990, because of the resulting domino effect of slower GDP growth. Dividend yields looked low by American standards until the recent fall of U.S. dividend yields to historically low levels. But Japanese dividend yields were actually higher in relation to Japanese interest rates than American dividend yields in relation to its interest rates, even before 1990.

Japan has the largest number of listed ADRs in Asia, followed by China. The two best-represented sectors are autos (Honda, Nissan, Toyota, and, formerly, Subaru), as well electronics companies such as Hitachi, Matsushita, Nintendo, TDK, and others, many of which are covered by Value Line. These companies, as well as Tokio Fire and Marine, and Ito Yokoda, the retailer, are often Graham and Dodd investments on a book-value basis. This is seldom true of Nippon Telephone and Telegraph (NTT), which was once the most expensive major company in the world, or Mizuho (a bank conglomerate). Among U.S. mutual funds, Martin Whitman's Third Avenue Value Fund invests heavily in Japan, perhaps too much so. He prefers financials, although he got burned by Long Term Credit Bank.

China, on the other hand, is an emerging market. Its ADRs are concentrated mainly in chemicals (Jilin Chemical and Shanghai Petrochemical) and utilities (China Telecom, Huaneng Power, and Shandong Power), which are often Graham and Dodd–type investments. China has also listed a large number of shares in Hong Kong, which are usually expensive compared to assets. In addition, minority shareholder protections are relatively weak, even by the low standards of East Asia.

South Korea has only a handful of ADRs, but these are large, prominent companies, which together with Samsung Electronics (listed in GDR, but not ADR, form) make up about half of the Korean market cap. These include Korean Electric, known as Kepco for short; Pohang Iron and Steel, or Posco; Kookmin Bank; Korea Telecom; and South Korean Mobile Telecom. The first two are covered by a Korean-American analyst at Value Line. They were all Graham and Dodd turnaround investments after the "Asian flu" crisis of late 1997.

Other Asian ADRs are few and far between. They include Indosat and Telekom Indonesia, Taiwan Semiconductor, Creative Technology of Singapore, and Philippine Long Distance.

AUSTRALIAN, NEW ZEALAND, AND SOUTH AFRICAN COMPANIES

Australia and New Zealand are linked to East Asia geographically, but not culturally. Along with South Africa, they are former British colonies, and retain the British tradition and practice. Nearly all of Australia's main sectors are represented by ADRs, as well as two of New Zealand's most important—telecommunications and natural resources. In the early 1990s, the three Australian bank stocks, ANZ, National Australia Bank, and Westpac, were the main Graham and Dodd investments, while Broken Hill Proprietary (BHP) and Rio Tinto (zinc) were richly priced. By the late 1990s, the reverse was true, with the three banks having shot through the roof, while Broken Hill Proprietary, the mining and energy company had hit on hard times. A cyclical analysis might be appropriate here, with the 1990s clearly having been the decade for the banks, and the 2000s could be the decade for BHP, Rio Tinto, and Western Mining. (BHP merged with South Africa's Billiton in 2001 to form BHP Billiton.)

In other major sectors, Rupert Murdoch's News Corporation, the media company, was a Graham and Dodd–type investment in the early 1990s when it went to the brink of, then stepped back from, bankruptcy. Nowadays, it is a representative, if debt-laden, member of an industry that may be overpriced worldwide. Coles Myers, the retailer, and Telstra, the telecom company, have only recently become suitable for our type of investment. There are no electric companies listed on either the Australian or U.S. stock exchanges. The leading New Zealand stock is New Zealand Telecom, which sometimes sells below modified investment value. More obvious Graham and Dodd choices usually include the forestry and building material spinoffs of the former Fletcher Challenge. The energy and paper subsidiaries have since been acquired.

South Africa is known primarily for its resource stocks, which make up over half of the index, and many of which have ADRs. Names here include Anglo American PLC, Anglo American Platinum, Gold Fields, and Sasol. The companies had, however, earlier benefitted from the low-cost labor that was made available by the apartheid system, and will tend to be less profitable now that the system has been abolished. "Black empowerment" initiatives forcing resource companies to give contracts to less efficient black-owned firms might depress earnings further. There are a number of fine companies outside the mining industry that are listed on the London, but unfortunately not the U.S., exchanges.

LATIN AMERICAN COMPANIES

Latin America is probably the best Graham and Dodd region for the American investor. This is true for several reasons. First, this region has the most ADRs relative to its economic importance. Second, it is a value market, unlike Asia, which is a more of growth market. The third has to do with its geographical and cultural proximity to the United States. Latin American companies are more inclined to align their accounting—and in many cases, disclosure—practices with those common in the United States than are companies in most European or Asian countries other than England.

The five largest countries have New York Stock Exchange–listed telecommunications companies. The first to list was Telefonos of Chile, in 1990, followed by Telefonos de Mexico, otherwise known by its abbreviation, Telmex. The two Argentinian companies, Telefonica of Argentina (which serves the southern portion of the country), and Telecom of Argentina (which serves the north), listed in 1994, although the minority interest in Telefonica has since been acquired by the Spanish parent of the same name. Brazil's Telebras was the last of the larger companies to list, in 1995, although it made up for it by doing a "Baby Bell"–type spin off of its 11 regional companies in 1998.Telecom of Venezuela is also listed on the New York Stock Exchange.

The second most represented industry consists of companies in the beverage area. Beer companies include AmBev of Brazil, and Cervezas of Chile. Coke bottlers include Andina of Chile, and Coke Femsa of Mexico, which acquired Panamerican Beverages, a Panamanian listed company with interests in Mexico, Brazil, Colombia, and Venezuela. Chile also has a listed wine company, Vino de Concha y Toro. Elsewhere in consumer goods, retailers with listed ADRs include Pao de Acucar of Brazil, and Elektra and Comerci of Mexico.

Banks are fairly well represented as ADRs. These include Santiago of Chile and Banco Bradesco, Banco Itau, and Unibanco of Brazil. From the smaller countries, there are two Colombian banks, Banco de Colombia and Banco Ganadero; Credicorp of Peru; and the Panamanian bank, Bladex, which provides trade financing for much of Latin America. Most of these often sell at Graham and Dodd–type valuations, and are reasonably good plays on general economic growth prospects of their respective countries, although they are also more sensitive to local economic developments than would generally be the case for banks in the United States.

In the energy area, Chile has a number of large listed utilities. These include Endesa (of Chile), and Enersis, a holding company. Brazil has listed two small regional companies, Cemig and Copel. Argentina's electric utilities, being much smaller than Chile's, are listed only locally, although two gas distribution companies, Metrogas and Transportadora are listed on the New York Stock Exchange. Mexico's electric company is entirely state-owned and therefore not listed even in its home country. The same is true of the oil companies of both Mexico and Venezuela. Petrobras of Brazil listed on the New York Stock Exchange in 2000.

In the natural resources area, Cemex, the largest Mexican cement company (and the third largest in the world) has an ADR. Other obvious Graham and Dodd candidates include Peru's mining companies, Buenaventura and Southern Peru Copper. CSN of Brazil was formerly the national steel company.

The trend seems to be toward regional markets and customs unions. In 1993, Canada, the United States, and Mexico signed a North American Free Trade Agreement (NAFTA) that covers the Americas north of Central America. This customs union, for this is all it is just now, seems to be working fairly harmoniously. Chile, at the southern end of South America, is trying to enter this union through the "back door," through an economic treaty with Mexico. During the early twenty-first century, America's President George W. Bush began negotiations potentially leading to the creation of an Americas free trade area with most of the Latin American countries. This would likely lead to a convergence of bond yields and stock market ratios of bonds and stocks in those countries toward U.S. levels, a fact that Mexico experienced, not immediately (since a lot of economic progress was undone by the 1994 economic collapse), but around the turn of the century.

In 1999, a group of 11 European countries began a monetary union by establishing a common currency, the euro, between them. These included the original six Common Market countries, Belgium, France, Germany, Italy, Luxembourg, and the Netherlands, plus Austria, Finland, Ireland, Portugal, and Spain. Several eastern European countries such as Greece, the Czech Republic, Hungary, Poland, and others have since joined or are slated to join them. Notably absent from the grouping are Britain, Switzerland, and Sweden, although Britain and Sweden are part of the enlarged common market. Despite the single currency, these countries may actually be less similar in monetary policy and other economic variables than the North American participants. The European Union has no counterpart to the leadership of the United States and is led instead by a group of equals, notably France and Germany.

CHAPTER 13

A Graham and Dodd View
of Real Estate

Real estate is a financial instrument that combines the more attractive fixed income and relative safety features of bonds with the upside potential of stocks. In fact, at the risk of discouraging potential investors in stocks and bonds, this chapter will discuss the advantages of real estate, presenting a Graham and Dodd view of this type of investing. Toward the end of the chapter, there will be a discussion of how to minimize the disadvantages of owning physical real estate by using stock- and bondlike instruments that are a play on real estate.

Real estate is safer than stocks for the same dollar amount of investment, which is why lenders will allow a greater margin for borrowing, generally 80 percent or more on mortgages, versus 50 percent on stocks. The appreciation potential of real estate has historically been about one percentage point a year below that of stocks. Their cash yields are comparable to those of corporate bonds, typically 7 to 9 percent per year, and better than the dividend yields on most stocks most of the time, apart from exceptional years like those around 1932 and 1980. (The competitiveness of stock yields with real estate yields in those years should have been a signal to buy stocks.) So the total return potential of real estate, capital gains plus income, is actually about 2 to 3 percent a year higher than that of stocks. Such a purchase is actually similar to that of a value stock, for a combination of modest capital gains and income. (This income is explicit, if you are renting out your building; implicit if you are living in it yourself to save rent elsewhere.) Because of the leveraging potential resulting from greater safety and higher income, Andrew Carnegie and others have noted that the fastest route to wealth has been buying and owning real estate.

The relative stability feature of real estate means that you can't make quite as large or fast killings on invested capital as you would when stocks go wild. (You can, however, produce similar swings on equity capital by leveraging your real estate to the hilt.) A common objection to real estate is that it is less interesting than stocks because you don't see quotes every day as you would with stocks.

Even so, many people are intimidated by real estate, and rightly so. The absolute size of the investments are generally larger than in the case of stocks. In many cases, a house or other pieces of real estate form a large part of a person's net worth. It's not possible to buy $1,000 of real estate as it is in the case of stocks. Even if the actual cash outlay is small, the amount of investment controlled is typically in the tens or hundreds of thousands of dollars. In fact, it is the leverage feature, rather than the underlying security, that makes real estate a somewhat risky investment. For instance, if you bought a $100,000 home for all cash, and it went down $30,000 in value, you would have a 30 percent loss. This is painful, but that's the likely extent of your downside, whereas you can lose your whole investment in the wrong stock. If you bought the same house on so-called conventional terms, with $20,000 down and $80,000 in debt, and it went down 30 percent in value, your equity would be wiped out, and in addition, the value of the house would be $10,000 less than the amount of the mortgage. (In fact, the total losses on stocks usually occur in businesses that use too much debt, only to find that the amount of outstanding borrowings were greater than the value of the business.)

ADVANTAGES OF INVESTING IN REAL ESTATE

One of the advantages of real estate is that it can be financed much more easily than stocks. In fact, most real estate transactions are completed at least in part with borrowed money. The basic financing instrument is called a *purchase-money mortgage,* which is obtainable from most banks or savings and loans. Mortgages can come in terms of 5, 10, 15, or 30 years, with the last being the most common. If the interest rate on the mortgage will not change over the term, it is called a *fixed-rate mortgage.* If the rate does change with interest rates in general, it is a *floating,* or *variable-rate mortgage.* In this case, the rate is adjusted every year, after an initial period of three or five years when the rate is frozen. There is, however, usually a "cap" over the life of the mortgage above which a borrower cannot be charged. Adjustable-rate mortgages were popular in the 1980s and early 1990s during a period of high and wildly fluctuating interest rates; fixed-rate mortgages tend to be more popular in times of lower rates.

Most mortgages are self-liquidating; that is, there are monthly payments that cover both interest and a reduction of principal so the mortgage is paid off over a period of time, typically 30 years. A less common type of mortgage is a balloon mortgage, wherein only interest is paid until the maturity date, with the principal due at that time. This kind of a mortgage is like a typical corporate bond; in effect, the home owner becomes a seller of a bond (to the lender) rather than a buyer. A reverse mortgage is one in which the monthly payments are less than the interest, initially, so the principal builds up, at least in the early years. One form of a reverse mortgage is one in which older people, who own their home free and clear, "mortgage" their home to a lender and receive monthly payments, based on their actuarial life expectancy, and surrender their home upon their death.

The mortgage payment is set half a percentage point to a whole point above your interest payment to provide for principal reduction, depending on the maturity. Thus, in the early years, you are paying mostly interest and get a tax deduction. But as the principal is dented, the compounding effect works in reverse, so that each successive payment represents a greater proportion of the principal, and less of interest.

If anything, it may be too easy to get home equity financing. If you own a house, you can get essentially a line of credit that allows you to mortgage your house to the tune of up to 90 percent. Many home owners did so in the late 1990s and early 2000s, for everyday consumption. Such home equity financing probably contributed significantly to the economic boom around the turn of this century, and left the country vulnerable to a subsequent crash. In 1950, when the mortgage boom had gotten under way, the value of all mortgages to all homes was only about 20 percent; by 2000, it was more like 45 percent. When you account for the fact that a fair number of people owned their homes free and clear, the mortgagors had well over half the value of the their homes in hock. The 30-year mortgage term seems to be overly long; a 30-year old home buyer will not fully repay a 30-year mortgage until age 60.

You can pay more than the monthly payment or even prepay your entire mortgage, thereby saving interest expenses over the life of the loan. This may be a wise option if you have few other investment opportunities earning more than the interest rate on the mortgage, as was the case around the turn of the century. But if you can rent out the building for more than enough to cover the mortgage payment, the longer the interest rate makes up part of the total payments, the larger the tax deduction. Instead of prepaying the mortgage, you can use the funds to buy another building and get even more tax deductions.

Because interest makes up the bulk of the payments in the early years (and indeed, over the life of most loans), the true cost of the real estate is not the purchase price per se, but the total payments (on a monthly or annual basis) counting both interest and principal amortization. A high purchase price need not be particularly burdensome if accompanied by a low interest rate. (The extreme case is a zero-rate mortgage, offered occasionally in lotteries by banks.) Because house payments are basically a function of monthly income, buyers have limited flexibility in how much debt they can service.

As rates go higher, prices paid by buyers must go down, just as in the case of a bond, to prevent total service costs from rising as fast as interest rates. So it often pays to buy in times of high interest rates, locking in a low price (and mortgage), and refinance later when rates come down. This is like a company issuing a high-coupon bond and then calling it when rates fall.

With leverage, you can earn 40 percent or more a year on real estate equity, about the same as a good LBO (leveraged buyout). In fact, real estate basically operates on the same principles as an LBO. As it were, the purchase of property with a mortgage is a highly leveraged transaction—one that is likely to succeed. It is one of the few such operations that an average person, in the role of a home owner, has the ability to run. Only a few people can get credit from banks to buy companies, but most people can get credit from lenders to buy homes.

A related reason why real estate will make you rich is that it is the best way to make use of other people's money. Donald Trump explained this best in *The Art of the Deal*. When he was trying to buy what later became the Hyatt Hotel from New York City, he obtained a tax abatement from the city for $100 million. He borrowed $100 million from the bank. Finally, he put down $10 million of his own money. That's 20-to-1 leverage, and this, at the bottom of the market. The profits from this deal alone were almost enough to make him a billionaire.[1]

The average home owner, however, is using 4-to-1 leverage, by putting 20 percent down and borrowing 80 percent. If the value of the house grows at the national average rate of 7 percent seen in the second half of the twentieth century, that works out to 35 percent on your 20 percent down payment. Throw in a little more for the reduction of your mortgage, and the total return is about 40 percent.

DISADVANTAGES OF INVESTING IN REAL ESTATE

Real estate does have some disadvantages relative to financial instruments, particularly stocks. First, real estate can't be traded nearly as easily as stocks or bonds. The transaction costs are much higher. While one share of IBM is exactly like any other share of IBM, no two houses are quite alike in value (even if they are built on the exact same design like homes in the so-called Leavittowns, because of differences in location). This may be a good thing, because people tend to hold onto their real estate for longer periods than their stocks. (Day trading hasn't yet hit the property market.)

Normally, you will also deal with one seller (or a few buyers if you are selling), which makes it harder to get a bargain than in the case of stocks, wherein you are dealing with many potential buyers and sellers, some of whom may be in the mood to give you a great deal (a bargain selling price or an aggressive purchase bid). In this regard, buying real estate is more nearly akin to buying a small business. You have to operate it or oversee a property manager who operates it for you. Of course, if you are simply buying your own home on a mortgage, your day-to-day management problems are not an issue, because you are your own tenant. If you finance your real estate with a combination of a down payment and a mortgage, you are using both debt and equity for your purchase.

Real estate also differs from stocks insofar as you are buying a whole "company," a home or a building, rather than fractional shares of a corporation. For this reason, you can improve it with active management because you, not some "other" corporate officers, are the manager. In fact, some developers make a practice of selling fix-ups, otherwise known as handyman's specials. The rule of thumb is that one dollar of repairs will increase the value of the house by two dollars. The danger is that you price the house out of the typical range for the neighborhood. That's why it is generally good to buy the worst house in a good neighborhood rather than the best house in a bad neighborhood. If you do fix up a house, the three places to concentrate on are the kitchen, closets, and bathrooms. A fix-up can also be profitable in another way, by allowing the property to command a higher rent. If the tenant has a short lease (one or two years), you can raise the rent at the end of the term. Of course, the tenant may move, but then you can get someone else at the higher market rent.[2]

FINANCING REAL ESTATE TRANSACTIONS

Financing is the key to most real estate transactions, so if your are buying real estate for your personal use, consumer credit considerations are of paramount importance. Unlike the standard stock leveraging scheme, where the debt is capped at 50 percent of the principal value of the transaction, the standard debt-to-asset ratio in real estate, or what the banks call the loan-to-value ratio, is 80 percent, with a 20 percent down payment. In such an instance, the lender looks as much to the credit of the borrower as to the value of the property, to be sure of repayment. Hence, your record of payment of other debts, or lack thereof, will be a critical factor in whether or not you get credit for a home purchase. Other factors that come into play are your overall financial picture. If you have large amounts of other assets such as stocks, that will help. Retirement assets such as individual retirement accounts (IRAs) cannot be used to secure loans, but even they may indirectly count in a borrower's favor as evidence of financial astuteness.

If you are buying property for rental as a business, then more businesslike considerations apply. The bank will still want to evaluate loan-to-value and income-to-debt service ratios, but may give lesser weight to your personal financial situation. Your past business experience, either in real estate or in other areas, will be taken into account, as will your business credit record. In unusual cases, the lender may require you to sign for loans personally, in which case your personal financial situation will matter.

There are several types of lenders. The most common one is a financial institution such as a bank or a savings and loan. A second is government agencies such as Veteran's Administration or the Federal Housing Authority. The third source of financing is owner financing.

A bank will look at the borrower's income, relative to the proposed debt service payments. The rule of thumb during the middle of the twentieth century was that a mortgage should not be more than two and a half times income. A more current rule of thumb was that mortgage payments should not be more than 28 percent of income, and total debt service payments should not be more than 34 percent of income. In recent years, the latter ratio has been relaxed to as much as 40 percent, a financial stretch. A borrower can even apply for a loan with no income verification. Typically, however, the bank requires a larger-than-usual down payment, 25 to 35 percent or more, and a clean credit record.

Somewhat different requirements apply for a government loan. For instance, the Veteran's Administration will make loans to war veterans at low interest rates. Other government agencies target other constituencies such as low-income housing. If you have a good record of running multifamily houses, you may qualify for government loans for the development and management of low-income units. In such cases, your ability to get the loan is contingent on your meeting the particular political requirements. Also, government loans are more likely to have onerous terms such as prepayment penalties.

A third source of financing, if you find the right seller and are persuasive enough, is owner financing. A mortgage is nothing more than an IOU in which the buyer agrees to pay a lender the value of the house over a period of time. It is really a way of borrowing money using the house as collateral. The borrower issues a mortgage, and is known as a mortgagor, while the lender is known as the mortgagee. In this particular instance, the seller is also the lender of last resort. Occasionally, there will be home advertisements in the newspaper that say OWC, or owner will carry.

The buying and borrowing transactions are handled simultaneously by a closer. She will take the down payment, typically in the form of a certified check from the buyer, and the check from the lender for the amount of the mortgage. She will then take title from the seller and re-register the property in the name of the buyer. Finally, she will hand over the monetary proceeds to the seller. If the parties want to make absolutely sure of the validity of the transaction, they will close in escrow. For most transactions, such a level of detail is not necessary.

It is said that the three basics of real estate are location, location, and location. That is true, all other things being equal. It means that you should not buy in a poor location. But it also does not mean that you should necessarily "pay up" for the best. Just as with stocks, you can make money from an expanding multiple, as well as from rising rents. Some of the best multiple plays are in neighborhoods where the economies and the quality of the tenants is improving. These situations are most often found in large metropolitan areas like New York City.

The best deals can be obtained from motivated sellers, sometimes known colloquially as "don't wanters." Such a person may have recently gotten divorced (or married, or had a new child born), and no longer finds the house the right size. Otherwise, they might have been transferred or lost a job and want a house with lower payments. The classic case is someone on the brink of foreclosure. Some investors check court records of divorces, arrearages, and upcoming bankruptcy proceedings to find such people. Others will go to banks or savings and loans and ask to see a listing of the "real estate owned" (i.e., repossessed real estate). In the latter case, the bank may be holding property that it is willing to sell for a discount, because a down payment and part of the mortgage have been paid, rather than holding and managing the real estate.

The real secret is to buy only in situations in which debt servicing costs are less than rental income minus expenses. Investors most often get into trouble in negative cash flow situations. A bankruptcy in real estate terms is known as a *foreclosure*. This is when the bank or other lender takes possession of the building because the buyer can't meet payments for a period of time. Foreclosures are the closest thing to personal bankruptcy, and stay on a person's credit record for seven years. (Bankruptcy stays for ten.) A more amicable situation is one in which the owner hands title (as symbolized by the keys and the deed) to the property to the lender in lieu of foreclosure, but this also involves a seven-year record. One or more missed payments followed by a catch-up will not lead to foreclosure, but this information does damage a credit record for some years.

To buy in a turnaround, the most promising situation is one in which the neighborhood and properties are already being improved by the current owners. It is good sign if developers are moving in. (But this is smart money.) The largest profits are made just before the developer stage, when individuals are fixing up the property. The quality of the people is even more important than the quality of the buildings. A blue-collar neighborhood with stable incomes and families may be a better bet than one inhabited by young singles who move out every few years. Seattle, Washington, was a case in point when the aerospace industry laid off people.

Before buying any property, you should get an engineering report, to make sure that the main systems work; electric, gas, and water. There should not be any structural problems with these, the foundation, or the beams. There may be plenty of minor faults such as chipped paint, but these should be reflected in a lower selling price. You should welcome such defects because you can increase your profits by fixing them.

The bank will do an appraisal, but it will be a cursory one. Instead of trying to pinpoint the exact value for your house, the bank appraiser will use the selling price as a starting point, and then test it for reasonableness. A good (well done, not necessarily favorable) appraisal will tell you what the market thinks of the house and why.

Cash flow on real estate is pretty much discretionary, at least after the minimum debt service charges are paid off. You can reinvest it in the property to maintain or improve it, you can prepay your mortgage, or you can spend it, either on more real estate, or on other items. A property can even be "milked" for short periods of time by deferring maintenance, but that is not a wise long-term strategy. Any way you slice it, cash flow is what ultimately drives the return on real estate. If cash flow after expenses and debt service is negative, the property is priced too high and likely to go down in value. For this reason, one should not think in terms of sacrificing cash flow for "appreciation."

Real estate should be bought for intrinsic (i.e., cash flow) rather than resale value. This is true of stocks, but particularly true of real estate due to its lower liquidity. The story has been told in numerous places, most notably by John Paul Getty, of Florida swamp land in the 1920s, in which "investors" bought and sold binders, or contracts, on real estate, with the intention of "flipping" them within a short time. When one skeptical investor asked the agent to show him the land, which was under a swamp, the agent explained, "This real estate is for trading, not for owning."[3] When the craze is over, some hapless investor will be left with a worthless piece of property. An only slightly less insidious form of "real estate" is one that is uneconomical, except for tax breaks. Then the investor is hostage to changes in the Tax Code.

TYPES OF REAL ESTATE PROPERTIES

Real estate is supposed to be put to its "highest and best use." It comes in several varieties: residential, commercial, and industrial. Among residential properties, there are houses, apartment buildings, and other special-use properties such as time shares. Most areas are zoned for residential, commercial, industrial, or other forms of real estate. But sometimes you can upgrade real estate by building a more remunerative type as permitted, or by going to city hall to get the land rezoned for a higher type of use. Thus, an investor might be able to upgrade residential property for commercial use. If it were mixed residential and commercial, one might be able to convert it to all of one or the other, depending on which was the more profitable use in this area. A person might buy a building and adjoining land, and either erect another building on the spare land or sell the land for a profit. Industrial properties are the trickiest to deal with because they tend to consist of "single-use" buildings such as a factory, which are hard to convert to other uses if the business closes down.

Real estate can be owned in several ways. The most common way is as a stand-alone building, usually a house. A unit in an apartment can also be owned as a condominium. In such a situation, people own individual apartments within the building, while the manager of the building owns the lobby and other areas open to all that are known as common areas. Apartment owners pay a fee to the manager for the use of these common areas known as maintenance. If the building goes bankrupt, the lender will foreclose on the ownership of the common area, but individual apartment owners will not be affected. A less safe arrangement is a cooperative, or co-op for short. Here, a corporation owns an apartment building, and individual apartment owners buy shares in the building corresponding to the value of their apartment. The apartment itself is occupied under a proprietary lease. Here, if the building is mortgaged and defaults, the lender to the building can foreclose on the whole corporation, which is to say that individual apartment owners lose their shares in their apartments, and thus, the ownership of the units themselves.

Co-ops are much harder to finance than condos. In the case of a condo, the owner has title to the unit, which the bank can repossess in the event of a default. The unit can then be liquidated fairly easily, as in the case of a detached building such as a house. In the case of a co-op, the bank can repossess only the shares corresponding to the apartment, not the unit itself. This is a much weaker form of security because the co-op typically has an underlying mortgage on the building, and thus, the mortgage on the individual apartment is effectively subordinate to the building mortgage. Hence, lenders in many parts of the country will not make co-op loans. The ones that do are mainly in large cities like New York City, where such arrangements are fairly common, and they typically require an assessment of the building's financial condition, as well as the individual's finances. Many co-ops require buyers to either pay cash or, if the purchase is financed, to use consumer, not mortgage, credit, wherein the interest is not deductible for tax purposes, in order to screen out buyers. A most illustrative case was in the novel *Bonfire of the Vanities,* in which the hero, Sherman McCoy, needed $420,000 of pretax income in order to pay annual interest of $252,000 on his $2.6 million apartment. He was "going broke on one million dollars a year."[4]

Another arrangement is known as a time share. This applies mainly to vacation and resort homes, where a number of people purchase and own the right to use the home exclusively for a specified period of time, usually measured in weeks or months. The more desirable time slots (the "season") cost more, because what you're really purchasing is not the home itself, but the right to use it at a particular time.

Commercial real estate commands higher rents per square foot than residential, but it is quite a bit riskier. Except for the highest and lowest-cost properties, residential real estate will seldom be priced out of the market, because there will be always be someone "trading up" or "trading down," even if the original target market disappears. However, commercial properties such as stores, factories, or motels are basically "single-use" holdings that will have a tough time finding alternative users to its originally intended market. A private investor would do well to gain some experience with residential at first, before moving up to commercial. Office buildings are the riskiest. They are overbuilt in many parts of the country, which means high vacancy rates and soft rents.

EVALUATION OF REAL ESTATE INVESTMENTS

Real estate can be valued in much the same way as stocks. The most common benchmark is a multiple of rent, in a manner similar to the P/E ratio. Another valuation method is comparable building analysis: How much have other buildings that are similar in type, location, and other features sold for? The final way is the replacement cost. If building costs are going up, replacement cost is a fairly good indicator.

Ratios of purchase price to various forms of real estate income can be computed in a manner similar to the way ratios on stocks are calculated. For instance, one real estate metric has the purchase price as a multiple of rent. This is similar to a price–cash flow ratio. Most real estate specialists compute net operating income as rent minus operating expenses. A price-to-net operating income ratio is similar to a P/E ratio. Interest is not subtracted to arrive at this figure, because this is a function of the financing decision (how large a mortgage to take out), rather than a function of the price of the house. Depreciation, which is a real expense in the case of machinery and equipment, is more a tax deduction than anything else in the case of real estate, which tends to appreciate over time.

Replacement cost is primarily an issue for developers. You would build if the market rents support a greater value for a property than the building cost. The risk is that you have large amounts of money tied up for a relatively long period of time with a relatively uncertain return. If you don't want to develop property yourself, but want to play the development game, you can always back a developer. A replacement cost above the market price doesn't do the investor any good. When the bottom falls out of the real estate market, as it does from time to time, plenty of houses sell for below the building cost, forcing builders to take a loss, and crimping new development, until supply and demand come back into balance.

Taking comparables is comparing a house to similar buildings in the neighborhood and asking what you would pay in relation to other similarly situated buildings. Perhaps one unit has about the same as another except that it has a few extras in terms of a front porch or swimming pool. Then it might sell for 10 percent more than the first unit. The converse of this rule is not to buy a house with a lot of attachments. If you want attachments, buy them yourself, so that you can pick and choose the ones you want and save money in the bargain. For a fancy house, it may be worthwhile to hire an architect to redesign the building. That's because you are selling taste and lifestyle, rather than just shelter.

A HISTORICAL VIEW OF U.S. REAL ESTATE

The national average price for single-family homes roughly doubled every 10 years between 1940 and 2000, appreciating at a rate of 6 to 7 percent a year. Thus, the trend-line values for a median single-family home that sold for about $3,000 in 1940 would have been $6,000 in 1950, $12,000 in 1960, $24,000 in 1970, $48,000 in 1980, $96,000 in 1990, and nearly $200,000 in 2000. Actual values for this hypothetical home have come close to this trend.

The main exception to the preceding rule was during the depressed 1930–1940 period. In real estate, the $3,000 median-priced single-family home in 1940 compares with a value of nearly $5,000 in 1930. Using a similar relationship to 1930–1950 over the next two decades would imply that the $190,000 single family home in 2000 would go for $120,000 in 2010 and $240,000 in 2020. Housing appreciation would, in effect, go in reverse for a decade, specifically, the coming decade. The potential for a 35 percent loss in real estate is disquieting to most people, but in a 1930s-type environment, this loss will be substantially less than the likely losses on stocks.

The seemingly uniform type of appreciation took place in very different ways over three distinct time frames. These were the war and postwar period between 1940 and 1970, the inflationary period between 1970 and the mid-1980s, and the excess period between the mid-1980s and 2000 and beyond.

From 1930 to 1940, house prices fell by over 35 percent in nominal terms, but only about two thirds of that in real terms because of the 10 to 15 percent deflation that took place during the same period. People who owned their houses free and clear took a loss, but one that was relatively modest compared to returns on other investments such as stocks. It was, however, buyers who took out mortgages who suffered tremendously because these debts had to be repaid in more expensive dollars—at a time when wages and employment were falling precipitously.

By 1940, housing was the cheapest that it had been for at least a generation. Rental values of houses were high relative to prices. From 1940 to 1950, house prices rose significantly in nominal terms, but these gains were partly canceled out by the inflation that took place as a result of World War II. Still, the fortunate investors who could borrow money to buy houses probably came out well ahead because inflation reduced the real value of their mortgages. What's more, the young adults of the so-called World War II or GI generation were favored with a student loan program—the GI Bill, and later Veteran's Administration (VA) and Federal Housing Authority (FHA) loans at low interest rates. Rent savings covered mortgage servicing payments by a wide margin, leading to a boom in home purchasing and house prices, and a baby boom, which in turn created greater demand for housing. Housing appreciated more in real terms over the three decades than at any other time in the twentieth century.

The next period, the latter part of the Vietnam War and the decade following it, was not nearly as favorable to real estate values. Nominal growth rates maintained their postwar pace, but these were worth much less in real terms because of the raging inflation. House prices essentially maintained, but did not increase, their value in real terms during the early 1970s, before edging ahead in the late 1970s, as house prices moved ahead of inflation, and the early 1980s as inflation came down. The advantage of housing over financial assets was that stocks did not even maintain their value in real terms. Moreover, investors who borrowed money to buy real estate came out ahead on every dollar they borrowed, because interest on fixed-rate loans did not keep up with rising inflation, and mortgages were repaid in cheaper dollars than those at which they were borrowed. Young Baby Boomers caught onto this fact, and used debt in a manner in which their Depression era–schooled parents were afraid to.

The last phase, from the mid-1980s to the early 2000s, was the least healthy, leading as it did to an overvaluation of real estate similar to that of the late 1920s. At the end of the period, mortgage payments in most parts of the country were greater than the fair rental value, the classic sign of overvaluation. Buyers had learned the lesson too well from the preceding two phases that property "always"goes up. The final period was also characterized by "innovations" in finance that vastly increased the availability of mortgage credit and the desire to use it. The first change came in the Tax Reform Act of 1986, which took away the tax deduction on consumer interest but allowed a deduction for home equity loans. The second change came in the rise of home equity lending itself. The third expressed itself in a long period, from 1982, of falling interest rates, together with a boom in home refinancing that conditioned home owners to being able to carry increasingly large amounts of debt for the same mortgage payment (or increasingly lower mortgage payments for the same level of debt). The last was the growth of loose lending practices such as loan-to-value ratios of greater than 100 percent and "subprime" lending to people with bad credit. At the end, Americans with zero or negative cash savings were counting on their house to provide for their retirement, just as investors in the late 1990s counted on the stock market to provide for their retirement. A house no longer was just a place to live, it was largely an investment vehicle.

In the late 1990s, as money became progressively easier, the value of real estate rose to astronomical levels. This is *not* a mere coincidence, but rather a cause-and-effect relationship. If money is readily available to you, it is probably equally available to others, unless you happen to have been born a Rockefeller or into some other family with large inherited wealth. Couple that with the fact that wages rose to record high level in real terms in the closing decade of the twentieth century, and you have the makings of a real estate boom. Hence, most deals were done at prices that reflected the easy availability of money in that period.

An example from Graham and Dodd's 1934 edition of *Security Analysis* will illustrate how wild the U.S. real estate market had gotten by the year 2000.[5] In the example, a $10,000 house in the 1920s rented for $1,200 a year, or 12 percent of the purchase price. Assuming that one-third of the rent was needed for maintenance, $800 a year would be left for debt service. Assuming a mortgage of 60 percent of the value, or $6,000 at 6 percent, the interest would be $360, and the total amortization would be about $400, which would be covered two times by the $800 a year net cash flow. In the early 2000s, the same house would be worth about $100,000. Mortgage rates were around 7 percent, which was considered low by the standards of the previous two decades, but actually higher than the 6 percent in Graham's example. Meanwhile, such a house typically generated a rental income of 6 to 8 percent of cost, or perhaps $7,000 a year. Subtracting a third of this for maintenance leaves less than $5,000 a year to service debt. The "conventional" mortgage ratio was 80 percent, not the 60 percent of Graham's time, so the interest payment of $5,600 on a 7 percent, $80,000 mortgage would have been more than the net cash flow of $4,700 (two thirds of $7,000). This cash flow would barely have been enough to service a 7 percent mortgage on $60,000, based on the 60 percent 1920s ratio (annual interest of $4,200, plus principal reduction). Given that mortgages in the early 2000s were in many cases closer to 100 percent, rather than 80 percent of value, the average investor would have been further in the hole than in the preceding example. It is also easy to see how the availability of credit pushed house prices up to such absurd levels in the first place.

ALTERNATIVE WAYS TO PARTICIPATE
IN REAL ESTATE INVESTMENT

Another way of buying real estate paper is through the purchase of mortgages, usually second mortgages, held by private investors (including sellers of property), rather than first mortgages, which are held by banks. Second mortgages are vulnerable because they are a form of subordinated debt; that is, they are junior to first mortgages. Most second mortgages are sold by so-called "don't wanters" at a discount, to yield 15 percent. In the more extreme examples, there will be little or no equity, so the value of the house must be sufficient to cover both the first and second mortgages, hopefully with something to spare. The analysis of second mortgages is similar to the analysis of distressed securities in Chapter 5. In these instances, the ultimate security is the right to foreclose on the property and resell it, if the second mortgage isn't paid. But if the value of the property is less than the face value of the first and second mortgages (the first mortgage has priority), one will earn less than the presumed rate of return.

Mortgage obligations are considered about as safe as corporate bonds. They do, however, have one important and common risk that figures only occasionally in corporate bonds: prepayment risk. In the 1960s, over the protests of bankers, Congress gave borrowers the right to prepay their mortgages, even before the home was sold. In essence, borrowers were given a "call" option on their mortgages like similar call options on corporate bonds. This option became even more valuable when advances in financial institutions made refinancing a popular practice starting in the 1980s. Many bonds were issued with this feature, but companies, which have other uses for their cash, are not quite as zealous about retiring their debt as consumers.

This prepayment risk probably came to a low early in the 2000s decade. The Fed lowered the key borrowing rate to 1.00 percent, the lowest in the history of this financial variable, and pushing other interest rates to multidecade lows. Interest rates to which mortgage rates were tied were not likely to go lower, and if anything, stood to go higher. Investors had refinanced and leveraged themselves as much as they possibly could and were not likely to continue prepaying.

There are instruments for publicly traded real estate investment trusts (REITs) that are very much like stocks. By charter, the companies must pay 95 percent or more of their income as dividends (or else lose their tax-advantaged status). So the securities have very high dividend yields, typically 6 to 9 percent. Throw in the historical average annual price appreciation of 5 to 7 percent, and the total return—dividends plus capital appreciation—beats the historical returns on stocks by 2 to 3 percent a year, just like the underlying properties do. The absence of "double taxation" is an important advantage and one reason for their superior total return. The gains could be higher than this if you buy during time periods like the year 2000 when the REITs were underpriced relative to historical norms. At that time, many REITs paid dividends as high as 8 to 10 percent, a bit above their historical norm. This compensated for the fact that prospective growth rates were below their historical 6 to 8 percent range, with 4 to 5 percent being the expectation.

REITs are generally classified by the type of building. For instance, there are office REITs, apartment REITs, health care REITs, and hotel REITs, among others. There are even companies outside the industry such as Plum Creek Timber that are organized as REITs for the tax advantages. Each type of REIT has exposures to the vicissitudes of its particular market segment, over and above the issues that confront REITs in general.

Portfolio Management

CHAPTER 14

The Question of Asset Allocation

Investors want to place their money in investments that best meet their short- and longer-term needs, after adjusting for risk. Usually, but not always, this involves maximizing potential return. Often, this means investing in stocks. But that is not to say that stocks are the investment of choice all of the time. And even when you want to own stocks, you should seldom put all of your holdings in equities, on the one hand, or fixed-income instruments such as bonds and cash, on the other hand. The selection of fixed-income instruments has already been treated in Part 2. The book's bias, nonetheless, is moderately in favor of stocks. This case will be presented after a more neutral view advocated by Graham and Dodd, as well as a rather opposite approach by Michael O'Higgins, one of the best modern proponents of income investing.

A PASSIVE ASSET ALLOCATION APPROACH PER GRAHAM AND DODD

Ben Graham advocated putting between 25 percent and 75 percent of one's capital in stocks at any given time, with the balance in fixed-income securities. A reasonable "naive" strategy would be a 50–50 mix of stocks and fixed-income instruments. But their basic advice to someone who wanted to time the market was that the investor deviate from the 50–50 mix by only 25, not 50, percentage points. They were less forthcoming about the allocation between short- and long-term securities.[1] But this is a problem that at least one modern practitioner, Michael O'Higgins, appears to have solved.

The allocation of stocks between the low and high end of the 25 to 75 percent range would be based on the market valuation techniques as discussed below. Specifically, you should be highly invested in stocks when there are a large number of Graham and Dodd–type investments, with dividend yields competitive with good-quality bonds (i.e., offering at least two thirds of the yield on a AAA bond. A list of stocks meeting, or coming close to meeting, such a test can be found in the weekly index of Value Line.)

When individual stocks fall out of the value range, however, they should be sold one by one, and not replaced with other equities if the general level market was high, as in most of the 1960s and most of the 1990s. This process would be continued until the proportion of equities reached the lower limit of 25 percent.

Graham recommended that investors who wanted to manage their own account select between 10 and 30 stocks. In practice, this should be weighted toward the lower number. A higher number gives better diversification, but it is hard for most individual investors to monitor a large number of positions. A portfolio of 10 to 15 stocks gives adequate diversification, providing they're not in the same industry or industry cluster (e.g., banks, insurance companies, and stock brokerage houses, with some interest rate–sensitive utilities thrown in), and what one loses from lesser diversification, one may well regain from better control.

ACTIVE ASSET ALLOCATION BY SECULAR TREND[2]

The case for stocks versus fixed-income instruments can be summed up as follows:

- Fixed-income instruments underperform stocks over a whole cycle of 30-odd years.
- Fixed-income instruments keep up with or outperform stocks for significant portions of the 30-odd-year cycle.
- The time periods when stocks produce most of their superior performance can be identified with a high degree of reliability.
- Therefore, appropriately blending fixed income with equities, with emphasis on equities at the appropriate times, can substantially reduce the risk to a portfolio without sacrificing returns.

This, in fact, was the experience of Michael O'Higgins, who set forth this view in his book *Beating the Dow with Bonds*. The study covered a period of 30 years (1969–1998), and demonstrated that over a period of more than 20 of those years, an investor would have done at least as well by owning the appropriate fixed-income instrument, bonds or cash, as by owning stocks. Moreover, there was a clear signal to indicate when an investor "had" to own stocks in order not to be left behind for the course of the whole three-decade cycle. (That signal was *not* present during the late 1990s bull market.)

When are stocks a clear favorite? O'Higgins compares the earnings yield, the inverse of the price–earnings (P/E) ratio on stocks, to the yield on bonds. In most of the 30 years between 1969 and 1998, the yield on bonds has been higher than the earnings yield, making bonds more attractive in

O'Higgins's view. Accordingly, he would have been invested in either 30-year zero-coupon bonds or 1-year Treasury bonds in most of those years. The exception to this rule was the stretch between 1974 and 1980, when stocks would have been the investment of choice because their earnings yield was higher than the bond yield. This was the period surrounding the 1974 bottoming of the stock market, and the subsequent recovery, and this would be a time to be maximally invested in stocks.

The logic is simple. Over a whole market cycle encompassing three or four decades, stocks will outperform bonds or cash. But they may underperform over a significant period of time that could last a decade or two. This is particularly true when the valuation of the market was way above its multidecade trend line, as it was in 1966, and was almost certainly the case around the turn of the twentieth and twenty-first centuries. A young person with three or four decades of working life, plus at least one or two decades of retirement life in prospect, can play the mathematical averages. But an old person, with only one or two (mostly retired) decades of life remaining has to guard against the possibility that the remaining life span will contain the disaster period.

If one were to complete a round trip, encompassing a market upslope followed by a downslope, one would have done fully as well between 1995 and 2002 in five-year bonds as in stocks, even giving effect to the stock outperformance that took place in the late 1990s, followed, of course, by their subsequent underperformance. For reasons to be discussed in the last section of the book, a two-decade top probably occurred around the turn of the century. The danger lies in the investor's expecting too much out of an already high market, and then failing to take profits when necessary.

O'Higgins's hypothetical asset allocation strategy could be summed up in three parts:

1. He would compare the earnings yield on, say, the Dow with the bond yield to determine the choice between stocks and fixed-income investments.
2. He would use a quasi–Graham and Dodd strategy to select stocks in the few years when stocks were indicated. Specifically, his strategy was a modified version of the Dogs of the Dow, taking the five lowest-priced "Dog" stocks, the ones easiest for the average investor to buy. The merits of this strategy are discussed in the following section.
3. He would use the price of gold to determine whether to be in long-term or short-term bonds in the (majority of) years when bonds were indicated as the investment of choice.

What is interesting is that through much of this period between 1969 and 1998, specifically the second half, zero-coupon bonds returned more

TABLE 14.1   Comparative Returns, 1969–1998

Year	Treasuries	Zeros	DJIA	BTDS
1969	6.58%	−17.34%	−11.60%	−10.09%
1970	6.52%	24.33%	8.76%	−4.72%
1971	4.39%	19.96%	9.79%	5.03%
1972	3.84%	6.21%	18.21%	22.16%
1973	6.93%	−29.59%	−13.12%	19.64%
1974	8.00%	−15.43%	−23.14%	−3.80%
1975	5.80%	11.34%	44.40%	70.10%
1976	5.08%	32.54%	22.72%	40.80%
1977	5.12%	−10.78%	−12.70%	4.50%
1978	7.18%	−16.35%	2.69%	1.70%
1979	10.38%	−20.52%	10.52%	9.90%
1980	11.24%	−33.67%	21.41%	40.50%
1981	14.71%	−28.62%	−3.40%	0.00%
1982	10.54%	156.12%	25.79%	37.40%
1983	8.80%	−20.10%	25.68%	36.10%
1984	9.85%	20.44%	1.05%	12.60%
1985	7.72%	106.90%	32.78%	37.80%
1986	6.16%	74.45%	26.92%	27.90%
1987	5.47%	−25.90%	6.02%	11.10%
1988	6.35%	7.51%	15.95%	18.40%
1989	8.37%	45.25%	31.71%	10.50%
1990	7.81%	0.33%	−0.58%	−15.20%
1991	5.60%	35.79%	23.93%	61.90%
1992	3.51%	7.82%	7.35%	23.20%
1993	2.90%	39.47%	16.74%	34.30%
1994	3.90%	−26.28%	4.98%	8.60%
1995	5.60%	85.11%	36.49%	30.50%
1996	5.21%	−12.58%	28.61%	26.00%
1997	5.26%	29.22%	24.74%	20.02%
*1998		24.39%	0.46%	6.41%
1968–98		9.00%	11.70%	18.00%
1980–98		22.70%	18.60%	20.00%

*9 months to September 30th.
Source: Michael O'Higgins, *Beating the Dow with Bonds* (New York: HarperBusiness 1999). The column BTDS refers to the Beat the Dow Strategy.

than stocks, as shown in Table 14.1. For the 30-year period as a whole, bonds returned somewhat less than stocks, but not a whole lot less—9.0 percent per annum versus 11.7 percent for stocks. This period approximates the 30-odd-year-long cycle described in Chapter 20. This result contrasts sharply with the pre-1969 period when bonds returned much less than stocks. By the early 1970s, following a prolonged period of inflation, lenders were beginning to "wise up," demanding higher-than-historical bond yields and discounting bonds more quickly at the first sign of trouble, than had been the case earlier.

Another important point is that a pure-bond strategy could have been significantly improved by the simple expedient of substituting stocks for bonds in the handful of years in which the earnings yield on the Dow exceeded the bond yield. This hybrid strategy would have given the best of both worlds. The outsized returns of stocks in the high-earnings yield years would have compensated for the fact that they were the investment of choice in only a few of those years. The 18 percent Graham and Dodd–type return earned on O'Higgins's Beat the Dow strategy would have handily beaten the Dow over the whole 30-year period—18 percent to less than 12 percent.

To simplify matters, one might say that in the period from 1969 to 1974, the investment of choice was Treasury bills; from 1975 to 1980, the best investment was stocks, and from 1981 to the turn of the century, the best returns could have been obtained in 30-year zero-coupon bonds.

Graham and Dodd would not have taken as extreme a position as Michael O'Higgins and advocated getting out of stocks entirely after 1980. Instead, they might have scaled down their stock position during the course of the next decade and a half from 100 percent in 1974 successively to 75 percent in the early 1980s, to 50 percent in the early 1990s, to 25 percent in the early 2000s. The reasons are as follows:

- With the advantages of the Graham and Dodd–type investing, the allocation between stocks and bonds is not as clear cut as just discussed. For most of the 1980s, the earnings yield on selected Dow stocks exceeded the bond yield, even if this was not the case for the Dow as a whole. This not only vindicates the Dogs of the Dow strategy or Michael O'Higgins's variation thereof, but also makes a case for some equity weighting for this period.

- Stocks have an additional advantage over bonds, that of autonomous or internally generated growth, generally estimated at 2 percent a year. This number corresponds to the long-term rate of productivity growth and represents the advantage that makes stocks more remunerative than bonds in the long run. Put another way, stocks are a bargain relative to bonds not only when the earnings yield is greater than or equal to the bond yield, but in fact when it is somewhat less. How much less? An aggressive investor might add the whole two percentage points to the earnings yield when comparing it to the bond yield, while a conservative investor may add back only one percentage point or less to allow for the fact that the P/E ratio is, after all, based on an earnings estimate and the inherently greater risks of stocks than bonds.

So we would consider any differential in favor of the earnings yield as a call to be 75 to 100 percent in stocks, and a differential of less than two percentage points in favor of bond yields to be partially invested in stocks.

In the late 1990s, the earnings yield was 3.3 percent based on a peak P/E ratio of about 30. Adding two percentage points to this figure to allow for autonomous growth (a generous assumption) gave an adjusted earnings yield of 5.3 percent, which approximated the bond yield. This was a low margin of safety that called for a less than 50 percent commitment to stocks. If the addition of two percentage points to the earnings yield brought the adjusted figure to less than the bond yield, it would support a strategy of being out of stocks entirely.

A LOOK BACK AT THE PREVIOUS CYCLE

After the 1930s crash, the conventional wisdom was that bonds are the only sound investment. It actually held true for the better part of 10 years, but it was really a case of locking the barn door after the horse had escaped. It would have been much better to follow that advice or a similar thesis before the crash, which is what the author did in advance of 2000. But the main point remains. The fundamental driver of the 1980s and 1990s bull market rally was the falling of the inflation rate, which in turn led to a fall in interest rates that was good for both stocks and bonds. Thus, bonds were a better investment for most of the period immediately before 2000 than afterward.

There are four major time periods in the modern history of financial instruments. The first was from 1929 to 1941. This was characterized by moderate yields on bonds (typically 3 to 4 percent) and falling prices, or deflation. Real yields were higher than nominal returns because inflation was negative. This was a moderately good environment for bonds and a generally poor environment for stocks. The post-2000 environment may well resemble this period.

The second time period, 1942 to 1965, which included World War II and its immediate aftermath, was a period of rising inflation, coupled with strong economic growth. Bond yields got as low as the 1 to 2 percent range, as a carryover from the deflationary period. Inflation was, however, also in the low single digits and typically greater than bond yields. So real yields on bonds were negative. This inflation was accompanied by robust economic growth, which was good for stocks. Stocks went to high levels and were due for a fall by the mid-1960s.

The third time period, 1966 to 1982, was characterized by higher rates of inflation, coupled with minimal growth, a condition known as *stagflation*. So bond yields, which had risen to the mid- to high single digits were still below inflation as late as the mid-1970s. Later in the decade, inflation reached the low teens, pushing bond yields into the mid-teens. But bond investors suffered major capital losses during that period. Stock investors also suffered in some years as stocks overshot declining fundamentals on the downside. But equities were somewhat the better investment, and most of their advantage in the O'Higgins study occurred during the mid- to late 1970s.

The fourth and most recent period was a time of disinflation coupled with growth. Bond yields entered the period in the mid-teens, even when inflation was falling to the mid–single digits. As inflation fell, so did bond yields, but by a lesser degree, providing good total returns through a combination of yields and capital gains. This was a time period that was also good for stocks, which went to historically high levels. This, together with the economic developments in the United States and rest of the world discussed in Chapter 19, set up a replay of the 1930s.

It should be noted that stocks can underperform bonds for long periods of time. This was the case in the decade of the 1920s, after taking into account the 1929 crash. In a special 1999 investor edition, the Leuthold group, writing in *Fortune* magazine, published the results of a series of back tests and came up with a table of historical returns that can be encapsulated in the "Rule of 27." In condensed form, the result was that the average annual return for the following 10 years approximated 27 minus the prevailing market P/E ratio. With a 1999 P/E ratio of 25 (or higher), the prospective return on equities would be only 2 percent a year for the next 10 years. This is well under the yields investors could earn on bonds. (At the other extreme, a market P/E ratio of 10 would allow for average annual returns of 17 percent a year for the following 10 years, as was the case in the market trough of 1982.)[3]

A GRAHAM AND DODD APPROACH TO BEATING THE DOW

It is a well-known fact that few money managers beat the market averages. There are two reasons for this. One is that investing is now dominated by professionals, running mutual funds, as opposed to the retail investor. For them, to beat the market averages means to beat their peers, not a bunch of unsophisticated investors. The other problem is that money managers try too hard. For them to chase every opportunity for potential profit, as individual investors are pushing them to do, requires them to churn their stocks, running up commission costs. A typical portfolio turnover rate is over 100 percent.

A blind strategy of buying an index will have the merit of exposing the investor to the (generally favorable) vicissitudes of equity investing. But it has no inherent risk-control features except to ensure that he or she will not underperform "the market." Specifically, there is no check to see if the index as a whole is priced too high, or yields too little, or the components are overleveraged. Our goal, rather, is to start with the Dow or other index as a bogey, and then try to improve on the stocks in it. More often than not, some of the stocks in the index will have the desirable qualities sought. But under the Graham and Dodd methodology, we are prepared to look outside, to any company of reasonable size to fulfill our requirements. Specifically, we want to try to improve on such desirable qualities of a high-dividend yield, a high degree of asset support relative to price, or even growth.

A compromise can be found in the so-called Dogs of the Dow. This strategy calls for buying the 10 highest-yielding stocks of the index at the beginning of each year, and holding them for 12 months, until the next rebalancing. One of the strongest advocates of this method has been Michael O'Higgins, who focuses on the cheapest five (in absolute price) of these 10 Dow stocks. Since this is a value approach that follows the spirit (and in many cases the letter) of the Graham and Dodd methodology, (see Table 14.1) its results may be taken as indicative of the Graham and Dodd experience. In fact, the so-called "Beat the Dow with 5" strategy would have earned 18 percent over the whole period. This result, in fact, is very much in line with the original Graham-Newman Depression-era result of around 20 percent.

The reason such a strategy usually works is that the 10 (or 5) Dogs are demonstrably superior investment choices in one obvious respect, dividend yield. This is no small matter because the Dogs usually have a yield advantage of about two percentage points over the index, and more important, a larger advantage of three percentage points or more over the stocks that are not included in the Dogs group. The key assumption is that the Dogs are enough like the rest of the index in other important respects—soundness, earnings growth, susceptibility to favorable economic trends, and so on—that whatever disadvantages they might have in these regards are more than offset by the yield advantage. It is like a somewhat weaker player at chess or some other game receiving a material "handicap" that at least compensates him or her on average, if not more so, for a lesser ability to perform.

In fact, Graham and Dodd would argue (in their 1934 edition of *Security Analysis*) that a portfolio of stocks selling at or below net-net asset value is actually *safer* than a portfolio of bonds of the same companies. The reason for this paradox is twofold. First, the because of their strong asset backing, each individual stock with these qualities is almost as safe as a bond issued by the same company. Second, there is the chance, however small, that an unforeseen event would strike one or more companies, impairing the value of the security, even with this asset protection. Which portfolio is likely to provide better protection against an isolated problem? The stock portfolio. The other bonds in the portfolio can only pay interest plus principal at maturity, not compensating for the wayward one, but the other stocks can rise to a multiple of the purchase price.[4]

This strategy is particularly useful when there are a lot of stocks selling net-net. At such times, a large proportion of one's capital can be placed in stocks—75 percent or more. As the number of protected stocks declines, so should the proportion invested in stocks.

TIMING THE MARKET

Timing the market is usually a difficult task in which even the professionals do not succeed with any great regularity. Usually, this is the because of the numerous and conflicting signals and the differing weights to which knowledgeable investors would attach to various signals. Thus, the amateur investor should seldom time the market. Yet advice to never time the market would be just as wrong as an exhortation to the time the market continuously. More suitable advice would be not to time the market on a regular basis, but only when there are loud, clear, and unmistakable signals. One such signal that seems clear and unmistakable is the secular trend previously discussed, which in turn is based on the generational cycle discussed later in Chapter 20.

Perhaps the most well-known timing strategy is the so-called January effect that is particularly strong for small stocks, especially if they were losers in the previous year. This is because a lot of selling takes place in December for tax loss purposes. Also, portfolio managers like to clear their portfolios of controversial securities before the December reporting period. This process is known as *window dressing*. An investor who regularly played the January bounce could historically have earned an average of nearly 5 percent on his money, before parking it in bonds for the remaining 11 months of the year.

One timing tool is a "naive" approach that actually adds two percentage points or so per year to performance. The underlying belief behind it is that because one can't time the market, one should invest an equal amount of money at regular and predetermined intervals. This technique is known as *dollar cost averaging*. An example will show the advantages.

Suppose you spend $9,000 on shares of company X at $10 a share. In this case, you purchase 900 shares. Now suppose the same $9,000 is spent on the shares of company X over three time periods, or $3,000 in each period. In period 1, the stock is at $10 and you buy 300 shares at that price. In period 2, the stock drops to $5 and you buy 600 shares for $3,000. In period three, the stock rises to $15, and you buy 200 shares for $3,000.

Total cost, $9,000; total shares, 1,100—200 more than in the last example. This is true even though the arithmetic average price ($5 + $10 + 15)/3 or $10 is the same as in the previous example. But through the magic of long division, the geometric, or weighted average, price is less than $10, because the low $5 dollar price boosts the total purchases (600 shares versus 300 at $10) more than the high $15 dollar price hurts it (200 shares versus 300 at $10). This leads to a net gain, in this example, of 200 shares, for the same money.

Another asset allocation rule is to buy in the fall, around November, then "sell in May and go away." The bulk of the gains take place in the six months between November and April. Observance of this rule would have allowed one to avoid the major crashes that typically take place in October (1929, 1977, 1978, 1987, 1990, 2000), while participating in the "January effect," the tendency of small stocks to get off to a good start in the new year. The summer is typically not as remunerative for companies and stocks as the fall and winter months because of vacation schedules for workers, including investment professionals, and the resulting slowdown in economic activity.

For market timers, the author has his favorite method: the observation that stocks tend to do better on the whole in odd-numbered years than in even-numbered years. The reason is that every other even-numbered year (those divisible by four) is a presidential election year, with all the attendant uncertainties. But it is the off-election, even-numbered years that have provided some of the worst markets. These include 1974, 1978, 1982 (until August), 1990, 1994, 1998 (until the fourth quarter), and 2002 (until the fourth quarter). The middle to the end of these years presented good opportunities to buy at the bottom. Exceptions to the off-election year rule include 1986, which benefited from the first president to complete two full terms since Dwight Eisenhower and the fall in oil prices which boosted the economy. A partial exception was 1998, which also benefited so much from a fall in the prices of oil and other commodities, as well as three Federal Reserve interest rate cuts, that not even a threatened impeachment of a sitting president could turn the tide. By process of elimination, one would expect a good showing from the odd-numbered years, and the best years include 1983, 1987 (until October), 1991, 1995, 1997, 1999, and 2003. An exception to this rule was 2001.

Apart from this, when considering how Graham and Dodd investing will fare in various markets, there are nine major scenarios:

1. *When the market is high and rising.* This is the one scenario in which Graham and Dodd investing has limited usefulness. An example of such a market took place in late 1990s. There are two consolations. One is that Graham and Dodd methods still produce good absolute

returns, although less than those of the market. The second is that the market will fall outside of the bubble levels, usually well below, during the next crisis.

2. *When the market is high and stable.* Stocks as a group are going nowhere, and neither might Graham and Dodd investments. Here, the advantage of higher dividend yields is worth something, but the safest investment is in cash, which offers a decent real return because inflation rates are low. This was the situation in the late 1960s and early 1970s.

3. *When the market is high and falling.* Graham and Dodd methodologies preserve capital by preventing investors from getting into stocks that have fallen by "only" 10 to 20 percent and have a lot further to go on the downside. This was the case in 1973 and just after 2000.

4. *When the market is moderately priced and rising.* There are Graham and Dodd investments to be had, and an investor should participate in the market rally, with an above-average degree of safety. This was the case for much of the mid- to late 1980s and early 1990s.

5. *When the market is moderately priced and stable.* Graham and Dodd methodologies tend to outperform by leading the investor to buy relatively underpriced securities and selling them when they reach fair value. The higher dividend yields on Graham and Dodd investments become an important consideration. This was the case in the early 1950s.

6. *When the market is moderately priced and falling.* Graham and Dodd–type investing outperforms by emphasizing preservation of capital. This was the case in 1977, part of 1978, and 1981.

7. *When the market is low and rising.* This is perhaps the ideal Graham and Dodd environment, with plenty of bargains and a tailwind to lift the value of investments. This was the case for most of the rest of the period from 1975 to 1982.

8. *When the market is low and stable.* This is another fine Graham and Dodd environment that generates market-beating gains by buying cheaply, selling at fair value, and collecting fat dividends in the meantime. Given the turbulence of market swings, there haven't been many of these periods.

9. *When the market is low and falling* (e.g., as in 1974). Here, the Graham and Dodd approach does better at preserving capital and realizing a disproportionate share of the gains that can be had.

Of these nine scenarios, Graham and Dodd–type investing has a clear advantage in the three stable scenarios by emphasizing dividend income, and the three falling scenarios by focusing on capital preservation. It is also robust in two of the three rising scenarios, when stocks are low and moderately priced. Its clear disadvantage is in the high and rising scenario, which was the case in the late 1990s.

THE LIFE CYCLE IN ASSET ALLOCATION[5]

In the life of the average person, there are six events that signal life changes, which argue for caution in investments. These events, more than absolute ages, signal events that should incline the investor to favor bonds over stocks:

1. Leaving home, getting the first job, becoming financially independent.
2. Marriage and the birth of the first child.
3. The attendance of college by the first child.
4. The leaving of the last child, or the so-called empty nest syndrome.
5. Retirement and the letting up of economic pursuits.
6. The death of one spouse.

A single person who has just finished school and embarked on a career has the fewest obligations. As it were, however, this person typically also has the least experience and the fewest financial resources. The more enterprising of such individuals may want to begin investing in the stock market. Such a person should start slowly, putting aside several months' worth of savings against a rainy day in bank accounts or Treasury bills. Then he or she can enter the market gradually, at the rate of a few thousand dollars a years as financial means and experience allow. It must also be noted that many young people unfortunately begin their adult lives with significant debts from student loans. Such loans should be paid off, or at least covered by savings, before the person begins a serious program of investment. The most enterprising investors are often found among individuals with 5 to 10 years' business experience and no other obligations.

A newly married person usually faces a different situation. Early on, marriage may be even more conducive to savings and investment if the couple can realize economies (e.g., by living in only one residence and pooling household expenses). Nowadays, with dual-income couples, there is also a form of insurance, given the likelihood of at least one person's being employed at any given time. The thing to note is that marriage is conducive to the production of children, which brings about a new set of financial pressures. Children not only have an immediate impact on household expenses, but also require a round of investment for their long-term needs. At the same time, the presence of one or more dependents (plus the possibility that one of the parents may curtail work efforts in order to take care of the children) means that the risk tolerance is reduced.

As the children approach college age, the needs become more immediate. Now the tolerance for stock market risk is quite limited, unless the game plan is to play Russian roulette with the children's education. Such a posture should be avoided, except in the rare case of a financially strapped family whose chances of giving their children a college education are slim to none. This is a serious matter for the child because education is an important factor of production in the modern world.

The needs of the child are also an argument for the parents to buy term life insurance. There is no point in buying whole life insurance, which in effect is trying to insure against an event that will happen, namely one's death. If you really counted on beating the actuarial tables, you would be better served by a straight annuity product. But buying insurance against a premature death is another matter. This guards against the untimely upset of a carefully laid financial plan.

The empty nest syndrome signifies a letting up of financial pressure, and represents the one event when an investor can take a more, rather than less, aggressive posture. In this regard, this stage of life may be considered something of a second young adulthood. The problem is that this, like the first period of independent adulthood, is usually short lived as retirement looms. Nevertheless, it may be regarded as a second chance to rebuild a fortune that has been depleted by children in the most critical (and expensive) years of their lives.

Retirement is another matter. Here, the waters are largely uncharted. First, no one knows how long the average life has been extended. Second, generous retirement pensions were formerly provided by a large ratio of economically active workers to a small number of retirees. The old age survivors will get more numerous with each passing generation, while the trend to fewer children means that the total number of workers will barely increase from one generation to the next.

CONSIDERATION OF INDIVIDUAL CIRCUMSTANCES IN ASSET ALLOCATION

In addition to the overall market, one must take into account one's personal circumstances in making investment decisions. For instance, is the investor single or does he or she have a number of dependents? What is the age of the investor? How much of the investor's means cover everyday living expenses, and how much is left over for investment/speculation?

If the investor can barely cover living expenses, any available capital must be used to produce income to try to widen the margin.

If a definite sum is needed at a fixed time, say for a child's college education, the choice is simple. The investor cannot afford to invest this money in stocks. The choice must be one of cash or bonds, and not just any bonds, but ones with a maturity close to the time of anticipated need, as well as an instrument of the highest quality.

A longer-term investor can think of these rules in terms of income instruments, including common stocks with a dividend yield of two thirds or more the AAA bond yield. In cases in which a good-quality stock yields more than a bond, it can be said to have the income characteristics of a bond and the appreciation potential of a stock.

Where can such stocks be found? The obvious candidates are the utilities: electric, gas, and water. Others can be found among real estate investment trusts (REITs). A few slow-growing retailers that have seen better days offer high yields, but with significant risk. Major drug stocks, during the 1993 "Hillary" scare, offered yields competitive with those of utilities and better prospects for growth. These are sounder, if less exciting, investments than the popular "hot" stocks of the time. What you see is what you get. There is no pie in the sky or castles in the air on which to build a growth story, but disappointments are relatively mild. The bias for stocks is built, as it must be, on the inherently superior "yield" and return characteristics. Industrial companies typically earn a return of 15 to 17 percent on equity, a "yield" that compares favorably with a yield of 6 percent or so (on average) on bonds. If the stocks of such companies can be purchased around book value, for a prospective total return in the low teens, these returns will over the long term outpace the returns on bonds. One might be able to pay up to two and a half times book for a 15 percent equity return and still get a yield ($15\%/250\% = 6\%$) competitive with bonds (which is why acquirers typically pay that price), and why one should be eager to sell before that level is reached.

In constructing a portfolio of stocks, one would use these classic value income plays, while sprinkling the portfolio with asset plays that have takeover potential and growth stocks with redeeming value characteristics. Sometimes a security can serve more than one turn, as drug stocks did in 1993 (growth and dividends), and heavy industrial stocks such as British Steel (assets and dividends) did in 1999.

In the allocation between cash and bonds, there are also about nine major yield scenarios for consideration, and five postures regarding them. These include all bonds, 75 percent bonds and 25 percent cash, 50–50 bonds and cash, 25 percent bonds and 75 percent cash, and all cash, under nine different scenarios, as follows ("cash" instruments include money market funds and Treasury bills, with less than a year to maturity):

1. When yields are high and rising, then the attractiveness of long-term bonds engendered by their higher yields must be offset against the potential for capital loss. Our fixed income portfolio in this instance would be 50–50 bonds and cash. A case in point was 1981.
2. When yields are high and stable, then the advantage lies with long-term bonds, both for their higher yields and for their potential for capital gains. In this scenario, our fixed-income weight would be 75 percent bonds and 25 percent cash. This was the case for much of the late 1980s.

3. When yields are high and falling, it is the classic case for a maximum weight (100 percent) and duration in long-term bonds. The most recent example of this was in 1982.
4. When yields are moderate and rising, it is a scenario in which we would try to err on the side of safety. Our posture would be 25 percent bonds and 75 percent cash. This was the case as late as 1994.
5. When the yields are moderate and stable, it is exactly the intermediate case, and our fixed-income posture is also intermediate, 50–50 bonds and cash. This was the case for most of the late 1990s.
6. When yields are moderate and falling, as around the turn of the century, we would urge a mixture of courage and caution. Our fixed-income posture is 75 percent bonds and 25 percent bills.
7. When yields are low and rising, the most dangerous scenario, we would put maximum weight (100 percent) in Treasury bills or other forms of cash, and even consider shortening maturities below a year. This may be the case from time to time after the early 2000s.
8. When yields are low and stable, the environment calls for caution too, although not to the degree of the previous one. Our fixed-income allocation is 25 percent bonds and 75 percent cash.
9. When yields are low and falling, we would be cautiously optimistic, but just as cautious as optimistic. This was true shortly after the turn of the twenty-first century, when Fed Chairman Alan Greenspan aggressively lowered rates. Our fixed-income allocation is 50–50 bonds and cash.

CHAPTER 15

The Concepts of Graham and Dodd versus Modern Theories and Practices

This chapter will juxtapose the key concepts of the Graham and Dodd method versus others more in vogue among academics and Wall Street practitioners, and try to demonstrate the advantages of the methods advocated in this book. It was Graham and Dodd's belief that an investor should first try for a "satisfactory" result, and only later strive to be "above average." The two endeavors are not mutually exclusive, and one's affairs should be managed in such a way as to allow "average" (somewhat broadly defined to be in the mid-range) to be a fallback position.

KEY GRAHAM AND DODD INVESTMENT PREMISES

The first key Graham and Dodd investment premise is the central tendency, or reversion to the mean, of stock prices. For instance, the child of two tall parents is likely to be shorter than the parents, and the offspring of two short parents is likely to be taller. In both cases, the child is likely to move toward the mean. Likewise, if a stock valuation is extremely under- or overvalued by historical standards, it is likely to move toward a more median valuation compared to its history, provided, of course, that the fundamental character of the company has not changed in the meantime. Such character changes do happen occasionally, but far less often than changes in stock market valuations of companies seem to give them credit for.

Graham and Dodd also had a sensible approach to stock market risk. In this instance, risk is not measured by day-to-day fluctuations in the market value of a stock or even by a temporary break in the share price followed by an imminent rebound. *Risk* refers to a one-time break in the stock price with essentially no subsequent recovery. This is a loss beyond all hope of recovery, either eventually or at least in the meaningful future. The possibility that the principal can recovered in 20 or 30 years is not, in most senses of the word, the *meaningful* future. The time lost in such an extended recovery period is long in relation to most investing horizons, and indeed, to the life spans of most investors. A loss of this nature must be considered permanent. One important purpose of Graham and Dodd investing is to avoid such permanent losses. These risks are most likely to occur when a stock is so overvalued that once investors come to their senses, they would not accord such valuations anytime soon. Their second key idea was to buy stocks offering a "margin of safety," issues that were priced so low in relation to assets or other measures of value that they would not go down much in price, even if they failed to go up.

The goal, therefore, is to buy stocks with broadly average prospects at a below-average price and (in most cases) an above-average dividend yield. Success in this endeavor will lead to superior stock price performance, as below-average valuations correct upward to average, before the stock subsequently tracks the market. The above-average yield will also contribute to superior total return while "paying" the investor to wait for a turnaround in the fortunes of the company and stock. Occasionally, such a turnaround will fail to materialize and bring about a disappointing result. But the law of averages dictates that these cases will be the exception rather than the rule and, in any event, occur less frequently in the case of established companies in established industries than the collapse of companies and stocks in hot new industries such as the Internet. The new industry, of course, offers greater potential for great and immediate wins, but also the possibility— perhaps the probability—of large and sudden losses. Studies have shown that the average investor is actually a fairly conservative individual who fantasizes about, but doesn't have the stomach for, the roller coaster changes that accompany the fortunes of high rollers.

These concepts that were popularized by Graham and Dodd are fairly well understood but not always practiced by professional investors. That's because many professional investors do not have the luxury of waiting for several years for a policy to take its course. Instead, they have to live in the "here and now," which often means the current year or even the current quarter. Another problem is the tendency of professionals (including the author) to focus on and overemphasize current events and trends, losing sight of the fact that day-to-day fluctuations mostly cancel out. It is the longer-run trends that count, but that fact is sometimes forgotten in the hurly-burly of trying to make one's short-term numbers.

It is probable that a number of investors unconsciously measure risk in relative rather than absolute terms. That is, it is less important how much money they make in the absolute sense than how well they are doing relative to their friends, coworkers, or some other reference group. Perhaps a whole group of people are making big money on Internet stocks. In this instance, you are primarily concerned not with how you're doing in absolute terms, but whether you can maintain a lifestyle or retirement comparable to that of the reference group. In such cases, the aim is not so much to prosper as to "keep up with the Jones." If you lose money following a risky investment strategy, there is at least the consolation that the reference group is doing as poorly. If this is the case, then by all means get yourself a fund made up of the stocks in the Standard & Poor's (S&P) 500, Internet stocks, or other relevant index.

Among the most important of the principles in this book is basic investment value, as measured by book value plus 10 times the dividend. Graham and Dodd railed at length about the difference between investment and speculation, and even gave numerous examples. Investment, in their view and here, consists of buying stocks primarily for what they are worth today, while speculation consists of buying stocks "on the come," in casino parlance, for what they might be worth tomorrow, regardless of what they might be worth today. In the event of highly valued assets, "margin of safety" takes on a somewhat different meaning. The large premium over asset value would initially make an investment less safe than would otherwise be the case. But an appropriately priced growth security using the formulas proposed in earlier chapters, or some others that do no violence to the Graham and Dodd philosophy, would compensate for this by offering upside potential not normally found in Graham and Dodd–type investments. Provided that the investor can stomach the occasional but inevitable losses, the prospective returns compensate, perhaps more so, for the risks. Even so, the expectation of high rather than average growth is a risky one to have.

Occasionally, the price of a security will reflect the worst-case scenario. Then the investment would be suitable even if the likelihood were one of collapse, because then the investment would be recovered, perhaps with small interest. This would be the equivalent to our dice game in Chapter 1, of having the croupier call 1, breaking even if the die roll were that number, and making money if it were a higher number. Warren Buffett noted this in his purchase of Arcadia, wherein the collapse was not of the company itself, but of a lucrative government contract. He earned 15 percent on his arbitrage of the company's being taken over, and a lot more upon a judicial determination that the company had been wronged, and was owed a large principal by the government, together with significant interest payments that more than doubled the value of the original principal.

One investment method that does not earn the normal Graham and Dodd result is the investment of stocks of small market capitalization (below $500 million to $1 billion in most cases). Such stocks are often overlooked and tend not to participate in any general movement of either the stock market as a whole or of similarly situated but larger-capitalization-value stocks as a group. Money can be made in small stocks, of course, but generally by very sophisticated investors with highly specialized knowledge of the company and/or the industry. Money in small stocks tends not to be made on a steady, ongoing basis, but rather in bursts, as a small company becomes recognized.

Indeed, it is the *comparatively* cheap investment that often offers the greatest pitfall for value-oriented investors. The stock was too pricey at 100 percent of the market price–earnings (P/E) ratio of 25, but it is now selling at 80 percent of the market multiple, or a P/E ratio of 20, so let's buy and see what happens. The problem is that comparatively cheap works out to be expensive on an absolute basis. Here, a value investor can take a tip from a momentum investor and avoid trying to catch a falling knife. When stocks get to "bubble" levels and the bubble bursts, there are large amounts of air to be let out. The academics would stand this on its head by asserting that a stock price merely represents an arm's-length transaction between two informed businesspeople.

Great latitude is afforded when an acquisition is done with stock, and the stock of the acquirer is also overpriced. Then the relevant measure is not the acquisition price as measured in dollars, but rather the exchange rate of the acquirer's stock to the acquiree's stock, which represents a true price. If this were similar to the trade-off that might have prevailed if both companies' stocks were rationally priced, then the deal would make sense even if the nominal price were too high—or, as Warren Buffett would put it, part of company A sold to acquire company B. In fact, Buffett pointed out that the conglomerate chiefs were acting quite rationally when they used their overpriced stock to purchase more mundane businesses with genuine earnings. Unfortunately, most of these companies also loaded up on debt.

A recent example is the Internet craze. Even the stock of as staid a company as Sotheby's, the art dealer, shot up in price when it announced its intention to make sales online. Under such circumstances, the acquisition of a small Internet company, even at a ridiculous price, might give the acquirer enough cachet to boost its own price–earnings multiple.

Stocks fluctuate around a central trend line, and they also advance along trend. Which of the two are more important? Graham and Dodd would have given the emphasis to the fluctuations around the trend. Warren Buffett disagrees, paying more attention to the trend itself. But he knew how to dodge the bullets, cashing out his partnership at the market top in the early 1970s, and diversifying into fixed-income investments through the acquisition of General Re in the late 1990s.

Buffett is probably more nearly correct than Graham and Dodd, but only over the course of a whole 30-odd-year-long cycle. For roughly half of the cycle, including the upcoming half, the Graham and Dodd methodology is the more robust of the two. And it has much to teach us even in the growth phase of the cycle. In the course of a whole long cycle, P/E ratios will vary from high single digits, six or seven times, to a high in the low to mid-20s, or three or four times as much. For now, the risks are on the downside, toward high-single-digit P/Es from double-digit levels.

In testifying before a congressional committee, Ben Graham was asked why stocks would return to their value. He replied that he did not know, only that his experience taught him that they would.[1] There is an answer, the one that William Strauss and Neil Howe gave us, which is discussed in Chapter 20. In the United States, at least, it is tied to the rise and fall of generations of Americans.

MODERN-DAY EFFICIENT MARKET THEORIES[2]

The theoretical assumption of efficient markets lends itself to mathematical formulas and proofs regarding hypothetical "rational" investors. This assumption leads to several variations, all concluding that theoretically investors cannot systematically "beat the market" either through superior stock selection or market timing.

Among these theories, the most useful concept is called the *efficient frontier*, which postulates that there are two measures of stock desirability, *return* and *risk* (the latter measured by volatility or prices). This frontier is a smooth curve that depicts the trade-off between risk and return. Only some stocks are "efficiently priced" on a risk–return basis, either yielding the most return for a given level of risk, or displaying the least risk for a given level or return. Most stocks are inferior, either by offering less return than a similar stock with the same risk on the frontier, or by being more risky than another stock offering the same return located on the frontier. Therefore, one should construct a portfolio consisting only of stocks with superior risk–return characteristics. The concept of efficiency leads not to a search for efficiently priced securities, but rather focused on the trade-off between risk and return.

There are actually two types of risk in securities selection: *unsystematic risk* and *systematic risk*. The former is peculiar to individual stock and the latter is the result of stock market fluctuation and otherwise known as *market risk*. Unsystematic risk can be diversified away by assembling a portfolio of securities. Systematic risk cannot be eliminated, but it can be managed by recognizing the characteristics of individual stocks. By a combination of analyzing both types of risks, this theory underpins the importance of stock selection.

The systematic risk of a security can be compared to the systematic risk of the *market portfolio*, which is a hypothetical portfolio consisting of every stock in the market. Because of the diversification of the market portfolio, unsystematic risk has been reduced to a minimum and only systematic risk remains. By examining available historical data, the rate of return of a

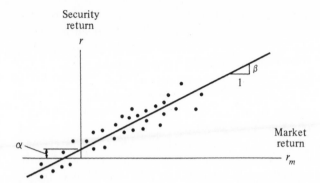

FIGURE 15.1 Determination of Beta Coefficient of a Security.

security can be plotted against the return from the market portfolio, which can be approximated, for instance, by using the Standard and Poor's 500 stock index as a proxy. Then, a theoretical line, referred to as the regression line, can be fitted by using a standard statistical technique, as illustrated in Figure 15.1. The small intercept on the y-axis is called the *alpha,* and the slope of the line is known as the *beta.* The alpha is the average value of the rates of return of the security due to unsystematic risk over time and in theory tends to approach zero. The beta represents the systematic risk of a security relative to that of the market portfolio.[3]

The characteristics of individual stocks, which may be classified as *aggressive* or *defensive,* are measured by the security market line as shown in Figure 15.2. A market portfolio will have a risk (relative to the market)

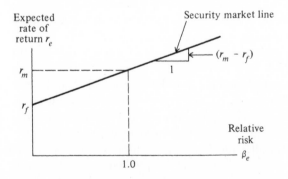

Source: Au & Au, *Engineering Economic Analysis for Capital Investment Decisions,* Englewood Cliffs: Prentice Hall, 1992, pp. 423–425.

FIGURE 15.2 Security Market Line.

of exactly 1. A more risky stock that fluctuates more than the market (e.g., a computer issue) has a beta greater than 1 and is called an *aggressive stock,* a less risky stock that fluctuates less than the market (e.g., a utility stock) has a beta less than 1 and is called a *defensive* stock.

The relationship between the expected return and the systematic risk of a security is established by the capital asset pricing model (CAPM), which is based on simple economic principles. The underlying theory is that with the same risk should have the same rate of return. Thus, the prices of assets in the capital market should be adjusted until equivalent risk assets have identical expected returns. Although some empirical data contradict this model, it is widely used because of its simplicity. The capital asset pricing model states that the expected rate of return on a portfolio should exceed the risk-free rate by an amount that is proportional to the beta of the portfolio.[4] This relationship is represented by the *security market line* as shown in Figure 15.2.

Let r_f be the risk-free rate of return (such as return from Treasury bills), r_m be the expected rate of return on the market portfolio, r_e be the expected rate of return on a security. Then, the relationship between return and risk for a security is given by $r_e = r_f + \beta * (r_m - r_f)$ in which $\beta * (r_m - r_f)$ is called the *risk premium,* and r_e is referred to as the *risk-adjusted rate of return* for the security.

For example, the expected return on the U.S. Treasury bills currently is 10%, and the expected rate of return on the market portfolio is 14%. The risk premium of return for a stock with $\beta = 1.5$ is found to be (1.5) * (14% − 10%) = 6%, and that for another stock with $\beta = 0.5$ is (0.5) * (14% − 10%) = 2%. The expected rates of return risk of these two stocks are, respectively, 10% + (1.5) * (14% − 10%) = 16% and 10% + (0.5) * (14% − 10%) = 12%.

The notion of diversification is rooted in the premise that if individual securities are more or less efficiently priced, then a large collection of them must be more so, and will represent a better chance to arrive at the efficient frontier.

This emphasis on risk minimization led to the least useful idea, the efficient markets theory (EMT). The EMT comes in three varieties: the weak form, the semi-strong form, and the strong form. The weak form says that current stock prices reflect all price history; the semi-strong form hypothesizes that stock prices reflect all publicly available information; the strong form says that stock prices reflect all information, publicly available or not. Therefore, the available information corresponding to each hypothesis does not give an "edge" to traders under that hypothesis.

Studies of technical analysis of prices appear to show that the weak form postulate—that one cannot profit from knowing past price data alone—is probably correct. Score one for the academics. The semi-strong form of the EMT is the most interesting and is the one that is most often debated. Publicly available information is widely known information. In theory, the general public knows all the public information, and one investor is not more well informed than the next, so this kind of information confers no advantage. The strong form postulates that even possession of nonpublic or "inside" information will not cause one investor to outperform another because knowledge by a small handful of traders would make the trading so competitive that the additional person does not obtain a benefit. This notion is ridiculous on its face. If the strong form of the EMT were true, there would be no need for a Securities and Exchange Commission (SEC). And there would be no charges for trading on "inside information," for such information would be fully reflected in stock prices. There would be no premium for any takeover bid, because such information would have been fully anticipated by the market.

There is another interesting wrinkle. Material information is data that would influence an average investor. Using material nonpublic information is illegal in most cases. (Courts have sometimes ruled that an investor who overheard or otherwise acquired "inside" information inadvertently would not be penalized for using it.) But under the so-called mosaic theory, an investor can make a decision using a combination of material public information plus nonmaterial nonpublic information. For instance, an investor, knowing Berkshire Hathaway's criteria for making acquisitions (material public information) and the fact that the chairman of such a qualifying company had taken a strong liking to Warren Buffett on their first meeting (nonmaterial nonpublic information), might take a "flyer" on that company's being acquired by Berkshire Hathaway. In another case, the author, while working for Value Line, emphatically lowered his recommendation on a troubled company based on a financial ratio analysis (of material public information) plus the uncharacteristic evasiveness of the investor relations person, normally a very voluble guy (nonmaterial nonpublic information).

Our claim is that the most significant returns come not from knowing information, but from properly interpreting information, which is the purpose of this book. The academic case is supported by the fact that most professional investors cannot beat the market. It takes very skilled investors like Warren Buffett to consistently outperform the indexes. In fact, Buffett has been referred to by academics as a five- or six-"sigma" event. This is an academic way of saying that the statistical probability of his having compiled his investment record by luck, rather than skill, is about one in a million.

Can the average investor beat the market using only publicly available information? It's a close call, but we'd like to think that a careful study of this book and/or its predecessors will provide an edge to the average reader. At the very least, we hope that this book will contribute, as did the original

Graham and Dodd text, to the development of a few future Buffetts who will compile five- or six-sigma track records.

A variation of the EMT is the random walk theory, which holds that stock prices move randomly. Therefore, there is no advantage in choosing one stock over another. It is probably true that there are few, if any, statistically significant moves on a day-to-day basis. Moreover, day-to-day fluctuations largely cancel out. But the theory ignores the fact that the cumulative impact of a number of "insignificant" daily moves might be significant over a period of time.

Warren Buffett had this comment on the academicians: "Observing correctly that the market is usually efficient, they came to the conclusion that the market is always efficient. The difference between the two premises is as the difference between night and day."[5]

How can an investor beat the market? According to the academics, only by taking more risk, since "markets," not individual security selection, determine returns. Their postulate that no one security is inherently better than another actually stands the original view of an efficient frontier on its head. If riskier stocks are priced to yield more return, then a portfolio of risky stocks will produce a higher return than a portfolio of average or below-average riskiness. True, the academics might concede, any given risky stock might underperform the market. But by diversifying away security specific risk, a large number of risky holdings should outperform the market. Then we would argue that if there are, in fact, variations in the performance of stocks within any given risk class, why not try to screen for the better-performing stocks in the lower-risk classes? If this were done successfully, then one could have a portfolio with a double benefit of greater return and lower risk. This is actually an argument much like the academics' efficient frontier.

A number of the better investment services rate investment managers not only on returns, but on the risks incurred to earn those returns. In other words, these measures adjust returns for risks, to come up with numbers for risk-adjusted returns. And a good investor needs to have a sense of risk control. While certain mileage can be gained by managing the beta or market risk, it is the alpha, or excess return, that is the more appropriate tool for Graham and Dodd investors.

PRACTICES COMMON ON WALL STREET

What is referred to as Wall Street is the so-called "sell side" of the investing business. The "buy side" consists of individual investors and mutual funds, while the "sell side" consists of brokers that sell stock to "buy siders." As recent revelations have shown, the "sell side" does not always have the interest of buy siders at heart. Worse, they have often persuaded many large buy siders to behave in ways that are inimical to investors, especially small investors. Put bluntly, some large, institutional buy siders have become "shills" in a "casino" run by the sell siders. Warren Buffett pointed out the difference between an investor like himself and Wall Street. While Buffett earns money based on the value of stocks he trades, Wall Street earns money on the volume.

In the best case, Wall Street firms act merely as matchmakers, matching up buyers and sellers of stocks. This is a riskless transaction, with the dealer collecting a commission at one or both ends, without having to worry about the risk of holding the stock. In other cases, "specialists," on the floor of the New York Stock Exchange or Wall Street firms, will buy or sell stock for their own account. This is done with an eye to quick, almost immediate, turnaround. These are called principal transactions, and they are based on an understanding of the market rather than the stock. In any event, Wall Street wants to place as much stock in customers' hands as possible, while collecting commissions or spreads on the turnover.

A broker will only rarely work within the overall context of a financial plan or strategy for a client. A bad broker will "churn" an account to generate commissions, while losing most of the client's money in the process. A more moral individual will at least operate within the limits agreed to with the client, with regard for the client's preferences and types of securities. A good and conscientious broker will trade with a high degree of skill while keeping the client informed. But in each case, there is an inherent conflict of interest. A broker does not make money based on how well the client does, but rather on how much trading takes place.

Wall Street likes to hedge its bets. This is related to, but not the same as, diversification. A hedge might be the purchase of one security, with an offsetting sale of a related security, and trying to capture the difference in value between the two. Hedging has become much more popular in the past 20 years or so, with the invention of new types of securities. These include not only stocks themselves but futures (the right to receive or deliver a basket of stocks at some specified date in the future), as well as options to buy or sell stocks. Although these techniques are used more often by the so-called hedge funds, Wall Street firms also sometimes have in-house hedging operations called "prop" (proprietary trading) desks.

In the 1960s, there arose a theory that maximum returns could be earned by concentrating a portfolio in a handful (5 to 10) of stocks. It was a theory practiced at the time (and later) by Warren Buffett himself. It was practiced, with variations, by the leading fund managers of the late 1990s. The Janus Twenty fund, for example, owns between 20 and 30 stocks, with a high proportion in technology stocks. (SEC regulations require "diversified" funds to own a minimum of 16 stocks.) But the risks of this became apparent when this fund collapsed shortly after the turn of the twenty-first century.

One risk-control idea actually makes a good deal of sense. If, for example, the most suitable investments followed one theme, say interest rate–sensitive or heavy industrials, one might go out of his way to admit stocks into his portfolio with the opposite sensitivities. Then he should not use maximum rigor for the candidates in the latter group, but merely screen to see that they were relatively cheap. In this manner, one can add balance to the portfolio. One might put half of the portfolio in the favored group and the other half in a basket quantitatively designed to minimize the industry risks, while leaving a good part of the company exposure on the table. This practice is called optimization and uses historical data. Ideally, the other, quantitatively designed half of the portfolio would beat or at least match the market.

Over the years, Buffett has earned the bulk of his money in a handful of stocks: *Washington Post,* GEICO, and Capital Cities/ABC from the late 1970s to the early 1990s, and Coca-Cola and Gillette, more recently. But he has protected his portfolio by putting roughly half of Berkshire's money either in other high-quality equity names, such as R.J. Reynolds and General Foods in the early 1980s, and more recently, Freddie Mac, Wells Fargo, and other banks, as well as McDonalds in the 1990s, or in fixed-income investments in the late 1980s, when equity values were unattractive.

If one sector, say high-tech or Internet, were dominating the picture, and our goal was strong relative rather than absolute performance, we might include the stocks, but only at maximum to their weight in the appropriate index. Our theory is that the lower valuation and higher dividend yields of our candidates would enable them to beat less moderately priced issues in their peer group, but not necessarily the sectors that we don't understand and might otherwise overlook. Under these circumstances, we fully expect to suffer if the market as a whole takes a bath, but expect our Graham and Dodd choices to rescue us by outperforming the part of the index that they are matched against. We would be somewhat uncomfortable with a Berkshire Hathaway–type portfolio anchored in a few high-value growth stocks like American Express, Coke, Disney, and Gillette.

The weakness of Graham and Dodd analysis is that it may select a collection of stocks with similar betas that are vastly different from the market as a whole. Hence, it may be desirable to balance part of the portfolio with other stocks whose market characteristics are notably different from the portfolio. For instance, in the late 1990s, the highest fliers, which generally lacked Graham and Dodd characteristics, were the high-tech stocks. Even so, there were a number of high-tech companies that sold for Graham and Dodd valuations or something pretty close to it.

As an antidote to these weaknesses, the managers of T. Rowe Price Funds observed around 1958 that the best prospective choices for stocks were the ones that had performed the best recently. This was the case at the beginning of an emerging growth phase. When stocks had been so beaten down for so many years so that excess valuations had been wrung out of them, then all the advantages would lie with the company with the superior earnings prospects. That is the basic case and is a useful approach for roughly half of a long (30- to 40-year) stock market cycle. It is when there are large differentials in valuations, based on perceived differences in earnings prospects that are greater than real differences, that a value approach works best. Such differentials appeared to be in place around the turn of the twentieth and twenty-first centuries.

The problems caused by growth stocks, and the laudable desire for hedging, led to a rather undesirable practice called portfolio insurance. Stripped to its essentials, this causes the investor to move in the same direction as the market; sell when the market is falling, and buy when the market is rising. The real reason is to avoid being out of sync with the market. The problem with portfolio insurance is that it requires investors, if they can be called that, to all be buying or selling at the same time, going in the same direction as many other investors. (Graham and Dodd, however, teaches that the best profits are made by going in the opposite direction as others.) If everyone wants to buy, there will be no stock for sale, and if everyone wants to sell, there will be no buyers. In essence, these contrasting methodologies interact somewhat like the children's game of paper, scissors, stone. Scissors beats paper, stone beats scissors, but paper beats stone.

In order to complicate the game, Wall Street invented what are called *derivative instruments,* or derivatives, for short. These included futures (contracts on "baskets" of stocks for settlement at a future date, rather than "spot" or normal settlement), and options, which are the right but not the obligation to buy or sell stocks by a certain date. These are instruments that are mentioned at the end of Chapter 4, but ones that the average investor—and certainly the Graham and Dodd investor—shouldn't try to trade. Their appeal lies in the fact that they provide other means for the smartest and quickest investors to outwit others in the market. The problem is that moves in the "real" (actual equity) and derivative markets are mutually reinforcing.

A word of warning: We base our formulas on easily obtainable information and use only arithmetic computations. Some of the professionals base their investments on arcane formulas that use calculus or other forms of higher math. A value investor is probably not at a disadvantage, except for the very short term, against such professionals. When one uses calculus to manage a portfolio, the calculations are necessarily very precise. In fact, they are carried to a degree of finesse that is often unwarranted by imprecise data. As such, they give their users a feeling of confidence that is not justified. A dose of common sense, accompanied by the use of grade school–level mathematics, might serve better in the long run. The "math wizards" at Long-Term Capital Management would have done well to remember this.

Regarding the principle of diversification, our feeling (and that of practitioners like Warren Buffett) is that we would rather have a few stocks with a large margin of safety rather than many stocks, each of which has a small or even negative margin of safety. To advocates of diversification, the main risk seems to be not that of losing money, but that of mistracking the market. We are more concerned about earning a satisfactory absolute rather than relative return. To this end, we will admit only those securities into our portfolio that meet our stringent criteria. Given market fluctuations, the number of qualifying securities will necessarily be larger at some times and smaller at others.

CONCLUDING COMMENTS

Although it has many merits, we admit to the deficiencies of the original Graham and Dodd methodology (as did its creators) and have done our best to repair them. The solution is to incorporate modern standards of value, as measured by earnings and cash flow and even dividends, as opposed to merely the balance sheet. The other is to relax the original criteria to allow for variations, or for combinations, of qualities that together offer compelling value, even if individual components, say assets or dividends, do not. For instance, in a bull market, there will be very few companies selling at net-net of working capital, but a much larger number that will be attractive on earnings, dividend yields, or some combination of assets and dividends.

There are two things that determine whether an investor comes out ahead. The first is the frequency of the wins, and the second, the size of the wins. This is true not only in investing, but in gambling games such as poker or bridge. All participants want the gratification that comes with a win, and most want that satisfaction immediately. Therefore, a momentum player will play for the frequent win by following the trend. The really big winners, however, are those that post sizable gains, even infrequently. And that often calls for running counter to trend. Another attribute of big winners is that they seldom suffer serious losses and never crippling ones. The foremost aim of a Graham and Dodd methodology is to allow the investor to live to fight another day.

Some investors will be troubled by the fact that the Graham and Dodd philosophy seems to be characterized by extremes. In our experience, it is under extreme, not moderate, circumstances that the most money is made. First, it simplifies the decision-making process. An extremely low valuation of a stock would signal either the presence of a large profit opportunity or an imminent collapse. Then one's energies need merely be devoted to examining the likelihood of collapse. As Sherlock Holmes said, when one has eliminated the impossible, what remains, however improbable, must be true. Put another way, heroic measures may well be called for, if our basic assertion, outlined in the last section of the book, is right that there will be troubled times ahead. History shows that the Graham and Dodd method works well for half, or a bit more, of a 30-odd-year stock market cycle, and specifically for the part of the cycle that we believe is about to come up. If this is the case, practitioners of such methods will soon be vindicated for the decade of the 1990s, which was probably the worst in American history for value-oriented strategies.

The reader must not take on faith our assertions that our system, or one similar to ours, can beat the market, either on the whole or over specified time periods, thereby confounding the academics, who maintain that it is impossible to systematically earn superior returns. You must rather consider carefully, first, which set of assumptions is more nearly correct and, second, which set of assumptions corresponds most nearly to your own beliefs and philosophies.

Your decision regarding our system may well turn on a fundamental law of economics—that the largest returns accrue to the possessors of the scarcest factor of production. The largest following appears to adhere to Wall Street, which is inclined one way, followed by academics, who, although representing a different camp, are now more nearly aligned to Wall Street than to us. The conservative value investor, however, appears to be in the smallest group. It is for this reason, as much as any other, that this investor is likely to come out best in the years ahead.

CHAPTER 16

Case Studies in Graham and Dodd Investing

The proof of the pudding is in the eating, so to speak. This chapter will cover some of the Graham and Dodd–type investments made by the author, and some that were missed, and 10 Value Line reports are attached to the end of the chapter for your reference (see Figures 16.1 through 16.10.)

FIVE SUCCESSFUL INVESTMENTS

Endesa of Spain, 1991–1994

Endesa, which is a Spanish acronym for Empresa Nacional de Espana, is the Spanish government–owned electric utility. It was formed in 1983 by the merger of several small utilities, the most important of which had paid dividends since 1949. The Spanish government had tried to encourage utilities to merge in order to realize economies of scale and operate more efficiently. Because Endesa was an efficient producer, it distributed one third of the electricity in the country despite having only 23 percent of the plant.

The company had a 50 percent–50 percent debt-equity ratio, which was moderately conservative. (Mentally, we subtract 20 percentage points from the debt ratio of a utility to arrive at a figure comparable to that of an industrial company, so Endesa's adjusted debt–equity ratio was about 30 percent–70 percent.) And the company's capital spending program was ending, so this ratio was likely to come down.

In 1991, the company had just overcome its main deficiency, its northeastern location, by acquiring Sevillana, which served the richest, most urban parts of the country in the east and south. Endesa now served a good one third of Spain by land area, and a larger percentage of that in terms of population and gross domestic product (GDP).

Volume growth in Spain was about 3 to 4 percent, but Endesa was located in the faster-growing part of the country, where volume gains of 5 to 6 percent could be achieved. In addition, the price regulation, which allowed a 3 percent price increase in real terms, was very favorable. Factoring a dollar inflation of about 3 percent (and assuming a normal purchasing power parity relationship), the company could increase revenues and earnings in dollar terms by about 10 to 12 percent a year. Profits probably could increase at the high end of this range.

The dividend yield was a couple of percentage points below that of a mature American electric utility, but the growth prospects were much better. A "crossover" dividend rate on the original cost would take place in four to five years. (That is, Endesa's dividend rate on the original purchase price would be higher than the other company's by that time.)

Endesa also had fast-growing subsidiaries in Latin America, specifically in Spanish-speaking Chile and Argentina, and would be in a position to bid on Brazilian electric companies if and when this government "privatized" these operations and opened them up to foreign investment. Latin America was considered a promising area for investment in 1991, although it has been discredited since then because of the recurring economic crises.

It was bought at a price of $21 in mid-1991, just above book. With an 18 percent return on equity (ROE), its modified asset value was $(18/15)$ * 2 = 1.44 times book, or about $29. Throw in a dividend of over $1 an American Depositary Receipt (ADR) (and multiply this by 10) and total investment value was nearly $40 a share. So the purchase price was just over half of investment value. It was sold in 1994 at a price of $54, having reached investment value.

Pioneer Financial Services, 1993–1995

Pioneer Financial Services was a small insurer in the life and health areas. It had a checkered past due to periodic waves of expansion and retrenchment, which eventually created a value opportunity. The full potential of this investment was not realized until the company's fundamental problem, inadequate size, worked to its advantage by making it a takeover candidate.

In 1990, the company lost money from operations because of overexpansion. The company seemed to pull itself together in 1991, but the following year, in 1992, the company's assets were overstated because of deferred acquisition costs and needed to be written down. The stock took a tumble when the charge was announced. But the company's earnings power was basically intact.

Early in 1993, some stock was bought at 5¼. We chickened out, and sold at 6½, and watched it go all the way to 14. The lower valuation had been just over four times 1993 share earnings of $1.25. As it were, the company's last major problem was in 1992. Given this premise, the $5 price was ridiculously cheap.

The stock was reentered the following year, below book, at $9. Further purchases were made at $11, and the last batch was purchased at $14, in 1995, just above book. The company was actually positioned in the better insurance areas, life and health. It had no property and casualty exposure. A final check of asset quality turned up no obvious problems and indicated that management had learned a lesson.

The fact that the chairman (and founder) owned 28 percent of the stock was encouraging, and other top managers owned a further 5 percent. Moreover, the company was aggressively buying back stock. So managers were positioned to think like owners. The company was generating cash, and its earnings were real. This is an important consideration when accounting has recently come under question for other companies.

It was troubling that Value Line gave the stock a low Financial Strength rating, C++, which corresponds to a B rating from Moody's or Standard & Poor's (S&P). This was probably because of $57 million of convertible bonds that they treated as debt. The bonds were convertible at a stock price of $11.75, so with the stock selling at $13, it could be treated as equity. The bonds had a maturity date five years hence but were callable in 1997. In 1995, the company made an exchange offer to convert some of the bonds into stock, a year and half ahead of the call date.

The company's ROE was in the 10 to 12 percent range, but the plan was to raise it to at least 15 percent. This would yield earnings growth above 15 percent during the transition period and 15 percent thereafter. At that time, a stock of this sort could sell at 13 to 14 times earnings, or twice book value. So whether one used a price–earnings (P/E) or price–book (P/B) valuation, there was a prospective doubling on valuation alone. An acceleration of growth would only be gravy. Earnings growth of 15 to 18 percent over a five-year period would lead to a further doubling or tripling of the price. The total impact would have been four to six times.

Although the company struggled through 1996, Pioneer Financial Services was taken over by Conseco late in that year for a price of $28 a share. The investment had more than doubled in two and a half years.

Dell Computer, 1996

Dell Computer might easily go into the "missed" category. It is an exercise in modified, rather than original Graham and Dodd, investing, because its ROEs are well over 15 percent. Consequently, it sells for a significant premium over book value, but its high ROE often compensates for this fact.

Dell Computer was started by a college kid, Michael Dell, who remains today as chairman. Its original market niche was in direct selling of computers and parts by mail order. This enabled Dell to cut out the middleman and, consequently, to sell at very competitive prices while maintaining a high degree of profitability. By the early 1990s, it was one of the most profitable computer companies in terms of net profit margins, even though gross margins were lower than that of its competitors. This direct sales model enabled Dell to gain market share from IBM, and also Compaq Computer, which was a somewhat larger firm. But the fact that Dell was the smallest of the three meant that even a small erosion of the existing share of the two competitors meant a large percentage gain for Dell.

In 1993, the stock had been hammered by trading losses on foreign currency. This was not an inconsequential problem—trading losses later brought Orange County to the brink of bankruptcy. But it was a one-time problem for the company that created a major investment opportunity that was missed.

The stock was bought early in 1996, at about twice book value, and actually half of modified investment value (which would be four times book value given a 30 percent ROE). This occurred when the prices of computer stocks were falling because prices were falling across the board for high-tech products in general. Moore's Law, promulgated by Gordon Moore, a founder of Intel, stated that computing power would double every 18 months, which meant that prices for a given amount of computational ability would fall by 50 percent every 18 months, or about 30 percent a year. But the prices of parts and chips were also falling by a comparable amount. So while unit prices were falling steadily, margins remained stable (because costs were dropped at roughly the same rate), but the lower prices caused unit sales to increase by a greater percentage than the fall in prices. (Demand was "elastic" in economic jargon.) Hence, the top and bottom lines gained significantly in a time of falling prices.

Two things helped the computer business. One was the mid-1990s "popularization" of tech products. The personal computer business had hit a "sweet spot" because the price of a PC was falling from around $3,000 a unit to less than $1,000 a box in the three years or so between 1995 and 1998. This put it in reach of the average family, in much the same way as TVs had become generally accessible after World War II. Demand was also helped by the popularization of computer games and the Internet, both of which were particularly attractive to younger people. This represented an audience that had previously been absent. The second factor was that a glut of chips by Korean and Japanese manufacturers caused costs to temporarily fall faster than selling prices, allowing for wider margins.

Dell was held briefly in 1996, for a gain of around 50 percent, missing a 500 percent gain that was achieved after it was sold. Thus, the growth story was missed, even though a value discipline allowed participation for a short period of time. It could have been a Warren Buffett–type long-term holding, and could have made the author richer earlier. Instead, the premature sale illustrates the weakness of the Graham and Dodd investment style. At the time the investment was made, we had only the slightest knowledge and understanding of the computer industry and were unable to compare the merits of one computer company to another.

British Steel, 1999

This had been a missed opportunity as early as 1992, when the ADRs sold for as little as $7, that was redeemed in 1999 at almost as favorable circumstances. The entry price was more than double the earlier price, but the value of the assets had also increased significantly in the meantime.

Steel is considered unattractive by many investors because it is clearly a commodity business, in one of the so-called "deep cyclicals." But the company had a virtual monopoly of steel in Britain. The fear was that of the European Union when trade barriers would collapse over most of the western part of the continent, outside of England and Scandinavia. The other fear was the collapse of Asian demand for steel and other metals in late 1997 and early 1998. There was finally the concern that a European steel company could not compete with low-cost producers in Asia and Latin America.

Fixed assets were in some cases obsolete and overstated on the books. So the company was worth somewhat less than the high $30s per ADR represented by book value. But British Steel had spent a good part of the early 1990s refurbishing many of its plants with new machinery and equipment. So part of its asset base was modern, just not the whole amount carried on its books. In order to clarify things, the company might have done well to shutter major portions of capacity and write them off. But the company had $20 an ADR in working capital, and about $13 an ADR net-net, after subtracting long-term debt. (Long-term debt was about $1 billion dollars, but the company had $7.5 billion dollars in equity at book, and $3.4 billion based on market capitalization.)

The company was paying a dividend whose yield was in the double digits. The dividend had been cut over a period of several bad years, but then substantially restored. The company had learned a painful public relations lesson about promises regarding dividend disbursements, and we believed it would not make the same mistake again.

Our calculation was that the company was worth almost $15 a share, on any *one* of the three measures—dividend stream, net working capital after debt, and fixed assets. This said, the company was selling at 30 to 40 percent of the sum of the value of these three components put together.

Financial strength was substantial. In fact, on a purely ratio-based calculation, without regard for the cyclical nature of the business, the company might qualify for the second-highest rating, say AA by Moody's or S&P or A+ by Value Line.

The chairman was Sir Brian Moffett, who had been chief financial officer when the company had sold below working capital. Taking its investment value as only net working capital, plus the 10 times the dividend, allowing nothing for the fixed assets, yielded a figure of $30 per ADR. Our cost was half of that.

The company was finally merged with one of its smaller rivals, Hoogovens of the Netherlands, and the combined entity took the name the Corus Group. This began a long process of rationalization in the European steel industry that would eventually help all the players. (Its main rivals, Usinor of France and Acelia of Spain, would merge a few years later.) As a parting gift, there was a $5 per ADR special dividend, after which we sold our holding with total return of 60 percent in less than a year. It was an investment that Andrew Carnegie would have made.

Philip Morris, 1999

This was *the* stock of the 1980s in our personal portfolio, powering the account to average annual percentage gains in the mid-20s.

Philip Morris's main business was tobacco. But it also had a major food operation, having used its cash flows from tobacco to acquire General Foods and Kraft Foods in the 1980s and Nabisco Foods around 2000. It also had Miller Beer, which it sold to South African Breweries in 2002. In fact, the value of the food operations tends to approximate the market value of the whole company when the stock hits its lows, meaning that the tobacco operations were assigned a value of zero at such times.

The stock (and those of other tobacco companies) had "always" sold at a low P/E ratio because of the threat of tobacco litigation. Hence, it was a reasonable value investment that provided above-average dividend yields along with steady, low-to-mid-teens percentage growth. Nevertheless, the stock moved steadily upward during the 1960s, 1970s, and 1980s. The 1990s would prove to be the exception to the rule as tobacco litigation came to a peak in that decade.

There was probably a reason that the tobacco crisis came to a head in the 1990s and not during some other decade. Published in 1991, the book *Generations*[1] (discussed at length in Chapter 20) presciently warned that the "new Puritan" Baby Boomers, born just after World War II, would "strike like blow after blow against tobacco" as they entered midlife. The spirit of the times was much like Prohibition of the 1920s, which was brought about by the post–Civil War babies, as they entered their middle years. The generation that preceded the Boomers, the Silent generation, had set the stage for this by being the most litigious generation in American history. A member of this Silent generation is Mayor Michael Bloomberg of New York City.

We had dumped our Philip Morris stock for technical reasons early in 1993. For the first time in many years, the stock had been quoted lower at the end of 1992 than at the end of the previous year. Thus, the growth trend appeared to have been broken.

Our assumption in 1999 was that the worst case scenario would slice the company in half, causing earnings, dividends, and assets to be only 50 percent of their current levels. (This assumed that the plaintiffs would take half the company in a settlement rather than killing the goose that laid the golden egg.) Under this assumption, the P/E ratio of 7.5 is really 15, and the dividend yield of 8 percent is more like 4 percent at our entry price of $24. We assumed, moreover, that growth will continue, albeit a depressed base. In fact, the stock rebounded to the low $40s, where we sold it, then continued into the low $50s, where it was fully valued, after allowing for continued litigation risk.

The company was dealt two more blows, in 2002 by a $28 *billion* jury award to a Rhode Island woman, and by a campaign waged against tobacco by New York City Mayor Michael Bloomberg, who saddled cigarettes with a prohibitively high city tax, and who pushed to ban smoking in public places such as restaurants.

Our best guess is that demand for tobacco, hence Altria shares, will rebound later in the 2000s decade, as the Baby Boomers start retiring, and the midlife managerial (and prosecutorial) slots are taken over by the more pragmatic Generation X, who now provide the bulk of the nation's smokers. Also, if economic times prove to be anywhere near as hard as we believe they will be, smoking will enjoy a revival in popularity. (It may well be that the "boom" times of the 1990s discouraged smoking by encouraging people to focus on "higher-order" needs.)

FIVE OVERLOOKED INVESTMENTS

This group of investments was considered by the author, but was missed because they were not fully understood at the time the opportunity presented itself.

Ericsson of Sweden, 1987

Ericsson is a maker of telecommunications equipment. That is a sexy business today, but was considered unglamorous at the time. It's true that the old wire-line phone business in developed markets was mature. But this was a good steady business. It was the premier company of Sweden, the General Electric of that country. Ericsson also had a reputation for technological sophistication, albeit in a field that was considered somewhat dated.

The stock was selling below the company's working capital and a fraction of book value. The company had suffered an earnings reversal compared to a strong 1986, but was still profitable. The dividend was a not-insignficant 5 percent. The main drawback was that this company was too large a player in its industry to be a takeover candidate, even if the Swedish government would have allowed a takeover. The stock skyrocketed by several times in the late 1980s to a multiple of book value.

There was a second chance in 1992, when the company was selling for twice book, or at 1 times modified investment value, given its high ROE, but the opportunity was missed again. This company and others were rescued by several important changes. First, important new applications such as cellular phones and data transmission networks were invented. This led to a second communications revolution for which Ericsson, as well as Nokia of Finland and Motorola of the United States were in a perfect position to capitalize on. Second, emerging markets in Latin America and East Asia became important customers of phone products. In fact, in a number of countries, demand for cellular telephones exceeded demand for wire-line products as these country tried to leap-frog their way into a modern level of interconnectivity without having to install phone lines and other infrastructure for more standard products. This effect was particularly pronounced in Finland, where there were relatively few people in a relatively large country located in or near Arctic latitudes, and in South Korea, where the relative affluence of the population caused demand to explode. In fact, by the late 1990s, roughly one third of the company's sales were made to the above-mentioned markets.

Value stocks can become growth stocks, but if you buy them on a value basis before growth takes off, you can get the "best" price. Put another way, if you do the right thing in the Graham and Dodd sense of the word, you will sometimes get lucky and be rewarded for something that you didn't expect. It could have been a long-term "evergreen" holding for the whole of the 1990s, but you would have had to get out as the new century dawned in order to preserve your capital gains.

Ericsson was eventually outcompeted in the handset market by Nokia of Finland. All three wireless companies suffered during the collapse of the tech boom, but Nokia suffered a bit less than the other two. Many of the same things that applied to Ericsson also applied to Nokia. Unfortunately for American investors, Nokia was listed as an ADR only in 1994, after the stock had begun to leave Graham and Dodd territory.

Wells Fargo, 1990

This was ultimately a miss that initially started out as a hit. In the fall of 1990, we began the purchase of Wells Fargo at a price of $50. It was selling below book, for about five times 1990 earnings, and paid a dividend that provided a generous yield at that price. It was thrilling to read a few weeks later that these purchases had been made in the company of Berkshire Hathaway. Nevertheless, when the stock shortly bounced up to $55, the entire holding in the issue was sold, cutting and running with a mere 10 percent gain, on the theory that "you don't go broke taking a profit."

Wells Fargo was chaired by Carl Reichart, who was famous in a notoriously profligate industry as a cost cutter. This fact alone ensured that the institution would be more profitable over the long term than most other banks. But the California location was a big question mark because the U.S. economy was going into a recession, and California, having been one of the greatest beneficiaries of the foregoing boom, would likely suffer more than most other parts of the country.

In the 1990 Berkshire Hathaway annual report, it became clear that Warren Buffett had considered some of the same issues we had. The first risk he cited was one of an earthquake in California. A more pressing concern was "the possibility of an economic contraction or financial panic so severe that it would endanger almost any highly leveraged institution, no matter how intelligently run." The last and most realistic fear was the collapse of real estate values and loans, especially in California, to which he said, "Wells Fargo is thought to be particularly vulnerable." He then suggested that losses on such loans could reduce 1991 earnings to zero but considered this a "low level possibility, not a likelihood." Even if this were to occur, he would not be greatly disturbed because few other companies "could then be expected to earn 20 percent on growing equity."[2]

Our less sanguine view was the more nearly correct one for 1991. We saw rightly that the breakeven scenario outlined was a probability, not merely a possibility, because most banks were in the process of "kitchen sinking" all of their bad loans at one time. Wells Fargo did the same; earnings disappeared as a result, and even more distressing, the dividend declined as well. Surprisingly, the stock bounced past $100, early in 1991, on the back of the Persian Gulf War euphoria, but then fell back to $57 by mid-1992. ROE for that year was only 14 percent, not 20 percent. Even so, the bank was clearly in a recovery mode, and the dividend would shortly be reinstated, albeit at a fraction of its earlier levels. So we had a chance to repurchase our shares in 1992 slightly above where we sold them a year and a half earlier (actually below the sales price of $55, adjusted upward for interest income), under much more favorable circumstances than the earlier purchase, and failed to do so.

The moral of the story was that we were right about near-term prospects, but Buffett was more correct about the longer term, which ultimately was the one that counted. The company did return to a 15 to

20 percent ROE after 1994. The California location, after having been a disadvantage early in the 1990s, was an advantage later in the decade because there was much less competition, at least from local institutions (Bank of America was not particularly well run). A chance to improve on Buffett's performance was missed, and the net result was a lost opportunity.

Following the retirement of Mr. Reichart, the company overreached in 1996, paying too much in the acquisition of California's First Interstate. It was acquired in turn in 1998 by Norwest Corporation of Minneapolis, which renamed the combined company Wells Fargo.

Citicorp, 1995

Citicorp, based in New York City, was the largest commercial bank in the United States. It had a broad franchise that included the nation's largest consumer loan (read credit card) portfolio, as well a large domestic corporate banking operation, and an international bank of world-class dimensions.

Citicorp had been plagued by bad loans to developing countries, notably in Latin America. In the mid-1980s, its outgoing chairman Walter Wriston had substituted the assertion "countries don't go bust" for credit analysis. As a result, the virtues of the consumer and domestic commercial banking were obscured.

The incoming chairman, John Reed, had in fact, built a Citicorp for the future. A graduate of the Massachusetts Institute of Technology (MIT), he had risen through the "back office," using technology to build an automated teller machine (ATM) credit card operation, and generally position the bank for the 1990s and the twenty-first century. His main failing was his initial difficulty in dealing with problems inherited from Wriston and his former peers on the corporate lending side. In fact, given the dominance of the corporate credit culture, it was something of a miracle that he had risen to the chairmanship of the holding company. (His mentor had suggested to Wriston that the top three members of the new generation be put through a horse race, which Reed proceeded to win).

Citicorp had approached bankruptcy in the early 1990s. At that time, the stock dipped below $10 a share, just more than one quarter of book value. But it had been saved by a timely capital infusion from an Arab investor, Prince Alwaleed bin Talal. The stock reflected this fact during the latter part of 1992 and through 1993. Like Warren Buffett's GEICO, this was a turnaround situation in the classic Graham and Dodd sense, but too complicated and risky for the average investor.

As a result of the seven interest rate hikes by the Fed in 1994–1995, Citicorp stock, along with that most other money center banks, fell back into

Graham and Dodd territory. At the beginning of 1995, it was selling at $39, or approximately year-ahead book. Adding in its dividend, it was also selling below investment value. The bank offered limited earnings growth in 1995 because 1994 earnings had been tax advantaged. After adjusting that year's earnings for taxes, the bank had earned only about $5.25 a share in 1994, a much more realistic base against which to compare 1995 earnings of over $6 a share. So Citicorp had the dual advantages of good earnings growth and a bargain price. Given these factors and the concern's prominence in the world economy, we and others should have followed the Prince's lead and made this a foundation holding in the early to mid-1990s. (His later investments in high-tech companies proved to be far less astute, however.)

In 1998, the value of Citicorp's franchise was underscored when it merged with Traveler's Group, headed by Sandy Weill, to form Citigroup, thereby becoming one of the Dow 30 stocks. In order to allow the merger to go through, the U.S. Congress had to repeal the 1930s Glass-Steagall Act which prevented banks and investment companies from being under the same roof. Citigroup now offered a full-scale commercial bank and a major investment bank (Smith Barney) under one roof. The stock skyrocketed because the combined company sold for over two times book, and earnings had also grown significantly between 1995 and 1998. The "merger of equals" would lead to an interesting, if somewhat uncertain, future because of the power-sharing arrangements (Sandy Weill and John Reed became co-CEOs until Reed's departure) and the differences in corporate cultures.

International Aluminum, 2000

International Aluminum met many of the criteria for Graham and Dodd investment. It was in a "boring" commodity business, selling aluminum siding and parts for home building. Falling profitability had depressed the stock price, putting it at a substantial discount to book value. After some deliberation, we finally decided not to undertake an investment here. Part of the reason was its small size, which did not qualify it for a Graham and Dodd investment. But a more important reason was our nagging doubts about management's ability to engineer a successful turnaround. This was a missed investment that was rightly passed, although with the benefit of hindsight, the stock did rebound meaningfully from our proposed entry point.

Slowing sales and the margin squeeze had depressed profits. The company struggled to rein in geographically and operationally far-flung operations, the legacy of an ill-conceived acquisition program. The main problem was that there were too many product lines and sales channels to manage easily. But the company failed to squeeze much cash by selling or shutting down peripheral operations, and if anything, they appeared to be users of funds as International Aluminum (IAL) tried to turn them around instead of downsizing them.

The low net profit margin was not as good a measure of the company's lack of profitability as the low and falling ROE. In its best days in the mid-1990s, it had actually shown an ROE in the mid-teens. Now each dollar of shareholder equity was earning one third that, or 5 percent. Surely margins and returns wouldn't remain this low forever. Our best guess was that "average" profitability was represented by an ROE of about 8 percent.

The company's charm was its balance sheet. It had no debt and a book value of $29 a share, and half of that was in the form of working capital. At $14 a share, or less than half of book value, we were sorely tempted to enter into this situation. With this price, even a "normalized" ROE of 8 percent made this an enticing proposition. With a dividend payout ratio of 50 percent, the dividend distribution rate was 4 percent. But this distribution of 4 percent of book value led to an 8 percent yield, based on an entry price of half of book. The retained earnings rate of 4 percent would theoretically lead to 4 percent growth. So the theoretical total return was 12 percent for the company on an "as is" basis. Given a commodity business and a management we believed to be only mediocre, there was still a meaningful upside. And there was always the chance of takeover or management buy-out at or near book, which would increase the return above the indicated 12 percent level.

In fact, a private investor, who owned about 7 percent of the stock, tried to take over the rest of the company with a bid of $18.25, a slight premium to the stock's low. But management refused the offer. Realizing that the company had a problem, it made several high-level changes in a last-ditch attempt to preserve some continuity of control.

Even after the personnel changes, management was worse than mediocre—it was below average. The company failed to capitalize on the housing boom of 2001 and 2002. Instead, it suffered all sorts of misadventures, including a labor strike and the loss of key customers. The ROE continued to deteriorate, bringing into question both profitability and the sustainability of the dividend. With such poor operating fundamentals, even a strong balance sheet and a bargain entry price could not make this an attractive investment. Other, more sanguine investors did take the stock price back up to the low 20s.

Wolohan Lumber, 2001

This is the flip side of International Aluminum, a small-cap company that should have been bought. Of course, this is said partly with the benefit of hindsight. But there were numerous, if subtle, signs that this was an investment situation worth pursuing. These signs were, however, missed until it was too late.

Wolohan Lumber also served the relatively mature housing market. Like International Aluminum, Wolohan Lumber had hit a brick wall in terms of sales growth, because of commodity (lumber) prices, and margins were also under pressure from competition. Unlike IAL, Wolohan's management reacted appropriately to create value for themselves and for other shareholders. It sharpened its focus on its core businesses, divesting operations that did not fit the focus. Also, the company introduced new value-added products and services, generating cash flow and shrinking the asset base. Hence, the relatively low ROE of 6 to 7 percent was maintained.

Book value was over $20 a share, and current assets represented nearly half this, yet the stock was selling in the low teens. Management had reduced the share base by nearly 25 percent in open-market purchases below $15 a share in 2000–2001. Even so, the balance sheet remained strong, as debt was reduced at the same time as equity. That was an indication that the company had very strong cash flow. A look at the flow of funds statement showed that this was the case, even though the income statement looked lackluster. The company was tightening control of working capital and also generating significant funds through the sale of assets. Given this fact, the bargain purchase price represented a real discount to a progressively more liquid asset base.

Management, specifically James Wolohan, now owned just under half the stock. Having already pursued a shareholder-friendly course of action, management was ready to complete a major restructuring such as a management buyout. Nevertheless, the stock dipped to $10 a share and was selling at less than half of book value. The thing that limited our interest was the low dividend. Nevertheless, we should have taken the share repurchases into account in calculating the dividend distribution rate.

It was likely that management would do a leveraged buyout. In fact, the company made a tender offer at $15 a share for any and all public stock, in order to "provide liquidity" to shareholders. The purchase would be effected partly from internally generated funds, and partly from long-term debt. Most but not all outside shareholders accepted the offer, and the stock continued to trade in small amounts. It rose to about $20 a share, approximating book value.

Management finally took the company private at $25.75 a share in August 2003. The company is now in effect a personal holding company of James Wolohan, who owned a majority of the shares. There are severe IRS restrictions on net-net working capital of personal holding companies, which is taxed at a high penalty rate in order to force the owner to pay out dividends. This stricture does not apply to working capital offset by long-term debt. The company had to borrow money to do the buyout, but it's likely that as the company continues to generate cash and pay down debt, it will reissue shares in the open market to reduce the owner's interest to less than 50 percent.

In sum, Wolohan Lumber shared with IAL the dual characteristics of an attractive balance sheet and anemic income statement. What set the two companies apart was the former's much more cash-generative statement of changes in financial position. This was a sign that true economic profitability was greater than accounting profitability, and led to a monetization of outside shareholders' claims.

1988	1989	1990	1991E	Year
15.87	19.13	22.82	**24.00**	Revenues per ADR
4.97	5.61	6.96	**7.65**	"Cash Flow" per ADR
2.27	2.60	3.38	**3.85**	Earnings per ADR
0.80	0.70	0.90	**1.18**	Dividends per ADR
13.95	13.82	17.92	**20.75**	Book Value per ADR
260.01	260.01	260.01	**260.01**	ADRs (mill.)
12.0	14.1	18.1	20.0	ADR Price (year low)
3120.1	3666.1	4706.2	**5200.2**	Market Cap (mill.)
5.3	5.4	5.4	**5.2**	P/E Ratio
0.9	1.0	1.0	**1.0**	P/B Ratio
6.7%	5.0%	5.0%	**5.9%**	Dividend yield
4127.1	4974.4	5933.9	**6700**	Revenues (mill.)
591.4	677.7	887.4	**1040**	Net Profit (mill.)
54.8%	55.2%	50.2%	**46.0%**	Long-Term Debt Ratio
45.2%	44.8%	49.8%	**54.0%**	Shareholders' Equity Ratio
7.8%	12.6%	12.8%	**13.5%**	Return on Capital
16.3%	18.9%	19.0%	**19.1%**	Return on Equity
8.3%	13.0%	12.9%	**13.4%**	Reinvestment Rate
8.0%	5.9%	6.1%	**5.7%**	Dividend Distribution Rate
51%	69%	68%	**70%**	Retained Earnings Rate
49%	31%	32%	**30%**	Dividend Payout Ratio

Bold figures were Value Line estimates or derived from them.
Source: Value Line Publishing Inc.; author's calculations.

FIGURE 16.1   Summary Statistics for Endesa 1988–1991.

1993	1994	1995	1996E	Year
1.26	1.58	1.85	**2.00**	Earnings per Share
0.00	0.15	0.18	**0.21**	Dividends per Share
10.24	14.35	14.35	**16.65**	Book Value per Share
6.72	5.92	10.08	**10.50**	Shares (mill.)
4.6	8.5	8.8	15.0	Share Price (year low)
30.9	50.3	88.7	**157.5**	Market Cap (mill.)
3.7	5.4	4.8	**7.5**	P/E Ratio
0.4	0.6	0.6	**0.9**	P/B Ratio
0.0%	1.8%	2.0%	**1.4%**	Dividend Yield
703.7	774.2	800.1	**930**	Total Income (mill.)
12.2	17.1	21	**29**	Net Profit (mill.)
1108	1076	1559	**1700**	Total Assets (mill.)
92.5	90	165.8	**175**	Shareholders' Equity (mill.)
13.1%	19.1%	12.8%	**16.5%**	Return on Equity
10.9%	15.9%	10.9%	**15.2%**	Reinvestment Rate
2.2%	3.2%	1.9%	**1.3%**	Dividend Distribution Rate
83%	83%	85%	**92%**	Earnings Retention Rate
17%	17%	15%	**8%**	Dividend Payout Ratio

Bold figures were Value Line estimates or derived from them.
Source: Value Line Publishing Inc.; author's calculations.

FIGURE 16.2 Summary Statistics for Pioneer Financial Services 1993–1996.

1993	1994	1995	1996E	Year
37.88	43.79	56.67	**77.35**	Sales per Share
-0.09	2.19	3.30	**4.20**	"Cash Flow" per Share
-0.53	1.58	2.74	**3.60**	Earnings per Share
0.00	0.00	0.00	**0.00**	Dividends per Share
4.54	6.61	10.35	**14.10**	Book Value per Share
75.86	79.36	93.45	**95.00**	Shares (mill.)
6.9	9.6	19.8	**23.0**	Share Price (year low)
523.4	761.9	1850.3	**2185.0**	Market Cap (mill.)
NMF	6.1	7.2	**6.4**	P/E Ratio
1.5	1.5	1.9	**1.6**	P/B Ratio
0.0%	0.0%	0.0%	**0.0%**	Dividend Yield
2873.2	3475.3	5296.0	**7350.0**	Sales (mill.)
30.7	33.1	38.0	**42.0**	Depreciation (mill.)
-35.8	149.2	272.0	**360.0**	Net Profit (mill.)
510.4	719.0	1018.0	**1150.0**	Working Capital (mill.)
100.0	113.4	113.0	**0.0**	Long-Term Debt (mill.)
471.1	651.7	973.0	**1340.0**	Shareholders' Equity (mill.)
NMF	20.30%	25.70%	**27%**	Return on Capital
NMF	22.90%	28.00%	**27%**	Return on Equity
NMF	21.5%	27.7%	**27%**	Reinvestment Rate
NMF	1.4%	0.3%	**0%**	Dividend Distribution Rate
NMF	94%	99%	**100%**	Earnings Retention Rate
NMF	6%	1%	**0%**	Dividend Payout Ratio

Bold figures were Value Line estimates or derived from them.
Source: Value Line Publishing Inc.; author's calculations.

FIGURE 16.3   Summary Statistics for Dell Computer 1993–1996.

1996	1997	1998E	1999E	Year
57.79	57.85	**58.60**	**60.60**	Sales per ADR
4.86	4.34	**3.60**	**4.10**	"Cash Flow" per ADR
3.33	1.89	**1.00**	**1.50**	Earnings per ADR
1.55	1.77	**1.77**	**1.77**	Dividends per ADR
38.05	38.49	**39.15**	**39.90**	Book Value per ADR
203.58	203.76	**198.14**	**198.00**	ADRs (mill.)
24.9	20.8	16.4		ADR Price (year low)
5069.1	4238.2	**3249.5**		Market Cap (mill.)
7.5	11.0	**16.4**		P/E Ratio
0.7	0.5	**0.4**		P/B Ratio
6.2%	8.5%	**10.8%**		Dividend Yield
11775	11463	**11600**	**12000**	Sales (mill.)
485.7	486.8	**510**	**520**	Depreciation (mill.)
505.3	372.9	**200**	**295**	Net Profit (mill.)
5258.1	3858.4	**4250**	**4500**	Working Capital (mill.)
1038.3	1193	**1000**	**975**	Long-Term Debt (mill.)
7753.9	7626.3	**7750**	**7900**	Shareholders' Equity (mill.)
6.2%	4.7%	**2.5%**	**3.5%**	Return on Capital
6.5%	4.9%	**2.5%**	**3.5%**	Return on Equity
2.2%	0.5%	**NMF**	**NMF**	Reinvestment Rate
4.3%	4.4%	**NMF**	**NMF**	Dividend Distribution Rate
34%	11%	**NMF**	**NMF**	Earnings Retention Rate
66%	89%	**NMF**	**NMF**	Dividend Payout Ratio

Bold figures were Value Line estimates or derived from them.
Source: Value Line Publishing Inc.; author's calculations.

FIGURE 16.4 Summary Statistics for British Steel 1996–1999.

Year	1997	1998	1999	2000	2001	2002
Sales per Share	29.71	30.61	33.61	36.38	41.78	39.43
"Cash Flow" per Share	3.3	2.91	4.01	4.63	5.06	5.26
Earnings per Share	2.58	2.20	3.19	3.75	3.87	4.49
Dividends per Share	1.6	1.68	1.84	2.02	2.22	2.44
Book Value per Share	6.15	6.66	6.54	6.79	9.12	9.55
Shares (mill.)	2425.5	2430.5	2338.5	2208.9	2152.5	2039.3
Share Price (year low)	36	34.8	21.3	18.7	38.8	35.4
Market Cap (mill.)	87318	84581.4	49810.05	41306.43	83517	72191.22
P/E Ratio	14.0	15.8	6.7	5.0	10.0	7.9
P/B Ratio	5.9	5.2	3.3	2.8	4.3	3.7
Dividend Yield	4.4%	4.8%	8.6%	10.8%	5.7%	6.9%
Sales (mill.)	72055	74391	78596	80356	89924	80408
Depreciation (mill.)	1700	1690	1702	1717	2337	1331
Net Profit (mill.)	6310	5372	7675	8510	8560	9402
Working Capital (mill.)	2369	3851	2878	-8711	-2866	-1641
Long-Term Debt (mill.)	11585	11906	11280	18255	17159	19189
Shareholders' Equity (mill.)	14920	16197	15305	15005	19620	19478
Return on Capital	25.8%	20.9%	30.8%	27.2%	25.4%	26.0%
Return on Equity	42.3%	33.2%	50.1%	56.7%	43.6%	48.3%
Reinvestment Rate	16.1%	8.6%	21.5%	26.6%	19.2%	22.2%
Dividend Distribution Rate	26.2%	24.6%	28.6%	30.1%	24.4%	26.1%
Earnings Retention Rate	38%	26%	43%	47%	44%	46%
Dividend Payout Ratio	62%	74%	57%	53%	56%	54%

Source: Value Line Publishing Inc.; author's calculations.

FIGURE 16.5 Summary Statistics for Philip Morris (Altria) 1997–2002.

Year	1987	1988	1989	1990	1991E	1992E
Sales per ADR	29.08	26.66	31.01	39.03	37.60	38.35
"Cash Flow" per ADR	1.65	1.83	2.65	4.29	2.50	2.45
Earnings per ADR	0.59	1.05	1.69	2.89	0.95	0.90
Dividends per ADR	0.31	0.34	0.45	0.62	0.63	0.65
Book Value per ADR	7.79	8.26	9.69	12.85	13.00	13.20
ADRs (mill.)	190.81	191.07	204.87	205.73	207.50	208.50
Share Price (low)	5.1	5.3	11.7	25.5	15.4	
Market Cap (mill.)	973.1	1012.7	2397.0	5246.1	3195.5	
P/E Ratio	8.6	5.0	6.9	8.8	16.2	
P/B Ratio	0.7	0.6	1.2	2.0	1.2	
Dividend Yield	6.1%	6.4%	3.8%	2.4%	4.1%	
Sales (mill.)	5548.0	5093.1	6353.3	8029.2	7800.0	8000.0
Depreciation (mill.)	201.9	150.4	204.0	276.2	325.0	325.0
Net Profit (mill.)	112.5	199.8	339.0	606.1	195.0	190.0
Working Capital (mill.)	2061.6	1895.7	2121.1	2566.9	2400.0	2500.0
Long-Term Debt (mill.)	557.7	496.7	341.0	188.5	150.0	150.0
Shareholders' Equity (mill.)	1487.0	1577.5	1985.4	2643.9	2700.0	2750.0
Return on Capital	6.4%	10.8%	15.5%	23.1%	8.0%	8.2%
Return on Equity	7.6%	12.7%	17.1%	22.9%	7.4%	7.7%
Reinvestment Rate	3.3%	8.5%	12.8%	18.3%	2.4%	2.2%
Dividend Distribution Rate	4.3%	4.2%	4.3%	4.6%	5.0%	5.5%
Earnings Retention Rate	43%	67%	75%	80%	33%	29%
Dividend Payout Ratio	57%	33%	25%	20%	67%	71%

Bold figures were Value Line estimates or derived from them.
Source: Value Line Publishing Inc.; author's calculations.

FIGURE 16.6 Summary Statistics for Ericcson Telecom 1987–1992.

Year	1989	1990	1991	1992	1993	1994
Earnings per Share	11.02	12.05	0.04	4.44	10.10	14.78
Dividends per Share	3.30	3.90	3.50	1.50	2.25	4.00
Book Value per Share	48.08	57.44	54.00	57.44	65.86	66.77
Shares (mill.)	51.08	51.44	52.00	55.19	55.81	51.25
Share Price (year low)	59	41.3	48	56.5	74.8	127.1
Market Cap (mill.)	3013.7	2124.5	2496.0	3118.2	4174.6	6513.9
P/E Ratio	5.4	3.4	NMF	12.7	7.4	8.6
P/B Ratio	1.2	0.7	0.9	1.0	1.1	1.9
Dividend Yield	5.6%	9.4%	7.3%	2.7%	3.0%	3.1%
Net Profit (mill.)	601.1	642.8	21.0	283.0	612.0	841
Long-Term Debt (mill.)	2541	2417.2	4220	4040	4221	2853
Shareholders' Equity (mill.)	2860.9	3359.8	3271	3809	4315	3911
Return on Equity	21.00%	19.10%	0.60%	7.40%	14.20%	21.50%
Reinvestment Rate	14.1%	12.4%	NMF	4.1%	10.1%	14.8%
Dividend Distribution Rate	6.9%	6.7%	NMF	3.3%	4.1%	6.7%
Earnings Retention Rate	67%	65%	NMF	55%	71%	69%
Dividend Payout Ratio	33%	35%	NMF	45%	29%	31%

Source: Value Line Publishing Inc.; author's calculations.

FIGURE 16.7 Summary Statistics for Wells Fargo 1989–1994.

Year	1990	1991	1992	1993	1994	1995E
Earnings per Share	0.57	-3.22	1.35	3.53	6.40	6.35
Dividends per Share	1.74	0.75	0.00	0.00	0.45	1.20
Book Value per Share	24.34	21.22	21.74	26.04	34.38	40.40
Shares (mill.)	336.51	346.25	366.49	366.49	395.08	425.00
Share Price (year low)	10.8	8.5	10.4	20.5	28.3	38.5
Market Cap (mill.)	3634	2943	3811	7513	11181	16363
P/E Ratio	18.9	-2.6	7.7	5.8	4.4	6.1
P/B Ratio	0.4	0.4	0.5	0.8	0.8	1.0
Dividend Yield	16.1%	8.8%	0.0%	0.0%	1.6%	3.1%
Net Profit (mill.)	318	-914	722	1919	3422	3450
Long-Term Debt (mill.)	23187	23345	20136	18133	17894	21000
Shareholders' Equity (mill.)	9679	9526	11217	13980	17769	20175
Return on Equity	3.30%	NMF	6.40%	13.70%	17.70%	17.0%
Reinvestment Rate	NMF	NMF	4.5%	11.5%	14.9%	17.0%
Dividend Distribution Rate	NMF	NMF	1.9%	2.2%	2.8%	0.0%
Earnings Retention Rate	NMF	NMF	71%	84%	84%	100%
Dividend Payout Ratio	NMF	NMF	29%	16%	16%	0%

Bold figures were Value Line estimates or derived from them.
Source: Value Line Publishing Inc.; author's calculations

FIGURE 16.8 Summary Statistics for Citicorp 1990–1995.

1999	2000	2001	2002	Year
56.99	50.78	50.16	45.64	Sales per Share
3.92	1.98	2.86	1.88	"Cash Flow" per Share
2.41	0.29	1.09	0.24	Earnings per Share
1.20	1.20	1.20	1.20	Dividends per Share
29.99	29.29	29.16	26.11	Book Value per Share
4.29	4.24	4.24	4.24	Shares (mill.)
23.4	14	17.8	15.5	Share Price (year low)
100.4	59.4	75.5	65.7	Market Cap (mill.)
9.7	12.8	16.3	64.6	P/E Ratio
0.8	0.5	0.6	0.6	P/B Ratio
5.1%	8.6%	6.7%	7.7%	Dividend Yield
244.6	215.5	212.9	193.7	Sales (mill).
6.5	7.2	7.5	7.0	Depreciation (mill.)
10.3	1.3	4.6	1.0	Net Profit (mill.)
69	63.6	66.1	58.0	Working Capital (mill.)
0	0	0	0	Long-Term Debt (mill.)
128.7	124.3	123.8	110.8	Shareholders' Equity (mill.)
8.0%	1.0%	3.7%	0.9%	Return on Capital
8.0%	1.0%	3.7%	0.9%	Return on Equity
4.0%	NMF	NMF	NMF	Reinvestment Rate
4.0%	NMF	NMF	NMF	Dividend Distribution Rate
50%	NMF	NMF	NMF	Earnings Retention Rate
50%	NMF	NMF	NMF	Dividend Payout Ratio

Source: Value Line Publishing Inc.; author's calculations.

FIGURE 16.9 Summary Statistics for International Aluminum 1999–2002.

1998	1999	2000E	2001E	Year
81.09	80.31	**72.20**	**77.65**	Sales per Share
2.73	2.70	**2.20**	**2.80**	"Cash Flow" per Share
1.05	1.19	**0.50**	**0.90**	Earnings per Share
0.28	0.28	**0.28**	**0.28**	Dividends per Share
17.78	19.27	**21.10**	**22.35**	Book Value per Share
5.55	5.03	**4.50**	**4.25**	Shares (mill.)
8.4	10.8	8.1		Share Price (year low)
46.6	54.3	**36.5**		Market Cap (mill.)
8.0	9.1	**16.2**		P/E Ratio
0.5	0.6	**0.4**		P/B Ratio
3.3%	2.6%	**3.5%**		Dividend Yield
449.9	404.0	**325.0**	**330.0**	Sales (mill.)
6.8	6.3	**2.5**	**4.0**	Net Profit (mill.)
53.2	52.3	**45.0**	**50.0**	Working Capital (mill.)
17.1	12.6	**9.0**	**11.0**	Long-Term Debt (mill.)
98.7	96.9	**93.0**	**94.0**	Shareholders' Equity (mill.)
6.8%	6.4%	**3.0%**	**4.5%**	Return on Capital
6.9%	6.5%	**2.5%**	**4.0%**	Return on Equity
5.0%	5.0%	**1.1%**	**2.8%**	Reinvestment Rate
1.5%	1.5%	**1.4%**	**1.2%**	Dividend Distribution Rate
73%	77%	**44%**	**69%**	Earnings Retention Rate
27%	23%	**56%**	**31%**	Dividend Payout Ratio

Bold figures were Value Line estimates or derived from them.
Source: Value Line Publishing Inc.; author's calculations.

FIGURE 16.10   Summary Statistics for Wolohan Lumber 1998–2001.

CHAPTER 17

A Real-Time Experiment

George Soros once demonstrated his investment technique with what he calls a "real-time experiment." In this chapter, the author uses the trades in his individual retirement account (IRA) in such an experiment for one year, calendar 1999. The accounting is simple, because there are no inflows or outflows of funds, and the reporting is handled by Charles Schwab. Moreover, it is a tax-deferred (read tax neutral) account, so that is where all the trading can take place without fear of tax consequences. This is not a wholly artificial condition, because roughly three fourths of the country's investment funds are in tax-deferred entities such as pension funds, IRAs, 401-k's, and annuities, or in tax-advantaged instruments such as municipal bonds. The size of the account is in the six figures, a small pool of money that won't incur "market movement" costs (those that result when a major fund moves the stock against it by the very act of trading it), or other liquidity problems associated with buying small-cap stocks, but is large enough to represent and be managed like "real money."

THE RUN-UP TO 1999

For some years before 1999, the portfolio had been primarily in the shares of Berkshire Hathaway (Class A). This holding began every year since 1993 (when it was bought) at a price moderately above investment value, but the results during the course of most years justified the premium. The main exception so far was 1996, when the stock underperformed, because it started the year selling for a price at which Warren Buffett averred, "Charlie and I would not buy it." It outperformed so much in 1997 and 1998 that it has doubled since early 1996 without a fully commensurate increase in underlying value. So 1999 was a year when it was likely to underperform again. At any rate, it provided a good opportunity to break loose from an overdependency on one holding. In the fall of 1998, the holdings of the Berkshire, then representing over 60 percent of the portfolio, were sold, and the proceeds reinvested in value stocks. This one weighting has been coupled with a heavy cash position, typically 30 to 40 percent of the portfolio. Nevertheless, the portfolio managed to beat the S&P 500 in 1998 by some five percentage points. This result, in fact, meant dodging a major bullet since value investors underperformed both growth investors and the Standard & Poor's (S&P) 500. (The 1997 result, however, was less than spectacular because Berkshire's good performance was not enough to offset the drag of the heavy cash position.)

At the end of 1998, the portfolio was realigned for 1999. This is because the fourth quarter of the year is used to get a first glimpse of likely stock performance in the new year, and also to reposition the portfolio before the starting gun, if possible. The author has always been a value investor, but is now going full tilt with a hard core version of this philosophy. The new investments going into 1999 included:

- *Filene's Basement.* This used to be a $6 stock, and is now less than $2. Another $2 stock is Morgan Products, a maker of household interior products such as doors and windows. Both investments are below book value. Both stocks were at the bottom of Value Line's bargain "basement" screen.

- *British Steel.* This stock has an unbeatable yield of almost 12 percent. Steel is down now, but will likely snap back when Asia comes back. Earnings are puny, maybe nonexistent, but the company can earn $5 to $6 an American Depositary Receipt (ADR) in a good year, just over $2 an ADR on average, enough to cover a dividend of around $1.75. And the company has $20 an ADR of working capital, and $13 of net working capital, after taking out debt, versus the $15 investment. The hard assets have a book value of $25 an ADR, a true value of perhaps half that. But one is getting a large steel business for $2 per ADR, net of working capital, or about $400 million in market capitalization terms.

- *Calloway Golf.* This was a fallen growth star selling in the low teens. The founder, Ely Calloway, is unhappy about recent performance, and is determined to do something about it. (The company has a potential investment value of around $20 a share, assuming a successful turnaround.)

- *Stewart and Stevenson.* It is selling at two thirds of book value, and yield is close to 4 percent. So investment value of nearly $17 is nearly twice the current price of $9, and insiders are buying.

- *Case Corporation.* A recommendation of John Dorfman, formerly of Dreman Value Management. He is put off by the large amount of debt. But Value Line credits the company with just over $500 million of debt (not the $1.3 billion that appears on Bloomberg) because the rest is attributable to the company's finance subsidiary.

- *Stratus Computer.* We don't generally like tech stocks, not because of the nature of the industry, per se, but because we don't like to pay generally elevated prices for what is basically a commodity industry. But this company was selling for book value, which is what we would pay for it. This was taken over by Ascend Communications, late in 1998, which in turn was taken over by Lucent, early in 1999. Given the takeover premiums, the two deals tripled the original investment.

Our investments fall into one of three categories: asset plays, dividend yielders, or fallen growth. British Steel and Stewart and Stevenson fit into both the asset and income categories, while Case Corporation is basically an asset play, since its dividends are minimal. Calloway Golf is a fallen growth company. More on dividend yielders in the future.

THE 1999 EXPERIMENT

January 1999

- *Landry's Seafood Restaurants.* It's a choice between this one and Luby's Cafeteria. Not knowing the way around the restaurant industry, picked Landry's. The fact that there was a favorable writeup in *BusinessWeek* doesn't hurt. At any rate, they're both value investments.
- *Rowan Companies.* Oil field service company; relatively little financial leverage. From my experience as a Value Line oil analyst, oil prices have nowhere to go but up. Other oilfield service providers, including (distant) past favorites Global Marine and Parker Drilling, are too highly leveraged. Traditional oil stocks, however, are too expensive.
- *Titanium Metals.* A producer of strategic metals selling at half of book value. More a post-2000 theme than anything else.
- *Seattle Filmworks.* Problems with aggressive accounting. But the company's balance sheet is strong, and sales have been growing at a rapid rate. A look at owner's earnings tells a different story than the recent reported losses. Capital spending needs are modest, so most cash flow is "true earnings." Good enough for a flyer.

The one that was crossed off the list was Gymboree. Late in 1998, it skyrocketed from $4 to $9 a share, and now sells above book value of $7 a share, and it no longer qualifies as an asset play. It can be a fallen growth company.

February 1999

No activity this month.

March 1999

Bought a few shares of Ampco-Pittsburgh, a steel company, at a price of $11. It has a dividend yield of 4 percent, and is selling for about half of investment value. Added another driller, Ensco, at 1½ times book.

April 1999

■ *United Dominion Realty.* Some investors don't like it because of its liberal stock options policy. But the main source of total return is the 10 percent yield. Even allowing for some action on the part of management, the portion of total return expected from capital growth is one half or less.

Warren Buffett likes real estate investment trusts (REITs). Of course he would. One starts with roughly a 10 percent dividend in hand. Growth rates are also in the 8 percent to 10 percent range, actually exceeding the corporate averages modestly. Real estate stocks have been hurt by concerns about overbuilding in many parts of the country. So the 30 percent or so premium that REITs used to command over net asset value by and large has disappeared. REITs are typically selling at about 10 times reconstructed earnings, and 6 to 8 times funds from operations, the nearest measure to cash flow. Indicated total return is almost 20 percent a year.

Stewart and Stevenson has found a new CEO. He was a former GE executive, that perhaps was passed over just because there was too much competition (it happens to everybody there at some point, unless his name is Jack Welsh).

Despite a cautious policy of holding 35 to 40 percent in cash, the account has earned 13.5 percent at the end of April, ahead of the less than 9 percent on the S&P 500. This is a good result for a basically defensive posture in a bull market. This point can be illustrated by the story of an ancient Chinese king who asked his top general, a man by the name of Sun Tzu, whether or not there was a way to win a best-of-three horse race bet with a rival king. The king noted that his best horse was about as good as the other king's best, the second best horse was comparable in speed to the other's second best, and the third best evenly matched against its counterpart. The general replied, "I think so. Run your number 3 horse in the first race against the other king's number 1 horse and lose; run your number 1 horse in the second race against the other king's number 2 horse and win; then run your number 2 in the last race against your opponent's number 3 horse and win— thus winning two out of three." The first and second horses are expected to win, but the third horse is expected to lose. But after the author ran his first horse against the market's second with a convincing lead in the 1980s, he's not losing even with the third horse in 1999 (and he expects to run his second horse against the market's third past the year 2000).

Sold Morgan Products with a gross profit of nearly 70 percent and sold Conseco (a carryover from previous years) at a loss. This should have been done earlier. It had been acquired in a takeover of Pioneer Financial Services, a company bought at book value in the mid-1990s, as outlined in Chapter 16.

Rebalanced the portfolio, by selling Case Corporation in the low $30s. It is close to investment value, priced attractively enough that a rational investor would want it, but it no longer meets the most exacting Graham and Dodd standards. As it turns out, it was sold too soon because it continued to rise on talks of a takeover by the U.S. subsidiary of New Holland N.V., a Dutch company. The buyout price is $55 a share, all cash, nearly twice investment value, and versus an implied takeout value in the low to mid $60s. But the agriculture business is a year or two away from recovery. On this basis, $55 seems like a reasonable discounted value relative to a theoretical $65, payable in a year or two.

Here is an object lesson for investors. What were they doing, paying $70 a share a year ago for Case when a "strategic" buyer is willing to pay only $55 a share today, based on economies of scale in production and distribution. An investor could go broke paying dollar bills for three quarters. But the classic was a supposedly nifty company called Snapple. Adjusted for stock splits, it came out at $10, went all the way to $30, descended to $5 (which was probably about what it was worth), and was taken over by Quaker Oats, supposedly a strategic investor, for $14, costing the $30 buyer over half his investment. It is interesting to note that the Quaker Oats executive who engineered this $14 a share deal was ousted a year or so later, an indication that $14 a share was an overpayment, even for an "informed" strategic investor.

Replaced Case with Allied Products, which produces agricultural and industrial equipment, $5 a share of book value, and a $3 stock price. Their one problem is their heavy debt load.

REITs are a depressed area right now, so the thing to do is to buy a basket of them. One is Omega Healthcare, which supports hospitals. The second is United Dominion Realty, a shopping center REIT. The third is Sunstone Hotels, featured in *Forbes* a week or two ago. Tried to buy Tanger Factory Outlet (a Warren Buffett personal holding) but the price got away.

Sold half of the British Steel position to lighten up on steels. Replaced it with La Salle Re, a recommendation of Third Avenue Value Fund. It is based in Bermuda, which possibly may lead to corporate governance problems. But other large companies Ace Limited and Excel Limited are also selling at low multiples. La Salle Re pays a dividend at a $1.50 annual rate, or 10 percent, although they have indicated their intention to adjust, read cut or eliminate it, in 2000. The account's cash position has been reduced from 40 percent to 35 percent.

A Value Line graph inspired us to apply the investment value model to the Dow. The results are striking. From 1950 to 1990, the Dow tracked investment value more or less, with some undervaluation in the mid-1970s. It was overvalued, by almost 100 percent, in October 1929. The investment value of the Dow was about 200, versus a market quote of 381.

The Dow was trading at some variation of modified investment value in the spring of 1999, because of the high returns on equity. Thus, Alan Greenspan and Warren Buffett opined, timorously, that the high valuations might be sustainable if companies maintain their high returns on equity. This assumption probably will not hold up, if only because of the Generations model outlined in Chapter 20. Two of the most eminent members of the so-called Silent generation might hesitate to take a stand on this matter. But the economy and corporate world are now basically being driven by Baby Boomers (some in middle management, and some at the very top like Bill Gates, Steve Jobs, Scott McNealy, and President Clinton) in a stock-friendly, turbocharged fashion. When Generation X starts to take over the middle management slots in 5 to 10 years' time, there will be a less investor-friendly ethos. Imagine people like Ally McBeal (an alienated and neurotic 28-year-old TV sitcom character) as the nation's shift supervisors, and what that will do to the economy.

June 1999

Bought Tab Products over $6 a share on pique, if the truth be told. Was looking at it around $5, but couldn't quite pull the trigger. Two pieces of news, back to back, pushed it up. The first is that Joseph Harrosh, a noted value investor, has taken a 5 percent stake. The second, a day or two later, is that the company has sold a major business, which will bring in cash and plump up its already strong balance sheet.

Time to pull the trigger on another company, Viasoft, that has been under observation for two months. At $4\frac{1}{2}$, it's down from a peak of over 60. People were right to sell it earlier, at much higher prices, and then forgot to stop. It now has book value of $5.50 a share, no debt, and working capital of about $4 a share. Seems that its main application is Y2K software, so they're working themselves out of a job. But they have skilled developers, a business franchise, no debt, and best of all, assets in excess of the stock market value. Although this book does not particularly favor tech stocks, it's not tech, per se, that is offputting, but rather the prospect of paying high prices for the equities. And the experience of steel, aluminum, and chemicals all show that yesterday's "tech" is today's cyclical, a fact amply demonstrated by this company. If a software company can be obtained at the wholesale prices normally associated with metal benders, fine.

Blair Corporation has shot up. A day or two later, the mystery was solved. Joseph Harrosh, the renowned value investor, has taken a 6 percent stake. Too late for us to get in. Hancock Fabrics, on the other hand, is basically a dividend play. It's in the textile business, which is suffering from hard times. As such, it fits the depression valuation thesis.

July 1999

This is a month in which many of the portfolio's investments are being snapped up in whole or in part by purchasers.

Allied Products has announced major negotiations. They are selling an 80 percent interest in the agricultural business for $120 million. This is almost exactly the amount of short-term debt. It represents a "cap shrink." Instead of having two high-leveraged divisions, they own one division free and clear, plus a 20 percent equity interest in the other. The remaining 20 percent of the agricultural division is worth, in an arm's-length transaction, $30 million. The $40 to $50 million market cap implies a value for the industrial division of $10 to $20 million when in fact it is worth probably $100 million or more, after the company's debt problem is resolved. Looked at one way, we are getting the industrial division at 10 to 20 cents on the dollar; looked at the other way, with the remainder of the Ag division left in, we are getting the company at 30 cents on the dollar. This is Graham and Dodd investing at its purest. Surprisingly, the stock, which had worked its way almost back to 5, fell on the news to the low 4s. Thus, 1,000 shares was added at a price of 4¼ to the original position of 1,500 shares, a near-doubling of the position in dollar terms.

A modest addition was made to Seattle Filmworks at $3. Once the company gets over its amortization problems, its basic earnings power is 25 to 30 cents per share for a (P/E) ratio of 10 to 12 times earnings. But its Internet operations are going for nothing, even though they might be worth quite a bit someday.

Sunstone has said that it plans to go private in a leveraged buyout (LBO) for $10.35 a share. Management is buying back the company on the cheap, but the portfolio is being taken out at a premium to the purchase price.

Another addition is Luby's Cafeteria. A restaurant company, not a favorite industry, but yield is over 5 percent. Finally, Rowan Companies and Ensco, which both look fully priced at twice book, were swapped for Transocean, which was cheaper, selling at 1.5 times book. The price of Transocean, at $30, is about three quarters the sum of the combined prices of Rowan and Ensco. So replacing two 500-share positions with a like quantity of the third also pulls out about $5,000 in cash.

Lucent has been hammered, retreating to the low $60s from a peak of $80. Part of it was the skittishness over tech stocks in general. But part of it was the departure of Carleton "Carly" Fiorina, the president of the company's most important division, for the CEO job at Hewlett Packard. *Fortune* knew what it was talking about last year when it nominated her as the most powerful woman in American industry in 1998. It's strange, but she wasn't among the top five executives at Lucent, which makes a statement about the company or about her.

August 1999

Gibson's Greetings now has a market cap of $80 million, down from almost $500 million a year earlier. The company has very little debt, but recurring problems with asset quality. Put another way, it is a survivor, but has a habit of giving investors fits, which is why its stock price is subject to large swings. The trick here is to remain more coolheaded than panicky investors who have problems evaluating either its up- or downside. The purchase price of just under $5 compares with (written down) book value of perhaps $15 a share and net working capital of $7 to $8 a share, of which over $6 is represented by cash (if one assumes that the current liabilities are paid off with other current assets). Its normalized earnings power is about $1.50 a share, and over time, it is a no-growth company. Based on this, it should return to the $15 to $20 range, and previous price dips and recoveries suggest that the "workout" time will be about two years, a Grahamite waiting period. The potential gains are better than the Graham 50 to 100 percent, but the safety and asset support are Graham-like.

This one has an interesting history. It was bought in the early 1980s by William Simon (the former Treasury Secretary) and a partner for $80 million in an LBO, and sold for $200 million. The kicker is that Simon and the partner each put up only $1 million apiece, borrowing the rest, so they made a killing on the $120 million accretion. The partners bought this basically sound company when it had hit a patch of hard times. It's an object lesson, that this $80 million stock will probably go back to $200 million or even $400 million. Unfortunately, the account won't be able to take advantage of Simon's high leverage, but hopefully we will participate in the cyclical upturn.

Gymboree has a good business selling toys to young children, who are now members of the so-called Millennial generation. Its recent track record has been that of a cyclical company, but it has a good balance sheet, so these cyclical swings are likely to continue, rather than terminate. Our purchase price around book gives a lot of downside protection, so hopefully the continued cyclicality will be on the upside.

Another investment was Salient 3 Communications, a maker of telecommunications equipment. The company has shown no growth, but the stock is selling at a deep discount to book, with very little debt.

A few weeks after our purchase, there is a takeover attempt on Viasoft. The offer is $9 a share in cash, which seems adequate but not overly generous. Even so, we're talking about a near-doubling of investment in a matter of weeks. We sold at $8 and change, just to be able to increase the cash position.

Ditched that Lucent at $61, because it has provided only headaches in the short time it's been held and it's a stock I don't understand. This came about because it was never bought, but rather acquired in back-to-back stock swaps (see the discussion on Stratus Computer early in the chapter). Sold Titanium Metals at $11, and half of the Stewart and Stevenson at about $13.5. Exited Ampco Pittsburgh with a gain of almost 20 percent, but which has been stuck in a trading range for two months. The account is now officially about 37 percent cash, but when one considers the positions in Sunstone a cash deal, the true cash position is more like 45 percent.

According to Bloomberg analytics, only 4 percent of the mutual funds gained in the past month (July). The portfolio's gain of 1.8 percent during that time (mostly due to Viasoft), was stellar within this context. Just how stellar is best illustrated by a year-to-date comparison. If the portfolio were a mutual fund, its year-to-date rank, given its gain of 23.9 percent, would be number 1 out of 388 balanced funds ranked by Bloomberg, handily beating the "official" number 1, which showed a gain of 19 percent. This is probably the true benchmark, since the portfolio has held 30 to 40 percent of its assets in cash. But even against other peer groups with (mostly) all-equity funds, it would also rank third out of 416 equity income funds, tenth out of 199 small-cap funds, and twentieth out of 534 mid-cap funds. Among peer groups, it was a submedian performer only against natural resource funds. This stands to reason, because natural resources (and capital goods producers) were basically the hottest sector so far this year, and the portfolio is not a dedicated natural resource investor. Even so, the other statistics show the importance of latching onto the right concept as was done with British Steel, the oilfield services companies, and others.

Safeco, a property casualty insurer, looks interesting, with a 4 percent yield, but it is not selling at enough of a discount from investment value.

September 1999

Bought some Safeco at $27 with a yield above 5 percent. Also Fremont General, which has tanked from the low $20s to $8, classifying both of them as fallen growth companies, although either could be considered an asset play. With a yield of over 5 percent, Safeco also qualifies as a dividend investment. Sold LaSalle Re. It has just eliminated its dividend. Neverthe-less, it preserved its value better than either of the other two during the period in which it was held, and served a useful function as "parking place." Naturally, it would have been better not to have owned it at all, and held cash (which is not trash), but such is the imperative of portfolio man-agement. Meanwhile, the broad market (S&P) averages have given up most of their gains in the third quarter, being up less than 4 percent for the nine months. We are up nearly 20 percent for the same period, with a lead ver-sus the market of more than 15 percentage points. The experiment has been a great success so far.

October 1999

No major activity in the portfolio this month. The main activity is in the major indexes, where the tech stocks have exploded, taking the S&P 500 back up with it. What a reversal of fortune. We are still leading this index for the year, but by only half of our September-end margin.

November 1999

Continued the portfolio upgrading process. Sold Luby's Cafeteria at a 20 percent loss. Replaced it with Enesco, a gift producer, which has lost much more from its mid-$20s peak to its present price of $13, and now offers a higher yield, and has a better, debt-free balance sheet. The company has been buying back shares for years. Sold United Dominion Realty (UDR) at breakeven, and replaced it with New Plan Realty, which now trades at yield parity with UDR, versus its formerly lower yield. Sold slow-growing Tab Products at a slight loss and replaced it with Office Max, a fallen growth company selling below book.

Initiated a position in Western Resources, a utility with a yield of over 9 percent. Management is under something of a suspicion for its acquisitive ways, and the fact that the dividend is under pressure. But the low $20s purchase price is below book value of $28, which represents a lower bound for investment value, assuming the dividend is eliminated entirely. It's worth about $40 a share, assuming a 50 percent cut, and perhaps $50 a share if it is maintained.

Titanium Metals is trading around $6 versus our exit price of just under $11. This helps illustrate the value of trading, even high turnover, for a Graham and Dodd–type portfolio. The portfolio is notably short of "ever-green" investments that should be held for the long term, and is predicated on basically one-time gains (or avoided losses, in this case), of 50 to 100 percent.

Bought a token amount of Philip Morris just below $24, mainly for presentation purposes to other value investors, even though the account is no longer hugely fond of tobacco stocks for moral reasons, and there is still litigation risk. Absent the litigation factor, the stock is worth about $60. The simplifying investment assumption that is used is that the plaintiffs' bar will divide the value of the company in half with the shareholders, leaving a value of about $30, postlitigation. On this basis, the stock looks cheap in the low $20s.

Another takeover, this time of Gibson's Greetings. Increased the position by 25 percent at about a 10 percent discount to the takeout price of $10.25 making it a risk arbitrage play.

December 1999

This is the payoff month. First a concept. Our preference for buying stock at one half of investment value represents a high level of discipline. But this necessary condition is not sufficient to bring relative success this year. That's because a well-chosen investment should have a prospective total return, the sum of its growth rate and dividend yield, of about 12 percent, roughly that of stocks in general, as well as sell at one-half investment value. This return doesn't have to come entirely or even primarily from growth by any means. For instance, British Steel, with its 11 percent yield and 2 percent prospective growth qualified, when it sold for half (or less) of investment value. So does Safeco (which has fallen to $24) with its 9 percent growth and 6 percent yield. A stock with a 6 percent growth rate (which is moderately below average) and 3 percent yield selling at investment value would not qualify for inclusion in the portfolio. But if the price were halved, the original 3 percent yield would become 6 percent, causing the stock to meet our return, as well as value, criteria.

The less promising investments have a prospective total return well below this 12 percent figure. Blair Corporation, with a prospective 4 percent growth rate and 4 percent yield at a price of $14 may not be a bargain even at one-half investment value. (It would look more interesting at one third of investment value, which would make its yield 6 percent and underlying return 10 percent, while its additional attractiveness as a takeover candidate would compensate for the shortfall from 12 percent.)

Hancock Fabrics has cut its dividend by 75 percent. It plans to use the savings to buy back stock, which is now selling below book, never mind its (reduced) investment value, a certifiably smart thing to do. What was not smart was the purchases (slightly) above book and at more than half investment value without sufficient regard for a possible dividend cut. The entry price was just below current investment value at around $5 a share, which is too much to pay for a struggling company in a tough industry.

Seattle Filmworks' book value has been written down by half, although its share price is hanging tough around 3. The interest is still the Internet marketing, which is why it's a " hold," not a "sell." The bad news is that asset quality problems were worse than originally thought, which basically disqualifies it as a Graham and Dodd–type investment, preventing additional purchases.

The account lost its November-end lead against the S&P 500, and then some. One reason was the relatively poor absolute performance of the portfolio in December. But a much more important factor was the explosion of NASDAQ. This index, which is dominated by high-tech stocks, advanced some 48 percent in the fourth quarter of 1999, leading to a gain of 84 percent for the full year. It also had a spillover effect on the S&P 500, which at the end of the year had over one third of its weight in tech stocks. The result was an increase in the total return on the S&P 500 from less than 4 percent at the end of the third quarter to over 20 percent for the whole year. In order to lock in relative performance (starting with our big lead), the portfolio could have been indexed in the fourth quarter. But the one-quarter explosion of the major indexes was probably a once in a lifetime event.

Nonetheless, the full-year return of nearly 16 percent was about 10 percentage points better than that of the average value investor. It was also about 5 percentage points above the S&P mid-cap index. These results were achieved with a cash position that averaged just 40 percent, a posture that hurt this year, but would serve well in future years; had the account been fully invested, it would have beaten the S&P 500. As it was, it did very well against a universe of balanced funds, although not against a full universe that includes growth funds invested in tech stocks. The month-to-month results are summarized in Table 17.1.

TABLE 17.1   Year to Date, 1999 IRA Performance vs. S&P 500

Month	IRA	S&P*	Difference
January	3.30%	2.00%	1.30%
February	−0.40%	0.70%	−1.10%
March	0.50%	4.70%	−4.20%
April	13.60%	8.60%	5.00%
May	13.50%	5.90%	7.60%
June	21.70%	11.70%	10.00%
July	23.90%	16.10%	7.80%
August	20.00%	7.40%	12.60%
September	20.30%	3.80%	16.50%
October	18.40%	10.90%	7.50%
November	18.10%	13.00%	5.10%
December	15.90%	19.50%	−3.60%

*Price appreciation only. S&P full-year total return was 21.0%.
Source: Charles Schwab & Co.

POSTMORTEMS

A number of the positions in the portfolio were taken over after 1999. Comp USA was acquired for $10.10 a share, more than 50 percent over cost. The buyer was a Mexican conglomerate, Grupo Carso, named after Carlos Slim, the Warren Buffett of Mexico, and his wife Soraya. This looked like a steal for Carso, versus a back-of-envelope calculation of $15 to $20 a share. Of course, Slim, like Buffett, got to be Mexico's richest man by buying things for 50 to 60 cents on the dollar. Even so, we are grateful to such a sophisticated investor for monetizing our investment so quickly. But Comp USA proved to be a disappointment for Mr. Slim. We also went in with Slim on a U.S. office equipment company, Office Max, although we sold too soon in 2002 with a small profit, and didn't get the benefit of a takeover bid by Boise Cascade in July 2003 that would have doubled the original investment.

Hancock Fabrics skyrocketed to the high teens over the next two years, after it was sold in disgust. Ben Graham had noted in *Security Analysis*[1] that cotton fabric stocks underperformed in the 1920s, but did relatively well after the depression hit in the 1930s. This statement deserved more attention. Arguably, the market crash, and hence the outperformance of this stock, began in 2000, three years earlier than the 2003 target.

The position in Gymboree was doubled at 2⅝ in January 2000, and sold above 10, in December 2000. This was one of the two drivers of the portfolio for the year. Despite some important fits and starts, the company was successfully turned around early in the 2000s.

The portfolio rebought half of its original holding of Berkshire Hathaway A on March 10, 2000, the day of its two-year low, when it was out of favor as NASDAQ reached its peak of just over 5,000. Berkshire continued to behave in the opposite fashion from NASDAQ, recovering later in the year while NASDAQ crashed. It was sold early in 2001 for just under $70,000, because it exceeded the investment value estimate of just under $60,000. The stock continued to trade at prices bracketing the sales price for the next two years.

New Holland got into financial difficulties as a result of the Case acquisition, proving that even the $55-a-share purchase price was too high, and validating the discipline of selling this cyclical company at investment value.

Safeco proved to be a disappointing investment. Its troubles, and those of its industry, were long term, not temporary, and the company cut its dividend twice. Naturally, its growth rate came in below expectations, and the only redeeming feature was its cheap price relative to asset value that limited the loss on sale.

Salient Communications decided to sell off its assets and liquidate the company, a smart thing to do. It returned $12 a share in the first distribution, early in 2000, versus the cost of $8, and was distributing liquidating dividends even three years later.

The one "permanently" bad investment was Allied Products, which could not work out its problems, even after selling off its assets, because of high capital spending needs, and filed for bankruptcy, leaving stockholders with nothing. Most of the position was sold at a loss, but a token holding was kept as an "observer" position.

Stewart and Stevenson stock lived up to its promise, tripling from the lows under the new CEO. It was sold too soon, given a lack of faith in the analysis of the company's prospects.

Seattle Filmworks was sold at $7, early in 2000, a more than doubling, as tech stocks in general, and Internet stocks in particular, caught the popular imagination, realizing the fondest hopes on a short-term basis. But the fundamental weakness of its business model remained, and the stock collapsed soon after it was sold. This was a case of a good outcome based on a wrong premise.

Purchases continued in Enesco as it collapsed into the single digits, with the lowest price at just over $4, at half of book value, as the company eliminated the dividend. It was sold in 2002 at close to $9, making a small profit on the "blended" entry price.

Landry's Restaurant's, which was sold in July to make room for Luby's, skyrocketed in price in the following years, after its multi-restaurant format fired on all cylinders. It also started paying a dividend in 2000. The sharp contrast in performance to Luby's, which eliminated its dividend, shows that dividends are often a result, not a cause of good company and stock performance.

Western Resources (now Westar Energy) which was sold in the high teens early in 2000, dipped as low as $10 a share subsequently because of the failure of acquisitions outside of electricity, before returning to the high teens several years later. The dividend was slashed as well. Also of note, some former executives were indicted for bank fraud and conflict of interest in their dealings with the company.

Returns in 2000 were 19 percent, 29 percentage points higher than the S&P 500. The aversion to tech stocks was the main reason, and an important benefit was the strong performance (up 13 percent) of the nontech stocks in the index, although the account also managed to beat its "true" universe by nearly six percentage points.

PART SIX

Some Contemporary Issues

CHAPTER 18

A Historical View of the Dow and the "Market"

Since the Dow is a widely accepted proxy for "the market," it behooves us to take a closer look at the individual components. We need to know what we are trying to beat. The Dow is an artificial construct, put together by senior financial reporters at the *Wall Street Journal*, whose parent company is Dow Jones Incorporated. The weightings of the 30 stocks in the Dow are artificial and based on the prices, rather than the market capitalizations, of the various issues. Hence, a stock split will reduce the weighting of a company in the Dow.

A LISTING OF THE DOW STOCKS

On the whole, companies listed on the Dow are operating in key industries and are dominant players, usually number one or two, in those industries. Companies that long fail to meet one or the other criteria are usually candidates for removal. The current occupants include the following:

- *Alcoa.* The name is a contraction of Aluminum Corporation of America. It achieved prominence in the 1940s because of its contribution to the Allied war effort. Fueled by postwar growth, Alcoa is today the largest aluminum producer in the world, having maintained the industry dominance that has escaped other former Dow stocks including American Can, U.S. Steel, and American Smelting (Asarco, a copper producer) in their respective fields. Alcoa is a producer of both intermediate aluminum and aluminum products.
- *Altria* (formerly Philip Morris). Tobacco is a lucrative if somewhat despised business, and until recently, a good grower. Two decades ago, Morris acquired a former Dow company, General Foods, as well as Dart & Kraft and Miller Brewing (the latter two operations have been divested recently). Hammered recently by anti-tobacco litigation, it is still a force that is likely to be reckoned with for a long time to come.

- *American Express.* An offshoot of Wells Fargo in the late nineteenth century with a then revolutionary product called traveler's checks, it rocketed to fame with the introduction of a credit card in 1958. Since then, it has found it hard to stay focused. A disastrous foray into warehouse receipt financing (the "salad oil" scandal involving a large loan on phony collateral to a borrower that went bankrupt) was followed by almost as unsuccessful experiments in insurance, international banking, and brokerage house management. Dwarfed by the mergers of others, it is becoming a niche player in the financial services industry and may become a takeover candidate. A past and present Warren Buffett investment.
- *AT&T.* Otherwise known as Ma Bell, it has grown up with the telephone era. Its former virtual monopoly in long distance in the United States is under attack, and it was forced to divest its local operations through spin-offs of the "Baby Bells" in 1984. Its "stepchildren" include Lucent, the maker of equipment, and NCR, the former National Cash Register. Taken as a whole, the "family" is a major force in the stock market, but the parent is a shadow of its former self.
- *Boeing.* The world's largest aerospace company. Like Alcoa it enjoyed a burst of growth during World War II when air power played a key role in the Allied victory. Following the war, it benefited by the rise of commercial aviation that made air travel commonplace for both people and freight.
- *Caterpillar Tractor.* It remains the largest agricultural equipment firm, having outdistanced John Deere and International Harvester (a former Dow stock). It supplies end markets that are commodity-like in nature, but have a basic underlying demand. (People have to eat.) It has also become a major supplier of construction equipment worldwide.
- *Citigroup.* This was formed by a merger of Citicorp and a descendant of the former American Can (a former Dow stock). Citicorp has been discussed elsewhere in the book, so it is the American Can connection that is interesting. Under a former Wall Street gunslinger (Gerry Tsai of the Manhattan Fund), it diversified into financial services, renamed itself Primerica, and began divesting its industrial operations. This process was completed when it was merged with (i.e., was acquired by) Commercial Credit, headed by Sandy Weill, although the combined company took the name of the acquiree. Primerica acquired Travelers Group, and took the name of the acquiree, then assumed a name, Citigroup, that was basically a tweak of Citicorp in a "merger of equals." Along the way, Travelers had acquired Salomon Brothers by merging it with its Smith Barney subsidiary under the umbrella (pun intended) of Salomon Smith Barney. Citigroup then divested Travelers (Insurance).
- *Coca-Cola.* Founded in the late nineteenth century, it makes a sugary syrup that has since become the leading soft drink in the world. Unlike

much smaller rival Pepsi-Cola, it has mostly stuck to its beverage knitting, following some unsuccessful diversification attempts in the 1970s, and prospered as a result of its focus.

- *Disney.* Put together a set of cartoon characters and Hollywood, and one gets Disney Corporation. Although cartoons are still a staple, Disney is now a diversified entertainment company that grew big enough to buy Cap Cities, the owner of the ABC network, to provide a broadcasting outlet for its content. Warren Buffett had a major (financing) role in the original purchase of ABC by Cap Cities, and possibly a backstage role in Cap Cities's sale to Disney. In any event, Disney, Cap Cities, and ABC are all past Buffett investments going back to the 1960s and 1970s. Abroad, Disney is probably the third major symbol of America next to Coke and McDonald's.

- *DuPont.* Founded in the early part of the century by the DuPont Brothers as a producer of explosives. It got a second leg in 1940 with the introduction of nylons, a silk stocking substitute aimed at the mass market, and is now a diversified chemical company.

- *Eastman Kodak.* Named after founder George Eastman (with the name Kodak added on a whim), this company was a pioneer in photographic film. It has tried to leverage its strengths in imaging into the health care area, with only partial success. When it ran into financial trouble in the early 1990s, a newly hired chief financial officer (CFO), Christopher Steffen, earned the nickname "$2 Billion Man" because his appointment added that much to the company's market cap, while his departure subtracted that much. On balance, its recent problems make it a good candidate to leave the Dow.

- *ExxonMobil.* Exxon's roots include the largest and strongest of Rockefeller's Standard Oil (of New Jersey) companies. It merged with Mobil (formerly Standard Oil of New York) in 1998. With operations throughout the world, but particularly in the eastern and southern United States, it remains the dean of the oil industry, a key sector.

- *General Electric.* This concern dates back to the nineteenth century, and is the only one left of the 12 original Dow stocks. It is still barely a maker of electrical equipment. But it has branched out into other lucrative areas, including broadcasting (NBC), and finance (GE Capital). In doing so, it has left its nearest rival CBS (the former Westinghouse) in the dust. This company will almost certainly stay in the Dow for the foreseeable future.

- *General Motors.* Formerly the bellwether stock of American industry (boasting "What is good for GM is good for America"), now merely the dominant player in the U.S. auto industry. It, outlasted Goodyear Tire, and is a venerable company that is still representative of smokestack America.

- *Hewlett Packard.* This company was founded by William Hewlett and David Packard in the late 1930s, at the beginning of the electronic age. Initially built on electronic products such as calculators, HP is now mostly a computer and imaging company. It has outlasted most contemporaries in the computer industry other than IBM, and merged with much younger Compaq in 2002.
- *Home Depot.* An offering in the "do-it-yourself" home repair market. It is noted for its store format and marketing model, as much as any particular products, making it a "category killer" in its own industry. Founded in 1979, it is a rapid success story like Microsoft.
- *Honeywell.* The core of this company was formed by the merger of two former Dow components, Allied Chemical and General Signal in the mid-1980s. It has retained businesses in auto parts, defense, and specialty chemicals, while divesting others. It took a quantum leap in size by buying Honeywell in 1999, signaling a tilt toward the defense and parts business, and taking the acquiree's name. Concurrently, it closed down many operations in chemicals such as nylon.
- *Intel.* A demonstrator of Moore's Law (Gordon Moore was its original founder) that improved chips could cause computing power to double every 18 months. Within the technology area, it works like Levi Strauss's idea of selling clothing and tools to gold miners, benefiting from the growth of the computer industry without regard for individual winners and losers, making it a close runner-up to Microsoft and General Electric in market cap.
- *IBM.* It is still the dominant maker of hardware, but passed up a chance to partner with Microsoft in operating systems and other software when the latter was still a small company. Tried to play catch-up later in 1995 with the acquisition of Lotus, a much weaker company than Microsoft. This effort was only partially successful, but IBM turned its core business around and remains the dominant player in the hardware portion of the computer industry, as well as software development and consulting.
- *International Paper.* A carryover from smokestack industry days. Dominant in its industry, it may someday nevertheless go the way of International Harvester and International Nickel, both of which have left the Dow.
- *J.P. Morgan Chase.* With one of its components named after its founder, this institution has long been synonymous with banking. Mergers involving major rivals (one formed by the successive mergers of Chemical, Manufacturer's, and Chase banks; another by the successive mergers of Primerica, Travelers Insurance, Salomon Brothers, and Citicorp) forced the namesake company to give up its independence

and join the former group. Still, Morgan remains the leading banking service purveyor to the high-net-worth market, a posture that it has parlayed for better or worse into emerging markets (where wealth is concentrated in the hands of a few people).

- *Johnson & Johnson.* Founded by two brothers of that name shortly after the beginning of the twentieth century, this is a leading medical products company. It has a drug subsidiary, Ethicon, but its main thrust is in hospital supplies. With people living longer and geriatric care becoming more of an issue, J&J will have an important franchise well into the twenty-first century.
- *McDonald's.* Its golden arches are the symbol of the good life in the United States, especially for children, and represents Americana abroad. Founded in the middle of the twentieth century by the McDonald brothers (and commercialized by Ray Kroc, the first chairman), it built a service organization based on that great American manufacturing virtue, mass production. McDonald's has the potential to become another Coca-Cola. Indeed, it is one of the largest servers of that soft drink.
- *Merck.* It has been the leading drug company since the middle of the twentieth century. That's because it spends more on research and development than anyone else. It occasionally loses out to someone with a hot new drug (e.g., Pfizer with its Viagra) or is outdistanced in sales by companies with important nondrug operations. But it is the proven long-distance runner.
- *Microsoft.* Sometimes the largest market-cap company in the world, which made its founders three of the richest men in the world because it was built in barely one generation. Specializes in software, the driving force behind the modern invention, computers.
- *Minnesota Mining and Manufacturing (3M).* An innovative company and a major force when its original business, adhesive chemicals, enjoyed its heyday. Diversifications into sexier growth areas, information technology and life sciences, have been only moderately successful. But the sum total still adds up to a very substantial company.
- *Procter & Gamble.* Founded in the middle of the nineteenth century, its name has practically become synonymous with household products such as soap and toothpaste. Its other claim to fame is a powerhouse marketing organization.
- *SBC Corporation.* Formed by the merger of Southwest Bell and Pacific Telesis, two of the westernmost "Baby Bells," it is a proxy for the local phone market in the fastest-growing part of the country. Later, the company acquired Midwest-based Ameritech. More than other U.S. phone companies, including AT&T, it has diversified abroad, taking a large stake in Telefonos of Mexico.

- *United Technologies.* Formerly United Aircraft, it has expanded beyond its original aerospace roots to include household and building equipment such as heaters, ventilators, air conditioners, and elevators.
- *Wal-Mart.* This retailer was created by the late Sam Walton with a strategy of "everyday low prices" and superior service. It grew up at a time when information technology led to large economies of scale in retailing. Such "learning curve" effects induced it to grow for growth's sake, leading it to surpass both Woolworth and Sears, both leading retailers in their day. Wal-Mart's high-growth days may be over, but with its sheer size, it is a fair proxy for the retailing industry, especially low-end retailing.

THE CHANGING FACE OF THE DOW

It is a truism that the stock market should be a mirror of the future. It is almost equally true that the stock market is a reflection of the immediate past. It is unfortunately this immediate past, and not a considered view of the future, that usually dominates most investment thinking.

It is noteworthy that the Dow of today is rather different than the Dow that Ben Graham analyzed in his last book, the 1973 edition of *The Intelligent Investor,* which is featured in Table 18.1. General Electric has been in the Dow during the course of the twentieth century. Other standbys from the earlier era include Alcoa, AT&T, DuPont, Eastman Kodak, General Motors, International Paper, and Procter & Gamble. ExxonMobil is the Standard Oil Company of New Jersey under a new name; Honeywell is the successor to Allied Chemical, as is true of United Technologies vis-à-vis United Aircraft. But Wal-Mart has replaced Woolworth as the leading retailer, and American Brands has been replaced by the larger and more diversified Altria (formerly Philip Morris), which acquired General Foods. American Can is unrecognizable in its original form, having gone through several transformations described above to become part of Citigroup. U.S. Steel and Bethlehem Steel have both left the index, as have Anaconda Copper and International Nickel. In their places are consumer names such as Coca-Cola, Disney, and McDonald's; financial concerns such as American Express and J.P. Morgan Chase, and health care companies like Johnson & Johnson and Merck.

Other former Dow stocks fell on hard times. Chrysler has left the country altogether, having been bought by Germany's Daimler. Johns Manville filed for bankruptcy because of asbestos liabilities. International Harvester changed its name to Navistar and had to be recapitalized years later. In part because of financial problems caused by uranium contracts and lending by its financial division, Westinghouse Electric downsized these operations, shed its namesake electric business, and bought CBS in order to find a partner for its broadcasting operations, taking its partner's name in the

TABLE 18.1 Price vs. Investment Value for Dow Components, 1971

Stock	Price	Book Val.	Dividend	Invest Val.	P/IV
Alcoa	45.5	55.01	1.80	73.01	62.3%
American Brands	43.5	13.46	2.10	34.46	126.2%
American Can	33.25	49.01	2.20	71.01	46.8%
AT&T	43	45.47	2.60	71.47	60.2%
Anaconda	15	54.28	0.00	54.28	27.6%
Bethlehem Steel	25.5	44.62	1.20	56.62	45.0%
CBS[a]	96.5	33.67	1.80	51.67	186.8%
Chevron[b]	56	54.79	2.80	82.79	67.6%
Daimler Chrysler[a]	28.5	42.4	0.60	48.40	58.9%
DuPont	154	55.22	5.00	105.22	146.4%
Eastman Kodak	87	13.7	1.32	26.90	323.4%
ExxonMobil[a]	72	48.95	3.90	87.95	81.9%
General Electric	61.5	14.92	1.40	28.92	212.7%
General Foods	34	14.13	1.40	28.13	120.9%
General Motors	83	33.39	3.40	67.39	123.2%
Goodyear	33.5	18.49	0.85	26.99	124.1%
Honeywell[a]	32.5	26.02	1.20	38.02	85.5%
Int'l Nickel	31	14.53	1.00	24.53	126.4%
Int'l Paper	33	23.68	1.50	38.68	85.3%
Johns-Mansville	39	24.51	1.20	36.51	106.8%
Navistar[a]	52	42.06	1.40	56.06	92.8%
Owen Illinois	52	43.75	1.35	57.25	90.8%
Procter & Gamble	71	15.41	1.50	30.41	233.5%
Sears Roebuck	68.5	23.97	1.55	39.47	173.5%
Swift	42	26.74	0.70	33.74	124.5%
Texaco[b]	32	23.06	1.60	39.06	81.9%
Union Carbide	43.5	29.64	2.00	49.64	87.6%
U.S. Steel	29.5	65.54	1.60	81.54	36.2%
United Technologies[a]	30.5	47	1.80	65.00	46.9%
Woolworth	49	25.47	1.20	37.47	130.8%

[a]Current name of the company except for CBS, now part of Viacom.
[b]Chevron was the name of Standard Oil of California before the merger with Texaco. They are listed separately, because they were both in the Dow in 1971.
Source: Ben Graham, *The Intelligent Investor* (New York: Harper & Row, 1973):187; and author's calculations.

"marriage." Even in the capital goods area, Boeing, Caterpillar Tractor, Hewlett Packard, IBM, and Minnesota Mining and Manufacturing (3M) are considered more "modern" companies.

In the "hollowing out" of America's industrial sector, other cyclicals such as U.S. Steel and Anaconda Copper suffered greatly. This was due to events that were largely unforeseeable, and one should not fault an investor for not taking them into account. In the Graham and Dodd view, an investor is some-one who buys a stock based on what it is putatively worth in relation to assets, earnings, and dividends, while a speculator will buy an issue, regard-less of price, on the theory that it is likely to go "up." This is shown by the fact that in the late 1990s, the Dow got way above what it should sell for, based on the book's investment value formula of book value plus 10 times dividends (see Tables 18.2 and 18.3). Where we would find fault is in the

TABLE 18.2 Price vs. Investment Value for Dow Components, 1999

Stock	Price	Book Val.	Dividend	Invest Val.	P/IV
Altria	23	6.54	1.84	24.94	92.2%
Alcoa	41.5	8.50	1.41	22.60	183.6%
American Express	54.2	7.53	0.30	10.53	514.7%
AT&T	39.46	24.69	0.88	33.49	117.8%
Boeing	41.44	12.80	0.56	18.40	225.2%
Caterpillar	47.06	15.38	1.25	27.88	168.8%
Citigroup	38.95	10.64	0.41	14.74	264.2%
Coca-Cola	58.25	3.85	0.64	10.25	568.3%
Disney	29.25	10.16	0.20	12.16	240.5%
DuPont	65.88	12.39	1.40	26.39	249.6%
Eastman Kodak	66.25	12.60	1.76	30.20	219.4%
ExxonMobil	40.28	18.25	1.67	34.95	115.3%
General Electric	51.58	4.32	0.49	9.22	559.4%
General Motors	72.69	33.33	2.00	53.33	136.3%
Hewlett Packard	44.38	18.21	0.64	24.61	180.3%
Home Depot	68.75	5.36	0.11	6.46	1064.2%
Honeywell	57.69	10.81	0.68	17.61	327.6%
Intel	41.16	4.88	0.05	5.38	765.1%
Int'l Business Machines (IBM)	107.88	11.23	0.47	15.93	677.2%
Int'l Paper	56.44	24.85	1.00	34.85	162.0%
Johnson & Johnson	46.63	11.67	1.09	22.57	206.6%
J.P. Morgan Chase	51.79	65.20	3.97	104.90	49.4%
McDonald's	40.31	7.14	0.20	9.14	441.0%
Merck	67.19	5.69	1.10	16.69	402.6%
Microsoft	116.75	5.37	0.00	5.37	2174.1%
Minnesota Mining and Manufacturing (3M)	98.88	15.77	2.24	38.17	259.1%
Procter & Gamble	108.72	7.79	1.14	19.19	566.5%
SBC Comm.	48.75	7.87	0.97	17.57	277.5%
United Technologies	65	14.24	0.76	21.84	297.6%
Wal-Mart	69.13	5.80	0.19	7.70	897.8%

Source: Value Line, author's calculations.

TABLE 18.3 Premiums and Discounts of the Dow vs. Investment Value (IV)

Year	Dow	IV	Prem/Dis
1926	157	130	20.8%
1927	241	138	74.6%
1928	300	182	64.8%
1929	248	219	13.2%
1930	165	202	−18.3%
1931	78	171	−54.4%
1932	60	82	−26.8%
1933	100	114	−12.3%
1934	104	112	−7.1%
1935	144	129	11.6%
1936	180	156	15.4%
1937	121	176	−31.3%
1938	155	137	13.1%
1939	150	157	−4.5%
1940	131	170	−22.9%
1941	111	179	−38.0%
1942	119	171	−30.4%
1943	136	176	−22.7%
1944	152	184	−17.4%
1945	193	190	1.6%
1946	177	206	−14.1%
1947	181	241	−24.9%
1948	177	275	−35.6%
1949	200	298	−32.9%
1950	235	355	−33.8%
1951	246	365	−32.6%
1952	292	367	−20.4%
1953	280	405	−30.9%
1954	404	424	−4.7%
1955	488	488	0.0%
1956	499	515	−3.1%
1957	436	515	−15.3%
1958	584	511	14.3%
1959	679	546	24.4%
1960	616	584	5.5%
1961	731	612	19.4%
1962	652	634	2.8%
1963	763	660	15.6%
1964	874	729	19.9%
1965	969	740	30.9%
1966	786	796	−1.3%

(Continued)

TABLE 18.3 (*Continued*)

Year	Dow	IV	Prem/Dis
1967	905	779	16.2%
1968	944	814	16.0%
1969	800	881	−9.2%
1970	839	988	−15.1%
1971	890	916	−2.8%
1972	1020	966	5.6%
1973	851	1043	−18.4%
1974	616	1118	−44.9%
1975	869	1159	−25.0%
1976	1005	1212	−17.1%
1977	831	1299	−36.0%
1978	805	1376	−41.5%
1979	839	1369	−38.7%
1980	965	1472	−34.4%
1981	875	1538	−43.1%
1982	1047	1423	−26.4%
1983	1259	1451	−13.2%
1984	1212	1522	−20.4%
1985	1547	1565	−1.2%
1986	1896	1657	14.4%
1987	1939	1729	12.1%
1988	2167	1880	15.3%
1989	2753	2306	19.4%
1990	2633	2363	11.4%
1991	3168	2229	42.1%
1992	3301	2206	49.6%
1993	3754	2127	76.5%
1994	3834	2406	59.4%
1995	5117	2533	102.0%
1996	6448	2725	136.6%
1997	7908	2970	166.3%
1998	9181	3283	179.7%
1999	11497	3413	236.9%
2000	10787	3036	255.3%

Source: Value Line; author's calculations.

cases in which one bought into obviously overpriced situations hoping to be bailed out by subsequent events. If an investment at least meets the quantitative tests of acceptability, as many "old economy" stocks did in 1973, one should accept the investment as being reasonable and put the burden of proof on subsequent events to prove it wrong, whereas if the investment did not meet our quantitative tests, one should put the burden of proof on the

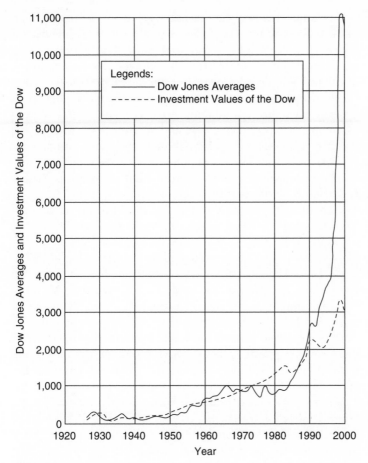

FIGURE 18.1   Dow Jones Averages versus Investment Values of the Dow.

advocate. The relationship between the Dow averages and the investment values of the Dow from 1926 to 2000 is shown in Figure 18.1.

Robert Hagstrom made a similar point in his latest book, *The Warren Buffett Portfolio.*[1] In an analysis of the Standard & Poor's (S&P) 500 entitled "Not Your Father's Index," Hagstrom pointed out the differences in composition between 1964 and 1996. The fastest growing sector was finance, which had gone from 2 percent of the index in the earlier year, to nearly 15 percent 32 years later. This growth area explains why Buffett has had a heavy concentration in this sector, including GEICO, Freddie Mac, Wells Fargo, American Express, and Citigroup. The next biggest gainer was a nearly fivefold growth in the health sector from just over 2 percent to over 10 percent. This is an area where Buffett has been notably absent, because of the difficulties in understanding the "technology" of medicine. He and Charlie Munger have said that they would buy a basket of the leading health companies if they were priced right. Technology more than doubled from 5.5 percent to 12 percent. It is noteworthy, though, that IBM a relatively slow grower in the last few decades, was an even larger part of the technology group in the 1960s than in the 1990s. Hence, the technology area excluding IBM would have shown a dramatic growth, from less than 2 percent to about 10 percent. Consumer goods and services grew their share only moderately. But their stability, especially of brand name companies, were a big attraction to Buffett. The big decliners were energy, utilities, and basic materials. These were slow growth concerns that often compensated by paying high dividends. Better that than reinvestment.

When Ben Graham rightly expressed his concern about the valuations in mid-1970, he referred to the Dow in the *Intelligent Investor*. By superimposing on his table our investment value calculation, one finds that most stocks in the Dow actually sold below estimated investment value in 1973, as shown in Table 18.1. The exceptions were American Brands, DuPont, Eastman Kodak, General Electric, General Foods, General Motors, Goodyear, Procter & Gamble, Sears, Swift, Westinghouse, and Woolworth. American Brands had a high return on equity (ROE) of 33 percent and sold at a price well below modified investment value. Most of the others were clearly overvalued, as subsequent events showed. However, the individual components of the Dow were selling for far more than investment value by 1999, as shown in Table 18.2. For the Dow as a whole, Table 18.3 shows that it was far more extended early in the 2000s decade than it was in the previous peak (late 1960s to early 1970s), or even in the late 1920s.

As the Dow flirted with 10,000 in 1999, *Barron's* ran an article by an analyst who pointed out that the addition of another zero to the Dow has always been a traumatic experience.[2] This 10,000 mark was "not another number," contrary to Alan Greenspan's statement. Instead, it would be a landmark for a conscious decision about the level of the market. Investors were reminded that the market that was already overvalued as a result of a process that had gotten way out of control. Hence, the history of such landmarks is almost certainly instructive.

A HISTORICAL VIEW OF THE DOW[3]

The Dow first reached 100 in 1906, and then languished around this level for more than 18 years, about one generation, before moving decisively above this level late in 1924. From there, it advanced in spectacular fashion, three and a half times in five years, to 381 in 1929, and then crashed to 41 three years later, a nearly 90 percent drop. The Dow did not regain its prewar high in nominal terms until 1954, and did not maintain this level in real terms until late in 1958, or some 29 years after 1929. It was not until 1966, about two generations after 1929, that the Dow approached the next figure, 1,000, just about doubling the 1929 peak in real terms. It closed at 995 early in 1966, and did not surpass 1,000 (on the close) until 1972, six years later. After that came the crash of 1973–1974 to below 600. The Dow did not permanently exceed its 1966 peak in nominal terms until 1982, and did not regain that level in real terms until 1995 (around 4,700), some 29 years later. The most recent bubble was a race to a level representing the modern-day equivalent of 1929 or 1966.

In the 1973 edition of the *The Intelligent Investor,* Ben Graham recalled that he had viewed the stock market as "dangerously high," at 575 in 1958, and as "too expensive" at 892 in 1964. The Dow peaked at 995 in 1966, eight years after the 1958 watershed, before plummeting to 577.60 in June 1974, eight years after 1966. The subsequent record shows that Graham was clearly right in 1964, but more to the point, he was even right about 575 in 1958! Thus, an investor who had sold the Dow in 1958 and invested the money in bonds would have been vindicated 16 years later when the Dow was below 600, while the dividends on stocks had been less than interest on bonds. Similarly, an investor who had sold his stocks in 1921 and sat out the "Roaring Twenties" in bonds would have been ahead by 1930. An investor who had sold all stocks in the mid-1990s, placing the money in Treasuries, was vindicated seven years later in 2002.

A history of the Dow Jones Industrial Average versus its underlying investment value (as calculated by book value plus 10 times dividends) shows a surprisingly high connection between the two over time, as shown in Table 18.3. (The calculations are based on data supplied by Value Line.) As late as 1926, the Dow traded reasonably close to its investment value. It rose significantly ahead of investment value in 1927 and 1928, reaching a premium as high as 75 percent by the end of the latter year. The market peaked at 381, at nearly twice its investment value, and started a correction process in 1929 that seemed to be completed by the end of 1931. But the bottom fell out in 1932. This was the year of 25 percent unemployment, when dividends were cut, and investment value fell by more than half, to 82. The Dow plunged further, more than reflecting the fall in investment value. It bottomed out at 41, demonstrating the book's dictum that a price of one half of investment value represents a bargain.

Business conditions improved through 1935, with the National Recovery Act, taking the stock market up to a premium. But there was a relapse in 1937, leading to another plunge in 1938. For a period from 1939 to 1958, a period of 19 years, the Dow traded below its investment value. It was not until the regaining of confidence that a premium was reattained in 1959. This lasted until 1968. The Dow actually traded at close to investment value through the early 1970s, until the 1973 oil shock caused a plunge that pushed the Dow below investment value, a condition that lasted until the end of 1985. (The year that fooled even the value investors was 1974.) In the late 1980s, the Dow traded at a modest premium to investment value, as leveraged buyouts (LBOs) and corporate restructuring promised to raise earnings growth above their historical trendline. The Dow widened its premium after the Persian Gulf War and the collapse of the Soviet Union in 1991. The premium became a chasm in 1995, and remained that way several years into the twenty-first century.

For over 20 years, since the 1982 watershed, not only the dividend yields, but even the earnings yields on stocks have been less than bond yields. Until 1999, the difference has been less than the two percentage points represented by an estimate of the autonomous growth factor of companies. Stock valuations closed most of this 2 percent "gap," by early 2000, just as the autonomous growth factor was being called into question. It is noteworthy that dividend milestones were breached at about the same time that stocks went into "dangerous" territory. In 1958, for the first time, the dividend yield on stocks was less than the dividend yield on long-term bonds. In 1992, dividend yields went below 3 percent for an extended period of time. Companies paid a smaller proportion of earnings as dividends (in many cases, using cash to buy back stock, thus taking out their least dedicated holders).

The reason appears to be rising ROEs for the Dow as a whole, through the course of the 1990s, accelerating after 1994, which could allow one to price the Dow on modified investment value. Both Warren Buffett and Alan Greenspan conceded that the high levels of the market might be sustained if the high ROEs were also maintained. But it is interesting to find that the improvement in the aggregate figure has been the result of turnarounds at American Express and IBM, coupled with improvement in the fortunes of cyclical companies such as Caterpillar Tractor and DuPont. (And because the Dow is price weighted, some of these stocks had a disproportionate influence on the Dow, more than either an equal weighting or market cap weighting would suggest.) At one level, the market seems to be saying that the business cycle has been repealed. As a warning, one should note that GM and J.P. Morgan Chase actually had significant declines in ROE during the decade.

Perhaps the greatest predictor of the crash starting in 2000 was the widespread notion of a "new era," that "this time things are different." After all, it was Irving Fisher—a Yale professor no less—who suggested "a permanent plateau of prosperity" in 1929. One of the weaknesses of the late 1990s market was that the performance was concentrated in the Dow (actually about 20 of the 30 stocks therein), plus a handful at the top levels of the S&P 500. These included a number of large NASDAQ stocks including Microsoft, Cisco Systems, and Intel, of which the first two each took a turn as the stock with the largest market capitalization in the world! The "average" stock, including about 300 issues in the S&P 500 had not participated in this rally during the "boom" year of 1998. The latter group, as well as smaller stocks not in the S&P 500, often offered a far better relation of price to investment value.

When Fed Chairman Alan Greenspan warned of "irrational exuberance" as early as 1996, with the Dow at 6,400, he was taking the long, not the short, view. It may take 10 years or more from his statement before it happens, but he will probably eventually be vindicated, by the Dow's going back below 6,400, just as Graham was when he warned of "dangerous" markets in 1958 and in the early 1960s. Likewise, Greenspan's comments that America cannot remain forever "an oasis of prosperity" will probably prove true, but only in the long run. These are careful, considered comments by a man who has been charged with the country's monetary policy, at progressively higher levels of responsibility, for 50 years.

Another sign of the top was the dangerous but prevalent belief that "anyone" can become rich in the stock market through no particular effort of their own. In "normal" times, success in this or any other endeavor has been the result of superior wisdom and painstaking effort. But these weren't really normal times. When things are changing as fast as they were in the 1990s (or the Roaring Twenties—hence the name, roaring), blind luck will sometimes produce fantastic results.

Another sign was the popular fascination with technology. Instead of being treated for what it is, the ability to facilitate existing processes, technology was regarded as a cure-all for whatever may be missing in the current economy. In the late 1990s, the highest multiples were paid for companies ending in .com. This was reminiscent of the electronics boom in the 1960s, wherein the most popular stocks ended in -onics. In the 1920s, the newfangled gadgets, cars, radio, and airplanes had the cachet. It is hard to remember that GM and Ford are the main survivors of tens of automobile companies that either folded up or were absorbed by larger concerns (the latest one being Chrysler).

Careful calculations by both Buffett and Graham, as reported in Chapter 9, indicates that the stock market can support price–earnings (P/E) ratios in the mid-20s, as it has recently, and at times in the past. The Graham calculation, for instance, of 8.5 plus 2 times the earnings growth rate gives a P/E ratio of 22.5 based on a growth rate of 7 percent, 24.5 based on a growth rate of 8 percent, and 28.5 based on a growth rate of 10 percent. It must be noted, however, that these figures are achieved only in periods of seemingly ideal economic circumstances such as those that were believed to exist around the turn of this century, prior to September 11, 2001. Similar ratios existed in the 1920s, the 1960s, and very briefly in the first three quarters of 1987, prior to the celebrated crash. But history teaches, and analysis shows, that such ideal economic conditions, and hence elevated stock prices, cannot exist forever.

That's because investors were beginning to take a long-term, perhaps 30-year view. On this basis, the classic growth stocks were "appropriately" priced in 1999, as the authors of *Dow 36,000*[4] (now!) would argue. But how long had this long-term view been held? It took hold only after 20 years of a bull market more or less, depending on whether one measures it from 1974 or 1982 to the turn of the century, and was held only for a handful of years. If history is any guide, a deeper economic downturn than that of 2001 will collapse these long-time horizons. People will become fearful of investing for a 3- to 5-year horizon, never mind 30 or more. The result will be a disproportionate collapse in stock prices (of say, 50 percent for a 5 percent decrease in the real economy).

There was talk, for instance, of investing Social Security money in the stock market, and not only allowing, but even encouraging, novice investors to do the same with payroll tax money earmarked for retirement. What an easy way to solve a very real problem of how to provide for the large number of people expected to live to a ripe old age. But it is noteworthy that this idea is a consequence, and not a cause, of the bull market of the 1990s. However, when presidential candidate Ronald Reagan made a similar proposal in 1975, in the depths of a bear market, he was wrongly derided by many as being dangerously delusionary. Yet one can see with the benefit of hindsight that the mid-1970s, near the bottom, was the optimal time to implement such a policy, while history will probably show that the late 1990s was the worst time. (However, it was in the go-go late 1960s that it became fashionable for colleges and foundations to put their money into stocks.)

Another worrisome feature of the 1990s stock market gains was that much of it was due to changes in the composition of profitability, rather than net gains. If ExxonMobil's profitability declines by $1 billion and Microsoft's profitability increases by a like amount, there is no gain in the gross national product (GNP). What was likely to occur, however, is a gain in stock market value. That's because the P/E ratio of Microsoft, the "new age" company, is about 60, or roughly three times that of Exxon's 20. So a mere transfer of wealth to the high P/E company leads to expectations of more of the same, hence a high market valuation.

Smaller companies can reasonably sell at up to two times investment value because of the prospect of a takeover. But the companies on the Dow, by definition, are the least likely candidates for merger. In fact, the companies whose stocks on the Dow, by their very size, are least likely to show improvements in earnings growth prospects, having done so in the past. At one point, for instance, if IBM had maintained its 20 percent growth rate for another 20 years, its total sales would have equaled U.S. gross domestic product (GDP). A similar thing could be said of Microsoft today.

Some mileage can be gotten, of course, by individual companies. Exxon, the largest U.S. oil company, could meaningfully increase its size, hence produce the verisimilitude of growth, by taking over Mobil, the third largest company. In another era, this would have been grounds for antitrust action. But it was not seen as worrisome, in large part because Exxon and other American players in other industries were seen as running into foreign companies in a globalization of competition. For instance, ExxonMobil will face a combination of British Petroleum-Amoco-Arco (now just BP). Antitrust probably would become an issue, and in more than one country if Exxon took things to the next step and tried to buy BP or Royal Dutch/Shell. And even if that next step were taken, Exxon would eventually run out of meaningful purchases. Exxon could, of course, buy any number of small independent producers, but that would not be enough to make a difference to its bottom line.

In fact, it has been the hollowing out of the "middle class" (the medium to largish but not the largest companies) that has brought about the transformation of many an industry—and the interruption of valuation growth for the behemoths. IBM faces major challenges now from a new generation of competitors such as Dell, Hewlett Packard, and others, but many don't remember that IBM crushed a previous generation. Companies like Burroughs, Control Data, DEC, and Wang Laboratories, not to mention a group of smaller companies like Commodore, have mostly been forgotten. This success did not lift IBM's stock price to the heights.

In the late 1990s, the author developed a model for studying the market trend and came up with the belief that the U.S. stock market was approaching a major crash. The model originally called for a top in the year 2003, although the top probably took place a few years earlier, in 2000. This was based on a time series of previous market tops of 1892, 1929, and 1966, which took place 37 years apart. As the previous years show, from top to bottom is a long way down, far more than the down move between 2000 and 2002, which was more of a correction than a crash. Although the original guess of the peak year was wrong, it motivated the defensive strategy used as early as 1999 in the real-time experiment discussed in Chapter 17.

How low can the Dow go? Ironically, the answer may be found by asking "How high did the Dow go (last)?" The historical experience from the twentieth century suggests that stock values grow at nearly 7 percent real (assuming that dividends and inflation offset each other). At this rate, they would double every 10 years, go up four times every 20 years, and eight times every 30 years. Knowing this fact, and hypothesizing that previous peaks will not be regained for almost 30 years, one can divide the previous peak by 8 to arrive at a discounted interim value for the Dow, in much the same way one could do with a zero-coupon bond. Dividing the 1929 peak of 381 by 8 gives a value of 48, a useful approximation of the low value of 41 in 1932. With the benefit of hindsight, the inflation-adjusted 1995 equivalent of the 1966 peak was nearly 4,700. Dividing this number by 8 gives 588, a useful approximation of the 578 low that the Dow reached in 1974. Rounding the year 2000 peak (upward) to 12,000 and dividing by 8 gives 1,500 as an indication of how low the Dow could go past the year 2000. This figure is roughly one half of the 3,000 "investment value" that was calculated in Table 18.3, a relationship that approximates the previous market bottoms in 1932 and 1974. The Dow may trough at a somewhat higher number, but mainly because of adjustments for inflation.

There is probably a causal factor—the generational model discussed in Chapter 20. Although the date could only be guessed at, the world financial system seemed likely to unwind, and sooner rather than later. A look at past crashes may give a clue as to how the ongoing crash will shape up. The stock market as a whole, as measured by the Dow, or the S&P 500, will likely decline by well over 50 percent in nominal terms from its peak, as the NASDAQ already has. Real estate in most parts of the country, which is supported by the vast creation of wealth through the stock market and through the currently artificial liquidity of the banking system, will decline by perhaps half as much. The cutting-edge stock of the 1920s, Radio Corporation of America, declined by over 90 percent off its peak between 1929 and 1932, and the same has pretty much happened to America Online and other leading Internet stocks—the ones that survive anyway. Unemployment will go back into the double digits of the 1970s or 1980s, although probably not the Depression-era level of 25 percent, given the safety nets that are now in place. Likewise, there will be a total contraction of GDP in the high single or low double digits percentage-wise, although probably not 25 percent.

William Gross of the Pimco Bond fund made the point more emphatically when he estimated fair value on the Dow as 5,000, supporting the thesis of a more than 50 percent decline from 11,722. He pointed out that annual real earnings growth for blue-chip U.S. stocks was barely more than one half of one percent in the twentieth century. (According to him, the difference between this figure and the average yearly 2 percent real capital gains was due to P/E multiple expansion.) Put another way, the return behavior of such stocks should approximate that of the Treasury inflation-protected securities (TIPs) by providing an inflation fighter and a dividend yield and not much more. Thus, over a 30-odd-year period, the total real earnings growth of blue chips is only 20 to 25 percent. The huge volatility (in real terms) of stocks over such a period was due mainly to market fluctuations, not to real growth. This is the most powerful argument for value investing (buying stocks at prices below historical value trend lines) over growth investing (buying stocks for the robustness of their trend lines).

A stock can be analyzed as being composed of a fixed income vehicle and a call option. When Gross estimated the "bond value" of the Dow as 5,000, he was saying that there was a "call option" in the Dow quotation of almost 5,000 points (based on a Dow of just under 10,000). Our "investment value" calculations are even more conservative than Gross's because they assume a risk premium for corporate bonds over Treasuries. And Table 18.3 shows that there have been times in the past when Dow stocks have traded at a discount to "investment value," meaning that the "option value" was negative.

"But the Dow is different today," many would protest. "It now includes growth companies like Microsoft, Home Depot, and Intel." The fact of the matter is that these are former growth companies. They were included in the Dow after, not during, their period of spectacular growth, in the same way as IBM or 3M of a previous year. Each of the three newer companies is now the leader in its industry, and Microsoft runs neck-and-neck with venerable General Electric, Pfizer, and ExxonMobil for the world's largest market cap, with the other two not far behind. By definition, the former growth companies are blue chips, and as such, they can't collectively beat the "market" because they are proxies for the U.S. economy itself. (Someone who had bought them a decade or two ago when they were small-cap stocks and held them until they entered the Dow would have gotten rich, however.)

A Graham and Dodd investor would not believe that the world is in anything like a new era, except for a few minor details. Instead, the world is probably following a pattern that has been displayed many times before. It is manifested in a willingness to ignore time-tested principles in the name of "progress." This pattern has always led to massive misery in the past and can hardly avoid doing the same this time around. A French proverb sums it up best, "Plus ca change, plus c'est le meme chose." Or in Ben Graham's English version, "The more things change, the more it's the same thing."[5]

CHAPTER 19

Some Disquieting Thoughts on Excessive Credit Creation

The fundamental issue of our time is world credit creation, or more exactly, the problems that are likely to accompany the collapse of the credit pyramid at home and abroad. It has been said that the key to wealth in the past three or four decades was not an abundance of resources, but rather access to credit. But this is a shaky foundation on which to build lasting prosperity. The more likely outcome is that most of the world, the United States not excepted, after having ingested economic steroids, is about to feel the aftereffects. This is reflected in the overvalued stock markets of the 1990s and early 2000s in the United States and western Europe. It is more likely that this represents the twilight of an old era rather than the dawn of a new one.

Although the problem began overseas, it will eventually spread to the United States. The international problems will be considered first, because they can't be separated from purely domestic ones. But there are enough weaknesses in the U.S. economy for a major domino effect to take place. The historical experience has been that an economic phenomenon overshoots, and on both the up and down sides, although the efficient markets academics may try to deny it.

EXCESSIVE CREDIT CREATION ABROAD

With the benefit of hindsight, history will probably show that an extended period of world economic crisis began, or rather first became apparent, in Asia in 1997 and 1998. First Thailand, then Indonesia, Malaysia, the Philippines, and finally South Korea were forced to devalue their currencies. This was considered surprising because most of these countries were large exporters that usually ran large surpluses on their balance of trade. The problem was that in order to support these exports, they had to borrow heavily to finance the purchase of capital equipment. But these moves turned out to be unprofitable for most of the Southeast Asian companies involved when the prices of commodities and semifinished products fell sharply. It means that the value of the exports had been overestimated, relative to the cost of producing them, causing their producers to lose money.

The crisis also highlighted the weaknesses of the Asian model of state-sponsored enterprise. At its worst, it consisted of crony capitalism, wherein government contracts and subsidies were awarded to the friends or even children of the rulers, as in Indonesia. But in general, this operated in a more insidious form. Strategic industries such as steel, machinery, or electronics were targeted for state-supported finance. This practice began in Japan after World War II, and was adopted by most Asian countries. In effect, the governments encouraged companies in these strategic industries to leverage their balance sheets far beyond prudent levels, and then persuaded banks to support such leverage by giving implicit guarantees of the resulting debt. The governments in turn had to borrow abroad from private (usually Western or Japanese) banks, or from the multilateral agencies such as the International Monetary Fund (IMF) or the World Bank to fund such loans. Thus, in country after country, a shaky credit structure was established that was only as strong as its government, as the ultimate guarantor.

So the Asian economic miracle rested on weaker foundations than previously thought. And the sense of false prosperity led to incredible waste. For instance, Malaysia tried to build the tallest building in the world. In all fairness, the building of the Empire State Building perhaps reflected American hubris of the 1920s and signaled a subsequent fall. (The same was probably true with the construction of the Sears Building in Chicago in the 1960s.) There was in the American case, however, the important difference that the world's tallest building represented also the very real economic achievements of that country in those eras. The Malaysian version had the hubris without the achievement.

Latin America has a somewhat different set of problems. Like developing countries in East Asia, the region has a deficit on the current account. Unlike the other countries, Latin Americans also have a deficit on the trade account. This is probably because of the so-called "demonstration effect" of American affluence, that makes Latin Americans peculiarly dependent on imported goods from the United States (including travel to that country). But this trade deficit is one that is shared by the United States. The central problem of the Americas, North as well as South, is the large trade deficits owed to continents offshore, in Europe and Asia. As of mid-2003, the U.S. balance of payments deficit was running at over $40 billion a month, nearly $500 billion a year.

Over a century ago, a president of Mexico said of his country, "Poor Mexico, so far from God, so close to the United States." This is true, to a greater or lesser degree, of just about every country in Latin America. This came to a head in the 1994–1995 Mexican currency crisis that saw the local currency, the peso, lose over half of its value in 12 months.

Brazil's problems, which led to a currency devaluation early in 1999, were in some sense an extreme version of the Latin American malaise. After a period of hyperinflation dating back to the early 1960s, it had tamed inflation through a combination of tight monetary policy and an overvalued currency in the mid-1990s. The last necessary ingredient, and the one that was hardest to achieve, was a responsible fiscal policy. The country needed to close a large budget deficit through a combination of privatization of state companies, lower spending, and higher taxes in order to shore up the confidence of international lenders. The asset privatization, which was managed by the federal executive branch, proceeded fairly well, although it was hampered by falling prices occasioned by problems in other emerging markets. But other reforms proved to be difficult to pass in a highly fragmented, multiparty Congress. The last straw was the governors' revolt that threatened to default on state payments to the federal government. The result was a devaluation of the real in January 1999.

As if the problems in emerging market economies weren't bad enough, they are being accompanied by problems in one of the key world markets, Japan. That country's growth recession, which lasted the better part of the decade, became an actual recession late in the 1990s. But the country was slow to undertake the most necessary reform: cleaning up its banking system. Although a few of the worst cases were allowed to go under, many other economically brain dead companies were maintained on the fiscal equivalent of life support. And other corporations were dominated by gangs representing the Japanese Mafia, not unlike Russia. As a result, the country was in the direst straits since the 1930s.

Japan, in fact, was perhaps the single country most responsible for the Asian crisis. The overbuilding of property and commodity industries across the region was the result of Japanese bank lending, which in turn had been inspired by Japan's own success in these areas. And the problems were massive, because during the 1980s, the top 10 Japanese banks had grown to the point of being somewhat larger in total assets, and much larger in terms of market capitalization, than American counterparts such as Chase, Citibank, J.P. Morgan, and Bank of America. The Japanese activity resembled, on an even larger scale, the foolish American lending to Latin American countries in the 1970s and early 1980s, which had in large part been the cause of American banks' being overtaken temporarily by the Japanese.

China is a rather different case. To its credit, it dodged the Asian crisis of 1997. (It is being discussed in this section rather than emerging markets because of its probable emergence as a future Great Power.) It is a vast country with great potential but important growing pains, due to the restructuring of its state-owned enterprises. These are communes run by a

Communist government that is now trying to take on the trappings of capitalism with a minimum sacrifice of state power. But these organizations had to be downsized, with the consequent loss of jobs and the exposure of their fundamental overleveraging. The result was a deflation that put the brakes on economic growth and threatened a devaluation.

The Soviet Union and China have different versions of the same problems. Both of them are trying to wean the populace off a communistic, state-sponsored system. Russia reverted to an updated version of feudalism. Tens, perhaps hundreds of thousands, of petty authorities exercised local control over small economic and political units. The result was a partial breakdown of previously existing economic relationships and a resulting collapse of living standards. China has been decidedly more successful in its effort. One or two hundred million people, mostly in the cities, now live a more or less capitalistic lifestyle approaching what others might enjoy in more advanced Asian countries such as Hong Kong or Taiwan.

China's basic problem is that it has too many people. To provide all 1.2 billion people with an American lifestyle would require a gross domestic product (GDP) of four times that of the United States. Even if the country's GDP were to approximate that of the United States, spreading it among four times as many people would mean a per capita income comparable to that of the United States in the early twentieth century. The large population forces China to have a "one child" policy, which creates two subsidiary problems. First, it creates a relatively old population because the current crop of young adults will (theoretically) produce only half as many members of the next generation. And because boys are more valued than girls, female infanticide and prebirth sex screening and selection mean that there are 15 to 20 percent more young men than young women. This is likely to lead to social unrest or worse, as this next crop of children grow up. Investor Jimmy Rogers (author of *The Investment Biker* and *Adventure Capitalist*) considers this the single most important demographic fact today.[1]

Europe had its own problems. For centuries the continent has had a divided and even contentious coexistence between its individual countries. Now, they are trying to unify a set of vastly different cultures and economies. But these problems were exacerbated by the European Monetary Union, an awkward arrangement because it included 11 different economies at the start, some of which have diametrically opposing priorities. But there may be at least two Europes, a mostly northern, German-led bloc, and a southern, Mediterranean bloc containing Italy, Spain, Greece, and possibly Turkey.

In all fairness, any country would have faced at least some problems. It's a question of picking one's poison. A financier's bias is in favor of sound money and a sound fiscal balance, at some modest cost to growth. The result is an uneasy pact whereby America is a receiver of a larger share of the world's goods than it produced in exchange for providing liquidity to the world. But America cannot be the world's consumer of last resort without creating serious imbalances in its own economy.

Most disquieting is the following situation: No major country in the world has both fiscal and trade accounts in reasonable balance. Many Asian countries have fine trade balances and large foreign exchange reserves. But they are running large fiscal deficits. The United States, however, had temporarily brought fiscal spending back into balance in the 1990s after several decades of profligacy. But it is running a large deficit on its trade balance as discussed above, as well as a fiscal deficit in the 2000s.

The fundamental problem is the credit expansion that has taken place in the United States following, and in fact resulting from, the collapse of confidence elsewhere in the world. The end result is that there are more IOUs than there are resources to back those IOUs. This has already been seen in devaluation countries like Russia and those in Southeast Asia. Living standards plummeted precipitously when national current accounts were proved to be a fiction, and the countries owed more money abroad than they could possibly pay, except by squeezing the living standards of the average citizen. The United States has so far (with emphasis on *so far*) avoided this fate.

The bailout of emerging market countries by institutions like the IMF is like that of the debtor whose income can't pay monthly bills plus outstanding interest and principal amortization. Then the credit card company says in effect, "no problem, your credit limit has been raised." Unlike the 30-year mortgage, so-called minimum payments do not come close to amortizing the debt, even after 30 years. (Note that a lender who collects 18 percent annual interest for 30 years and then forgives the principal would earn 143 times the original loan instead of 144.)

Indeed, there has already been a rolling depression in the stocks of U.S. steel and machinery companies. Such weakness in basic industry (at that time, primarily the farm sector) occurred in the 1920s and was a prelude to the larger depression in the more modern sector, hence, a Graham and Dodd investor's preference for investments that already reflect depression conditions and are based on true investment value. If a depression does come, those holdings will be appropriately priced, with only ordinary downside risk, while other issues that currently sell well above investment value and even modified investment value will fall off a cliff.

For example, what are the implications of weakness in the agricultural sector? In the last three or four decades, living standards in a significant part of the world, East Asia, had been rising significantly. Nowhere was this more evident than in nutritional standards. As of the year 2000, children of East Asian parents are similar to American children in height, weight, health, libido, and a score of other ways that their parents were not. Until the 1997 crisis, all but the poorest segments of the population in most East Asian countries had ample amounts of grain and adequate amounts of meat and vegetables. The crisis changed all that by forcing drastic reductions in the consumption of meat and vegetables, and even calling into question the adequacy of a diet of grain for many people. Put bluntly, the U.S. farm crisis occurred because people ate far less well than they did a few years ago in parts of Asia.

In 1998, the U.S. personal savings rate dropped to nearly 0 percent. Americans didn't feel the need to save out of their earnings because of the appreciation of their investments. Individual net worths were rising even without the addition of fresh capital. But these capital gains could go on only if other people, either inside or outside the country, saved and then invested in the United States. Asian countries had amassed huge savings through hard work and self-denial. But they have so far been unable to use such capital efficiently, as measured by returns on equity (ROEs) of companies. Americans have been less assiduous at capital accumulation, but they are better at deploying capital to earn maximum returns.

Here, there are the makings of a Faustian bargain. America was allowed, even encouraged, to engage in its profligate ways, because it was good for the world economy. The American stock market boom encouraged large spending stateside, which in turn led to large imports that kept the rest of the world's export-oriented economies growing—a virtuous circle, so far as it goes. But it is one in which the links are too complicated, and one broken link will lead to an avalanche.

RELATED PROBLEMS IN AMERICA

The United States has so far escaped such a fate because foreign investors have been content to roll over their investments in U.S. stocks and bonds, thereby financing the above-mentioned deficits. The plight of Latin American countries is instructive, because they are closer to home, both literally and figuratively, than problems in either emerging Europe or Asia. For one thing, an economic collapse, particularly in Mexico, would likely set off a wave on refugee emigration. More importantly, people in the Latin American countries have adopted watered-down versions of American economic and social mores and lifestyles without the means to support them. This process not only attenuates the Latin American countries, but holds up a mirror to our own weaknesses. The fact that the United States has had until recently a regional trade surplus only with South America underlies the main point, that foreign debt is fundamentally an *Americas* problem.

The drive for transparency, however, has some important side effects. Money fled the Far East, and to a lesser extent, Europe, including western

Europe, in the 1990s, because of the lack of transparency and the resulting loss of confidence. It came, instead, to the United States, where both financial reporting and corporate governance were demonstrably superior to those in just about every other part of the world, although Enron and other corporate scandals have greatly reduced this advantage. The problem is that the American business environment is better, but probably not to a degree as to justify the high valuation of American stocks at the turn of the century. But the real benefit of transparency is not for outside investors but for the managers themselves.

The growth rates of the United States in the 1990s, while above their own historical trend, were unexceptional by the standards of the developing countries. (They compared favorably with Europe and Japan, however.) What was regarded as exceptional was the security and certainty of that growth. "Security and (presumed) certainty"—in a word, confidence—form an unstable foundation on which to base investment values. After all, there was similar confidence in Asia in the late 1980s, and with exception of Japan, into the early 1990s, that led to overvaluations in those markets. Are we likely to be different?

The key to wealth in the past two decades or so has not been access to productive capacity, but rather access to monetary liquidity. This recent economic expansion has been fed by the secular trend toward greater financial sophistication, which in turn has led to a massive expansion of liquidity. The changes include things like automated teller machines and electronic banking. Credit analysis has gotten more sophisticated, though not more accurate (the major credit agencies were slow in calling the problems at Enron, Worldcom, and elsewhere), as has advertising. Consumers can now be identified with almost pinpoint accuracy and are pursued ruthlessly through targeted appeals that include affinity marketing and telemarketing.

Preapproved credit cards are an example of this trend. In the old days, no credit could ever be granted unless the lender had first met the borrower. This most important factor in the credit decision was the lender's evaluation of the character of the borrower. This character evaluation could be undertaken only in a face-to-face meeting. But a preapproved credit card skips the face-to-face process and thereby omits the most important part of the credit analysis. Consider the case of a man who, in the space of six months, had received preapproved credit cards for his four-month-old son, his dog, and his computer (which had a cybermoniker). All of these entities had excellent "negative" credit histories (no records of previous problems). But credit was approved to them on the basis of information that was otherwise incomplete. These mistakes would not have been made face to face.

In response to the soaring bankruptcy rate, the credit card companies have pushed for new laws to limit bankruptcy proceedings. An argument can be made that bankruptcy is too easy and should be made more difficult. But the credit card companies are the last entities who should be making this argument, because they are a significant part of the problem. They have no real interest in people being more careful in incurring debt. Instead, they use the most sophisticated forms of market segmentation and advertising to encourage spendthrift behavior, and then harness the force of the law to force unsophisticated borrowers to pay the full price for loans that they were foolishly induced to take. In essence, their mode of operation is similar to that of a narcotics dealer who wants his "collection" activities to be backed by the force of law, when they are, in fact, receiving the natural consequences of risks that they willingly, even eagerly, took on. And yet, this profligacy has been a key ingredient in world economic growth, first in the United States, then Europe, and most recently in Southeast Asia.

Company after company loaded up on debt in the 1990s, after having spent long decades following World War II with prudent balance sheets. One company after another reduced or eliminated dividends during times of prosperity, not the least of which was AT&T, which maintained its payout during the whole of the Great Depression. Meanwhile, high P/E ratios all but eliminated the yields even of companies that pay a respectable portion of earnings as dividends. John Paul Getty made the point in *How to Be Rich* regarding companies with 100 P/Es. "Even if every penny of earnings were paid out in dividends, shareholders would be receiving only a 1 percent return on their investment. But if this were the case, the company would have no money left to spend on expansion. That, of course, would eliminate the possibility of capital growth."[2]

Classical inflation stopped in the past decade. But the inflation of the prices of financial assets continued. Indeed, it is this form of inflation, and not that of the real economy, that probably worries the Federal Reserve the most. If present trends were to continue, it would completely transform the historical relationships between the real and financial sectors of the economy. Rather than merely being a mirror of the real economy, its traditional function, the financial sector would be the arbiter of economic activity. The whims and worries of central bankers, and "street" traders in financial centers around the world, would determine whether or not various goods were sold, and at what price.

To a greater extent than is generally believed, America has been plain lucky, rather than smart. The country has been on a course that would ordinarily lead to significant inflation. But this was offset by a raging global deflation, which serendipitously created the so-called Goldilocks economy in the late 1990s, where the "porridge" was "not too hot, not too cold, but just right." This was supported by an apparently successful "fine tuning" of the economy that economists had first attempted in the 1960s, but had finally achieved in the 1990s, thanks to the growth of information technology.

Indeed, many consider the major risk to the world economy to be deflation. But deflation is just the opposite of inflation, comes the argument. It's just a matter of lower prices. In a rational world, like the one hypothesized by the "rational expectations" school, there is no money illusion. People adjust their calculations according to the current price level, and all is well. But the true risk from deflation is not a falling price level, but rather disintermediation. This is a process in which liquidity dries up more or less across the board. The result is a major reversal from hyperspeed to retreat in the real economy. Instead of excess liquidity to finance borderline—or even more foolish—projects, there is a lack of liquidity to finance projects of genuine and demonstrable economic merit.

There is, supposedly, excess capacity in the world. Is there really a lack of demand? That's hard to believe when there are large numbers of poor people in Africa, Asia, and Latin America. What is lacking in developing countries is effective demand, as measured by purchasing power. Traditional markets have been saturated, and insufficient attempts have been made to open up new ones. Put another way, billions of people who would like to participate in the abundance of the world markets cannot do so because they don't have access to credit and other resources that would give them a stake in the world economy.

For some decades now (not years), world GDP growth, at roughly 3 percent a year, has been greater, by a factor of two, than that of the expansion of demand for oil, metals, or other basic materials. Instead, the gains have come primarily in areas such as health care, technology, and services— things that most benefit affluent people who already have met basic needs such as food, clothing, and shelter. At the turn of the century, average American family income was approximately $40,000 a year in 2000 dollars. This compares roughly to a figure of $10,000 a year in 1900, a quadrupling (and $2,000 to $3,000 a year at the turn of the eighteenth and nineteenth centuries—another fourfold or so increase). Americans are living in larger houses than they were a century ago, but not four times larger. They're certainly not eating four times as much food or wearing four times as many clothes.

Because of a century of misgovernment and war, the average Russian, was not appreciably better off in 2000 than in 1900, despite a century of technological progress. This person has somewhat greater access to cars and TV sets, expressed as fractional ownership of these items "on average." But the Russians are actually eating less well than their grandparents. Life expectancy, after having advanced early in the twentieth century, is no longer today than it was shortly before World War II, and has actually dropped during the course of the 1990s. In other parts of the world, especially most of Africa, the standard of living is lower today than it was 100 years ago.

A SOBER VIEW OF THE FINANCIAL MARKETS
IN THE NEXT DECADE OR TWO

The trauma early in the twenty-first century will be the fight over whether the world development model continues to favor the affluent nations and people through the greater production of services rather than goods, or whether this will go on the back burner to allow a larger number of the world's people to follow the path that America traveled over a century ago, which entailed a greater production of goods. The latter would be good for the world in the long run but would cause shorter-term problems in the United States by reversing the conditions that created the "Goldilocks" economy and soaring stock market of the 1990s.

How could this come about? Central banks across the developed world, including and especially the United States, will be concerned about inflation, especially of asset prices, and take steps to rein it in. Local lenders will cut back on credit, especially to consumers. Consumer spending will be thrown into reverse, causing a contraction in the real economy. With this backdrop, international markets, particularly emerging markets, are seen as riskier, and money stops flowing to them. Trade dries up as countries pursue a "beggar my neighbor policy."

The following has happened within the experience of many people on the earth today: A major country enjoyed a period of substantial economic success over a period of two or three decades, which in turn fueled a stock market boom. This financial boom was particularly evident in the most recent decade, when money flowed into mutual "funds," which drove up the stock market to astronomical heights. This in turn led to an orgy of both consumption and investment. Meanwhile, the economic environment slowly and subtly changed into one that was less favorable. So the overvaluation of the stock market could no longer be sustained, and it crashed. This exposed the folly of earlier investment and placed a huge damper on consumption. The country was stuck in a long period of anemic growth, coupled with deflation. Far-fetched? This was the story of the United States in the first four decades of the twentieth century. More to the point, it was the story of Japan in the past three decades. As of the beginning of the twenty-first century, the United States had experienced the first two decades of a similar cycle, a decade or so behind Japan. The final phase is all but inevitable for America. Coupled with Japan's recent depression experience, it will have very serious consequences for the world economy.

Mr. Greenspan and most of his team may be among the most capable economic managers the world has known, at least in modern times. But it may be their very success at managing what have been decent-sized problems that may cause the world to put too much faith in their ability to head off the big one. What's more, it's likely that their very ability to put out the smaller fires will eventually lead to a far bigger one. Every general knows how to win the last war. But this knowledge is available to everyone, so the preparations should all be for the next war, although they usually aren't.

An analogy exists in medicine. Pharmaceuticals, particularly antibiotics, have largely reduced the number of diseases that kill people before their time. But through a process of natural selection, the germs have also gotten tougher and more disease resistant. At the end of the day, it is not clear who is ahead, bacteria or antibodies. While it appears likely that the current level of economic management is a sufficient antidote to the valuation excesses of the 1920s, those excesses are far greater as of the turn of the twentieth and twenty-first centuries. Thus, the better the economic policy, the greater the excesses.

Why do business cycles occur? And why would there be a crash? Again, modern medicine has cured a number of diseases like polio and smallpox, and has made important progress against cancer. People's life expectancies are nearly 30 years longer than they were a century ago. But medicine still cannot keep people from dying. In much the same way, macroeconomic policy can prolong business cycles or moderate their effects. But they cannot prevent them from coming to an end.

The answer was not that monetary policy was too tight or that there were too many barriers to trade, or things of that nature. Instead, the problems lay in the real economy, as a result of the cycle. The Social Security debate is an example of this phenomenon. The real issue is not whether Social Security can exist, but the level of benefits supportable by the current level of taxes, or alternately, by raising payroll taxes. Social Security became the "third rail" of American politics as a black or white proposition, when it should have been couched as a question of living within one's means. The continuance of Social Security should never have been in question, only the level of benefits.

Social Security has been wrongly referred to as a "contract between generations." This terminology is nonsense. A contract presupposes the agreement of two equally knowledgeable, willing parties. In fact, Social Security is more like the "tyranny of whoever happens to be walking around the earth at a given time." It is a burden imposed on younger generations, including those who are in fact unborn, by others in the prime of life, who worry about their old age. It is an arrangement that unborn generations had no say in, and that our dead ancestors may well have disapproved of.

But perhaps the biggest Ponzi scheme was the turn-of-the-century stock market. The so-called new paradigm went something like this: The reduction of cyclical and political risk in the early 1990s fueled a stock market boom, which in turn fueled a rise of consumption. The resulting economic expansion fueled a further rise in the stock market. Through the attainment of stock price levels well above investment value, the market was capitalizing the earnings, not of today, but of one generation hence. In this manner, fortunate participants of today's market were offered the chance to increase their own consumption by appropriating the capital of their children and grandchildren.

The technological revolution has been a mixed blessing. Early in 2000, technology accounted for nearly one third of the S&P 500, and an even larger share of smaller-cap indexes such as NASDAQ. That was a huge bet on a somewhat dicey proposition. Even as the indexes made new highs late in the fall of 1999, the number of new lows (mostly of nontech stocks) exceeded the number of new highs by a factor typically of three or four to one. That's because fast-growing tech stocks were sucking capital out of other sectors of the economy and stock market. Put another way, if investments were being made in the tech sector based on the proposition that earnings (and stock values) would grow at 15 to 20 percent for the foreseeable future, the prices of nontech stocks will have to fall in order for their (rising) dividend yields and potential price appreciation to compete. That, as much as anything else, was the reason for the 1970s Nifty Fifty phenomenon and its modern equivalent. That said, the prospective returns on certain nontech issues are now as attractive as they have been any time in the past two decades.

The astronomical compensation (admittedly in the form of cheap options on expensive stock, rather than cash) of Internet executives, and others that serve them (such as Wall Street) are a case in point. These packages were justified if the tech fulfilled its promise of historically outsized returns, but not otherwise. The risk was that huge sums of money would have been expended for genuinely large—but ultimately insufficient—returns, destroying rather than creating value in the process. Because of their significance, such a result would not be limited to the tech sector but would have ripple effects throughout the whole economy.

Another example was the oil shocks of the 1970s. There were actually two crises, one in 1973 and one in 1979, both of which, in theory, should have been bad for the U.S. stock market. The 1973 event certainly was, with the market declining nearly 50 percent in 1973–1974. But stocks actually rose in 1979. Apparently, the markets had discounted both events (and nearly a decade of high commodity prices) at one go. A similar situation probably existed with the Internet and tech revolution. The phenomenon itself should unfold well into the first decade of the twenty-first century, but it appears to have been priced into the stock market in one go around the turn of the century.

The tech revolution was welcomed because it led to productivity gains that support a high level of growth without inflation. For instance, if raw materials are being used in a wasteful fashion, then improved technology can conserve such resources, extending their use and reducing costs. But if supplies are already taut, the law of diminishing returns comes into play, and expanded supply, not greater efficiency, is the solution. Likewise, productivity gains are welcome during a period of turbocharged demand. But if demand falls off, then rising productivity leads to greater unemployment. In a sense, the so-called Phillips curve model, which assumes that lower inflation is matched by higher unemployment, may not have been abolished, but rather gone dormant.

Some people suggested that the tech revolution was equivalent to the Industrial Revolution, which revolutionized the whole production process and society as a whole. If this were the case, then perhaps the premises of this book are wrong. Clearly, a paradigm shift was under way, but it appears to have been more on the order of the 1970s oil crisis or the 1920s radio craze. Put another way, it appears to have been the kind of event that occurs once or twice in the average lifetime, not once or twice in the average millennium. The tech revolution appears to be a temporary acceleration of normal growth patterns, not the dawning of the Dark Ages and the feudal system, which brought economic growth to a halt, or the Industrial Revolution, which awakened it from its slumber.

There are too many flies in the ointment to believe that the world economy will go straight up. The collapse of the Asian economic miracle is both a roadblock and a warning as to what could well happen in the United States. The debt spiral provides a ready mechanism for a meltdown of global credit and hence economic growth; fears that have already been ignited by the near collapse of Nobel Prize winner–led Long-Term Capital Management. The unevenness of global economic growth is an issue that will have to be addressed, hopefully peacefully, but not necessarily so. Economic history has always been about the race to increase production fast enough to keep up with rising desires for consumption, but the 1990s exuberance raised the bar further on what is usually a high hurdle.

Lawrence Sloan, in his 1931 book *Every Man and His Common Stocks,* posed three rhetorical questions about the economic conditions then gripping the United States (and the rest of the world). Was the country in a severe and possibly prolonged economic downturn? Almost certainly yes. Were there clear signs ahead of time? A qualified yes. The last question was: Could it have been foreseen? Here, Sloan made a mixed case. In his opinion, the indications of trouble were present, but only to someone who was predisposed to look for them. But there were enough other confusing and positive signs that someone with an optimistic, or even neutral, view of the world would probably have been led astray.[3] For reasons outlined above, the author was inclined to uncover danger and found plenty to worry about. But it has been difficult convincing others, before the fact, that the world is on the brink of the mother of all economic crises.

Clearly, the U.S. financial markets, which have been a pacesetter for the world, cannot maintain the same pace early in the twenty-first century as in the late 1990s. In a best-case scenario, the U.S. and world stock markets would move sideways for a decade or two, allowing economic growth and earnings to catch up, after having enjoyed an unjustified expansion around the recent turn of the century. But history teaches that markets are seldom that patient. A long period of withdrawal would be a painful experience after the recent "high." And there are too many possibilities of exogenous shocks, economic "accidents," and just plain human emotions to make this relatively good scenario the more probable one, with the terrorist attack on the World Trade Center in September 2001 being an unfortunate case in point. The more likely prospect is that the world is headed for a situation similar to the last time that the Graham and Dodd methodology was most effective, a period characterized by stock market crashes and a global depression, possibly followed by a world war.

CHAPTER **20**

Generational Cycles in the American Stock Market

A whole stock market cycle appears to last 35 to 40 years, or roughly two generations. This may come as a surprise to those investors who evaluate investments relative to say, a 10-year (or shorter) time frame. Instead, there have been at least two U.S. market tops in the twentieth century, in 1929 and 1966 (the latter after adjusting for inflation because stocks went higher in nominal, but not real, terms, in later years), or 37 years apart. This finding is supported by a previous market top, 37 years before 1929, in 1892.* Straight-line calculations would give another market top shortly after the turn of the century (adding 37 years to 1966 gives the year 2003), although the top may have been reached a few years earlier, in 2000. This discrepancy occurred because 2003 was a "point" estimate, when in fact, a "range" estimate is more appropriate.

Historically, 1892, 1929, and 1966 represented important turning points in the U.S. economy, with several different meanings. The first turning point, 1892, ushered in a period of "good deflation" and moderate economic growth following the depression and stock market crash of 1893. The second turning point, 1929, is the most famous because it was characterized by deflation and depression. The third turning point, 1966, was followed by "stagflation"—stagnation plus inflation. Given these precedents and the likelihood that 2003 is another turning point, what is likely to occur? The turning points in 1892 and 1966 were marked by the transfer of managerial power to "Silent"-type generations described below. However, 1929 was characterized by the ascendancy of the "Lost" generation. The present turning point is more likely to resemble 1929 than the other two because the coming midlife

---

*Technically, 1892 was not a market peak. It followed a correction and a rebound, but is treated as a top in the literature because it was the "last stop" before the Crash of 1893. The author now believes that 2003 will perform a similar function in modern times.

generation is the "new Lost" Generation X. The first manifestation of this was the hiring of Sallie Krawcheck, a 37-year-old-Gen-Xer, to a senior position at Citigroup to clean up that firm's "tainted" stock research. This, in turn, was an unfortunate but necessary consequence of the social and stock market "boom" engendered by the previous two generations.

A LOOK AT THE GENERATIONS

The operative word is probably *generations,* a phenomenon for which there may be a sociological explanation. According to the pathbreaking book *Generations,* by William Strauss and Neil Howe,[1] there are alternating strong and weak generations in American life (*dominant* and *recessive* in Strauss and Howe's terminology). Strong generations, such as the Baby Boomers, run the American economy in overdrive. Weak generations, like the preceding Silent generation and succeeding Generation X, rein in the excesses of the strong generations. Each leaves its mark on the American economy and culture, especially during its managerial midlife years, roughly between the ages of 40 and 60. The four generational types are Idealist (Baby Boomers and the post–Civil War generation), Reactive (Generation X and the Lost Generation before it), Civic (the World War II generation or what Strauss and Howe call the GI generation, and probably today's youngsters), and Adaptive (the Silent generation and most children to be born shortly after the year 2000). A stock market cycle of 30-odd years then encompasses one strong and one weak generation.

The recent generations and their birth years are:

- *The GI generation, aka the World War II generation, 1902–1925.* This formulation differs slightly from Strauss and Howe's GI generation, which they peg as beginning in 1901 and ending in 1924.
- *The Silent generation, 1926–1942.* Strauss and Howe use 1925 as the starting year.
- *The Boom generation, 1943–1961.* The starting year is the same as Strauss and Howe's; the ending is a year later, based on who had turned 40 years old before the tragic events of September 11, 2001, at the World Trade Center. Strauss and Howe stand the conventional wisdom (that the baby boom started in 1946 and ended in 1964) on its head by arguing that the demographic boom was the consequence, and not the cause, of the cultural changes that took place around the end of World War II. This book basically agrees.
- *Generation X, 1962–1979.* This definition is shorter at both ends than Strauss and Howe's version. A recessive generation is supposed to have fewer years and members than a dominant generation, if only because

people on its borders identify themselves as members of the stronger generation.

■ *The Millennial generation, 1980–1999(?)*. The ending year, especially, is a guess, but this figures to be another civic generation and, most likely, another "GI" generation.

Going back in time from the GI generation, there are:

■ *The Lost generation, 1883–1901 (18 years)*. This was the generation of Fitzgerald and Hemingway in literature, as well as Graham and Dodd in finance.
■ *The Missionary generation, 1861–1882 (21 years)*. This post–Civil War generation had its "rendezvous with destiny" under leaders like Franklin and Eleanor Roosevelt.
■ *The Progressive generation, a hybrid "civic" and "silent" product of the Civil War, 1843–1860 (17 years)*. Representative members include Presidents Theodore Roosevelt and Woodrow Wilson.
■ *The Gilded generation, a "pre-Lost" generation, 1821–1842 (21 years)*. These included the "robber barons" like John D. Rockefeller, J.P. Morgan, and Andrew Carnegie.
■ *The Transcendental generation, 1792–1820 (28 years)*. Personified by Abraham Lincoln and Nathaniel Hawthorne, it is the last of the very long generations.

Beginning with the Gilded generation, there have been a number of 21 year generations alternating with 16- to 18-year generations, for an average of nearly 20 years. The longer generations (except for the Gilded) were those of the dominant cohorts, shorter ones those of recessive peer groups. But beginning with the Baby Boomers, a dominant generation, what used to be the long 20-plus-year generation was only 18 years long. Hence, the generational cycle itself may have shortened from 80-plus years in colonial times to 75 years or less in modern times. While the periods between the crises that Strauss and Howe describe are roughly 80 years, the difference was actually 85 years between 1776 and 1861, and exactly 80 years between 1861 and 1941. An 80-year cycle would predict a crisis and possibly a war around the year 2021. This is close to the right time frame, but at the rate events are progressing, the climax could come just a bit earlier, in the mid- to late teens.

SIMILARITIES OF THE LAST TWO GENERATIONAL CYCLES

Thus, the period preceding the Depression and World War II coincided with the arrival to midlife power of a strong-willed, idealistic group of elders that were much like the Baby Boomers in the 1990s. Early in the decade of the

1920s, the so-called Missionary generation had pushed the country into Prohibition; later, they caused an economic crisis by passing the Hawley-Smoot tariff. The problem had been exacerbated by the free-spending ways of the next-younger group, the so-called Lost generation, in the 1920s. The two groups together created an "inner-driven" ethos much like the 1990s that had actually started in the 1980s. (The 1910s did not play a similar role because they preceded America's rise to Great Power status, and were punctuated by World War I.)

In the 1920s, just as the automobile, or "horseless carriage," put an end to the "horse-and buggy" era, there was a miraculous invention that put a number of electric boxes in houses all around the nation, which could receive transmissions or "broadcasts" from a station located anywhere in the country. It was called radio, and like the Internet of today, it was the wonder instrument of its time. Its main producer, Radio Corporation of America (RCA), commanded lofty valuations reminiscent of Internet stocks such as America Online (AOL). RCA lost over 90 percent of its value in the crash of 1929–1932, in a manner similar to most Internet stocks.

The author's "take" on the 1990s can be summed up by the statement that the Internet craze was the modern version of the 1920s radio craze. Radio was invented shortly after 1900; took over 20 years, until the 1920s, to capture the popular imagination; and required another 25 years, until the 1950s, to become commercially profitable. The Internet was invented in the mid-1970s; took over 20 years, until the mid-1990s, to become popular; and will probably require another 25 years, to around 2020, before companies in the field start making a significant amount of money. (By then, an Internet portal will probably be a good investment.) The mass use of a new invention is seldom achieved by the peers of the inventors, but rather a new generation who grew up with it as children.

A number of "back of the envelope" calculations done in late 1999 showed that the tech stocks all appeared to be discounting likely earnings for the year 2010, not for 2000. Put another way, the market was saying that an amount of economic and social progress that normally requires a decade or two was going to take place in one to two years. All it required was for the year 2000 to progress, and for people to realize that the hoped-for timetable would not be achieved, for the market to retreat.

The ethos around 2000 was best exemplified by a social event, the Multimillionaire Marriage on Fox TV in February of that year. The instant "marriage" (and almost equally quick breakup) between a Baby Boom man and a Gen-X woman itself represented the "roaring" nature of the times.[2] A joke that was told shortly afterward went, "How are Internet start-ups like the multimillionaire marriage?" Answer: "They were both sold by shameless promoters to greedy investors as a form of instant gratification." Cole Porter said it best, regarding the 1920s, "For day is night today, and black is white today, and the men that women prize today . . ." instead of "silly gigolos," one could say, "multimillionaires." And the punch line was "And heaven knows, anything goes." As was the case around 1970, the nation was losing its collective mind, courtesy of the same Baby Boomers.

An editorial in the *Wall Street Journal* in February 2000 made a crucial point. When Rick Rockwell, who, with a net worth of $2 million barely qualified, was the "last" available unmarried multimillionaire, it meant that Bill Gates, Michael Dell, Mark Andreeson, and a host of other more obvious (mostly tech) moguls had recently gotten married, were starting families, and were about to take their feet off the gas pedal at work.[3] (In fact, Bill Gates shortly afterward relinquished the CEO slot in order to concentrate more fully on other job functions and his family.) This, in turn, would mean a moderation of the turbocharged tech growth, as well as more moderate U.S. GDP growth in general, thereby cutting down one of the main underpinnings of the overheated stock market. From a larger social standpoint, this more family-friendly ethos wasn't necessarily a bad thing. But pressures for more "family leave" are likely to lower productivity until, perhaps, the Millennial generation figures out a way to better combine work and family responsibilities, possibly through networked home-based workplaces. If so, they are likely to produce another demographic and cultural baby boom.

The 1920s were also characterized by a period of rising mechanization through the widespread use of the assembly line. Efficiency had been introduced a decade earlier by pioneers of the Missionary generation like Frank Bunker Gilbreth and, above all, Henry Ford. Likewise, the modern Idealists, or Baby Boomers, created the tech revolution that mechanized computational processes through the use of computers and local area networks. This rising efficiency, however, is a blessing only during a time of tight demand. In a period of demand reversal, it is likely to cause a high level of unemployment. Moreover, the technological innovation created a corporate prosperity that was characterized by falling costs during a period of barely rising prices and sales. Hence, most of the economic benefits flowed to the owners and managers of cost-cutting technology, rather than to the population as a whole.

Another recent throwback to the 1920s was mentioned in a 1996 *Barron's* article that contained the tagline "A Seventy-Year Anti-Tobacco Cycle?"[4] That was exactly the contention of *Generations,* although Strauss and Howe might have argued that the cycle was 80-odd years in length rather than 70-odd. The cycle may have been modified slightly, so 70 years (more like 75, actually) is operative.

When the World Depression hit in the 1930s, creating what Strauss and Howe call a "crisis" era, it was up to the reactive Lost generation to clean up the excesses of the 1920s. One prominent member was Britain's John

Maynard Keynes. Earlier, he had warned against the damage to Europe (and the world) of the reparations imposed on Germany, the economic engine of Europe, by the Treaty of Versailles at the end of World War I. In 1936, he expounded on the role of government spending in combating a world depression.[5] In the United States, meanwhile, stock market teachers like Graham and Dodd warned investors how to sidestep trouble, but found few listeners.

The post–World War II period, or "outer-driven" era, was characterized by a time of innovation in nuclear science and space exploration, the development of new industries in computers and electronics, plus the perfection of mass-production processes (e.g., of Liberty ships). The comparable post–Civil War period was marked by advances in metallurgy and steel, plus the development of related industries such as railroads and telecommunications. Each gave rise to a postwar prosperity in which industry could be directed toward the needs of the consumer. These periods were also characterized by large-scale organization, large corporations (and the organization man) after World War II, and trusts after the Civil War. The resulting production of wealth in the post–World War II period fueled a stock market boom. Toward the end of the period, morals loosened. With the Missionary generation dead or dying, it was up to the members of the Lost generation (e.g., President Dwight Eisenhower) to preside over a steady economic expansion, powered by the now midlife workers and managers of the GI generation.

The passing of the Lost generation and the ascension of the GI generation to elderhood created another crisis in the 1960s that brought the stock market gains to a halt. First, the GIs had spawned another idealistic generation, the Baby Boomers, who are much like the GIs' Missionary generation parents. Nurtured in a prosperous but intellectually sterile environment, the younger generation started a "consciousness revolution" upon coming of age, creating a new "awakening." Peace marches, demonstrations, and campus riots disrupted the social fabric of the nation. The problem was exacerbated by the Vietnam War, which veteran GI generation elders tried to fight with dollars (e.g., saturation bombing) rather than the blood of their Baby Boom children. (The GIs' idealistic parents had no such compunctions about sending them off to war.) The war was not only unsuccessful, but it contributed to the inflation that rocked the country and threatened GI retirements, which is probably why these elders called it off.

The GIs also tried to buy social peace without raising taxes. This also unbalanced the budget and caused inflation. But the youngsters could not be mollified. "You've never been to hell unless you grew up in Scarsdale," characterized the ethos of the time. This was accompanied by the dilution of the workforce by a large number of young Boomers who were not really work ready. Meanwhile, the midlife managers were members of the Silent generation born between 1926 and 1942, who ran corporations and the economy far more loosely than the GI generation. It is probably no accident that the stock market sputtered between 1966 and 1982 as this generation turned 40.

The 1960s, like the 1920s and late 1990s, were characterized by a cyclically high level of interest in mutual funds. The public was willing to bear market risk as long as it could put money in the hands of professionals who, hopefully, could manage to diversify away company-specific risk. It is a general rule that market risk is greatest when people are most willing to bear it. The Vietnam War was a festering sore during this time. It caused a massive inflation. It also gave an artificial stimulus to the U.S. economy that was far from healthy. For instance, it prevented the credit crunch of 1966 from leading to recession. The alternative was worse: a decade of stagflation in the 1970s. This was marked by a conglomerate boom. Because of elevated stock market levels, companies took over others for stock, not cash. Warren Buffett pointed out that such acquisitions might be accretive to the acquirers (and a bad deal for the selling shareholders). This phenomenon was repeated in the 1990s.

Meanwhile, economic trouble was brewing overseas. Because of the high costs of the Vietnam War (as well as American imports), a flood of dollars had found their way abroad. There was far more U.S. currency available to foreigners than could be redeemed by American gold reserves (in Fort Knox) at the then prevailing fixed price of $35 an ounce. Under (GI generation) President Richard Nixon, America went off the gold standard and floated the dollar, which in effect, meant devaluation. This set off a time of troubles, with the rise of oil prices, the fall of the U.S. dollar, and the accelerating deterioration of the American balance of trade and payments.

Under (GI generation) President Ronald Reagan, America pulled out of its 1970s funk during the 1980s, returning to the "inner-driven" type of environment like the 1920s. A stock market boom, or rather recovery from the depressed 1970s, took place. But this turnabout did not reach its full flowering until the 1990s. The defining events of this decade were the dual "wins" of 1991, victory in the Persian Gulf War and the collapse of the Soviet Union, presided over by the last of the GI generation Presidents, George Bush, Sr. These two events restored America's position, temporarily, to that of the single, great, unchallenged world superpower. After the Vietnam War reverse in the 1960s and 1970s, America regained its credibility as the world's policeman. This led to the leadership role that the United States took in the Bosnian crisis. The result was that both U.S. and foreign capital returned to this political safe haven. This, together with the corporate restructuring (and explosion of new companies) caused the

American stock market to lead the international indexes. This lasted until the next pothole, the early 2000s equivalent of the Vietnam War and oil crisis, following September 11, 2001.

With the retirement of the GI generation, economic leadership had passed to the steady don't-rock-the-boat Silent generation (of Alan Greenspan and Robert Rubin). But the Silent generation is notably underrepresented in the political sphere, particularly the executive branch, where the presidency, long dominated by GIs, now appears to be firmly under Boom control. So it was a Boom, and not Silent ethos, that recently dominated the American political and economic scene.

When the author was growing up in the 1960s, cars, houses, and TV sets were getting bigger every year. This "bigness" was the ethos of his parents' peers, the then midlife members of the GI generation. Among the most admired and successful companies were those with "General Issue"–type names—General Electric, General Foods, General Mills, and General Motors; or perhaps "American," as in American Brands, American Home Products (now Wyeth), American Hospital Supply, and Rapid American. In the author's middle age around the year 2000, however, computers, fax machines, and phones have been getting "smarter" on an annual basis. Many of the most successful and admired companies have "invented" names: Microsoft, Intel, Cisco Systems.

A period of relative calm set in for another generation, roughly 1983 to 2001, as the Boomers moved into middle age and middle and top management positions. The corporate restructuring programs that they executed were the catalyst for a renewed boom in the stock market. So was the technology revolution led initially by people like Steve Jobs at Apple, and later by others like Bill Gates of Microsoft and Larry Ellison of Oracle, to name just a few. The 1980s represented a rebound following the depressed 1970s. But the 1990s proved to be surprisingly robust as well, extending the boom for a whole generation, but not beyond.

Warren Buffett made a similar observation, although he did not coach it in generational terms. He observed in *Fortune* magazine at the end of 1999 that the stock market went practically nowhere between the end of 1964 and 1981 (the Dow was at 874 in the earlier year and at 875 in the latter), roughly the midlife tenure of his Silent generation. Then it boomed during the midlife of the Baby Boomers, from 1982 to 1999. Observing the cycle of 17 fat years and 17 lean years (a term we borrowed from the Bible's reference to seven-year agricultural cycles in ancient Egypt), Mr. Buffett forecast that the 17 years from 2000 to 2017 would likely be lean as well. He predicted total returns for that span averaging 6 percent nominal, well down into the single digits, and 4 percent real, assuming 2 percent inflation. And he noted that if he were wrong, returns would just as likely be lower as well as higher.[6]

This book argues that results for the next decade and a half may be worse than Buffett prognosticates (and he raised his total return estimate to 7 percent for the balance of the period 2002 to 2017 in an update in *Fortune* in the fall of 2001, to partly reflect the hit that the market had already taken during the two intervening years). But fundamental factors seem to be deteriorating worldwide. Hence, the U.S. economic recovery in 2002–2003, which seemed to be built around a false foundation, was not reassuring. If that's the case, the market retreat—and it was no worse than that of 2000–2002, would be a dress rehearsal for something far worse in 2004–2006.

During 1930 and 1931, it looked like what later became the Great Depression would be nothing more than a severe recession. In the fall of the latter year, President Herbert Hoover predicted that "Prosperity is just around the corner," quite possibly with good reason. But the seminal event that turned the retreat into a global economic collapse was the collapse of the Credit Anstalt Bank in Austria, which plunged Europe deeper into a decade-long Depression (and brought Adolf Hitler into power in Germany), while infecting the United States. This time around, the crisis, if it comes, will be in Asia. The "fall guy" could be the Taiwan Trust Bank or the Korea Savings Bank. (These are made-up names to illustrate places where the trouble is likely to occur.) The consequences will be severe for the whole region, but particularly for China.

Likewise, the boom of the 1920s was due largely to the Allied victory in World War I, and the reduction of the main economic competitor, Germany, just as the 1990s benefited from the comparable events of 1991 mentioned above. During such times, idealistic midlifers tend to produce patriotic GI-type children (and vice versa two generations earlier or later). The most recent crop of children, which Strauss and Howe dub the Millennials, represent a baby boomlet, a demographic bulge. They have already spawned new child-oriented businesses such as Gymboree and Motherworks (which are fast growers, but only occasionally good Graham and Dodd investments). Looking ahead, producers of such things as yearbooks and class rings will likely see a renewed prosperity in the 2000s decade.

If there were any doubts that the Boomers were producing another GI generation, they were largely dispelled in April 1996 when Jessica Dubroff, a seven-year-old girl, crashed an airplane trying to set an age record at the behest of her New Age parents, who were trying to teach her, among other things, not to show fear. Her father also died in the crash. (Members of civic generations are particularly close to their fathers, or to put it another way, their fathers take a particular interest in them.) The remarkable thing was not that she failed to fly an airplane in a cross-country flight, but that several other children, aged 11, 10, and 8, had already succeeded. The urgency was due to the fact that Jessica would have turned eight in a month, and she was confident that if she could set the record at age seven, that it would stand, because no one would be allowed to make the attempt at age six. The prowess of these young children echoes the heroism of Charles Lindbergh, an (older) young man, who successfully completed the first transatlantic flight.

It may not be an accident that Jessica was a female. Traditionally, the stars of civic generations have been men. But the main thrust of the most recent 70-year cycle has been a push for gender equality, one that will almost certainly be completed during the lifetime of the idealistic Boomers. A year later, a foreign (and female) member of Generation X, Louise Woodward, was convicted of second-degree murder for the death of a child in her care in, of all places, Massachusetts. (This state had been the site of the Sacco and Venzetti trials of foreign Lost generation "anarchists" in the 1920s. It was also the locale of the Salem witch trials three centuries ago.) The baby had apparently been injured some weeks earlier, and it may have been these injuries, rather than Ms. Woodward's rough handling, that was the actual cause of death. But the real indictment was that a member of the recessive "reactive" generation (herself hardly more than a child) had failed to take sufficient care of a highly prized member of the dominant "civic" generation.

Although what has been called the "greatest generation" is generally referred to as the World War II generation, a better term is Strauss and Howe's moniker, the GI generation, after the soldiers that defended American freedom in the 1940s and made possible American prosperity in the second half of the twentieth century. Likewise, the "Continental" soldiers of what Strauss and Howe call the "Republican" generation that fought and won the Revolutionary War, were members of what one would nowadays call a "GI" generation, before the term was invented. There was no civic generation in the mid-nineteenth century because of the destruction wrought by the Civil War.

The young civic generation born in the 1980s and 1990s will not, of course, be a "World War II" generation. But it could very well be a GI generation, with Private First Class Jessica Lynch as one of its earliest members. And it will probably build on a fundamental principle that Boomers preached (but didn't always practice), of equal rights for women. Hence, another symbol of this generation is Jessica Dubroff, who was already the female Charles Lindbergh of her time at a very young age, and who would almost certainly have been a GI, had she lived to see a war in her young adulthood. The new civic generation made one of its first public appearance during the Winter Olympics of 1994 when Michelle Kwan, the dutiful daughter of Chinese-American parents born in 1980, stood in sharp contrast to the older, fractious rivals, Tonya Harding and Nancy Kerrigan of Generation X.

ECONOMIC CONSEQUENCES OF CHANGING GENERATIONS

Let's translate this phenomenon of generations into economic terms. The Boomers, as idealists, can be called a founder generation. Under the leadership of visionaries such as Steve Jobs and Bill Gates, they created the information technology revolution, just as Henry Ford and Lee deForest of the analogous Missionary generation introduced mass-produced automobiles and radio, respectively. The civic children of idealists are an inheritor generation. They are the most dutiful group because they stand to inherit the "family business." The reactive generation, sandwiched in between, will probably be a disinherited generation, who will have been leapfrogged in the idealist–civic succession. They will be understandably bitter about their plight but acquiesce in the end. The last (a "silent") generation, could be characterized as the ward generation. As the "baby" of the generational family, it is taken care of by the three older ones.

As seen above, the performance of the stock market seems to be dictated by which group occupies the midlife managerial positions. Thus, perhaps your investment policy should be driven by your age location relative to the generations immediately ahead of and behind you. This generational analysis therefore stands much of the conventional wisdom about life-cycle investing (including the more conventional view presented in Chapter 14) on its head. It is true that early-born members of "strong" generations should invest cautiously in their young adulthood, because of their lack of experience, most aggressively early in midlife because of their peak in earnings and experience, and conservatively in old age. But, by definition, these are the ones who are least likely to follow this pattern, especially the latter part regarding old age. Instead, this formula works best for late-born members of "weak" generations whose economic fate is determined by their being one step ahead of stronger generations immediately behind them. However, late-born members of strong generations and early-born members of weak generations ought to reverse the cycle. Thus, they should be aggressive as young adults to take advantage of strong generation ahead of them in middle age, cautious in their own middle age because of the weak generation right behind them, and then aggressive in old age, because of the succeeding strong generation who will then be in middle age.

The risks of the tech boom were aggravated when members of the GI generation threw caution to the winds and jumped into tech stocks early in the year 2000. This has always been a generation of joiners, first in the armed forces, later in the large corporations, and finally in "senior" communities that seem to have been planned especially for them. What's more, their life cycle always had a happy ending. They had won World War II in their youth, landed a man on the moon in middle age, and benefited mightily from the Reagan Boom in their dotage. In previous centuries, normal mortality would have ensured that the last occurrence would have been the end of the story. But rising living standards would add another chapter to their lives.

This generation, by definition, has during its lifetime been America's last line of defense against danger. As oldsters, they were the country's wealthiest age bracket. To a degree that had never been true of previous generations, they held the country's last financial reserves, just as they had commanded the nation's reserves of physical energy when they were younger. In their youth, they had utilized these reserves wisely, under the direction of a wise post–Civil War generation they revered. In old age, this supremely energetic generation largely lacked the "vision thing," and followed the risky patterns of more "with it" people who were younger. When these reserves were committed, America's financial security was at risk.

Some may shrink from the contemplation of a major war, but this may be a precondition for another bull market. Note in this context that the 1920s bull market followed World War I, the 1950s bull market followed World War II, the 1970s bear market followed the Vietnam War, and the 1990s bull market followed the dual victories in the Persian Gulf and Cold Wars. (Graham and Dodd investors, however, will do relatively better in a pre- rather than postwar scenario.) One can't eat steak without killing a cow, and maybe America can't have a bull market without winning a major war. If anything, the mini-bull markets of 2001 and 2003 merely confirmed this thesis by taking place after the United States won relatively minor wars against terrorists in Afghanistan and Iraq. Moreover, Chapter 19 outlines a number of economic reasons why a war with China is likely, a conclusion supported by the Crisis of 2020 theory in Strauss and Howe's *Generations*.[7]

Thus, the dual victories in the Persian Gulf War and the Cold War were responsible for much of the roar of the 1990s. By the same token, America in the year 2000 should not have been optimistic about the stock market, since the country had not won any wars in the immediate past. In fact, as a number of journalists observed, Pax Americana stood under heavy challenge. The terrorist bombing and near-sinking of the USS Cole represented an unraveling of one of the main preconditions for the bull market. And this was just symptomatic of the fact that America was losing its grip on key world flashpoints in the Balkans, the Middle East, and East Asia, much as the country was unable to control events in Central Europe, North Africa, and East Asia in the 1930s. Challenges to American dominance then rose in the form of Nazi Germany and other aggrieved countries who formed a loose alliance that posed a threat to the American economy, stock market, and, ultimately, world power.

Strauss and Howe's *Generations* predicts a crisis of 2020, which this book seconds. It will almost certainly have economic roots, but will carry major social and political ramifications, not only in the United States, but worldwide. How will the crisis unfold? A possible interpretation of world history for the first half of the twentieth century is that the world, with American help, spent three decades or so, from World War I to the Marshall Plan, working out Europe's economic problems. Likewise, the most probable cause of world problems in the near future will be an Asian crisis. The Great Depression actually started in Europe in 1923 and 1924, five or six years ahead of the American crash of 1929. A two-decade Asian economic depression was probably incubated in 1997 and 1998, which could spread to America some years later, by the mid-2000s.

Meanwhile, East Asia may have similar cycles, two generations ahead of, or behind, the Western world. For instance, the East Asian peers of the Baby Boomers, who saw capitalism unleashed in their adulthood, may be the Oriental equivalents of the GI generation. (World War II had a debilitating, not empowering, effect on East Asian countries, probably delaying their social progress.) A guess is that the Tiananmen Square incident in 1989 was inflicted on China's "Silent" generation, the one most concerned about civil rights, just as America's Silent generation suffered the consequences of fighting for the rights of African-American people. The spoiled "little emperors" of China's one-child families could be the equivalent of America's Baby Boomers, proving that the rise of an Idealist generation is a cultural, not demographic, phenomenon. There has been the beginning of student demonstrations in other parts of Southeast Asia reminiscent of the America's own campus riots of the 1960s. This seems to prove the dominance of economic and social cycles, not "American" or "Asian," or even "Eurocentric" values in world events.

This holds a promise for America. If the U.S.–China confrontation that seems almost certain to come to a head in the first half of the twenty-first century takes place around the year 2020, it will probably be settled on America's terms. This is not only because of the earlier time period, but because of the generational lineup. In that year we will have idealistic elders and civic-minded young adults, as we did in World War II, while China likely will have the reverse, a Vietnam War era–type roster. If the confrontation takes place around midcentury, however, China will have the World War II lineup with "little emperors" and their children, and America will have another Vietnam War setting.

This is not idle speculation. It is a major reason for a belief in a critical commodity shortage sometime after the year 2000. Although it will not be the only force in the stock market, the looming U.S.–China rivalry will create many of its undercurrents, in much the same way that U.S.–Soviet rivalry underlay most of the stock market action between 1945 and 1991. And while it is outside the scope of this book to predict whether there will be a world war as a result, or whether the diplomats and politicians can avert one, it is well within an economic purview to forecast that there will be a level of economic stress worldwide sufficient to produce a world war by 2010, as was the case in the 1930s.

This problem came to a head in 1998, when a Taiwanese-American scientist, Wen Ho Li, was accused of stealing American nuclear secrets and selling them to China. This follows a number of other suspicious "leaks" of information to China. The espionage episodes are measures of China's desperation, and show that China is a nouveau riche country in our time, much as Nazi Germany was years earlier. The fight for Taiwan, or what China calls a "One China" policy, is the modern version of Nazi Germany's "Anschluss" with Austria. China will probably take an "opportunistic" foreign policy, which, if opposed, could lead to war.

Second, the growing strength of Asian countries, combined with their rising expectations and resulting discontent, will pose a threat to U.S. world power in much the same way as a miserable and resurgent Germany challenged America's rise to world power the last time around. Already, in the late 1990s, we saw clashes on human rights between the West and China. And this was during a period of relative prosperity, when the economies of both America and China were growing at historically high rates. In a time of economic turmoil, the political struggle will only be all the more acute, with flashpoints in Hong Kong, Taiwan, North Korea, and elsewhere in Asia.

Indeed, Great Power confrontation will probably have its causes in economic problems. Because of its profligate ways, the United States has once again become the world's largest debtor, followed closely by its Latin American emulators south of the Rio Grande. The world's largest creditors, meanwhile, are in Asia, including "Greater China," China, Hong Kong, and Taiwan. This will create massive economic tensions, which, combined with existing political and cultural animosities between the countries, will carry the potential for a major war. World War II was brought about by the Great Depression, which in turn stemmed from the burden of Germany's reparations payments to the Allies. The Civil War was brought about by the economic failure of the slave system, the South's resulting debts to the North, and the threat that this failure posed to the social system of the South. The American Revolution was fought on the issue of "No taxation without representation," based on America's unwillingness to pay its debt to England for support in the French and Indian war.

The Boomers, as old idealists, will be the least tolerant generation of challenges to American power that occur during "their" watch. And their children, the peers of Jessica Dubroff and Jessica Lynch, will be the most war-ready generation since the GIs of the early twentieth century. These young soldiers would be led by the Eisenhowers and Pattons of Generation X, who have already seen small "practice wars" in the Persian Gulf, Somalia, Yugoslavia, Afghanistan, and Iraq.

The resulting world environment will be one that is the most recognizable to today's very oldest members. (Fed Chairman Alan Greenspan should not be counted among them because he was only three years old in 1929). Graham and Dodd were members of the Lost generation (most of whom are now deceased), but their 1934 warnings about the "New Era" mentality ring true today. Their baton was picked up here by a late member of the Boom generation, who is within hailing distance of the "new Lost" Generation X. As such, he invested aggressively as a young man, turned cautious as he approached middle age, and foresees opportunities to invest with uncharacteristic aggression as an oldster.

Endnotes

Chapter 1

1. The "Graham and Dodd" criteria are scattered throughout Benjamin Graham and David Dodd, *Security Analysis* (New York: McGraw Hill, 1934), but the best summary is in John Train's *The Midas Touch* (New York: Harper & Row, 1987), p. 13.
2. There are plenty of books on Warren Buffett. Two of the best are Andrew Kirkpatrick, *Of Permanent Value: The Story of Warren Buffett* (New York: McGraw Hill, 1998), and Roger Lowenstein, *Buffett, The Making of An American Capitalist* (New York: Doubleday, 1995).

Chapter 2

1. Much of the technical material in this and the next section is drawn from Tung Au and Thomas Au, *Engineering Economics For Capital Investment Analysis* (Englewood Cliffs, NJ: Prentice-Hall, 1992), now out of print, Chapter 3, Sections 4–6, and Chapter 5, Sections 5–11.

Chapter 3

1. The bond math can be found in any number of texts, but the "classic" is Frank Fabozzi, *Fixed Income Analysis* (New Hope, PA: Fabozzi Publishing, 2000).
2. The algebraic formulas were adapted from Au and Au, *op. cit.*, Chapter 10, Section 3.
3. Cited in Lowenstein, *op. cit.*, p. 119.

Chapter 4

1. The financial statement analysis is drawn from Au and Au, *op. cit.*, Chapter 14, Sections 2–3.
2. Scattered discussions of discount bonds and preferred stock can be found throughout Ben Graham's *The Intelligent Investor* (New York: Harper & Row, 1973).

Chapter 5

1. Buffett's bond investments are best recounted in Kirkpatrick, *op. cit.,* various chapters.
2. Bryan Burroughs, and John Helyar, *Barbarians at the Gate* (New York: Harper & Row, 1990), second half.
3. The statement of changes in financial position analysis is drawn from Au and Au, *op. cit.,* Chapter 14, Section 4.

Chapter 6

1. Much of the technical material on costs and depreciation is drawn from Au and Au, *op. cit.,* Chapter 11, Sections 4–7, and Chapter 13, Sections 2–3.
2. Much of the technical material in this section is drawn from Au and Au, *op. cit.,* Chapter 15, Section 12.
3. Yuji Ijiri, "Recovery Rate and Cash Flow Accounting," *Financial Executive,* March 1980, pp. 54–60.
4. Thomas Wolfe, *Bonfire of the Vanities* (New York: Farrar, Straus, and Giroux, 1987), pp. 69–72.

Chapter 7

1. John Maynard Keynes, *The General Theory of Employment, Interest, and Money* (New York: Harcourt, Brace, 1936), Chapter 11.
2. The best account of Buffett's purchase of Berkshire Hathaway is found in Lowenstein, *op. cit.,* Chapter 7.

Chapter 8

1. Geraldine Weiss, *Dividends Don't Lie* (Chicago: Longman Financial Services, Publ., 1987), Chapter 1.
2. *Ibid.,* Chapter 4.
3. The last part of the chapter summarizes Michael O'Higgins and John Downes, *Beating the Dow* (New York: HarperCollins Publishers, 1991).
4. Warren Buffett, *Chairman's Letter,* Berkshire Hathaway 1991 Annual Report. The discussion is found under the section "Twenty Years in a Candy Store."

Chapter 9

1. Value Line's *Subscriber's Guide* (New York: Value Line Publishing, 2000) has a discussion about how the company uses earnings to evaluate stocks.

2. Dreman, David N., *The New Contrarian Investment Strategy* (New York: Random House, 1982), Chapters 7–8.

Chapter 10

1. Warren Buffett, *Chairman's Letter*, Berkshire Hathaway Annual Report, 2002. The discussion is found under the section, "Derivatives."
2. Ken Fisher, *Super Stocks* (Homewood, IL., Dow Irwin), 1984.
3. John Kenneth Galbraith, *The New Industrial State* (Boston: Houghton Mifflin and Company, 1967), pp. 59–71.

Chapter 11

1. Warren Buffett, *Chairman's Letter*, Berkshire Hathaway 1993 Annual Report. The quote is taken from the section "Common Stock Investments."
2. Warren Buffett, *Chairman's Letter*, Berkshire Hathaway 1988 Annual Report. The quote is taken from the section "Borsheim's."
3. John Train, *The New Money Masters*, (New York: Harper & Row, 1989), pp. 152–153.

Chapter 13

1. Donald Trump, *The Art of the Deal* (New York: Warner Books, 1987), Chapter 6. Jerome Tucille, *Trump* (New York: Jove Books, 1987).
2. Much of the discussion in this paragraph was drawn from Suzanne Brangham, *Housewise, The Smart Woman's Guide to Buying and Renovating Real Estate For Profit* (New York: Perennial Library, 1988), Chapter 9.
3. John Paul Getty, *How to Be Rich* (Chicago: Playboy Press, 1965), p. 173.
4. Wolfe, *op.cit.*, p. 142.
5. Graham and Dodd, *op. cit.*, p. 115.

Chapter 14

1. Graham, *op. cit.*, p. 8.
2. This section is a brief summary of Michael O'Higgins, *Beating the Dow with Bonds* (New York: HarperBusiness, 1999).
3. *Fortune*, August 16, 1999, p. 94.
4. Graham and Dodd, *op. cit.*, pp. 504–507.
5. The last part of the chapter is excerpted from Donald Nichols, *Life Cycle Investing* (New York: Dow Irwin Press, 1987), Chapter 2.

Chapter 15

1. Lowenstein, *op. cit.,* pp. 57–58.
2. There are many sources for the discussion of academic theory, but the "classic" is Richard Brealey and Stewart Myers, *Principles of Corporate Finance* (New York: McGraw Hill, 1984).
3. Au & Au, *op. cit.,* p. 423.
4. *Ibid.,* pp. 424–425.
5. Warren Buffett, *Chairman's Letter,* Berkshire Hathaway 1988 Annual Report. The quote is taken from the section "Efficient Markets Theory."

Chapter 16

1. This quote is drawn from William Strauss and Neil Howe, *Generations* (New York: Harper & Row, 1991), p. 399. A further exposition of Strauss and Howe's generational theory takes place in Chapter 20. Strauss and Howe mention the stock market only in passing, so the economic interpretation of the generational cycle, as opposed to the cycle itself, belongs solely to the current author.
2. Warren Buffett, *Chairman's Letter,* Berkshire Hathaway Annual Report, 1990. The discussion on Wells Fargo is found under the section "Marketable Securities."

Chapter 17

1. Graham and Dodd, *op. cit.,* pp. 35–36.

Chapter 18

1. Robert Hagstrom, *The Warren Buffett Portfolio,* (New York: John Wiley & Sons, 1999), p. 181.
2. *Barron's,* March 22, 1999, p. 23.
3. A history of the Dow from 1900 to the mid-1970s, and Ben Graham's opinions on it, can be found in Graham, *op. cit.,* Chapter 3.
4. Glassman, James K, and Hassett, Keven, A., *Dow 36,000,* (New York: Random House, 2000), Chapter 8.

Chapter 19

1. *Barron's,* May 6, 2002, p. 22.
2. Getty, *op. cit.,* p. 164. The whole chapter, "The Wall Street Investor," contains an excellent exposition on Graham and Dodd Investing.
3. Lawrence Sloan, *Every Man and His Common Stocks* (New York: McGraw Hill, 1931), Part IV.

Chapter 20

1. Strauss and Howe, *op. cit.*, Chapter 4.
2. Rick Rockwell, *What Was I Thinking?* (Commercial Communications, Inc. 2002). The author knows Mr. Rockwell.
3. "Advice to the Lovelorn: Sell," *Wall Street Journal*, February 24, 2000, p. A18.
4. *Fortune*, November 22, 1999, pp. 212–218.
5. Keynes, *op. cit.*
6. *Barron's*, October 14, 1996, pp. 37–42.
7. *Fortune*, December 10, 2001, pp. 80–94.
8. Strauss and Howe, *op. cit.*, Chapter 13.

Bibliography

Au, Tung and Au, Thomas P., *Engineering Economics for Capital Investment Analysis*, Englewood Cliffs, NJ: Prentice-Hall, 1992.

Brangham, Suzanne, *Housewise, The Smart Woman's Guide to Buying and Renovating Real Estate For Profit*, New York: Perennial Library, 1988.

Brealey, Richard, and Myers, Stewart, *Principles of Corporate Finance*, New York: McGraw Hill, 1984.

Buffett, Warren, *Chairman's Letter*, Berkshire Hathaway's 1988, 1990, 1991, and 2002 Annual Reports.

Burroughs, Bryan, and Helyar, John, *Barbarians at the Gate*, New York: Harper & Row, 1990.

Dreman, David N., *The New Contrarian Investment Strategy*, New York: Random House, 1982.

Fabozzi, Frank, and Fabozzi, T. Dessa, *The Fixed Income Handbook*, Chicago: Irwin Press, 1995.

Fabozzi, Frank, *Fixed Income Analysis*, New Hope, PA: Fabozzi Publishing, 2000.

Fisher, Kenneth, *Super Stocks*, Homewood, IL., Dow Irwin, 1984.

Fortune Magazine, November 22, 1999.

Galbraith, John Kenneth, *The New Industrial State*, Boston: Houghton Mifflin and Company, 1967.

Getty, John Paul, *How to Be Rich*, Chicago: Playboy Press, 1965.

Glassman, James K, and Hassett, Kevin A., *Dow 36,000*, New York: Random House, 2000.

Hagstrom, Robert, *The Warren Buffett Portfolio*, New York: John Wiley & Sons, 1999.

Keynes, John Maynard, *The General Theory of Employment, Interest, and Money*, New York: Harcourt, Brace, 1936.

Ijiri, Yuji, "Recovery Rate and Cash Flow Accounting," *Financial Executive*, March 1980.

Kirkpatrick, Andrew, *Of Permanent Value: The Story of Warren Buffett*, New York: McGraw Hill, 1998.

Lowenstein, Roger, *Buffett, The Making of an American Capitalist*, Doubleday, 1995.

Nichols, Donald, *Life Cycle Investing*, New York: Dow Irwin Press, 1987.

327

O'Higgins, Michael, *Beating the Dow with Bonds,* New York: Harper-Business, 1999.

O'Higgins, Michael, and Downes, John, *Beating the Dow,* New York: HarperCollins Publishers, 2000.

Sloan, Lawrence, *Every Man and His Common Stocks,* New York: McGraw Hill, 1931.

Strauss, William, and Howe, Neil, *Generations,* New York: Harper & Row, 1991.

Train John, *The Midas Touch,* New York: Harper & Row, 1987.

Train, John, *The New Money Masters,* New York: Harper & Row, 1989.

Trump, Donald, *The Art of the Deal,* New York: Warner Books, 1987.

Tucille, Jerome, *Trump,* New York: Jove Books, 1987.

Weiss, Geraldine, *Dividends Don't Lie,* Chicago: Longman Financial Services, 1987.

Wolfe, Thomas, *Bonfire of the Vanities,* New York: Farrar, Straus, and Giroux, 1987.

Index